Anna Seghers

Social History, Popular Culture, and Politics in Germany
Geoff Eley, Series Editor

(continued on last page)

Anna Seghers

The Mythic Dimension

HELEN FEHERVARY

Ann Arbor

THE UNIVERSITY OF MICHIGAN PRESS

Copyright © by the University of Michigan 2001
All rights reserved
Published in the United States of America by
The University of Michigan Press
Manufactured in the United States of America
⊚ Printed on acid-free paper

2004   2003   2002   2001   4   3   2   1

A CIP catalog record for this book is available from the British Library.

Library of Congress Cataloging-in-Publication Data

Fehervary, Helen.
    Anna Seghers : the mythic dimension / Helen Fehervary.
        p.   cm. — (Social history, popular culture, and politics in
    Germany)
    Includes bibliographical references and index.
    ISBN 0-472-11215-5 (acid-free paper)
    1. Seghers, Anna, 1900—Criticism and interpretation.   I. Title.
    II. Series.
    PT2635.A27 Z635   2001
    833'.912—dc21   2001001996

Contents

Illustrations following page 52

Preface

My ability to conduct research and to see the writing of this book through to completion owes a great deal to individuals and institutions, and to each and all I express my gratitude. The National Endowment for the Humanities supported archival research in Berlin in 1994 with a Summer Stipend and Travel Allotment within the Initiative on the Emergence of Democracy. A three-month Deutscher Akademischer Austauschdienst (DAAD) Research Study Grant allowed me to continue library and archival research in the fall of 1994. Archival research in Budapest in 1997 was made possible by a Research Travel Grant from the International Research and Exchanges Board (IREX). The support of the Ohio State University College of Humanities and Department of Germanic Languages and Literatures allowed me to embark on my project with the award of a Faculty Professional Leave for the year 1993–94. College Grants-in-Aid in 1994 and 1996 helped fund research travel, and my department made possible additional travel support and adjustment in my teaching schedule. The staff of the Humanities Information Systems came to my aid in the conversion to a new programming system, and my continued education in electronics under the guidance of my colleague Gregor Hens was made altogether bearable by his serene company.

A number of people enabled me to conduct sustained research in archives and libraries. I acknowledge in particular the cooperation of the knowledgeable staff at the Akademie der Künste–Berlin am Robert-Koch-Platz, where I worked in 1994 and in years following, especially Renate Graßnick, who was responsible for the collection in the Anna-Seghers-Archiv until her retirement in 1999. Special thanks go to Marianne Berger of the Anna-Seghers-Gedenkstätte in Berlin-Adlershof for her readiness to respond to inquiries, whether in person, by mail, or by telephone, and above all for her keen interest in my project and trust in me, permitting me to work in the Seghers library undisturbed in 1994 and subsequent years in search of inscriptions, notations, and other clues among the over nine thousand books stacked in double rows on shelves reaching from floor to ceiling. The work was tedious, the findings all the more delightful, and without them, this would have become, if at all, an altogether different book.

I also express thanks to Friedrich Schütz, Director of the Stadtarchiv Mainz, for clarifying information pertaining to the history of the Reiling family; to Erdmut Wizisla, Director of the Bertolt-Brecht-Archiv in Berlin, for allowing me access to a variety of materials over the years; to the archival and library staff who assisted me at the Hungarian Academy of Sciences, the Petöfi Literary Museum, and the Széchenyi Library in Budapest; to László Sziklai and his staff at the Georg Lukács Archive and Library in Budapest; and especially to the Mannheim and Radványi scholar Éva Gábor, who generously gave of her time and provided insight concerning the Budapest Sunday Circle.

I am indeed fortunate to have had conversations over the years with individuals who knew Seghers intimately: Christa Wolf, Steffie Spira, Stephan Hermlin, and Seghers's children, Pierre Radvanyi and Ruth Radvanyi. I am particularly indebted to Ruth Radvanyi for generously giving of her time and offering hospitality in Berlin. I also wish to acknowledge Sonja Hilzinger for her interest in my work from the very start, and for the same, the scholars in the Anna-Seghers-Gesellschaft in Berlin, above all Frank Wagner, whose discernment and friendship did much to spur me on.

Here in the United States I have been heartened over the years by the interest and support of friends and colleagues; special thanks are due David Bathrick, Sander Gilman, Jost Hermand, Patricia Herminghouse, Robert Holub, Leila Rupp, Egon Schwarz, Marc Silberman, and Frank Trommler. Peter Beicken and Arpad Kadarkay kindly read the manuscript in the summer of 1999 when it was in its last stages. I am especially grateful to David Hayes, whose humanity and wit encouraged me to continue on a journey that took me into ever more uncharted territories; and to Erika Bourguignon, who read early drafts of the chapters and whose insights as an American anthropologist born in Vienna lent our discussions wide-ranging life perceptions and more than occasional good humor. I owe particular thanks to the series editor, Geoff Eley, for his initial interest and confidence in the manuscript, and to Liz Suhay of the University of Michigan Press for seeing it through the review process and offering sound editorial advice and encouragement.

Finally, I express my gratitude to Georgine Kopeczek Biedermann for help with some of the more subtle nuances of the Hungarian language; and to Maria Corvera Fehervary for countless hours of reviewing, rethinking, and reformatting, allowing me to be brought up to date at long last in the language of the computer—and no less for her request years ago that I read her *that* story: Anna Seghers's *Shelter,* about a German boy who loses his parents to the Nazis and is taken in by a French working-class family in Paris. The story hardly worked the more familiar wonders of the fairy tales, but it nonetheless became part of our household's new "canon," adding significantly to my appreciation of Seghers and thus providing a kernel of sorts for the later project of this book.

But the first idea for the topic, particularly for chapters 4–6, goes further back, to a casual remark made by Ferenc Fehér in the mid-1970s when I visited him and Ágnes Heller in Budapest. "You know, there are many interesting things in Lukács's life and his papers that have to do with Anna Seghers," he offered. "You're Hungarian, after all; you know the language; you should know there's quite a topic you could write about here." No, I didn't know, and in my youthful exuberance about more burning matters, I didn't much care. Years later I happily remembered Feri's words. To his memory, and to that of the other "wayfarers" who haunt its pages, this book is dedicated.

The following articles that I published during the course of my research contain the prolegomena to some of the ideas that are elaborated upon and transported into entirely new contexts in the separate chapters of this book: "Anna Seghers's *Seelenmalerei* and the Mannerism of Heiner Müller's Theatre," in *Responsibility and Commitment: The Ethics of Cultural Mediation,* ed. Klaus L. Berghahn, Robert C. Holub, and Klaus R. Scherpe (New York: Peter Lang, 1996), 225–41; "Brecht, Seghers, and *The Trial of Jeanne d'Arc*—with a Previously Unpublished Letter of 1952 from Seghers to Brecht," *The Brecht Yearbook* 21 (1996): 20–47; "Die Seelen-landschaft der Netty Reiling, die Stimmen der Jeanne d'Arc und der Chiliasmus des Kommunarden László Radványi," *Argonautenschiff: Jahrbuch der Anna-Seghers-Gesellschaft* 5 (Berlin: Aufbau Verlag, 1996): 118–36; and "Landscapes of an *Auftrag,*" *New German Critique* 73, special issue on Heiner Müller, ed. David Bathrick and Helen Fehervary (winter 1998): 115–32. The relevant sources are acknowledged in the pertinent notes to the chapters. I wish to thank *New German Critique* for permission to reprint in revised form passages from my article on Seghers and Heiner Müller (*NGC* 73, winter 1998) in chapter 6; and *The Brecht Yearbook* for permission to reprint in revised form sections of my article on Seghers and Brecht (*Brecht Yearbook* 21, 1996) in chapter 8.

The preparation of a text-critical, annotated, and commentated edition of Seghers's works using a text base of first editions is only just under way (Anna Seghers, *Werkausgabe,* 24 vols., ed. Helen Fehervary and Bernhard Spies, [Berlin: Aufbau Verlag, 2000–]). Where possible I have quoted from published English translations. Otherwise I have relied on the

reprint editions of individual novels published by Aufbau Taschenbuchverlag since 1993 and the six-volume Aufbau Taschenbuchverlag edition *Erzählungen 1924–1980* of 1994. These editions use the same text base
as the fourteen-volume *Gesammelte Werke in Einzelausgaben* authorized
by Seghers and published by Aufbau Verlag between 1977 and 1980. The
edition *Erzählungen 1924–1980* also includes previously unpublished texts.
Where I have quoted from Seghers's essays, my main source has been
Anna Seghers, *Über Kunstwerk und Wirklichkeit,* ed. Sigrid Bock, 4 vols.
(Berlin: Akademie-Verlag, 1970–71, 1979).

Unpublished letters and other archival materials quoted are so acknowl-
edged in the pertinent notes. I am grateful to the following for permission to
quote from such materials: Anna Seghers's and László Radványi's heirs, Dr.
Pierre Radvanyi (Paris) and Dr. Ruth Radvanyi (Berlin); Akademie der
Künste zu Berlin, Anna-Seghers-Archiv und Gedenkstätte and Bertolt-
Brecht-Archiv; Magyar Tudományos Akadémia Filozófiai Intézet, Lukács
György Archívum és Könyvtár; and Petöfi Irodalmi Múzeum.

Grateful acknowledment is made to Dr. Ruth Radvanyi, Berlin, for
permission to reproduce the original photograph of Netty Radvanyi
(Anna Seghers), 1925, and Joachim Cmok, graphic artist, Berlin, for pho-
tographic reproduction. Acknowledgment is further made to the British
Museum for permission to reproduce *The Three Trees* by Rembrandt; the
Staatliche Kunstsammlungen Dresden for permission to reproduce *The
Jewish Cemetery at Ouderkerk* by Jacob van Ruisdael; the Staatliche
Museen zu Berlin, Kupferstichkabinett, for permission to reproduce *The
Landscape with the Spruce Branch* by Hercules Seghers and *Ecco Homo*
and *Study after Leonardo's Last Supper* by Rembrandt; the Musée Jacque-
mart-André for permission to reproduce *The Supper at Emmaus,* 1629, by
Rembrandt; the Louvre for permission to reproduce *The Supper at
Emmaus,* 1648, by Rembrandt; the Rijksmuseum-Stichting Amsterdam
for permission to reproduce *Christ in Emmaus,* 1654, and *The Twelve-
Year-Old Jesus in the Temple,* 1654, by Rembrandt; the Bibliothèque
nationale de France for permission to reproduce *Christ Preaching* (*La
petite tombe*) by Rembrandt; and the Philadelphia Museum of Art for permission to reproduce *Head of Christ* (*Portrait Study of a Young Jew as
Christ*), attributed to Rembrandt.

A time-consuming task in the preparation of this book has been that
of translation. A significantly large number of sources from which I quote
are not yet available in English. These involve above all Seghers's shorter
narratives, essays, and letters, on which I draw in all eight chapters, as well
as published sources and unpublished archival materials in German and
Hungarian from which I quote especially in chapters 4–6. Wherever possible I have relied on existing English translations, as in the case of Seghers's

novels *The Seventh Cross, Transit,* and *The Dead Stay Young* and her narrative *The Revolt of the Fishermen;* and on translated works by Lukács, Benjamin, Brecht, and others. All published translations from which I quote are acknowledged in the notes to the individual chapters. Where I have deemed it necessary to make alterations in the translations, these adjustments are likewise accounted for in the notes. Unless thus indicated, all translations from German and Hungarian are my own.

Columbus, Ohio
August 2000

Introduction

When the living must keep silent, a proverb tells us, then the dead
speak.

—Anna Seghers, 1938[1]

Anna Seghers scholarship has focused in large part, and justifiably so, on
Seghers's place within the history and literature of German socialism and
antifascism. While ideological opinion has been wide-ranging, critics in
both East and West have interpreted her works by relying for the most
part on principles of mimesis and variations of the *Wiederspiegelungstheo-
rie.* However, this foregrounding of German history in respect to Seghers's
oeuvre has also limited our understanding of the aesthetic underpinnings
of that oeuvre and its place within the larger panorama of European and
world letters. Certainly I do not recommend that we separate her art from
her politics. This would be no less absurd than the effort to ignore the history of Latin America in a discussion of Pablo Neruda's poetry, or to dis-
count the political upheavals in South Africa in a reading of Nadine
Gordimer's prose. As a storyteller and chronicler, which she was above all,
Seghers in fact had more in common with these two writers than with
many of her German contemporaries. Indeed, her narrative manner
clearly indicates that she preferred Joseph Conrad's topographical style of
yarn-spinning to Thomas Mann's psychological musings on art and culture, Dostoyevsky's soulful character studies to the teleological middle-
class order of the *Bildungsroman,* the Dutch landscape painters' renderings
of the dynamics of everyday life to the quiescent provincial interiority of
the nineteenth-century German novella.

Seghers was one of the great modernists of her time, who from the
start wrote with a deliberately global context in mind. Her cosmopolitan
stance is evident throughout her work, from her first published story, *Die
Toten auf der Insel Djal* (1924, The Dead on the Island Djal), subtitled "a
tale from the Dutch retold by Antje Seghers," to her very last collection,

Drei Frauen von Haiti (1980, Three Women from Haiti). Her depiction of political resistance and liberation movements on an international scale—in stories about imperialist and revolutionary China, Jewish life in Eastern, Central, and Western Europe, anticolonial uprisings in the Caribbean, urban and rural life in Mexico, South America, and Africa—also assures her place within present and future discussions of postimperialist and postcolonial discourse.

Yet Seghers's narratives have little in common with the modernist quest for identity or postmodernist constructions of self that pervade the literary heritage of our time—from James Joyce and Marcel Proust to Manuel Puig and Jamaica Kincaid, from Thomas Mann and Robert Musil to Ingeborg Bachmann and Botho Strauss. The absence of narrative self-interest, indeed the lack of even vestiges of narcissism in Seghers's prose, is striking. Even in her most autobiographical work, *The Excursion of the Dead Girls,* written in 1943–44 in response to the Holocaust, the first-person narrator mourns the deaths of her parents and childhood friends, indeed the loss of childhood itself, but hardly engages in the pursuit of self. Self and other, mourner and mourned, are separate in this text, as in her other texts. Yet past and present are intertwined. As Walter Benjamin already noted in 1938,[2] Seghers's prose strives for redemption, seeking at once to affirm the living and liberate the dead. Her narratives are less concerned with the relationship of self and other, or self and self, than with the trials of the present in relation to the unfinished lives of the past. She wrote for the future, but not about the future, with urgency about a present that is always a *past* present, that is to say, an enchanted present inscribed by topographies inhabited by the dead.

Imbued with redemptive hopes and mythic meaning, Seghers's prose offers little enticement for reader identification in the postmodern era of identity and survival politics. Her narratives, wherein the ghosts of the past figure alongside the lives of the living, offer no sign of what Georg Lukács once lamented as the "homeless" nature of aesthetic creation in the modern era.[3] Nor do they provide the private gratification ascribed by Walter Benjamin to the reader who is "drawn to the novel . . . in the hope of warming his shivering life with a death he reads about."[4] At once hopeful and tragic, the world of Seghers's prose offers neither individual nor collective resolution. As readers, we are not so much invited to identify with a narrative subject as we are called upon to engage ourselves in the larger flow of the narrative. In so doing, our attention is often directed, as in Rembrandt's drawings and etchings, to the occasional observer or witness, the seemingly minor characters who figure at the edge of the action, who merely look and listen, indeed are barely aware of the significance of the events they attend nonetheless. This site of implication is where we the readers are ultimately called upon to recognize and identify ourselves—on the brink of time, at the edge of a precipice, as it were, distinct from the actors and their actions, but directly implicated in the events themselves, and ourselves at risk. Seghers's prose invokes the form of the chronicle and legend. As a modernist reutilization, it prefigures—through the eye of a detached yet nonetheless sympathetic viewer—what in contemporary idiom is known as the testimonial narrative. Here the truth as related by the storyteller, the credibility and skill of the witness, are at issue, not the identities of the narrated subjects themselves. This form of storytelling invokes the spirit of survival in the biblical stories of Joseph, Daniel, and Ruth, not the Greek instrumental reason of a Ulysses; the narrative deliberateness demanded by the trial of Scheherazade, not the epistemological uncertainties surrounding Oedipus the King; the epic sweep and resoluteness of a Nadine Gordimer, not the minutely detailed perceptions and introspections of Virginia Woolf.

There is little question that in terms of the quality of her narrative style and scope of her narrative vision, Seghers was the greatest German woman writer of the twentieth century. Moreover, she was one of the most intellectually astute, politically engaged, and, like her exiled contemporaries, politically persecuted artists of her culture and era. Yet the issue of gender has played no small role in allowing critics who may applaud the artistry of a man like Brecht *despite his politics,* as it were,[5] to suspend the same discretion in the case of the woman writer who was in every respect his contemporary and peer. But if literary criticism has revived interest in German, and more recently German-Jewish, women writers, one can hardly make the case of the marginal or minority voice for Seghers. She was, after all, internationally renowned during her years in exile in the 1930s and 1940s, thereafter served for twenty-five years as president of the German Writers Union in the German Democratic Republic (GDR), and, as a leading international voice in the intellectual life of her times, takes her place in history alongside such women contemporaries as Hannah Arendt and Simone de Beauvoir.

Surely she did not follow on the heels of a strong tradition of German prose authored by women. Virginia Woolf, whose younger contemporary she was, was nurtured by the legacies of Jane Austen, the Brontë sisters, and George Eliot; Colette and Simone de Beauvoir, by the urbane wit and romantic style of George Sand. Seghers, by contrast, inherited nineteenth-century traditions of women's writing that coexisted within the difficult history of Germany's national formation but rarely merged: on the one hand, a progressive but fairly insular epistolary tradition informed by the pietism of the German Enlightenment; on the other, the middle-class provincialism of the women's feuilleton and sentimental novel. An exception may be the turn-of-the-century writer Ricarda Huch, whose keen interest in history and epic style had some influence on Seghers, as did, among the Scandinavians, the novels and sea tales of the Swedish writer Selma Lagerlöf. In sum, due at least in part to the lack of a substantive body of middle-class women's fiction written in German before her time, Seghers's prose exhibits few examples of the kind of psychological introspection and differentiation of gender identity that characterizes the writings of her female contemporaries in England and France and, one generation later, those of her own protégée Christa Wolf.

To wit, unlike Emma Bovary, Seghers was a woman who much preferred landscapes to emotions. Like Balzac and Conrad before her, she created a body of work that is serial in character, a work wherein the same or slightly altered names, character paradigms, and topographies recur. Cedric Watts's observations on this aspect of Conrad's work are just as valid for Seghers's: "The recognition of such recurrent characterizations (and of recurrent localities) . . . strengthens the sense of authenticity and generates in the reader the sense of a meta-narrative—a large imaginative territory, closely related to actuality, from which all the individual existent narratives seem to arise as selections."[6] The resulting tension is heightened all the more in Seghers's work, whose thematic is not only the global expanse of colonialism and imperialism, but also the emergence of fascism, and, albeit less explicitly, Stalinism. The critic Hans Mayer has referred to "a deep dualism" in Seghers's writing, reminding us that despite all hopes for a better future, hers (incidentally, like Conrad's and Balzac's) was ultimately "a *tragic* world." And, as Mayer wrote in the same essay, "All the world in Anna Seghers is at once *mythic world*."[7]

This book is an attempt to identify some of the sources of that "mythic world" and to examine the shape it took in her work. It seems instructive in this context to place Seghers somewhere between Kafka, whose own no less "mythic world," like Seghers's, was steeped in Jewish lore, and whose "nasty fairy tales for grown-ups," as she called them, decisively influenced her;[8] and Brecht, with whom she shared a lifelong interest in early European and East Asian art, a more or less "plebeian" epic-chronicle style, and a generally progressive, in her case essentially messianic, worldview. All three authors, of course, drew heavily on the Bible, Kafka focusing on Old Testament and Talmudic tradition, Brecht on the New Testament and the Lutheran Psalter, Seghers on Jewish legend in Palestine and the diaspora as chronicled in the prophetic books of the Old Testament, the New Testament Gospels and Epistles, and the apocryphal writings. However, her reliance on biblical material is not as indebted to the hermeneutics of language (Kafka), imagery (Brecht), and parable (Kafka and Brecht) as it is to its iconographic mediation via the architecture, sculpture, and painting of northern Europe from the Gothic period to seventeenth-century Holland. Notably, she studied art history and sinology at the University of Heidelberg from 1920 to 1924 and completed her doctoral dissertation on the topic "Jews and Judaism in the Works of Rembrandt," favoring what she called Rembrandt's "overrealism" in his late Christ portraits.[9] The dissertation is not only biographically interesting to the Seghers scholar, but crucial to an understanding of the author's work, for it contains her only systematic commentary on aesthetic criteria that subsequently informed her own narrative art. Née Netty Reiling, Anna Seghers took her pseudonymous patronymic from Rembrandt's most radical and perhaps most modern contemporary, the seventeenth-century Dutch landscape painter and engraver Hercules Seghers.[10]

The chapters that follow examine aspects of Anna Seghers's life and work that were entirely unknown or largely ignored heretofore: the influence of art and art history, particularly the Dutch landscape painters and the drawing style of Rembrandt; her lifelong indebtedness to the ideas of the young Georg Lukács and the Budapest Sunday Circle; her relationship to and, so I argue, influence on Walter Benjamin in the late 1930s; and, finally, her friendship and collaboration with Brecht. In light of her biography, which I take into account in the pertinent chapters, Seghers's reliance on biblical and Netherlandish influences should become self-evident, and the chapters devoted to them require no further introduction. Much the same can be said for my discussion of Seghers and Benjamin regarding the period of exile in the 1930s, and of Seghers and Brecht in exile and in the GDR. In the relevant chapters I discuss these influences and correspondences in some detail. Seghers's relationship to Lukács and the Budapest Sunday Circle, the topic of chapters 4–6, is a different matter, first, because much of the material I discuss has simply been unknown heretofore, and second, because its evidence alters in a significant way what we have previously surmised about Seghers (not only in her early years), and about the political, aesthetic, and philosophical concerns that underlie her entire oeuvre.

Seghers research, conducted largely by German scholars, has virtually ignored the influence of the man with whom she lived in an exceptionally close marital and working relationship for fifty-three years: the Hungarian philosopher László Radványi, one of the youngest members of the Budapest Sunday Circle, who first introduced her to the thought and writings of the young Lukács, the sociologist Károly (Karl) Mannheim, the poet and film critic Béla Balázs, the poet and folk artist Anna Lesznai, and the art historians Károly (Charles de) Tolnay and Arnold Hauser, as well as other members of the circle. This circle, whose occasional members also included the composers Béla Bartók and Zoltán Kodály and the psychoanalyst René Spitz, held weekly meetings during World War One after Lukács's return to Budapest from Heidelberg in 1916. The meetings continued during the revolution of 1918 that brought in the liberal Károlyi government and during the spring and summer months of the Hungarian Council Republic of 1919, in which most members of the Sunday Circle were active participants, notably Lukács as Commissar of Education. After the defeat of the Council Republic in August of 1919, most of the Sundayers, as they called themselves, fled to Vienna, where they continued to meet well into the 1920s, albeit under quite different circumstances. Like Karl Mannheim, László Radványi soon moved on to Heidelberg, and it was here, in the winter semester of 1920–21, that he met Netty Reiling, later known as Anna Seghers, who was quickly drawn into the exiled Sunday group in Heidelberg. Radványi studied with Heinrich Rickert, Emil Lederer, and Karl Jaspers (Netty Reiling also attended their lectures), and in 1923 a committee headed by Jaspers awarded him *summa cum laude* for his dissertation on chiliasm, a study containing ideas that would have a major impact on Seghers's subsequent creative work.[11] They married in 1925 and moved to Berlin, where Radványi, at first still calling himself Johann (after the apostle John), thereafter Johann-Lorenz Schmidt, became director of the Marxistische Arbeiter-Schule, or MASCH, whose international faculty included members of the Sunday Circle—Lukács, his wife Gertrud Bortstieber, Béla Balázs, Béla Fogarasi—as well as such Germans and Austrians as Karl Korsch, Walter Gropius, John Heartfield, and Hanns Eisler.

In the pertinent chapters I argue that the philosophical, aesthetic, and political questions debated by the members of the Sunday Circle for over a decade in Budapest, Vienna, Heidelberg, and even Berlin assume a significant place in the "mythic world" of Anna Seghers's narrative prose. Although Seghers, unlike Thomas Mann, for example, was not one to paint psychological portraits but rather created more or less composite characters, one can recognize traces of the Sunday Circle, especially the life journey of the exiled "philosopher-king" Georg Lukács, in some of the chiliastic figures that permeate her early prose and also recur in later works. For Thomas Mann, the young Lukács was the brilliant, ugly Jew Naphta who appears as quite an aberration in the misty environs of the Magic Mountain. For Anna Seghers he was akin to the first-century Jewish apostle in the diaspora—soul of a failed revolution, melancholy captain of a tiny craft navigating cautiously to avoid shipwreck as it sails toward the horizon on rough seas.

If Seghers had been Simone de Beauvoir thus writing of Sartre, or Hannah Arendt of Jaspers (or Heidegger!), the world of letters would surely have taken more serious note. But previous cold-war barriers to the elucidation of the rather cryptic "Hungarian" dimension in Seghers's work have been not only Western in origin, nor have they been primarily cultural or linguistic, although this last factor must also be taken into account. It is well known that after his pivotal role in the Hungarian Revolution of 1956 Lukács once again, as in the 1920s and again in the late 1940s, came into official disfavor within the Hungarian Communist Party, whereupon he was permanently retired from his university professorship and all other public service; he retreated to a life of internal exile in his apartment overlooking the Danube, where he devoted himself to his late writings on ontology and aesthetics.

This situation was hardly conducive to the exploration by GDR and East European scholars of Lukács's, especially the *young* Lukács's, influence on Seghers—nor to its acknowledgment by Seghers herself. Thus, *mutatis mutandis,* a virtual hold was put on any major new findings in subsequent Seghers scholarship at the very time that Brecht scholarship, for example, was reinvigorated by discussions of his early writings, thus bringing about a crucial redefinition of his work as a whole. The less fortunate state of affairs in Seghers criticism—in part because Seghers was still alive to alternately guide and befuddle even her best-intentioned critics—is particularly lamentable in the case of the progressive young GDR critics of the 1960s and 1970s, for example, Friedrich Albrecht, Inge Diersen, Frank Wagner, and Seghers's first German biographer, Kurt Batt, himself a devoted Lukács scholar.[12] Their painstaking studies of Seghers's writings prior to her return to the GDR attempted to dispel the official GDR image of Seghers as a mere "socialist realist," yet they were compelled, at least on paper, to forgo excursions into the very issues that might have given them new keys to the understanding of her work. Nonetheless, these GDR studies of the sixties and seventies are still among the best that exist, and they laid the basis for Seghers research undertaken by a younger generation of scholars, many of them women, in the Federal Republic of Germany and subsequently in the United States.[13]

Christa Wolf's preoccupation with Seghers, as revealed in more than ten essays and interviews, also belongs in this context. The beautifully crafted and quite moving essays Wolf devoted to her mentor are well known to have had enormous resonance. But in the interviews Seghers granted to Wolf, and others, one senses in their cautiously phrased questions how much some interviewers surmised but were unable to pursue in dialogue with an author who was extremely guarded about her own person and work, refusing clarification of whatever she had decided in a given work to leave ambiguous in the first place. Especially when it came to her early years in Heidelberg and Berlin, to the influence of the young Lukács, or to the impact of the later Soviet purges and trials, Seghers's responses were predictably vague and even misleading. For example, when confronted directly about her preference for legends and tales in "times of great danger," as Christa Wolf once had the audacity to suggest, the elder writer quickly withdrew behind the explanation that she just plain "invented" the material for such stories or drew on already "existing *Märchen* and tales."[14] There is of course some truth in this. But such utterances, taken all the more seriously because we have so precious few of them, have occasionally inspired more literal-minded exegetes than Wolf to peruse Seghers's work for motifs in the more politically subdued spirit of the collections of the Brothers Grimm.

The reappraisal of Lukács after his death in 1971 was made possible by the somewhat more fortuitous circumstances in Hungary, where Lukács's students, notably Ferenc Fehér and Ágnes Heller, set about editing his work and, after their own exile to Australia in the mid-1970s, continued to stress the significance of his early period for an understanding of the work as a whole. This endeavor, spurred by the discovery of the early Heidelberg manuscripts and other writings, quickly brought about renewed interest in the Hungarian avant-garde movement between 1900 and 1919, in which the artists and intellectuals of the Budapest Sunday Circle of course played a crucial role. Significantly, this avant-garde movement was destroyed by the Horthy regime as many as fourteen years before the victory of the National Socialists in Germany, that is, in 1919, when most of its members dispersed throughout Europe, while those few remaining in Hungary were arrested or went more or less underground. The specter of the failed revolution that already figures so prominently in Seghers's work of the 1920s and continues to be a decisive paradigm in her later work is modeled on *this* avant-garde project that culminated in the Hungarian Council Republic of 1919, or, as its defenders called it, the Commune. What I am saying is that Seghers's narrative prose has little to do with the Stalinist model or subsequent revisionist utopias of the German Communist Party that some critics have claimed to identify in her work.[15] As Siegfried Kracauer already noted in 1932 about her first novel, *Die Gefährten* (1932, The Wayfarers), Seghers's prose offers the reader a "martyr chronicle of today."[16] It is entirely in keeping with the spirit of Seghers's work that it was Rosa Luxemburg, not Lenin, or, *horribile dictu,* Stalin or Ulbricht, who pointed out more than one parallel between the lives of the early Jewish Christians and the socialist movements of the modern era.[17] My examination of Seghers's connection to Lukács and the Sunday Circle also leads me to conclude that, as revealed in any number of her tales, it was again not Stalin, but the recalcitrant Jewish intellectual and political "heretic" Leon Trotsky whose legacy came closer to embodying the chiliastic spirit of revolution to which most of the Sundayers continued to cling long after the defeat of the Hungarian Council Republic of 1919.

The textual readings and arguments offered in this book are quite new and, I believe, overturn a good deal of what has previously been taken for granted regarding the aesthetic, philosophical, and political underpinnings of Seghers's oeuvre. Without a doubt, my work has profited above all from the original research I conducted in archives in Berlin and Budapest, from my conversations with Seghers's contemporaries, family, and friends, and, last but not least, from countless hours of reading and rereading Seghers's own words in the forms she had them assume in her creative legacy. For lack of archival evidence in the form of letters and other documents pertaining to the crucial Heidelberg (1920–24) and early Berlin (1925–33) years, the Seghers library holdings were vital to my research. The collection has over nine thousand titles ranging from books from the author's childhood to the years prior to her death in 1983. It includes significant Judaica, titles in sinology, art books and prints from the years in Heidelberg and Berlin, and philosophical works that influenced discussions within the Budapest Sunday Circle, as well as an illuminating collection of Hungarian avant-garde writings acquired by Radványi before and shortly after his exile in 1919. Due to my Hungarian birth and facility in the language, I developed a greater interest in László Radványi than other scholars have shown, and I was able to find significant Hungarian materials in the Seghers-Radványi library in Berlin and in Budapest archives. My knowledge of Hungarian also allowed me to decode linguistic curiosities in Seghers's prose previously overlooked or dismissed as obscure. I have identified some of these as phonetic transcriptions of Hungarian words whose meaning is vital to our understanding of the entire oeuvre.

"Criticism is an art and not a science," Lukács noted in his introductory essay, written in the form of a letter to Leo Popper, in *Soul and Form*.[18] Surely it was due to my long-held attraction to Lukács's writings, and to the essay form per se, that in spite of my conversance with the secondary literature on Anna Seghers, I also hungered for more. Thankfully, I found such nourishment in those critics and writers whose essays on Seghers give evidence of Lukács's inspiration and, not coincidentally, whose skillful use of critical association and suggestion also reveals a deep understanding for the art of Seghers: Hans Mayer, Christa Wolf, Walter Benjamin, Hans Henny Jahnn, Stephan Hermlin, and also Heiner Müller, in many of whose plays both a kinship with Lukács and the language and topographical texture of Seghers's prose are embedded.[19]

This having been said, I see my work as having built on a significant body of the more conventional historical, biographical, and textual studies. While I cannot acknowledge them all, I wish to single out the contribution of Erika Haas, whose study of 1975, *Ideologie und Mythos: Studien zur Erzählstruktur und Sprache im Werk von Anna Seghers,*[20] represents the first attempt to differentiate Seghers's myriad uses of myth and mythic structures. Unlike scholars who tend to ascribe a vaguely defined "Christian" symbolism to Seghers, Haas locates the biblical references within the appropriate Old Testament and Jewish-Christian traditions. While my own study is concerned with identifying paradigms and contextualizing them within a larger set of intellectual discourses and histories, those readers wishing more specific textual enumerations and categorical detail will find Haas's book valuable.

As yet, there is no definitive bibliography of the extensive international secondary literature (*The Seventh Cross* alone has been read in over forty languages!), but significant listings of titles in major languages can be found in the bibliographies compiled by Maritta Rost and Peter Weber (1975), Manfred Behn-Liebherz (1982), and Sonja Hilzinger (1992).[21] More recent publications by Ute Brandes, Andreas Schrade, Alexander Stephan, and Christiane Zehl Romero contain useful select bibliographies.[22] Select bibliographies, as well as a fairly comprehensive listing of Seghers's works, can be found at the end of my encyclopedia entries in English, "Anna Seghers" and "Das siebte Kreuz" (*The Seventh Cross*), in the Fitzroy *Encyclopedia of German Literature.*[23] The publications of the Anna Seghers Society since 1992 contain a treasure-house of information: releases of archival material and biographical data; scholarly articles, essays, reviews, and debate; heretofore unavailable letters and literary texts authored by Seghers; and new theoretical-historical readings that recontextualize Seghers's work.[24] The pictorial biography of 1994 (reissued in 2000), edited by the Seghers scholar Frank Wagner, her former Aufbau Verlag editor Ursula Emmerich, and her daughter Ruth Radvanyi, contains theretofore unknown letters and documents that shatter previously held cold-war perceptions.[25] The 1998 English volume of critical essays, edited by Ian Wallace, contains a diverse range of new studies by international scholars; especially useful is Ute Brandes's well-researched examination of Seghers's political difficulties in the GDR.[26]

The lack of a definitive text-critical, annotated, and commentated edition of Seghers's works has posed a serious impediment to past and current scholarship. The twenty-four-volume *Werkausgabe* currently under way, edited by Helen Fehervary and Bernhard Spies, with individual volumes edited by an international corps of Seghers scholars, will surely provide a solid foundation for more critically exacting Seghers research. Unlike the fourteen-volume Aufbau edition *Gesammelte Werke in Einzelausgaben* (1977–80), the new twenty-four-volume critical edition uses first editions as the text base and accounts for variants. Moreover, its editors are able to rely on letters and other documents previously sequestered by the heirs. The *Werkausgabe* also presents new textual material released since 1990 and foresees two volumes of letters.[27]

A final word about Seghers's Anglo-American reception. Her work first appeared in English in 1929 (London; New York, 1930) in Margaret Goldsmith's translation of *Aufstand der Fischer von St. Barbara,* published in German in 1928. In a prefatory note Goldsmith informed her readers that *The Revolt of the Fishermen* was "one of the most outstanding examples of the new German prose," that "both in matter and manner Frau Seghers is a notable representative of this new style," that the author's "technique . . . plays a very definite part in conveying the atmosphere of her story," and that she "occasionally enters the minds of her characters and describes their thoughts without indicating that she is no longer describing the immediate happenings."[28] Yet Goldsmith (or her publisher) felt obliged to omit one taproom song that she "feared might offend English and American readers."[29] The song, which I have translated in the notes to chapter 2, is sung in a harbor tavern by the prostitute Marie. Today's readers would easily recognize it as a characteristic example of late Weimar culture, indeed perhaps even mistake it for a song rendered by Lotte Lenya in the legendary productions of *The Threepenny Opera* or *Rise and Fall of the City of Mahagonny.*

Seventy years later, stylistic provocation needs no defense, and sexual material can be more or less explicit. But the reasons for Seghers's later success in the Anglo-American world, and subsequently the virtual disappearance of her name from the pages of English-language newspapers and journals, are more directly political. In 1942 Seghers became renowned throughout the Western Hemisphere as the author of the antifascist novel *The Seventh Cross,* a best-selling Book of the Month Club selection in the United States that was later republished as part of the war effort in a special armed forces edition. The novel was also turned into a popular comic strip syndicated nationwide and, more memorably, into a successful Hollywood film directed by Fred Zinnemann. The film starred Spencer Tracy, Hume Cronin, Jessica Tandy, and Signe Hasso, with Brecht's wife Helene Weigel in a stunning mute appearance as a concerned janitress who dutifully reports to the Gestapo a tenant harboring an escaped concentration camp inmate in his apartment.[30] Two years later, as the war was nearing its end in 1944, there was far less interest in the publication of *Transit,* Seghers's novel about the plight of European Jews and other political refugees trapped in Paris and Marseille in 1940–41.[31] The publication in English of *The Dead Stay Young* in 1950, a novel spanning the period of the rise and fall of National Socialism between 1919 and 1945, barely found critical resonance.[32] By this time Seghers was already living in the German Democratic Republic, and the rest of this particular story, we might say, vanished into the depths of the political and cultural divide that marked the more than forty-year history of the cold war.

The book I present is the first major study of Seghers in English and the first in any language to situate her within the larger context of Central and East Central European intellectual history. As we celebrate the centennial of the author's birth in the year 2000, it is my hope that publication of the book can help rekindle interest in the legacy of an extraordinary German-Jewish woman writer of her generation and era, a writer whose life work gives rare artistic testimony to the hopes and trials of a century few among us may soon forget.

CHAPTER 1

Mythic Topographies: Art and Art History in Mainz and Heidelberg

I'll side with the man in Shaw's *The Doctor's Dilemma,* who when asked what he believes, answers: "I believe in Michelangelo, in Rembrandt, and in Velázquez."

—Anna Seghers, 1948[1]

Anna Seghers's creative imagination was not psychological and musical like Thomas Mann's, nor dialogic and lyrical like Brecht's. She was instead the quintessential pictorial writer. Everything she wrote revolves around pictures and derives its significance from them. If we can speak of an aesthetic credo behind her work, it is inextricably bound to the visual arts. Their influence is apparent everywhere in her prose. In one of many such memorable scenes in her famous antifascist resistance novel *The Seventh Cross* (1942), the unfortunate acrobat Belloni, one of the novel's seven concentration camp escapees, crouches gargoyle-like on the roof of the Hotel Savoy until he is shot "into the feet" from below. Summoning "all his strength," he rolls down to the railing, swings himself over it "before they could get to him," and plunges into the hotel yard. Long afterward he remains ingrained in the memory of onlookers, "floating above the roofs for hours, part ghost, part bird."[2]

In the same novel the fugitive Georg Heisler experiences a moment of clarity before the vastness of space and time represented by the great Romanesque cathedral in Mainz, where he finds refuge for a night:

In the meantime the bells had ceased. The sudden silence in the square and the absence of the reverberation in the wall against which he was once again leaning made him realize how strong and powerful their sound had been. He took a step forward and looked up at the spires, but grew dizzy before he found the highest one. Above the two squat steeples near by a single spire towered into the autumn sky with so effortless a daring and ease that it hurt him. Suddenly it occurred to him that in so vast an edifice there ought to be no dearth of chairs. He looked for the entrance; it was a door, not a gate. Still marvelling at actually being able to get in, he collapsed on the nearest end of the nearest bench. "Here," he thought, "I can rest." Only then did he look about him. Not even under the vast expanse of the sky had he felt so tiny. When he saw the three or four women scattered here and there, as tiny as he himself, realized the distance between himself and the nearest pillar, the distance between one pillar and another, and realized too that from where he sat he could see no ending either above or in front of him, but only space and again space, amazement rose within him. And perhaps the most amazing thing of all was that for a moment he forgot his own self.[3]

The depictions of Heisler's subsequent encounters with the statues and painted images in the cathedral's interior bring the individual perspective face to face with the archetypal aspect of art and thereby translate subjective experience into the stuff of myth:

Across the aisle fell the reflection of a stained-glass window, possibly lighted up by a lamp in one of the houses facing the cathedral square or by a passing car. An immense carpet, glowing with all the colors of the rainbow, suddenly unrolled in the darkness. . . . "Ah," thought George, "these must be the two who were driven from paradise; these the cattle gazing into the manger that sheltered the child for whom there was no place anywhere else; there the supper, when he already knew that he was being betrayed; there the soldier thrusting the spear as he hung on the cross." . . . Anything that transcends solitariness has the power to comfort. Not only what others suffer at the same time as we, but also the suffering others have endured before us.[4]

Seghers's interest in the redemptive power of the arts—one might well call it her *faith*—also had a significant conceptual dimension, and whereas so much is written about her as an author in ideological terms, it was in fact her fundamentally aesthetic frame of reference that allowed her to conceptualize her larger worldview. This view, the hope for a more just, economically as well as politically democratic world, comes directly to the fore in her many speeches and essays, and here, too, examples from the visual arts abound. In a 1961 speech as president of the Writers Union, for instance, she rather ingeniously referred her audience to the example of Giotto and the so-called primitive frescos of the early Italian Renaissance in order to make a statement about the desired popular or plebeian form of realism within the new East German socialist culture. As Seghers put it, Giotto was "not the first and not the only painter at the beginning of the Renaissance who placed his haloes around the heads of the native peasant girls. In this way he gave the new content of his time a valid expression."[5]

One of her most moving testimonies is the essay "Glauben an Irdisches" (1948, Faith in the Terrestrial), which she presented as a speech in Poland shortly after her return to Europe. Here again she placed her faith in the transparency of stained glass that allows light to break in and illumine an otherwise dark, empty, colorless world. Responding to the awesome task of postwar reconstruction, Seghers reminded her audience of the "almost senseless" strivings of the mystics and artisans of the Gothic period who in more or less equally dismal times had built the Sainte-Chapelle in Paris, a city most recently occupied by the German army: "At that time, shortly after 1200, a construction where not the walls but the windows were all-important, not the stones but the plates of glass, may well have struck many people as being almost absurd, almost 'abstract.'"[6] Removed to safety during two world wars, in 1948 the glass windows were reinserted for a second time into their iron frames as the world powers deliberated the future of Europe—and Europe hovered on the brink of yet another world war. Comparing the restoration of the glass windows to Pablo Neruda's phrase "reawakening in fleeting souls a faith in the terrestrial," Seghers concluded her essay with her own "almost absurd, almost 'abstract'" utopian view:

> If our watchfulness allows the windows of the Sainte-Chapelle to be completed undisturbed, the fairy tale of red and blue glass will once again be aglow. People will once again, like children, forget their troubles and sorrows for a few moments within these walls, a shelter that is like no other, because it is the work of artists. A marvel will conclude the second millennium: glass windows before which bullets retreat.[7]

Seghers's earliest impressions of art came from her personal experience of the historic topography and architecture in and around her native Mainz:

> As children we were told that across the blue chain of hills beyond the Rhine the Romans had drawn their *limes,* the boundary between the Roman Empire and the wilderness. That stirred up something in me. . . . On the walls of the cathedral's great crypt we were shown the drawings of apprentices from the Gothic period, and were told how the cathedral's towers were built even earlier—by means of circular

wooden stairways for the mules that hauled up the building materials. All that played a part in my relationship to the arts.[8]

During her Mexican exile in the 1940s she was able to draw a connection between her abiding interest in the early "primitivism" of European art and the indigenous influences on surrealism in Latin America:

We know that Diego Rivera decorated the Cortez house in Cuernavaca with images taken from the history of Mexico. I had the experience of watching a peasant who came to the house with his family, tied up his mule at a tree, then went inside to contemplate the frescos with his people. In those frescos they found themselves anew—their lives and their history.[9]

Seghers's later narratives, written after her return from exile, often reveal the attempt to express the essence of a picture in the rhythms of prose. For example, the slow, steady movement of sentences at the beginning of *Das wirkliche Blau* (1968, The Genuine Blue) simulates the weariness and fragility of Mexican life among the poor as enacted by the plodding strides of a mule laboring under a potter's wares. The scene also reminds us of the medieval Mainz of Seghers's childhood and its legends of toils by men and mules who erected the towers of its great Romanesque cathedral:

Benito climbed slowly down the slope with his laden mule and his family toward the outskirts of the city. Luísa walked behind, her youngest child in her rebozo. Andrés, the eldest boy, went alongside the mule, cautiously, like his father, so that nothing would break. Gabriél, the middle son, went a bit ahead. Now and then he forgot himself and jumped or plucked at something, for after the rains everything was sprouting and flowering. The meadows were dotted with all kinds of colors, and a purple hue of bougainvillaea hung over the white houses at the city's edge.

The mule walked with care. It knew very well what it was carrying. Even on its own it could have transported safely all the way to the market in Mexico City the entire stock of ceramic wares its master Benito had shaped and fired, painted and glazed.[10]

Anna Seghers, that is, Netty Reiling, was born on 19 November 1900 in Mainz, a city with a rich two-thousand-year history and culture situated southwest of Frankfurt on the left bank of the Rhine across from where it is met by the Main. First established as a Roman fortification under the emperor Durus, as early as the ninth century the city enjoyed significant periods of independence and prosperity within the Holy Roman Empire under the rule of its powerful bishops. The old Jewish cemetery, a short walking distance from Parcusstraße 5, where Netty Reiling was born, dates back to the eleventh century. During this time Jewish economic and intellectual life flowered in Mainz, and its Jeshiva became a leading rabbinic school within the larger Ashkenazic communities of culture and learning. Equidistant from Paris and Berlin, the city had historic ties to France during the Enlightenment and the French Revolution. In 1792 its citizenry declared the Mainz Republic, defeated one year later by the armies of the German aristocracy. The siege was described by the poet Goethe, who accompanied the Duke of Weimar and his troops to Mainz. The Germans were ousted by the French in 1797, and the city officially became part of France until Napoleon's defeat. In 1816 Mainz was incorporated into the Grand Duchy of Hesse-Darmstadt. After 1870 and Germany's victory in the Franco-Prussian War it became part of the German Reich. At the time of her birth in 1900 Netty Reiling's parents wanted her name registered as Jeannette but were refused by the official in charge with the explanation that it was "French." Thus she officially became Netti, later known as Netty. Her father did not sign the birth document because it was the Sabbath.[11]

Netty Reiling appears to have been precocious and somewhat indulged as a child. "I was a terrible child," the author later said of herself. "I gave my parents a lot of trouble."[12] Her cousin Pablo Arfeld recalled that whenever they disagreed about something as children, she would say: "I happen to have my own ideas, and what I think is toll free."[13] Her friends thought of her as "intelligent and impertinent, smart, mature for her age, modest, and somewhat different from us."[14] A former schoolmate of Netty Reiling told the writer Christa Wolf that when Netty visited her she sat on the floor of her room (not in a chair!) and provoked her with the question: "Which one do you really love more—your father or your mother?" "I ask you," the now aged woman said to Christa Wolf, "how is one supposed to answer a question like that?"[15]

Netty Reiling's parents had liberal-democratic leanings, and they raised their only child in the religious and cultural traditions of Judaism and the spirit of the Enlightenment as it developed over the centuries in Holland, Germany, and France. Her mother was widely read and tried to inculcate a taste for Schiller and Goethe in a daughter whose active fantasy life was inclined to the magic of Andersen's tales, *Robinson Crusoe,* and the *Thousand and One Nights.*[16] Hedwig Fuld Reiling was a woman with a strong social commitment who became a founding member of the Mainz Jewish Women's League and participated in numerous voluntary projects on behalf of the disadvantaged. She belonged to the distinguished Fuld family in Frankfurt, who traced their Rhenish ancestry back over the centuries. Herz Salomon Fuld, the patriarch of the family during the early Enlightenment, can be dated back to 1675.[17] The brother of Netty Reiling's maternal grandmother Helene Goldschmidt Fuld was the renowned Frankfurt jeweler and antiquities dealer Julius Goldschmidt. The firm J. & S. Goldschmidt had subsidiaries in Paris, New York, and Berlin and was the sole agent for the Rothschilds worldwide.[18] One century later, descendants of this family dispersed to all corners of the world. Hedwig Fuld Reiling herself perished after being deported to the Piaski ghetto near Lublin on a transport of one thousand Hessian Jews that left Mainz on 30 March 1942. Her husband Isidor Reiling died in March 1940, two days after being forced to relinquish the art and antiquities firm he and his brother Hermann inherited from their father.[19]

It was undoubtedly the memory of her Frankfurt lineage, coupled with her father's more humble ancestry, that inspired Anna Seghers to write her novella *Die Hochzeit von Haiti* (1949, Wedding in Haiti) after her return to Germany from Mexico in 1947. Set at the time of the French Revolution, the novella relates the story of a Jewish family of jewelers that expands its business to Haiti on the recommendation of its patron Count Evremont, who owns one of the largest plantations on the island. The move to the New World is a profitable one for Samuel Nathan, but unsettling to the rest of the family: "How could he suddenly go so far away? Away from his loved ones? Away from his community? To an island where there was no community?"[20] His father-in-law Mendez, "the smartest and cleverest of the family" (13) and of Sephardic origin, is skeptical of the French aristocracy and would prefer the part of the island under Spanish rule, were there any prospects there, which there are not. And so Samuel Nathan's business acumen prevails, and his wife, daughters, and father-in-law soon follow him across the ocean. On this island far removed from Europe Samuel Nathan is privileged and financially successful, yet he "belongs to no particular group of whites and to no particular group of mulattoes." But he "wouldn't in the least have been astonished by this, just as a mango tree isn't astonished to find itself standing among coconut trees. It was what it was" (12). His only son Michael stays behind in France to complete his education and is a supporter of the Revolution by the time he reluctantly complies with his father's wishes and makes the voyage to Haiti twelve years later. Soon after his arrival he witnesses the first successful anticolonial revolution in the New World led by former slaves. Thereupon his family returns to France along with the plantation owners, whereas Michael Nathan becomes a supporter of Toussaint L'Ouverture and marries a black woman. After her death and the defeat of

Toussaint, Nathan rejoins his family in Napoleonic France, enters into an arranged marriage, and is sent to open a new branch of the family business in London, where he soon dies.

Netty Reiling's father Isidor Reiling and his brother Hermann owned an art and antiquities firm inherited from their father David Reiling, who first came to Mainz dealing in dry goods. The brothers turned the family trade into one of the city's thriving businesses. The firm soon acquired a European reputation, and its regular customers included members of the Hessian, Prussian, and Russian courts. The large, renovated three-story building housing the Reiling brothers' art and antiquities firm—only a few steps behind it the girls' school attended by Netty Reiling—was located on Mainz's Flachsmarkt. From here the narrow Schusterstraße, lined with the city's Jewish businesses, led to the central square around the Romanesque cathedral, where Isidor Reiling, whose daughter would later describe its details from memory in *The Seventh Cross,* was consulted on curatorial matters. The Reiling brothers' firm was also only a few steps away from the synagogue in the old Jewish sector, where by the end of the nineteenth century the wealthier Jews in Mainz, among them David Reiling and his family, no longer lived.[21] When a more spacious, modern synagogue was built in the recently developed northern part of the city, Isidor and Hedwig Reiling remained loyal to the old community and continued to attend services at its small Orthodox synagogue decorated in the Moorish style. The attributes of personal loyalty, determination, and devotion to community that the child Netty evidently observed on the part of her parents surely influenced her own adherence to these values as an adult—her commitment to her marriage that lasted more than five decades, to her children and grandchildren at whose side she stood firmly over the years, and to friends and associates whom she supported in myriad ways, and finally, despite many disagreements and increasing disenchantment, her unflinching loyalty to the German Communist Party, to which she belonged from 1928 until her death in 1983.

Although she broke her official ties to Judaism after her marriage and move to Berlin,[22] Anna Seghers was firmly rooted in its religious life and traditions. As a child she accompanied her parents to services and was familiar with the prayers, rituals, and readings that would have been expected of someone of her background and education. At school she received instruction in the "Israelite" religion from her favorite teacher Johanna Sichel, known to readers of *The Excursion of the Dead Girls* (1946) as Fräulein Sichel, who also taught German and English literature.[23] We can assume that the Reiling family library held devotional literature and other Judaica, which for the most part was lost or destroyed under National Socialism.[24] We can assume that it also held an impressive selection of the German and European classics, and of course art books. Netty Reiling could boast of a good number of such titles in her own library, and she rigorously pasted her ex libris "Netty Reiling" into the books belonging to her at this time.[25] Prone to sickness as a child, she learned early on to read, draw, and illustrate her own stories.[26] Because of her frail health her parents took her to spas and resorts as far away as St. Moritz, and with more regularity to the Dutch seacoast, which she later described in her narratives. Netherlandish art and the history and culture of Amsterdam, where Jews had found sanctuary over the centuries, would have a strong impact on her writing.

Predictably, Netty Reiling went on to study art history. She began her studies at the University of Heidelberg in the spring of 1920 after completing her *Matura* in Mainz, where she attended the Höhere Mädchenschule und Lehrerinnen Seminar (Upper Girls' School and Teachers College). Her major course of study in Heidelberg was art history, with a significant number of courses in sinology, including a practicum at the Institute of East Asian Art in Cologne. The official record of her eight semesters of study also indicates a good number of lectures and seminars in history and philosophy, several of the latter taught by Emil Lederer and Karl Jaspers.[27] The courses for which she registered during her first semester in Heidelberg indicate the general range and direction of her interests at the time: Introduction to Egyptian Art, Modern Chinese Language Study, General History of the Nineteenth Century, The City in the Middle Ages, Modern Life in China and Japan. Her courses in her last semester, in the winter of 1923–24, indicate a continued humanistic interest with a shift in concentration toward European art: History of German Art (Carl Neumann), Greek Sculpture (Ernst Robert Curtius), Greek Painting (Curtius), Painting in the Renaissance, History of Christianity, Buddhism, Ethics (Jaspers), Early History of the German People, History of German Literature, History of the French Revolution, François Villon.[28] In 1924 she completed her dissertation under the renowned liberal art historian Carl Neumann on a theme—"Jude und Judentum im Werke Rembrandts" (Jews and Judaism in the Works of Rembrandt)—that wove together many of the threads in her life up to this point. She received her doctorate in November of the same year, and her first story, *Die Toten auf der Insel Djal* (1924, The Dead on the Island Djal), appeared six weeks later in the *Frankfurter Zeitung* under the name Antje Seghers. She never used her academic title and henceforth published her work under the Netherlandish pseudonym Seghers.

It was during her studies in Heidelberg that Netty Reiling began writing creatively. Half a century later she remembered this process as having been connected from the very beginning to the visual arts, particularly as they provided the evidence for a topographic setting or landscape:

> When I was only a young thing I already had a great love for painting and architecture. But this had less to do with my family and upbringing . . . than with my active fantasy life. When I looked at something built in Roman times I didn't just think of history, I also made up stories. I lived out these stories in my imagination, got excited by them, and was disappointed that my friends didn't experience things in this way. I would spin stories like crazy. . . . My university studies absorbed me completely. But my imagination worked and worked, yet produced nothing. Then one day when I did begin writing it broke out of me like a torrent: I wrote, studied, wrote, studied—like a madwoman, and it went on like that to the point of utter exhaustion. Then I knew I couldn't maintain both for long, and I chose writing.[29]

The actual process of finding her vocation seems to have been a relatively slow and arduous one. As a girl alone with her "active fantasy life," later an aspiring writer with few female German-Jewish models before her, she seems to have experimented by placing herself within a variety of more or less mythic settings. If her early childhood fantasy propelled her back to Roman and medieval times by way of the architecture and topography in and around Mainz, at the University of Heidelberg she was quickly exposed to the orientalist trend prevalent in the arts at that time. And here Netty Reiling's fascination with sinology and ancient art from the Mediterranean basin to India, Indonesia, China, and Japan allowed her to identify physiognomies and topographies that would accommodate her Jewish heritage by acknowledging its ancient non-European roots and at the same time take her beyond the more or less assimilated bourgeois German-Jewish identity she inherited from her family.

Like the poet Else Lasker-Schüler, who had experimented similarly two decades earlier, the less exhibitionistic Netty Reiling nonetheless went so far as to physicalize her mythic identifications and even stage them with her own body. For lack of other documentation from her early years, we must rely on evidence from her library, in this case a general history of ancient Mediterranean and East Asian art that served as one of Netty Reiling's textbooks. Whereas it was her habit since childhood to affix her ex libris "Netty Reiling" to the inside cover of her books, in this instance she veered from this custom and pasted it facing page 17, which introduces the section on Egyptian art. The positioning of the ex libris close to the binding directs one to look at the color plate on the full reverse side of the page, which shows the following: the casket of a woman from Thebes (nineteenth dynasty), King Seihos I before Osiris, a wall painting from a cliff grave in Thebes, the casket of a priest (circa twentieth dynasty), and the mummy and casket of a woman from Abussir (late period).[30] The positioning of the ex libris "Netty Reiling" pointing to ancient topographies of the dead hardly seems accidental if we consider the title of Seghers's first published story, *The Dead on the Island Djal,* or the title of her 1949 novel *The Dead Stay Young,* or indeed if we bear in mind the crucial thematic of death and the testimonial significance of the dead throughout her work.

We need not ascribe to mere adolescent rumination Netty Reiling's mythic identification with mummified kings, priests, and women of old (and presumably with other sacred figures depicted in this book and similar books available to her). That this kind of identification continued to have meaning for the author Anna Seghers is indicated by a page from the French newspaper *L'Humanité,* presumably from the 1950s, which she folded between the pages of this very same art history textbook some thirty years later. The page from *L'Humanité* contains an article about the sacred grottos and treasures of Dunhuang in northwest China, as well as two large photographic images from the grottos that bear a remarkable resemblance to the physiognomy of Anna Seghers: the famous *Buddha couché* (673–820 A.D.), with his serene, youthful smile and eyes closed, and the *Guerrier gardant l'accès du Temple* (763–820 A.D.), with his smiling open mouth and eyes, rounded cheeks, thick eyebrows, hair parted in the middle of the forehead, and loose bun at the back of the head.[31]

One is struck by the uncanny resemblance to photographic images of Anna Seghers's physiognomy as a mature woman: the soft repose of her slender, slightly rounded figure; her beautifully proportioned oval face, serene expression, prominent thick eyebrows, translucent irises, and slanted eyes; and the fine strands of long hair pulled loosely into a bun at the nape of her neck. Seghers had a modest interest in fashion but, unlike Else Lasker-Schüler, for instance, hardly dressed in an exotic way, so it must have been the more interior quality of her demeanor that struck many of her contemporaries, not a few of them male admirers, as fascinating and unusual. During their Paris exile in the 1930s the Austrian-Jewish writer Manès Sperber, a student of Alfred Adler, even thought she looked more "Chinese" than either "German" or "Jewish." In his words, Anna Seghers was

> a young German Jew whose round bright face with its clear features looked neither German nor Jewish. . . . The most astonishing thing about the face of this German writer was her penetrating glance, the sudden flashing of her eyes. It reminded one of China; this was the

surprise, for there was nothing Chinese about Anna's face, but when one learned that she had studied Sinology, one was no longer so surprised. It is an undeniable fact, though one not easily explained, that Chinese features develop in older Sinologists, usually after an extended sojourn in China. Anna, however, was young and had never lived in China.[32]

In two photographs taken of her during her student years, Netty Reiling appears in "oriental" attire and assumes attitudes and gestures resembling those of Tai Chi.[33] At this time she was particularly interested in what she once described as Lao-Tse's "great Tao with its principle of 'doing by not doing.'"[34] Netty Reiling seems to have practiced the teachings of the *Tao* even in her everyday bearing. The writer Carl Zuckmayer, who attended art history classes with her in Heidelberg, remembered her as being "very quiet, with a friendly reserve, almost shy, and—how can one say this—quite unconventionally 'sweet and fair' (which is how Thomas Mann describes the young Joseph). Her eyes, agate brown, concealed her intelligence behind an expression that always gave the appearance of being somewhat childlike and astonished, occasionally even sleepy." Zuckmayer also remembered that one of their art history teachers, Wilhelm Fraenger, likened Netty Reiling's demeanor to "the gracefulness of a Javanese temple dancer at rest."[35]

As compared with a writer like Brecht, whose somewhat later interest in East Asian art and philosophy is documented in a variety of ways, thus providing critics with an important key to his work, Anna Seghers left us practically nothing to go on beyond her literary oeuvre itself. Although more opaque in this respect than Brecht's work, it exhibits no less of an East Asian influence.[36] We do know that in her German copy of the *Tao* the student Netty Reiling inscribed Chinese characters in pen beside the fifty-sixth maxim, which appears to have been especially significant to her:

He who knows does not talk
He who talks does not know.

May life be integrated,
Dissipation excluded,
Sharpness blunted,
Confusion clarified,
Blinding softened,
Demeanor made ordinary:
 This is depth in community life.

> Beyond glory,
> Beyond shame,
> Beyond honor,
> Beyond contempt:
>   This is virtue in community life.[37]

We can gain a glimpse into the aesthetic questions that preoccupied her as a student of sinology from a book on Javanese architecture and sculpture in which she highlighted the following:

> All questions of art and the creation of art are rooted in this central point: The complex of the artistic . . . is wholly integrated into the metaphysical. Thus in the last analysis artistic production is not based on the power of the individual intention or will, but on the power of the metaphysical experience of pleasure, and artistic forms are subjected not to aesthetic but to philosophical limits.[38]

Another passage marked by her ends with the sentence "Sculpture as the potential of substance is the potential of reality, that is, it makes life processes visible"[39]—a sentence that can throw light on her later inclination as a writer to rely on mythic topographies, from painting as well as architecture and sculpture, in order to "make visible" the yet unfiltered nature of more contemporary events.

In the concept of art described above there is no place for the idealistic representation of ideas that so preoccupied the neoclassical mainstream of Western art. Instead, everything described here seems to emerge from life itself in relation to infinity, from the reality of nature and substance in relation to the barely "visible" life and shape of the soul. In the course of her studies in Heidelberg Netty Reiling gradually shifted her focus to the art of northern Europe, and here she concentrated on issues that were not unrelated to the formal principles and philosophical traditions inherent in East Asian art. Based on her "love for the kind of art that one falsely calls primitive,"[40] she eschewed the idealistic and imperial traditions of Greco-Roman antiquity that culminated in the Italian high Renaissance and Baroque. Instead she turned her attention to the artisan and early middle-class traditions of northern Europe from the medieval period to the art of seventeenth-century Holland. This concentration comprised the stone and glass work of French, Flemish, and German artisans inspired by the mysticism of the Gothic age, the early Renaissance realism of van Eyck and Matthias Grünewald, and the flowering of landscape and genre painting in seventeenth-century Holland. Thus it was not the more or less egocentric assertion of the individual self, as in the Davids of Donatello and

Michelangelo, that would later inform her own style of narrative art, but the serenely unselfconscious, at once earthly and otherworldly bearing of the Gothic peasants and saints; not the idealized humanity and aesthetic perfection of Albrecht Dürer's portraits and settings in the Italian vein, but the often unflattering, yet always soulful momentary aspect captured in the probing, tentative style of Rembrandt and the Dutch landscape painters and engravers.

As indicated by the courses in which she enrolled at the university, the books she collected in her library, and the figures she later created in her own writing, there existed in the mind of Netty Reiling/Anna Seghers a free-flowing yet interactive, and for her work as a writer ultimately quite productive, relationship between the contemplative heritage of Asian art and the mystical religiosity that manifests itself in the art of northern Europe. In this intricately topographic configuration of mind that would later express itself on the written page, we might identify variously positioned Buddhas from temple gardens alongside the happy enthroned Christ from the east portal of the Mainz Cathedral, or the wondrously smiling St. Stephen from the Adam portal of the Bamberg Cathedral. We might find the physically more expressive figures of Javanese art alongside such Gothic stone groupings as Maria and the apostle John weeping at the cross on the west wall of Naumburg Cathedral, or the clever and foolish virgins on the north transept portal of the Magdeburg Cathedral. We may even come upon Chinese miniature painting and the intricately embellished religious paintings of Hindu art alongside the detailed and colorfully decorated Madonna and Nativity paintings of the fourteenth and fifteenth centuries by the anonymous Rhenish painters and such German and Netherlandish masters as Stephen Lochner, Bartolomäus Bruyn, Martin Schongauer, Albrecht Altdorfer, Matthias Grünewald, Jan van Eyck, and Rogier van der Weyden. And alongside the simple, graceful female figures in Javanese painting we would see the exquisite Gothic Madonnas of northern France as well as German Marias with adolescent peasant faces in thirteenth- and fourteenth-century dress, such as the enthroned Madonna from the Liebfrauenkirche in Halberstadt, the fragmented wooden Madonna in Marburg, or the especially captivating standing stone Madonna in the Märkisches Museum in Berlin.[41]

Pictured in the art books owned by Netty Reiling, these female sculptures can be seen as prefigurations of the girls and young women that people Anna Seghers's later work. Indeed, just as Asian sculptures and Gothic statues were intended as variations attempting to "make visible" or "give life to" the at once original and legendary source, be it a Javanese female deity or the Judeo-Christian Madonna, Anna Seghers the writer is well known to have serially assigned the name Marie to many of the female characters in her novels, novellas, and stories. Indeed, a vast number of the names she gave to significant characters in her works—in several cases repeatedly, for example, Marie, Anna, Johann or Hans, Andreas, Katharina, Paul, Stefan—are derived from Judeo-Christian tradition as mediated by the history of art. In European painting, particularly that of northern Europe, the tumultuous events of the first century A.D. represent a watershed in historical, cultural, and religious development, and the iconographic ingredients of these events were used by generations of European artists to portray successive apocalyptic events in modern times. It is evident that Anna Seghers understood her role as a chronicler of her own time as standing firmly within this iconographic tradition.

By assuming a literary pseudonym—in 1924 Antje Seghers, in 1927 Seghers, and finally in 1928 Anna Seghers—she clearly had a more mythic identity in mind than women writers before her who for more pragmatic professional reasons chose to call themselves Currer Bell, George Eliot, or George Sand. Her choice of the patronymic Seghers, a name belonging to more than one seventeenth-century Dutch painter, may have been "the idea of a moment," as she later suggested,[42] but it was surely appropriate for a writer whose prose is replete with land-, sea-, and skyscapes inspired by the Dutch landscape painters. Indeed, it only seems consistent that a writer who first "made up stories" around Roman ruins, later identified with Egyptian mummies, and had herself photographed in "oriental" attire would eventually assume a more or less mythic pen name conjuring up its own iconographic topographies. The name recalls in particular that of the Dutch landscape painter and engraver Hercules Seghers (1589/90–1638), a contemporary whose landscapes and etching technique Rembrandt admired and to whom these aspects in Rembrandt's own work were indebted.[43]

Before the name Seghers she eventually put the less foreign-sounding name Anna, a Hellenized version of the Hebrew Hannah. The name, like Marie (Mirjam), recurs throughout the Bible. In the Christian tradition it is primarily associated with the mother of the Virgin Mary, who in painted depictions, notably by Leonardo da Vinci and the Italians, is found together with Madonna and Child and John the Baptist. But the former art history student who wrote a dissertation titled "Jews and Judaism in the Works of Rembrandt" is more likely to have drawn the name from the many outright Hannah figures depicted by Rembrandt. These include the mother of Samuel, the first of the major prophets, who anointed both Saul and David. Rembrandt depicted several times the particularly close relationship between this long-barren woman and her beloved son who only reluctantly but at her urging finally assumed his duties in the Temple (Samuel I, 1–3). Furthermore, in the apocryphal book of Tobit it was the blind Tobit's wife Hannah who complained of her husband's misfortunes until he was finally healed (Tobit 2:14; 5:17; 10:4). Rembrandt repeatedly pictured Hannah as the devoted wife at the side of her husband in his more than thirty depictions of the story of Tobit and his family, a milder and more hopeful version of the Job tale, one that the artist seems to have held especially dear.

However, it was not simply the mother or the wife, but the storyteller Hannah who ultimately would have interested Seghers as a writer, particularly as a Jewish writer whose works reveal a lifelong interest in the messianic legacies of the first-century Jewish Christians. Hannah is known to have been the last Hebrew prophetess, the woman who at the time of his presentation in the Temple proclaimed the infant Jesus as the Messiah (Luke 2:36ff.). She is shown standing at the side or in the background in several of Rembrandt's drawings titled *The Circumcision,* but his more remarkable painting *Hannah in the Temple* (1650) is devoted especially to her. The full-length portrait shows the aged prophetess seated in serene repose in the foreground, holding her eyeglasses and a book she has just closed, or is about to open, in her lap. A boy child kneels at her side and looks longingly at the book. In the dim background the infant brought in for the blessing and circumcision is held by an old priest while the young father's attention is averted as he looks forward into the distance toward the prophetess. The mood of the painting suggests a tension between the ritualistic custom of ancient law and the modern view of learning as enlightenment. It is significant that the prophetess is not depicted in magical terms as a seer, but as an enlightened reader and storyteller with book and eyeglasses from the contemporary humanistic perspective of Rembrandt's time.

This is surely how Anna Seghers herself perceived and indeed sought to fulfill the role of the writer within the turbulent events of her own epoch. Like Rembrandt, she inscribed the content of her era onto earlier topographies of myth. But if the artist Rembrandt relied on the Bible as his direct source of inspiration, whereby he was able to turn words into images, as it were, the writer Seghers was obliged to do the reverse, using as her main inspiration those iconographies from the history of art that would guide her in finding her own indelible words. The concept of Midrash, used rather loosely here in the sense of allegorical or legendary commentary and illustration, can be said to apply to them both. This may have been another reason for her decision to complete her studies in art history in November of 1924 with a dissertation on the topic "Jews and Judaism in the Works of Rembrandt." Only a few weeks later she published her first story, *The Dead on the Island Djal,* a narrative that has all the ingredients of a Midrashic commentary in the legendary anecdotal style of the Exodus narratives contained in the Haggadah. Quite deliberately, she appended to the story's title the imaginative explanatory note "a tale from the Dutch, retold by Antje Seghers" ("eine Sage aus dem Holländischen, nacherzählt von Antje Seghers").[44] It was a deceptively modest note that allowed her to declare, if covertly, her readiness to take her place among the legions of chroniclers and storytellers who passed on to subsequent generations the knowledge, fancy, and wisdom inherent in age-old traditions of legend and myth.

CHAPTER 2

Landscapes and Seascapes from the Dutch Masters

> Be it "The Crucifixion of Christ" or a folk uprising, a summer land-
> scape or a starving child, the reality the artist wishes to portray is very
> clear to him at first. . . . But as he works he is often restricted by what
> he feels are theoretical and technical defects. Only when he carefully
> removes these wrappings from his original conception does the work of
> art, if not damaged by the tearing of the wrappings, finally stand
> resplendent in greater clarity than reality itself.
>
> —Anna Seghers, 1946[1]

The landscapes and seascapes in Seghers's prose narratives are informed
by the works of the Dutch masters, from Rembrandt, Ruisdael, Jan van
Goyen, and Hercules Seghers to such nineteenth-century naturalists as
Jozef Israëls. Depictions of land, water, and sky in *The Revolt of the Fishermen* (1928), for instance, reflect the very narrative aspect of seventeenth-
century Dutch landscape painting that captured the continuity of nature
and everyday life in the small Dutch republic before a historical backdrop
of economic prosperity and colonial expansion. Seghers's novella, of
course, is concerned with events at the end of that era centuries later:

> The day was soft and grey, the wind came from so far inland that one
> longed to taste salt on one's tongue. Land and sea were covered with
> dust, somewhere the wind was buried; the people did not feel like
> making a noise. Only the birds, forced by the rain to stay close to the
> cliffs, were chattering. Down below, at the harbour, everything was as
> usual; there was no undue activity, but still enough: three, four steam-
> ers left at noon; red packing-cases, striped by the rain, were rolled
> from the piers across the market-place to the warehouses.[2]

Under the influence of naturalism, the narrative perspective often
resembles that of a camera whose subjective view captures emotions that

accompany the economic plight of the fisherfolk. The mood created as the body of the dead fisherman Kedennek is brought to his cottage evokes the mournful atmosphere in Jozef Israëls's *Victims of a Shipwreck* and *By Mother's Grave,* as well as any number of Israëls's cottage interiors. Seghers sets the scene as witnessed by an orphaned adolescent boy standing outside his uncle's cottage with the now dead man's youngest child in his arms:

> The stiff silence of the path and of the cottages, an inexplicable pressure in the air, some noise or other, made Andreas realize at once that down below, under the sky spreading over his village, something important was happening. . . . Kedennek's boys came running up; they were out of breath, they said: "They are bringing father."
>
> Andreas shook his head; now several other people were coming; a few fishermen were carrying Kedennek; his wife came too. Marie Kedennek pulled back the curtain from the alcove bed and helped them lay him down. The men stepped aside but remained standing near the door because it did not seem quite proper to leave at once. A few women, too, came into the cottage; they sat down at the table as a matter of course. Marie Kedennek wiped off the table and joined them. (127–28)

Only a few sentences later, in a narrative gesture characteristic of Seghers, the scene is brought to an abrupt, emotionally pointed conclusion as the fisherwoman takes her all-night vigil to the marriage bed: "When she had cleared things away, Marie Kedennek crept into the alcove bed and lay down to sleep beside her husband, as she had done the night before, as she had done every night before" (129).

Many of the scenes drawn by Seghers convey the somber shapes and hues of Rembrandt's drawings and etchings. The "few strands of rain" we first see in the following excerpt recall the long dark strands that stretch dramatically across the upper left corner of Rembrandt's famous 1643 etching *Landscape with Three Trees.* The fine curved lines scattered across the top of Rembrandt's etching indicate that his sky is also "in tatters." Here is Seghers's version:

> In the morning only a few strands of rain were stretched between the sea and the country sky. Sea and sky were completely in tatters, there was a smell of salt, and the wind was scattering pieces of yellow sunlight over the market-place. Formerly, when Saint Barbara was still the largest fishing harbour on the coast, buyers from everywhere had thronged to the market. But now Sebastian was three times as large,

Wyk at least as large. Formerly the shipowners had lived in the two beautiful gabled houses overlooking the market-place. The gables themselves still floated over the market—they floated, in fact, over the entire harbour like the outstretched wings of two birds resting in the air. (33)

The tenuous realism of the scene is undercut in the last sentence by a simile likening "floating" gables to the "outstretched wings of two birds resting in the air." Such devices are typical of Seghers's early work, which in the wake of expressionistic and surrealistic prose and film is built on a series of more or less realistic images of everyday life, cut one after the other as the narrative moves deliberately and without consolation from one image to the next. We find a similar, though less expressionistic, device at the end of the novella's final tableau. The scene is an eclectic composition combining the wide scope and colonial manner of seventeenth-century Dutch landscape painting with the closely focused naturalistic mood paintings of Jozef Israëls and the more impressionistic landscapes of the Maris brothers. The subjective emotion evoked by the scene depicting the departure of a ship is reminiscent of Israëls's *Fisherwoman.* The arrangement of perspective reminds one particularly of Jacobus Hendrikus Maris's *The Arrival of the Boats,* where as viewers we are also positioned, as if looking through a camera, behind a motley, wet group watching from the shore as fishing boats, in the case of the painting, approach from a turbulent gray sea:

The *Marie Farère* was the first ship to leave the harbour. The rain pricked the women's faces; their fresh bonnets were limp from the moisture and the outlines of their braided hair were visible at the back of their heads. When the trawler pulled the steamer round the pier, a small group of women moved away from the rest and ran to the end of the pier, holding their heavy damp skirts and their children. Now, once more, they saw their husbands' faces as distinctly as though they had been sitting opposite them at the dinner table.

For a moment each woman could, in fact, recognize that dark firm something which she had learned to know during the winter in her husband's eyes. Then they could distinguish only their husbands' faces, then only the outlines of their figures were visible, then only the ship could be seen. The trawler pulled in its chain and turned round; the *Marie Farère* turned at the same time towards the open sea.

The *Marie Farère* had hardly left the harbour, when the wish, which she had secretly suppressed for weeks, became apparent: she moved forward with incredible swiftness. Now the children could still recognize the Bredel Shipping Company's numbers painted on the sails of the ship, then the sails looked like shining red leaves. The ship moved more and more swiftly towards that visible line which separates what is near from what is far away. The ship had already forgotten the harbour, and the grief which she had felt at leaving the land had passed away.

The women on the pier began to realize that they were wet to the skin.[3] (170–72)

The text deliberately sets off the last sentence so as to underscore the disruption of a topos that threatens to become melodramatic: women and children left behind by a ship moving out of the harbor. The scene shifts radically from the barely visible, soon-to-be-imagined ship skimming the waters at the horizon, to the physical reality of women and children soaked to the skin as they stand on the fragile construction reaching into the water that constitutes the pier. The women's attention to the vulnerability of *this* reality breaks the aura of the greater vista, and we are ripped back into the moment, left with the image of a group of women about to leave the pier as if they were stepping off a stage. This prose variation of the emblematic conventions of *pictura* and *subscriptio* imparts a feeling of both stasis and recurrence, an understanding that the *pictures* to which we have been exposed form only a small part of a much greater mythic history and epic construction.

In *The Revolt of the Fishermen* naturalistic landscapes and seascapes predominate. Expressionistic and surrealistic elements dispersed throughout the text thus create the impression of an ultimately unresolved tension between myth and reality. Already at the beginning of her novella Seghers personifies the insurrection in the vein of expressionism but paints its physical surroundings with quick naturalistic strokes:

And Saint Barbara looked just as it did every summer. But long after the militia had left, long after the fishermen were back at sea, the insurrection hung, brooding, over the empty white marketplace which had a deserted, almost bald look in the summer time; here the revolt remained, thinking quietly of its own, of the men it had borne, reared, nursed and protected in preparation for that which was best for them. (9)

Die Wellblech-Hütte (1929, The Corrugated Iron Shack) experiments with a different style. Here there is no tension between naturalistic and expressionistic depiction. Nor are the landscapes merely suggestive of emotion. In the manner of van Gogh the landscapes themselves constitute the emotion, the story—the myth itself. *The Corrugated Iron Shack,* a fragment written shortly after the publication of *The Revolt of the Fishermen* in 1928, can in fact be seen as its sequel. The fragment does not focus on a group of people but on the fate of a single individual. Reminiscent of Kafka, whose novels appeared posthumously in the mid-1920s, Seghers gave her main character the at once anonymous, collective, and mythical name "L." It was not the dynamic-tragic aspect of his character during a failed insurrection that interested the author in her fragment, but his demeanor after his capture; not his splendor in view of the high seas, but his lonely journey into the desolation and trials of the desert. We are given a preview of L.'s fate in the figure of Hull at the end of *The Revolt of the Fishermen.* After his arrest, this instigator of a failed insurrection is escorted overland by soldiers in a horsecart behind the dunes. Thus doomed, he is separated from the age-old symbol of life and renewal—the sea:

> That same day Hull was taken to Port Sebastian by several soldiers. They did not go back by boat but went overland in a small tilt-wagon. The rest of that day, throughout the night and for a part of the next day, the sand road between the dunes stretched before them endlessly. . . . Hull felt only one wish: he wanted, just once more, to see a small strip of sea, he expected this sight of the sea would be quite close, at his lefthand side. But the flat wavy backs of the dunes followed one another with such incessant swiftness and persistency that his wish was not fulfilled. (169–70)

The scene is reminiscent of the dune scapes favored by Jacob van Ruisdael, as in *A Blasted Elm with a View of Egmond aan Zee* (1645) with its two figures walking on a sand road between the dunes, their view of the sea obscured by their downcast gaze and the undulating terrain. The mood of confinement and impending disaster evoked by the image of soldiers and prisoner riding in a fragile horsecart also echoes scenes from such van Gogh paintings as *The Drawbridge near Arles, Road with Cypress and Star,* or *Landscape with Carriage and Train in the Distance.* In *The Corrugated Iron Shack* the mood of desolation and despair is heightened and far more concentrated. Here realism recedes almost entirely before the reduction of surrealistic imagery, as in the following excerpt:

> L. was left behind with two new escorts. They sat down next to him under the platform roof. Obviously they were waiting for something. It couldn't be the train, because the tracks had ended. The sky was clapped over the yellow earth the way one claps a soup plate over a

flat one in order to put away leftovers of food. The wires above the roof ran toward the horizon.

The sun went down. The sky was ripped through. Streams of red and gold couldn't be held back anymore. The sky rose higher, as if it had been relieved of a wonder. L. was relieved, too, but disappointed as one is after great expectation. Then the command was: move on. His escorts had waited for nightfall so as to be able to march in the sand.

Now L. was alone. He walked in the middle, a pace ahead. Across their shoulders the soldiers carried a pole with supply bags that hit against his back. They walked along the rail tracks, then on the highway. . . . After Wheatley there wasn't a highway any longer, only the faint trace of a path under the wires. One after the other the telegraph poles rose doggedly out of the sand before them. L. walked with more difficulty. The supply bags hit more frequently against his back. Maybe his guards had changed places, he wasn't sure. His soles felt as if they were peeling off his feet. He began to reflect again, but with each step he returned to the same thought. His sentences made sounds, but no sense. With each step in the sand the threads that still connected him to his comrades were stretched more taut, and would soon break. Then he would be left all to himself. He wanted to speak to his escorts. They kept silent, as they were supposed to do. Perhaps he should have been more persistent, but then he let it go. Since it was better to hold on to something, his glance followed the wires that ran along with the sand and sky, not with humans. He contented himself with wondering whether after a few paces a pole would reappear. Then he calmed down, because the poles didn't move, they were fastened. The poles became more familiar than his escorts.[4]

Like van Gogh, Seghers focuses the narrative on single, isolated elements that tentatively constitute a landscape and are rendered by flat strokes in blunt, straight lines—train tracks, platform roof, soup-plate sun on horizon, telephone wires and poles, poles with supply bags, traces of a path. The technique of objectification is also evident in the depiction of light, as in the passage that follows:

The sky pressed out more and more stars, the old ones became lighter and lighter. After a while L., who by now was looking all around him, discovered far off a new tiny bright spot. They were heading toward it. As they came nearer the spot turned into a gleaming small cube. L. told himself, now the other [escort] will walk over there. But all three of them went. The cube was a small, flat hut. A light burned behind the window opening. The light ran along the grooves. A man stepped out of the hut and looked toward them. (131)

The affinity to van Gogh is only superficial, however, or symptomatic at best. Whereas van Gogh's art is inscribed by the modern experience of individual alienation, which in its extreme form becomes madness, Seghers's narratives render estrangement and suffering as the conscious memory of, enforced separation from, and persistent longing for community. In this sense (and only in this sense!) her narrative art can be said to be simultaneously romantic and political—which van Gogh's art surely is not. Moreover, Seghers situates the human experience of suffering within mythical landscapes rooted in traditions of Netherlandish art that culminated in the seventeenth century and whose iconography belongs to the Judeo-Christian tradition. Thus L. and his predecessor Hull, both transported into a sand-desert wilderness, are not simply modern revolutionaries (or "madmen," as in the version of modernism since van Gogh) but are bound iconographically, that is, via the history of European art, to the legacies of the Jewish apostles who dispersed after the crucifixion.

If the stars "pressed out" of the sky in the passage above remind us of van Gogh's *Starry Night,* the light that was at first a gleaming "small cube," then "burned behind the window opening," is more likely to have us think of the expression of religious feeling in the art of Rembrandt. Indeed, a significant part of *The Corrugated Iron Shack* is devoted to the existential differences and eventual brotherhood between L. and his fellow outcast and prisoner—the man seen stepping out of the hut at the end of the passage quoted above. Their conflicts make L. long for the old comrades he lost on his journey into the desert—"Why am I here with Brekoly? If only Thomas were in his place!" (136). But it is with Brekoly that he is forced to come to terms, a man with whom he has as little in common as the "rock" Peter had in common with the charismatic apostle Paul. As these two men, banished into the desert as criminals, struggle to understand each other, we are reminded more than once of the young Rembrandt's famous Leyden painting *Peter and Paul in Conversation* (1628): his eyes aglow, his finger indicating a passage in the book held by Peter, Paul passionately argues his point while Peter sits and listens in a calm, meditative pose, three-quarters of his back turned toward the viewer.

L.'s own response to the written word recalls the inspired physiognomies of the apostles depicted as reading or writing in other Rembrandt portraits, as in the 1627 painting *Paul in Prison,* even though L.'s somewhat plodding steadfastness, when compared to Brekoly's "wildness," seems to have more in common with the apostle Peter:

It was a small package, a pack of cigarettes and a letter. The letter was torn open and a sheet removed. Friends had used a piece of newspaper for packing. L. gave the cigarettes to Brekoly and smoothed down the piece of newspaper. These letters held a power that one needed only to touch in order to possess it. Whoever read them belonged to the community of all those who had ever read them. He was no longer alone. Besides that, the news was many months old. L. didn't know some of the names, others he missed. At that moment his homesickness was so strong that instead of oppressing him, it lifted him up. Everything became a bit easier. The horizon almost shrank up. Cities, ships, and human beings were still behind it. The hut was only a bit to the side, that was all. (140–41)

But the desolate landscapes in this fragment are ultimately indebted to the seventeenth-century painter and engraver Hercules Seghers, whose experimental technique already made a great impression on Rembrandt as it did later on the expressionists in the wake of van Gogh,[5] and from whom of course Anna Seghers, née Netty Reiling, took her pseudonymous patronym.[6] No two seventeenth-century Dutch artists were as different as Hercules Seghers and a painter such as Jan Steen. Whereas Steen's works present charming genre scenes peopled by colorful figures at work and play, the somber hues of Hercules Seghers's paintings and etchings erode the civilized trappings of everyday life and reduce perception to the bare minimum of timeless mythic experience—the meandering, seemingly endless road across cragged mountain cliffs and desolate valleys; the wanderer on his lonely journey along withered oaks and long, scrawny dead spruces fallen along or leaning across his path; the occasional resting places offered by the ruins of abbeys and fortresses from whose broken turrets sprout weeds and wild grass. These landscapes that still hold the memory of the Spanish occupation are at the same time topographical journeys into the life of the body, the mind, and the soul. Not coincidentally, examples of Hercules Seghers's rare deviations from his landscapes are an almost life-size skull, a black horse rearing, starkly drawn ships with barely an indication of sea or sky, and a large worn book. In his 1922 study of Hercules Seghers, Wilhelm Fraenger (one of Netty Reiling's teachers in Heidelberg) likened the struggle between religious hope and despair in Hercules Seghers's work to the "prisoner's dream" that weighs the pronouncements of the Old Testament prophets and the evangelists' promise of salvation.[7]

Hercules Seghers's etching technique, for which he is best known, displays no tendency toward illustration. Instead, the very *material* of the content is produced by the sharp lines and angles rendered by the process of etching itself—the strong, meandering, often multiple strokes indicating a road, the sparsely etched leafless, dead trees created by quick, seemingly careless strokes, the small curved lines suggesting the almost indistinguishable outline of a human figure. The wasteland topographies in the passages quoted above from *The Corrugated Iron Shack* are remarkably similar. It is as if Anna Seghers's iconographic arrangement of colorless technological requisites—platform roof, train tracks, telephone wires, telephone poles, pole with supply bags, corrugated iron shack—merely brings up to date, that is to say, modernizes, Hercules Seghers's mythic excursion into the existential suffering and wilderness ruins of his own time. As shown by the following excerpt, Anna Seghers's text stresses the specifically administrative quality of the modern justice system and its dehumanized distinction between the criminally banished and the socially integrated:

> The next day two soldiers walked across the sand. L. would have wanted to run out toward the two dots. He wanted to overwhelm them with questions. The soldiers brought supplies, unscrewed the light bulb, put another one in, tested the locks, tested the security devices. They left before anything might have passed between them other than a murmur between their coming and going. L. watched them until they became dots and disappeared. (135–36)

The setting of *The Corrugated Iron Shack* in a vaguely sketched penal colony located in a geographically remote "Oklahoma"-like wasteland gives evidence of the young Anna Seghers's familiarity with Kafka. The narrative can thus be seen as both a scenic variation of *The Penal Colony* and an elaboration of Karl Rossmann's journey in *Amerika,* alternately entitled *Der Verschollene* (The One Lost) and *Klassenverhältnisse* (Class Relations), after the dystopian depiction of Rossmann's experience in the Oklahoma Theatre is cut off. The political contours of Seghers's fragment, written in the wake of the first "modern" execution in the electric chair of the Italian American workers Sacco and Vanzetti in August of 1928, also bring to mind Bertolt Brecht's response to the Sacco and Vanzetti executions in *Rise and Fall of the City of Mahagonny,* whose inception was also in 1928–29. In *Auf dem Wege zur amerikanischen Botschaft* (1930, On the Way to the American Embassy), which she wrote in 1929, Seghers used a stream-of-consciousness technique to portray the thoughts of four people swept along by a political demonstration on the day of the Sacco and Vanzetti executions. In response to growing commotion after demonstrators hear that the executions have been carried out, police shoot into the crowd. Among the dead is the disconsolate man who flows aimlessly into the crowd at the beginning of the narrative, one of many such accidental martyrs found throughout Seghers's work. Like Hull in *The Revolt of the Fishermen* and L. in *The Corrugated Iron Shack,* he is a fundamentally lonely man driven by ethical principles, inner torment, and incessant wanderings.

Hercules Seghers's mythical landscapes also influenced Anna Seghers's later prose work. *Das Argonautenschiff* (1949, The Ship of the Argonauts), written after her return to her ravaged homeland in 1947, is a prose meditation on the demise of revolutionary hopes in the wake of National Socialism, Stalinism, and the political stalemate brought on by the cold war. The narrative revolves around the homecoming of the mythical Jason, who according to legend was crushed by his own ship. Like *The Corrugated Iron Shack, The Ship of the Argonauts* evokes such desolate landscapes by Hercules Seghers—"on the brink of three-dimensional and absolute space," according to Wilhelm Fraenger—as are found in the etchings *The Great Landscape of Cliffs with Four Trees, Landscape with Cragged Cliffs, The Hollow, The Great Landscape with Cudgel Terrain, The Great Landscape with the Broken Spruces,* and *The Landscape with the Spruce Branch.*[8]

The narrative line of *The Ship of the Argonauts* presents the progressive stages of the shipwrecked Jason's leveling on land. As the once renowned seafaring Argonaut now travels on foot from place to place, unrecognized by his own people, he appears as if engulfed by terrain that is both native and foreign to him. The Golden Fleece draped across his shoulders remains as the only signifier of an entire catalogue of heroic feats. Here we are reminded of Hercules Seghers's etching *The Landscape with the Spear Bearer:* a lone man, visible only from his shoulders and head, carries a long spear pointing upward within a hilly landscape of cliffs encircling him like a whirlpool and threatening to obliterate him entirely.

Jason finds momentary solace in a cool, shaded wood between plowed fields and the crest of a hill, a scene reminiscent of Hercules Seghers's faintly ominous *The Hilly Landscape into the Height.* As the Argonaut emerges from "between the cliffs," his fleece gleaming from afar "like metal in the sun,"[9] he encounters an old man who he senses is not a "shepherd," but a "gardener." He is in fact the "watchman" of a wood whose trees "bear holy signs," that is, decayed remnants of once illustrious ships (132). Only the most famous ship, the Argo, is still more or less intact, Jason learns, and in this curious version of a narrative within a narrative, he is told his own story. Then, continuing on his way through the wood, Jason comes face to face with the "famous ship." The startling positioning of its hull in the branches of a tree within a wooded terrain recalls the finely curved lines, evoking a ship's rigging, that are etched diagonally, from right bottom corner to top left, across one of Hercules Seghers's typically barren landscapes in *The Landscape with the Rigging of a Ship:* "An especially powerful tree bore the hull of a ship along with its moldered figurehead. Jason recognized the Argo in a moment, even though he had never seen it from below. A shudder ran down his back at the reunion" (134).

But the narrative retards the mounting terror and goes on to paint an almost idyllic setting. Heedless of the cares of the world, the weary Argonaut stops to rest under the great tree whose branches cradle the remains of his ship. Here we are reminded not of the morose abstraction of Hercules Seghers, but the soft brushstrokes evident in the bucolic landscapes with great trees painted by Jacob van Ruisdael and Jan van Goyen—Ruisdael's *Hilly Landscape with a Great Oak Tree and a Grain Field* of 1652, for example, picturing a woman seated in the shadow of a great oak; or Jan van Goyen's brightly lit *Landscape with Two Oaks* of 1641, where a traveler resting under two battered oaks on a hillock converses with a peasant who appears to have just approached him:

> Jason lay down on the earth under the tree. Even if he loved the sea more than anything, today it was good to have only green and specks of sun around him. Today he liked the smell of the woods better than the biting sea air. He was tired from the journey into the mountains. He cast off his fleece to feel the warm earth beneath his shoulders. He looked up at the ship, tied by its ropes to the branches, as it swayed imperceptibly in the wind. (135)

> Jason stretched out on the warm earth. He was intimate with the sea, with its storms and its perfidies, but at once it was good to see no more of it. Instead the earth sheltered him quietly and unassumingly in the afternoon sun—like a mother, as compared with a lover. He took a stalk of hybrid grass between his fingers, but didn't dare break it. The roaring in the tree grew stronger. The indistinct rumbling from the sea didn't trouble him in the least today. Whatever storms were brewing, they were not his problem. He put the stalk between his teeth. (136)

But before long we return to Hercules Seghers's orbit of influence, alerted to it by the mention of a cold shadow, which in *The Landscape with the Rigging of a Ship* takes the form of large dark patches covering the landscape. The atmosphere of doom is completed by the groaning of the rigging, the moaning of the tree, and the sudden swinging up of a branch, reminding us of *The Landscape with the Spruce Branch* and other etchings by Hercules Seghers in which a dried-up spruce tree or a split-off branch juts ominously into and across the barren landscape:

> Now the Argo swayed, and its shadow was cold. For one cloud chased after the next across the sun. Showers of acacia blossoms were sent forth. The ropes groaned like hawsers. The brittle planks of the ship cracked in all their joints, and even the living wood of the tree began to moan. Jason thought to himself: I should look for shelter before the old watchman returns. But he stretched and wrapped himself in his fleece.
>
> All at once there were many more birds in the wood. They even fled into the space between the ship's hull and its figurehead. A branch swung out high because one of the ropes had torn, and yellow billows of leaves scattered over the man on the ground. At first the birds thrust themselves into the crown of the tree, then they retreated as far below as possible, even further down than before; in their bewilderment they cowered up against the man in the grass.
>
> Maybe Jason could still have jumped up. But he folded his arms under his head, and his face was as bold as it had truly been bold only in his youth at the moment of greatest danger on the roaring sea. The storm broke. It burst the last cords with one blow. The entire ship's hull crashed down on Jason. He perished with his ship, as it was told long ago in legends and songs. (139–40)

The Ship of the Argonauts is a rare example of Anna Seghers's reliance on Greek mythology, interspersed here with wooded sequences borrowed from folk legends of Central and Eastern Europe. Certainly the topographic aspect of the Argonaut legend would have interested her especially, since the different versions of the story include a wide spectrum of sea voyages around the Adriatic, the Black Sea, and up the Danube River even to the Rhone.[10] But for the most part Seghers preferred to situate such extensive voyages of the mind, body, and soul within the diasporic geography of Judeo-Christian legend and its messianic traditions. After her six-year exile in Mexico, she often used to this end the topography of Latin America and the Caribbean Sea, as in the narratives *Die Hochzeit von Haiti* (1949, Wedding in Haiti), *Wiedereinführung der Sklaverei in Guadeloupe* (1949, Reinstatement of Slavery in Guadeloupe), *Crisanta* (1951), *Das Licht auf dem Galgen* (1948/1960, The Light on the Gallows), *Überfahrt* (1971, The Ship Passage), *Steinzeit* (1975, Stone Age), and *Drei Frauen von Haiti* (1980, Three Women from Haiti).

The Light on the Gallows, which in part was Seghers's response to the Hungarian Revolution of 1956, revolves around a failed uprising on the island of Jamaica in the wake of the French Revolution. Debuisson, one of the three leaders of the uprising and himself the son of a plantation owner, eventually betrays the mission. Another Jacobin—Jean Sasportas, a Sephardic Jew—is hanged for it. A third, Galloudec, manages to escape in a small boat to Cuba, where before long he also perishes, in a prison. Yet he lives long enough to relate the events he has witnessed to a fellow prisoner and to hand him a scrap of paper on which he has written a letter. Sewn into the prisoner's jacket, the letter eventually makes its way across the ocean to a reclusive Jacobin living a semi-underground existence in Napoleonic France. The letter's intricate journey recalls the epistles of the early Jewish Christians written in prisons or on ships, smuggled by way of myriad hands to the old and new communities in Palestine and in the diaspora. Indeed, the scenes of Galloudec's escape from Jamaica directly evoke New Testament and apocryphal stories of the dispersal of the disciples and their followers at the time of the crucifixion:

> He steered the boat toward the southern coast of Cuba. He was soon exhausted. The wind wasn't true to him. It was a southwester, which no one would have expected at this time, and he feared he might be thrown back to his previous refuge. He decided to head for a nearby island inhabited only by birds that he had heard about from sailors.
> It resembled the crown of a mighty tree rising up from the ocean floor. . . . The incessant screaming and screeching made him think the birds might attack and hack him to death. But they calmed down and only swirled around in their tree. He calmed down, too, and began to think things over. He decided to wait until the wind shifted and, once he had regained his strength, head out toward Santiago de Cuba. Then he could easily spot a Spanish ship, maybe even a French one. . . . He had already accustomed himself to the screaming of the birds and to the surf. He looked out toward Port Royal and thought to himself: Ann said Sasportas is to be hanged today. It seemed to him as if a light were shining toward him from the very top of the gallows. A year ago I would not have entrusted him with much, Galloudec said to himself. When I met him earlier in his life I had no idea what kind of life this would be. The light appeared only at its end.[11]

On first impression a passage such as this reminds us of the tranquil mood paintings of small boat, water, and wood crafted to perfection by the seventeenth-century Dutch landscapist Meindert Hobbema. However, by building the momentum of the text toward the light that seems to shine in the distance "from the very top of the gallows," Seghers situated her scene within an expanded, explicitly epic framework. Whereas *The Ship of the Argonauts* ends with a retardatory close-up that builds up and extends subjective tension before the final terror, in *The Light on the Gallows* Seghers wrote as if she were having us look through a wide-angle lens. What is significant here is not the subjective perspective of the martyr, but the larger view from the standpoint of the participating witness. It is in fact the physical presence and (at least temporary) survival of this witness, illuminated as he is by a light that *appears* to shine from the gallows, that in this case gives the most concrete assurance of an afterlife.

Seghers's attention to considerations of spatial distance and perspective in scenes such as these indicates how carefully she allowed her hand to be guided by the iconography and scenic composition characteristic of the crucifixion landscapes in late medieval and early Renaissance Netherlandish and German painting. The actual scene of the Sephardic Jew Sasportas's execution in *The Light on the Gallows* exemplifies once again her indebtedness to this tradition of painting:

> Since Sasportas refused to make a confession, his execution was prepared. Fashionable people came on horseback and in carriages, and they brought their slaves with them, so that these blacks would learn something from the spectacle. . . . The carriages and the individual spectators didn't wait behind the gallows, but in places on the side, as was usually the case, so that they could observe the entire procedure. Because the main event passed quickly, it was customary on such occasions to set up booths and market stands in these locations. Several hundred Negroes who worked on the docks and wharfs around the city were also sent up to gallows hill in Port Royal. Before the executioner put his hand on Sasportas a representative of the court stepped up to the condemned man, telling him to name his accomplices, because in this way he might still save himself.
>
> Sasportas replied: "I see many of my accomplices here, they're standing here and standing there."
>
> When the noose was put around his neck, he called out: "You Negroes, do it the way they're doing it in Haiti!"
>
> A minute later the executioner cut the rope. The corpse fell into the sea like a stone. No splashing was heard in the surf.[12]

In the novel *The Dead Stay Young* (1949) Seghers situated her crucifixion landscape onto the Russian front of World War Two. Here the traditional iconography is given a unique twist in that no light from the gallows illuminates the darkness that usually surrounds pictorial images of the crucifixion. Instead, the darkness itself promises the kind of salvation that will alleviate not only the spiritual suffering of the people, but their material and physical suffering as well. As indicated by the excerpt quoted below, this darkness heralds another kind of resurrection and light—the coming of the Russian winter with its power to bring invading armies to their knees under a gray-white blanket of snow. The scene is viewed through the eyes of a German soldier. Like the legendary Roman soldier who underwent a conversion after having witnessed the crucifixion of Jesus, the soldier Hans is moved to join the resistance on the front. Thereafter he, too, is executed. He is of course only one soldier among thousands of others who were left to die at Stalingrad, abandoned by their senior officers and their once admired *Führer:*

> The autumn was so golden it was hard to realize that this gold too would vanish. Into the faces of the peasants who stared at the strange soldiers came a new expression, carried perhaps on the wind that ruffled their shawls and their hair, while it scarcely stirred the heavy coats of the soldiers. Now the vast sky, as endless as the earth, began to grow dark earlier. The western sky shone bright, and everything beneath it was golden and smooth. Till now it seemed as if the winter had avoided them, but now the army had apparently come to a standstill; they still felt as if they were moving forward an inch at a time, as if they were merely pawing the ground in one spot as slowly, slowly, the snow came to meet them.
>
> At first it was as fine as flour, this snow that sifted down on fields and woods, covering them. And all at once Hans understood what the peasants had been waiting for, when gritting their teeth, they had been pressed into forced labor. They had looked up at the sky, even that woman whom they had recently strung up on the gallows on their march through the village square; for just before she mounted the steps she had raised her eyes to the sky. In her expression there had been none of the hope one turns on the Great Beyond; perhaps, thought Hans, even when she had the rope around her neck she had foreseen the gray twilight now settling down at last over them all.[13]

CHAPTER 3

Ecce Homo: The Legacy of Rembrandt

I think it's a splendid book. I know it by heart from A to Z, and if I
had to live one more time, I'd put it to memory all over again. You can
find all kinds in it, dumb and smart, strong and weak, hard and soft,
seafarers and men of prayer. As to the miraculous stuff, any one can
take with him as much of it as he can bear.

—Anna Seghers, 1924[1]

To describe something one need not have experienced it oneself. One
only has to look, really—and feel intense sympathy.

—Anna Seghers, 1978[2]

Anna Seghers's depiction of physiognomy, interiors, and milieu is
indebted to the drawing and painting style of Rembrandt. Like the art of
the seventeenth-century Dutch master, her prose captures the realism and
authenticity of experience in the glimpse of the moment. As she wrote of
Rembrandt's late portraits of Christ in her University of Heidelberg dissertation of 1924, *Jude und Judentum im Werke Rembrandts* (Jews and
Judaism in the Works of Rembrandt):

> He paints these faces the way he painted a dark, shabby backyard or
> a desolate, insignificant landscape that no one before him could see in
> its richness of expression and that one can only recognize again in the
> depicted image. . . . He doesn't really show us people suffering, but
> rather how they are struck by sudden or unusual misfortune. He
> wants faces that can suddenly quiver with joy or pain, faces in which
> the artist can capture the moment of agitation, not the condition of
> the suffering soul.[3]

Seghers's depiction of the embittered working-class wife and mother
Frau Bentsch in *Die Rettung* (1937, The Rescue) reminds us of Rembrandt's ability to compress deeply felt emotions in a few quick, short
strokes, as in his renderings from different perspectives of Abraham's

expulsion of Hagar (with Sarah looking on) in order to grasp the drama and complexity of the Genesis story in its momentary urgency. In the equivalent scene in Seghers's novel (where the woman is positioned between her husband and the memory of a younger man), Frau Bentsch tells of the love she felt as a young woman for her first husband, who died in the war. Related in the third person, the intimate scene unfolds from the perspective of the second husband, who observes the changes in his wife's face as he listens to her:

> That was her true face now, totally unfamiliar. When the things she was talking on and on about were the most fleeting, long gone and past, her face got brighter and brighter, as if there were something indestructible, an eternal clarity attached to these frail, fragile things. Only to them, not to the continuity of their life together. So that is how she could look, that is how she should look. But it was already over. Except for the bright dots in her eyes that from one second to the next became utterly repugnant to him.[4]

Another passage in the novel, concerning the men's reactions to the boy Lorenz, brings to mind the worried looks of concentration on the etched faces of the young Joseph's brothers as he stands before Jacob and tells him his dream, or similar physiognomic expressions and arrangements in Rembrandt's drawings and etchings of the young Jesus among the elders in the synagogue: "They all focused their attention solely on Lorenz, as if sooner or later what was most important would display itself on Lorenz's face. Bentsch and Franz watched him most intently of all. They were never caught off guard when his neck tightened, or when his ears turned red."[5] One is reminded, moreover, of the simple clarity of expression in the physiognomies of young Joseph and young Jesus in Rembrandt's drawings and etchings:

> Lorenz sat right down. He even seemed happy that he had been given something to do. With long, tough, thin fingers that skillfully accustomed themselves to any occupation, he peeled one potato after another, more finely and handily than Bentsch. Now and then Bentsch threw a glance at his helper's face. It was pensive and, as Bentsch noticed just now, had become fairer and calmer in recent days. It was starting to get dark, maybe from an approaching snowfall, maybe already from dusk. The long young face brightened a bit, its features became clear, as if the last finishing touches had been put on the face this very minute. And now at last it was ready—for the moment.[6]

The compositional style, manner, and narrative technique in passages such as these are particularly indebted to Rembrandt's numerous pen and wash drawings of scenes from the Old and New Testament. Seghers gained insight into the narrative possibilities inherent in Rembrandt's drawing style from the work of Carl Neumann, one of the great liberal art historians of his time, with whom she studied and wrote her dissertation at the University of Heidelberg in the early twenties. Toward the end of her life she remembered that as a teacher Neumann was "critically opposed to the artistic perpetuation of the Renaissance." This "rather curious theory," which first "troubled" her, soon proved decisive for her own work.[7]

Seghers's dissertation on Rembrandt and the painter's impact on her emerging self-concept as an artist as well as on the aesthetics of her own prose were certainly indebted to Carl Neumann's groundbreaking two-volume study of Rembrandt, which first appeared in 1901 and was published in 1921 in its third edition and in 1924 in its fourth, revised and expanded edition. In his foreword to the editions following World War One, Neumann argued against the nationalistic and racist concepts of culture that developed in the wake of Jakob Burckhardt's "cult of the Renaissance" and its promotion of a "Golden Age."[8] According to Neumann, Rembrandt was the epitome of the kind of artist to whom Burckhardt was absolutely disinclined. Politically, he embraced the democratic principles of the small Dutch Republic, which sought to guarantee civil liberties and religious freedoms to its citizens and foreign refugees. Philosophically, he was interested in the mysticism of Jakob Böhme and the ethical pantheism of such enlightened contemporaries as Spinoza. As a religious man he shared many of the beliefs of the free-thinking wing of the Mennonite community (Neumann conjectured that Rembrandt was raised as a Mennonite by his mother), and he was keenly interested in a variety of beliefs that prevailed at the time, as exemplified by his friendship with the Hebrew scholar and publisher Menasseh ben Israel. As an artist Rembrandt was dependent on the system of patronage but devoted himself for the greater part of his life to the portrayal of human life in its myriad external and deeply experienced emotional and spiritual forms. It was this democratic context that informed the artist's profound mysticism, Neumann argued, and only in this sense could he be understood as a "religious genius" and "painter of the soul" (646–93).

Neumann's argument in favor of Rembrandt's enlightened religiosity was an effort to counter the aristocratic racist conception behind Julius Langbehn's *Rembrandt als Erzieher,* which in the decades following its initial publication in 1890 was enormously successful in promoting the Dutch artist as a Germanic *Übermensch.* The three plates that Neumann chose to include in his long chapter "Rembrandt and Religious Life in Holland," for example, are indicative of his stance on Rembrandt's enlightened religious views: the artist's famous self-portrait as the Jewish-Christian apostle Paul; his equally well known portrait of Menasseh ben Israel; and the "so-called Faust," which, according to Neumann, Rembrandt took not from the German chapbook, but from a Dutch version of the legend. Influenced by his friendship with Menasseh ben Israel, Rembrandt portrayed a Faust who "pursues magic and Kabbala as science" before a background illuminated by Kabbalistic signs surrounding the inscription on Christ's cross (660; the plates face pages 658, 659, 688).

According to Neumann's introduction to a 1923 collection of Rembrandt's drawings, the artist's drawings were not preparatory for his etchings and paintings but were compositions in their own right, like "the vase images and narrative friezes of antiquity." Rembrandt did not simply illustrate stories from the Bible but continued the very process of composition that characterizes the Bible itself—in the form of drawings that were in and of themselves "narrative histories" ("erzählende Historien").[9] Thus the visual composition was not the illustration of a text, but narrative per se. Just as the wide-ranging books of the Old and New Testament contain similar stories told in different ways, Rembrandt returned in his drawings more than once to the same story or a group of stories—Abraham and Isaac, the expulsion of Hagar, Joseph and his brothers, David and Samuel, the trials of blind Tobit and his family, the life and preachings of Jesus, the woman at the well, the prodigal son—rendering them from a variety of considerations of light, perspective, composition, and milieu (6–7).

The cyclical quality of Seghers's own narrative work, its reliance on recurrent character types, topographies, and epic constellations, gives evidence of the same approach to subject matter that is at once immediate and timeless, at once historically specific and mythic. Moreover, the very prose style of Seghers's narratives exhibits the characteristics of Rembrandt's unique drawing style. In the words of Neumann, Rembrandt's pen stroke

> hardly produces a form enclosed within an abstract line. Since surfaces consisting of relationships that are continuously changing and crooked cannot be connected by continuous lines, the drawing makes allowances for this optical insight and has a multiplicity of lines crossing or curving and flowing through each other. These lines that glide, gambol, dart, and flash . . . seek to capture movement in the activity of the moment without the randomness of arbitrary scrawls, flourishes, or squiggles. Every stroke entails an awareness of form and despite all breathlessness is replete with artistic composure and confidence. . . . This newfound capacity to create form as movement

finds its appropriate field of application in the task of articulating the movement inherent in dramatic action. Here Rembrandt shows his ability to suggest the drifting and fleeting quality of that which passes with time, [as in] the drawings *Christ Carrying the Cross* and *The Lamentation.* (12)

The way in which a "multiplicity of lines" can create "form as movement" in Seghers's narrative prose is evident in the following passage from *Grubetsch,* first published in serial form in the *Frankfurter Zeitung* in March of 1927:

> The courtyard was quiet again. Somewhere somebody was beating a featherbed. A small boy with a combed part in his hair was trotting off to school, the first one. Then came two workers, then a couple of young things, chattering away in their colorful blouses. Then came a woman, yawning, with a basket of wash, then a swarm of children, then some more workers, then the last schoolchild, a boy with an apple. The day had arrived, hot and wearisome.
>
> The young lads, four or five of them, lay on the pavement in front of the door and waited for something to happen. They had no work. But the sun purled down their throats, painted shirts on their chests, shoes on their toes, and stopped the holes in their jackets. Paul, his hair lacquered brown, his teeth open and shining, stood with his legs spread apart, stiff with boredom. Toni plucked at his moustache, hummed again and again the same start of a song; his shoes full of holes were brightly polished, his nails were cut. The red-haired twins sat sleeping on the window ledge. Below them a tall blond lad, who for some reason or other tended to be coddled by the others, stretched his limbs. The smeary flood of sun that swept across the pavement had almost reached their feet. It was so quiet that one could hear the hissing of fat, whose sharp smell just now filled the courtyard, as it fried in some pan.[10]

The events in the narrative take place in and around a familiar locale—the urban courtyard, or *Hof,* surrounded by tenements that sprang up from the streets of Central European cities at the turn of the century. Seghers wrote *Grubetsch* soon after her move to the German capital in 1925, where her husband became the director of the Marxist Workers' School (MASCH). From her visits to the working-class areas where the school's offices and classrooms were located, indeed even from the back window of her apartment on Helmstedterstraße in Wilmersdorf, she would have had ample opportunity to observe the oppressive atmosphere of a Berlin *Hof* with its dark entrance corners and alleyways, its forbidding, shaftlike walls, and its almost total lack of sunlight in the dead of winter.[11] But the narrative's seemingly naturalistic attention to contemporary social reality belies its larger mythic scope and construction. Here again we are reminded of the art of Rembrandt, as exemplified by the very first image that introduces *Grubetsch.* The drab mood of expectation created by the interplay of light and dark around the cellar door—behind which the vagrant Grubetsch sleeps under the stairway, we learn several pages later—suggests any number of the weather-beaten barns and cottages pictured in their everyday settings in Rembrandt's drawings and etchings. The mention of a "few pieces of washing" at the end of this introductory paragraph also reminds us of those Rembrandt scapes of cottage life in which a small, sketchy figure is seen walking from the side or from behind, who, like the woman mentioned by Seghers, might have been hurrying to do chores or errands "ahead of the rain":

> If the lantern on the iron arm over the cellar door had borne a light other than this burned-down gas jet, it would only have lit up a puddle in a torn wooden plank, a discarded house slipper, and a pile of rotten apples. Like a pit lamp in the deep, it pointed the way for the rain that poured thinly and continuously into this shaft. Only somewhere halfway up did something move that was fluttering white and alive. It was the few pieces of washing hung by their owner in her kitchen window before she left for town ahead of the rain. (13)

From this concentrated retardatory focus the narrative's second paragraph moves quickly and abruptly to present us with the momentary image of a woman leaning out of a second-story window, and in its corner seconds later a young girl, to take a look at whatever might be going on down in the courtyard:

> But in the courtyard things must have been more carefree and gay than they were behind the windows, otherwise nobody would have pushed back the shutters on the left side of the second story, and the woman would not have stuck her head out the window with a long "Ah," and enticed by this, the girl would not have pushed up next to her in the corner. (13)

These are not characters in a modern psychological sense, but images gleaned from any number of renderings of everyday life by the Dutch masters, among them Rembrandt's biblical depictions—Sarah leaning on her ledge, watching with scornful pleasure as Abraham expels Hagar; or the mother of the returning prodigal son opening the shutter of her window to see him met by his father's embrace.[12] The image of the two women in the window in Seghers's text also brings to mind Rembrandt's attention to the windows indicated at the rear of the courtyard in his famous *Ecce Homo* etchings of 1655. Of these there are two main versions, the first with a motley group of figures in the foreground and on the two sides, the second with an emptied foreground under the figures of Jesus and Pilate showing two large dark, catacomb-like hollows. Whereas the first version suggests the presence of Jesus' supporters, the second is dominated by a mood that bespeaks doom. In both versions the setting indicates a courtyard of people having both biblical and seventeenth-century characteristics in terms of architecture, ornamentation, and dress. Jesus stands at the center with Pilate and his entourage on a large raised platform before a Roman-style arch that seems to jut out into the courtyard as if it were a Renaissance stage.

Prominently depicted in both *Ecce Homo* versions are two large second-story double windows behind the arched platform, one window on either side. In each of the windows we can see two figures looking out. On one side of the window at the left sits a woman with the restrained bearing and headdress of a lady, and next to her, on the other side of the baluster, a smaller figure whose features cannot be distinguished. In the right double window, which in his second version Rembrandt brought down lower and enlarged so as to balance it with the other, a man on the right leans far out and cranes his neck so as to catch a glimpse of the figure of Jesus exhibited at the front of the platform facing us; standing back in more reserved fashion is a woman on the other side of the baluster, which partially obscures her. We would need take no special notice of these particular parallels were it not for the fact that Seghers has her two women look out the window just as the text indicates a figure emerging from a cellar door to cross the dark courtyard, and we first hear mention of the title character. "Grubetsch is here again," the woman named Marie remarks to her young sister-in-law Anna. "That means there'll soon be another calamity" (14).

Grubetsch tells the story of a raftsman who spends the winters with a group of people living in various stages of dissatisfaction and misery around an urban tenement courtyard. Since only Grubetsch knows the freedom and fantasy of traveling "on the river," the tenement dwellers put their expectations and hopes in him. But Grubetsch hardly has the makings of a messiah or savior. He remains the lonely outsider onto whom others project their secret libidinal desires—and act accordingly. Thus Grubetsch's presence rips away the mask of reality behind which in his case is affection and the longing for community, but in others only fear, envy, greed, and self-destruction. Indeed, those whose desire for liberation is most desperate are the first who are brought to naught. Sebald, who once followed Grubetsch to work "on the river," dies soon after his return to the prison of his petty family life. Thereafter his sickly, battered son, whom Grubetsch befriends, dies from weakness and heartache while Grubetsch is away on a river raft. The frightened adolescent girl Anna who dreams of "red, glowing, gleaming calamities" (15) surrenders herself to Grubetsch and later resorts to prostitution. The prim, proper wife Marie, her long braids loosened and her breast bared, is also seen offering herself to Grubetsch in the tavern one night, after which she deserts her husband Martin and disappears. Martin's anarchic attraction to Grubetsch soon brings him, an exemplary worker and head of household, to drink and ruin. The remaining tenement dwellers, whose initial fascination with Grubetsch turns to hate, finally betray and eliminate him.

Grubetsch brings the legendary tale of the traveling teacher or prophet into the contemporary urgency of an urban tenement setting. One can find in the narrative as many elements from the legends of Lao-Tse and the teachings of the *Tao* as from the parables of Jesus and depictions of his life in the New Testament. The influence of Eastern mysticism is foremost in the presentation of the characters' thoughts as fabrications and illusions, while the Judeo-Christian influence manifests itself in aspects of messianic longing and the configuration of the passion.[13] In her embittered account of his abandonment of his home life to follow Grubetsch, Sebald's widow unwittingly reminds us of the meditative teachings of Eastern mysticism as well as Jesus' command to his disciples to leave whatever they have and follow him:

> "Grubetsch," said Sebald's wife, "he ate at our table, sat around with us, played with our boy. At first it was Sundays, then twice every day. He got really nice and comfortable. Not that he was pushy or sweet-talked anybody. Oh, he didn't need to do that. It was my husband who dragged him in. Funny, my husband, he was one of those with big plans, always contriving and trying to figure out something; if it got into his head he had to talk about it down in the courtyard and even in bed at night, and ever since we first got together he had some kind of plan, a small plot of land out in the country and wanting to move out there, and down in the yard he would say: 'Someday I'll have a house in the country.' So one day he came home and said: 'I met this man, Grubetsch, and he said, I'd sell that plot of land and go down the river.' So, believe it or not, he went and sold it. From then on he never said, 'I want a house in the country.' Now it was: 'If I could just go down the river with Grubetsch!'" (16)

The first meeting between Grubetsch and Martin is somewhat haphazardly modeled on Rembrandt's depictions of aspects of Jesus' life—his learned skill as a carpenter, his search for a community of friends and disciples, and his later encounters with the apostles as the resurrected Christ. In Martin's desire to touch Grubetsch's hand we are reminded of the doubting Thomas, and in the two men's brief exchanges we hear echoes of the conversation about current events on the road to Emmaus. Even the chronicle tone at the start of the narration suggests storytelling in the tradition of Luke:

> One evening Martin returned from work to go home for supper, and as he was passing through the gate he heard the noise of a saw. . . . At the end of the courtyard a man was working with his back turned to him. . . . That's Grubetsch, Martin thought to himself. If he turns I'll speak to him, oh, I hope he doesn't. Grubetsch broke off, put down the saw, breathed hard, and turned around. Martin came up to him, said hello. Grubetsch looked up at him, Martin was two heads taller. They exchanged a few words about the wood, oh God, how tired Martin was. I'd like so much to touch his hand, Martin thought to himself, oh, what nonsense. They talked about this and that, about the weather, about wood prices, about wages. Just to touch his hand once, such nonsense, Martin thought to himself. Had something happened? When had he felt so anxious before? . . . I like him, Grubetsch thought to himself, he's from the country. He reminds me a bit of Sebald. Yes, I like him, he's the right one for me. "You have no family?" asked Martin. "No, and you?"—"Yes, sure." They were quiet. The lights in the windows were already on. Suddenly Martin said: "Look at what I have!" and pulled the straw husk from the bottle. "Come up and drink with us." He took Grubetsch's hand—so, it had gone well. Once again small spots of joy blinked in Grubetsch's eyes. Yes—he'd be glad to come. "Then let's go," said Martin. He went ahead. His tiredness had flown. (21–23)

The ensuing scene in Martin's apartment creates the atmosphere of the supper at Emmaus. Extending across several pages, Seghers's images recount elements from Rembrandt's different versions of the supper at which Christ only gradually reveals himself to the two apostles who sup with him. Like Rembrandt, Seghers proceeds by presenting us with a genre painting—a guest at supper in a small family's modest apartment. We are shown the same kinds of details used sparingly and pointedly by Rembrandt to indicate the everyday quality of an event in contemporary life—the wife somewhat reluctantly welcoming the stranger, the white cloth on

Landscape with Distant View and Pine Branch, Hercules Seghers, n.d. (HB 27 I-e).
Etching, printed in green on light yellow colored paper, 132 × 197 mm. Courtesy
Staatliche Museen zu Berlin, Preußischer Kulturbesitz, Kupferstichkabinett. Photo
by Jörg P. Anders.

The Three Trees, Rembrandt Harmenszoon van Rijn, 1643. Etching, 21.1 × 28 cm.
Courtesy British Museum, London.

Les Pélerins d'Emmaüs, **Rembrandt Harmenszoon van Rijn, 1629. Oil on canvas, 15⅜ × 16½ in. Courtesy Musée Jacquemart-André, Paris.**

Les Pélerins d'Emmaüs, Rembrandt Harmenszoon van Rijn, 1648. Oil on canvas, 68 × 65 cm. Courtesy Musée du Louvre, Paris.

Ecce Homo, Rembrandt Harmenszoon van Rijn, 1655. Etching, 38.3 × 45.5 cm. Courtesy Staatliche Museen zu Berlin, Preußischer Kulturbesitz, Kupferstichkabinett. Photo by Jörg P. Anders.

Christ in Emmaus, Rembrandt Harmenszoon van Rijn, 1654. Etching, 211 × 160 mm. Courtesy Rijksmuseum-Stichting Amsterdam.

The Twelve-Year-Old Jesus in the Temple, Rembrandt Harmenszoon van Rijn, 1654. Etching, 9.5 × 14.4 cm. Courtesy Rijksmuseum-Stichting Amsterdam.

Le Christ prêchant (La petite tombe), Rembrandt Harmenszoon van Rijn, c. 1652. Etching, 15.5 × 20.7 cm. Courtesy Cliché Bibliothèque nationale de France, Paris.

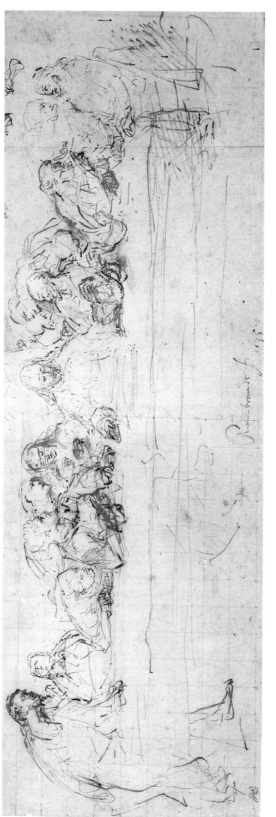

Study after Leonardo's Last Supper, Rembrandt Harmenszoon van Rijn, 1635. Pen and bistre, wash, white body color, 128 × 385 mm. Courtesy Staatliche Museen zu Berlin, Preußischer Kulturbesitz, Kupferstichkabinett. Photo by Jörg P. Anders.

Head of Christ (Portrait Study of a Young Jew as Christ), (attributed to) Rembrandt Harmenszoon van Rijn, 1650–1655. Oil on panel, 9¾ × 7⅞ in. Courtesy Philadelphia Museum of Art, The John G. Johnson Collection. Photo by Graydon Wood, 1999.

The Jewish Cemetery at Ouderkerk, Jacob van Ruisdael, c. 1660. Oil on canvas, 84 × 95 cm. Courtesy Staatliche Kunstsammlungen Dresden, Gemäldegalerie Alte Meister.

the table, the roast in the oven, the wallpaper, mirror, curtains, and lamp-shade. At the same time the mood of anxious solemnity created by the narrative retardation gradually makes us aware that within this genre painting there also resides a more universal meaning, as if the momentary, everyday event were only the *aspect* of a larger mythic significance. Like Rembrandt, Seghers is able to render, with a minimum of quick strokes, flashes of thought and feeling that reveal the deeper emotions of the characters. The careful attention given to the positioning of the figures in relation to each other and to the structural details of the interior space indicates, furthermore, that the author wished to mediate events, subjective feelings, and development in an architectonic way:

>   They came in the door. Marie got up, raised her eyebrows just a bit. There was no need to announce guests to her. The white cloth was already on the table, or had been laid out as quickly as if it had always been there. The smell of the roast didn't at all hint of rancid fat, but of Sunday, and Marie's eyes, and her lips, smiled in a welcoming way. But couldn't Martin have found a better guest than this starveling with no hearth, no home? She was sure these empty eyes would take in everything—the flowered wallpaper, the mirror, the new lamp-shade. This is the room, thought Grubetsch, this is the family, a woman and a man, and the child is back there under the featherbed, her little braid on the pillow. Martin got up. He slipped past the stove, tried to take as much of Marie with him, her hips, her hand, as the moment allowed. He closed the curtains, and Grubetsch watched him, saw the curtains too, flowery just like the wallpaper. Martin came back, took the lamp from the chest and put it on the table. He lit the lamp. Marie came with the pot of soup and sat down. The lamp laid its arm around the three of them. Nobody can know, thought Grubetsch, how things here will look in a few months.
>
>   Marie ladled out the soup, the thin little bracelets jangling around her wrists. "Peace to you," said Martin. They began to eat in silence.
>
>   I like this Martin, thought Grubetsch, I like him much better than I liked Sebald, no, he can't even be compared to him. I'm even sorrier for him than I was for Sebald. Marie's eyes shone, small sparks skipped across the two men. But Grubetsch pushed back a bit from Marie, closer to Martin. Their plates were so close now that the backs of their hands sometimes brushed against each other as they ate. All at once Martin felt great sympathy for Grubetsch again. He felt as though he had to comfort him about something, and he didn't understand that. I don't feel as sorry for anyone as I do for Martin, Grubetsch thought to himself. Martin jumped up. "Now let's drink," he

said with a smile. "I only drink on Sunday, weekdays I never drink."
Grubetsch looked up at Martin, took the glass with his two hands,
yes, he liked having a drink with a man like him.

Marie let out her soft "Aaah," and now Grubetsch looked over at
her too. They drank their glasses empty, then drank again. Like a
pitcher that fills slowly, the redness moved from Marie's white throat
up into her face. She turned up her sleeves over her elbows and served
the meat.

Martin became anxious again. Doesn't the food taste good to him,
he thought, doesn't he like it? Why doesn't he say anything? (23–24)

Rembrandt depicted the supper at Emmaus at least seven times, in
four paintings, two etchings, and one separate drawing. In them he was
careful to differentiate between the one apostle who is overcome at his
recognition of the risen Christ as he breaks bread, and the other, more
skeptical figure who recoils at the sight. Seghers's distinction between
Martin's hesitant but authentic attraction to Grubetsch and Marie's more
petty concerns reiterates this differentiation, albeit in the specific context
of her narrative. We find in the narrative different elements from Rembrandt's various depictions of the supper at Emmaus, as if Seghers had
been looking at these depictions while she was writing her text and, in having written it, were guiding the reader through these pictures once more.

Rembrandt's early painting of 1629, for example, is almost a pure
genre work. Other than the theme of light behind the Christ figure, there
are no direct biblical references in setting or dress, and the three clearly visible figures might well be replaced by Seghers's Grubetsch, Martin, and
Marie. The painting shows Jesus sitting in the right foreground, his
shadow side to the viewer, his face looking in profile up and out to the left
as he breaks the bread and the light blazes on his other side. In the left
background the small figure of a woman, clearly unapprised of the event
at the table, is seen busily tending a cooking fire. We recall that in
Seghers's text we also observe, that is, from the perspective of the table,
how Marie busies herself at some distance in front of the stove. We notice
her at the stove when Martin gets up from the table and slips past her to
close the curtains. That he then fetches the lamp from the chest, puts it on
the table, and lights it makes us aware of how radically the light has shifted
in this scene—from the distant, small light of the cooking fire and the
almost completely dark window, whose features are brightened by the
flowery curtains, to the deep, concentrated glow of the lamp on the table
in the foreground.

In Rembrandt's darkly shaded foreground between Jesus and the
viewer one can barely detect the figure of the apostle who has just fallen to

his knees at the apparition. This figure is appropriately absent in Seghers's text. But across the table sits a working man, not unlike Martin, both frightened and fascinated, who marvels in gaping terror at the sight. This working man is the central and only figure in the painting facing front, and it is his combined attraction and disbelief, not the miracle of the risen Christ itself, that constitutes its major theme. That Seghers herself so often subtly shifted perspective between her three characters suggests that she was fully aware of the changes in view that occurred in the course of Rembrandt's numerous depictions of the Emmaus story by Luke.

The small etching *Christ and the Disciples in Emmaus* of 1634 is also a genre work, if in a less obviously contemporary setting, but complete with a scraggly dog waiting for scraps in the right foreground. We would have no difficulty placing Seghers's Grubetsch, Martin, and Marie into the configuration at the table. Christ is seated in three-quarter view on the right, his large, strong hands breaking the bread, his friendly, ruddy, fleshy face and youthful, abundantly flowing hair surrounded by light. In the middle sits the older, somewhat disconcerted apostle, whose face shows only a slight disturbance while his hands remain preoccupied with his own bread. But the Christ figure is not concerned with him as he is with the second apostle, who sits in startled recognition, folding his hands in a loose gesture of reverence as Christ stares intently and lovingly at him across the table.

In Rembrandt's later depictions, between 1648 and 1654, the figure of the risen Christ faces directly forward at the center of the scene, as in an altarpiece, with one apostle seated on either side. In the 1648 paintings he no longer sits in the formerly relaxed manner of the man Jesus, but the contours of his body are still defined. In the 1654 etching, however, it is as if the radiance of his divinity is about to consume him and he will disappear in an instant. These later Rembrandt versions seem to have informed the second part of Seghers's depiction of Grubetsch's supper with Martin and Marie, which I quote below. Like these Rembrandt versions, in which the figure of a serving boy is added, Seghers's text also introduces a fourth figure—Martin's younger sister Anna, to whom his wife Marie leaves the menial household tasks. On this frightened, vulnerable girl Grubetsch's visit has its most immediate transformative effect, just as the radiance of Christ in Rembrandt's 1648 and 1654 depictions might have the most profound, if still unconscious, impact on the respective youth who is about to serve at the table or is caught by the radiance as he walks by. It is this moment to which Seghers responds in her text. Indeed, she goes one step further than her models by moving the fourth figure into the center of the action and, by way of a unique twist—as if Rembrandt's serving boy were about to rip the bread out of the hands of the risen Christ!—places the transformative moment in the desperate immediacy of human experience and action in the here and now:

> The rustling in the corner was louder now, then came the splashing of bare feet. Suddenly Anna appeared at the table. . . . "Let me have some too," she said softly, and took Marie's glass. Grubetsch put his head in his hands, looked her up and down. "That's not for you," said Marie, and took the glass away from her. "Let her be," said Martin, "she just wants to taste it." Anna took the glass and put it to her mouth. Grubetsch stood up. "Thanks for the meal, I've got to go now, good-bye." That very instant Anna was going to put her glass down, but something got into her hand. She quivered about at the edge of the table and stood the glass up in the air. Then, sweeping aside plates and glasses with her head and her thin arms, she threw herself straight across the table the way one throws oneself on the ground. She took the tablecloth in her teeth, ground away at it, and sobbed without making a sound other than the slight clicking of the china. Marie bent over her, stretched out her hand to stroke her hair, but just before her fingers touched the part they quickly pulled back. Anna had lowered her eyelids but couldn't prevent a smile from squirting from the corners of her eyes. "What's the matter with you?" said Martin, dumbfounded. He had turned quite pale and began rubbing Anna's feet with as much fury as he could muster, she had after all cried so much last winter whenever her feet froze.
> "Well, good-bye," Grubetsch said at the door. (26–27)

What, then, is the relationship between the biblical context and the contemporary milieu of Seghers's narrative? In her dissertation of 1924, which preceded *Grubetsch* by less than three years, Seghers addressed herself to this very question as it applies to the relationship between Rembrandt's genre style and the surrealistic quality of what she called his "willfully constituted overrealism" ("eigenwillig gestaltete Überwirklichkeit") (38). It seems to me that her explanation can apply just as well, with changes only in the details, to her own work:

> A large number of [Rembrandt's] drawings take us into the roomy quarters of a family of burghers, the home of a scholar, a respected merchant, or whomever else. The master of the house is depicted in various situations, distributing alms in his doorway, sitting before his bed, asleep in his armchair, etc. But each one of these scenes can have a dual nature. For in some cases one cannot at all elicit from the image what it is in our consciousness that recognizes it as a biblical

depiction. . . . The transition by which a scene from everyday life becomes a biblical one already takes place in the process of Rembrandt's own drawing, indeed in his very own gaze. In the same room whose table and window appear familiar to us from his other drawings, the master of the house receives a guest, and the reinterpretation of this genre situation into that of *A Man of God Comes to Eli* occurs solely in the mind of the viewer. As a fleeting impression taken from the street, Rembrandt's drawings often depict an old man together with a boy, walking along together or caught in a close embrace, which the eye accustomed to reading in this way will recognize as *The Return of the Prodigal Son.* There are no artistic means applied here in order to distinguish the biblical event from the real one; the biblical world coincides with the real. (38–39)

The coincidence of the "biblical world" and the "real" is no less evident in the genre scenes of working-class life in *Grubetsch.* The parallel to Rembrandt's drawings is even more striking in the courtyard settings, which far outnumber the genre interiors—the level courtyard, its wall shafts, gateway, multiple doorways, alleys, corridors, the hollow under the tavern stairway, and the corner tavern itself. The courtyard is the topographical landscape within which the characters in *Grubetsch* are observed and tested as they wait in expectation of a coming or hoped-for deliverance. It is the architectonic aspect that carries the narrative, not the dialogue, action, or any illustrative description or symbolic representation. Although some requisites of modern industrial life are indicated, the courtyard locales might just as well take us back to earlier times, indeed as far back as the first century A.D.

And so we begin to understand why Seghers foregrounds the courtyard in her text, and why so many of the encounters between the characters take place in its various spaces, corners, and crevices. We are given only quick, intermittent sketches of its distinguishing features. At one point it is described as having walls "like a fortress" (42), reminiscent of the Roman or Italian Renaissance proportions in Rembrandt's *Ecce Homo* etchings discussed earlier. But more often the hasty, irregular sketches of a doorway, a tenement corridor, a dark alleyway, or a corner of the gateway resemble Rembrandt's own rough outlines suggesting the more intimate but always open structure of the synagogue and its environs. Thus we can assume that Seghers's varied, and to the modern reader quite distinctive, arrangement of her figures in the courtyard setting—leaning casually against a doorway, standing idly in conversation, hunched against a corner of the gateway, kneeling to look into the window of the tavern, lying carelessly about, and so forth—was directly influenced by the late Rembrandt's depictions of the synagogue, wherein his own sparse use of background ensures that "the biblical world coincides with the real."

Seghers's dissertation tells us that Rembrandt depicted the synagogue in two fundamentally different ways. In his monumentally conceived painting *Christ and the Adulteress* of 1644, for example, he proceeded from artistic fantasy to create "an indefinite imaginary space" representing the synagogue as "the scene of the great moments in Jewish history." In order to verify that his invention was "historical Jewish reality," he relied on "a Hebraic inscription, a Temple item, a Torah scroll—things that constitute a reality of historical Judaism, but not the reality of Jewish being" (44). This historicizing approach, a kind of "orientalism," was obviously not the one that influenced Seghers's own writing. To describe the other in her dissertation, she drew on the example of Rembrandt's 1654 etching *The Twelve-Year-Old Jesus in the Temple,* in which only the rough outline of a large column indicates the synagogue, before which the boy Jesus, clad in a tunic faintly suggestive of trousers, is seen in intense discussion with a heterogeneous group of men, hardly all "elders," whose motley appearance and workingmen's dress place them as a group neither fully in Jerusalem of the first century A.D. nor fully in seventeenth-century Holland. "Here we have the same intention of depicting the synagogue," Seghers observed in her dissertation. "But here Rembrandt proceeds by rendering reality, namely, the soul of the people, the reality of its being, which he wants to have crystallized" (44).

Synagogue is the Greek term signifying Jewish places of assembly for prayer and instruction. Originally a small gathering in a private dwelling, the synagogue can possibly be dated as far back as the Babylonian exile of the sixth century B.C. Unlike the Temple, which housed the deity attended by priests, the synagogue was a lay organization that could function anywhere as the Jewish community's meeting place for the preservation of the faith and a way of life. By the first century A.D. every Jewish community had its synagogue, and these included the assemblies of the Jewish Christians. Just as Jesus regularly prayed and taught in synagogues in Nazareth and other towns, the synagogues in Palestine and in the diasporic communities were the sites of his apostles' preachings, notably the spirited visits of the apostle Paul, which often ended in quarrels and violence. From this point of view, the scale of events in and around the urban courtyard in *Grubetsch* can be understood as being paradigmatic.

In *Grubetsch,* then, the urban *Hof,* or courtyard, itself a place of community interaction and assembly, functions as a cipher for the first-century Jewish synagogue. For her models of the courtyard and the figures positioned therein Seghers relied on the very core of Rembrandt's late genre

depictions of Jesus' life, which she foregrounded in the text of her dissertation: the 1648 etching *The Synagogue;* the 1655 oil painting *The Tribute
Coin;* the two 1652 and 1654 etchings and the 1652 pen drawing *The
Twelve-Year-Old Jesus in the Temple;* the 1639 pen drawing *The Circumcision;* the 1649 etching *Christ Healing the Sick* (the "Hundred Guilder
Print"); and the 1652 etching *Christ Preaching* ("La petite tombe"). In this
respect, the dark, occasionally sun-splashed corners and alleyways in
which the tenement dwellers are huddled in gossip, conversation, and
argument, indeed even the tavern and its cellar stairway in whose hollow
Grubetsch sleeps, acquire no less a significance than the cavernous spaces
where Jesus preaches before motley crowds in more or less seventeenth-
century dress in "La petite tombe" and the "Hundred Guilder Print."

Seghers's dissertation of 1924 differentiates between, on the one
hand, the historicizing or orientalist elements that predominate in the
early Rembrandt's depictions of Jews and Judaism and, on the other, the
simpler but more essential "overrealism" of his later works. Nonetheless,
the author argues, the very multiplicity and range of Rembrandt's depictions went against the creation of stereotypes: "However the model is seen,
it changes its meaning, and in this same way the Jewish model could be
seen in different ways, whether as the ragged street figure, or the Oriental
draped with his valuables, or even as one fulfilled by a long, lonely life"
(32–33). Seghers's discussion acknowledges the differences between the
images of Jews created in Rembrandt's work and the historical reality of
Jewish life in Amsterdam during his time. But her interest was not simply
sociological, nor did she measure Rembrandt's art by his ability to create
images of Jews that would approximate the actual reality of "Jewishness"
or Jewish life. What makes Rembrandt unique as an artist, she argued, is
that he "does not present us with an image of the Jewish individual; his is
not an image that arises from the desire to depict the essential and ethni-
cally peculiar characteristics of a real model" (30).

What fascinated Seghers is how Rembrandt, especially in his later
years, was able to go beyond naturalism and, by means of an "overreal"
("überwirklich") depiction of Jewish character and Jewish life (36), was
able to fathom a deeper level of portrayal. As in his later drawings of the
synagogue, the mature Rembrandt's paintings also avoid the attempt to
depict stereotypical, that is to say, potentially anti-Jewish or antisemitic,
characteristics of Jews and Jewish life. As Seghers wrote at the conclusion
of her dissertation: "What is most essential and most astounding about
Rembrandt's depiction of Jews is that he arrived at the ability to portray
Judaism not by way of the Jewish idea complex of his time, but in spite of
it" (58). The evidence lies most obviously in Rembrandt's famous portrait
studies of Christ, she argued, beginning with his *Portrait Study of a Young*

Jew as Christ, approximately dated 1648. According to Seghers, it is precisely in these late Christ portraits filled with great depth of religious feeling that Rembrandt came closest to depicting the reality of Jewish life. By the very fact that as a devout Christian he saw his Jewish model as Christ and, conversely, Christ as a Jew, Rembrandt arrived at his most authentic and profoundly "realistic" depiction of a Jewish figure:

> Rembrandt wants to portray Christ in his human existence as a Jewish youth. He wants above all to portray Jewish reality, the unique quality of this reality. His portrait study of Christ is at the same time the portrait study of a young Jew, but what is expressed here about the topic of Judaism comes from his immersion in his model and the desire to render the meaning and essence of this Jewish reality. (31–32)

In creating the protagonist for *Grubetsch* Seghers may well have been thinking of the young Jewish man in Amsterdam—his clothing and manner suggesting a poor refugee from Eastern Europe—who sat as Rembrandt's model for his masterful portraits of Christ. If this otherwise anonymous man found resurrection anywhere, we can be assured it was in the world of art. Bearing in mind the late Rembrandt's series of oil portraits *A Young Jew as Christ,* which so preoccupied Seghers in her dissertation, we have an idea of how Grubetsch himself might have looked to the author. The narrative's protagonist is likened to Rembrandt's Christ figure in that he has no "typical" traits or characteristics but wears a "blue jacket" and appears "pale, plain, and quite neatly dressed" (18). When we are told more than once that his eyes light up with sparks (19, 61), we are reminded of Seghers's reference in her dissertation to "faces that suddenly quiver with joy or pain, faces in which the artist can capture the moment of agitation, not the condition of the suffering soul" (32).

Conditions are such in *Grubetsch* that human freedom and deliverance are postponed indefinitely, while ignorance and malice prevail. Indeed, the very man who might redeem others even participates in their gradual ruin. As the author noted in 1931 in one of her only references to the topical landscape of this early work, this is "a nasty yard [ein böser Hof], and in it a man who knows how to divine people's secret desires for self-destruction, and to fulfill each one of them in his way."[14] Hardly a savior, Grubetsch is nonetheless a martyr of a kind, and his own passion culminates in an appropriately mythic conclusion. Like the early Christian Jew Stephen (whose stoning Rembrandt also depicted), Grubetsch is finally lynched by a mob of tenement dwellers—foremost among them his close friend and onetime admirer *Paul.*

The ultimately clear distinction between two figures who have vied for leadership in the courtyard, or *Hof,* suggests the eventual co-optation of first-century Christianity, as represented by the Palestinian communities under the "rock" Peter, by the more ambitious Greco-Roman strivings of Saul/Paul. It was, notably, the apostle who had never known the man Jesus who insisted, at the expense of Jewish messianism, on the resurrection as an article of pure faith. In more contemporary terms, the distinction between the two figures in *Grubetsch* also brings to mind Comintern debates between Bolshevik hard-liners and left-wing internationalists, many of whom, like the participants in the council republics of 1919, were anarchists, pacifists, socialists, and communists inspired by Jewish messianism. These debates became increasingly critical with the vacuum created by Lenin's death in 1924. By March of 1927, when Seghers's novella appeared in serial form in the *Frankfurter Zeitung,* it was fairly clear that Stalin would soon be victorious over the members of the Left Opposition, foremost among them Leon Trotsky, who had been removed from the Politbureau in October of 1926. This changing of the guard within the revolutionary history of the early twentieth century represents no less a central thematic in Seghers's novella than do the parabolic allusions to political events in first-century Palestine.[15]

The narrative's epic-parabolic prose style, mythic construction, and story line culminating in the final lynching bring to mind the writings of Kafka. Seghers must have been particularly aware of *The Castle,* published in 1926, one year after the posthumous publication of *The Trial* and not long before *Grubetsch* appeared in March 1927. The similarities in plot are striking: a stranger moves into a community and participates in its everyday life but is denied permanent residency and membership. At the end of Kafka's novel the protagonist dies from weakness and exhaustion; in Seghers's narrative he is lynched (as is Joseph K. in *The Trial*). The similarities in the larger formal-conceptual construction are even more striking, even if in Kafka's case the text is grounded in Old Testament and Talmudic tradition, while Seghers's narrative, by way of Rembrandt's drawings, relies for the most part on the New Testament. The distinction is best exemplified by Kafka's fixation on the final authority of decisions made in the remote castle just beyond the village community (in mythic terms, the mysterious and forbidding Temple, wherein the deity is carefully guarded by priests), compared to Seghers's leveling of authority (based on the community-based proportions of the synagogue) to the interactions of more or less petty and quarrelsome "equals" around a tenement courtyard. Keeping in mind this distinction, we observe how Kafka's text focuses on the theological problem of knowledge and absolute authority, whereas Seghers's narrative is concerned with messianic-eschatological questions and the weight of subjective experience. It goes without saying that both Seghers and Kafka, fully aware of their indebtedness to religious and secular Jewish traditions, allowed their respective rootedness in these traditions to define their underlying narrative conceptions. In this respect, it might be no more difficult to interpret a narrative like *Grubetsch* as being a response to anti-semitism than it is to do the same in respect to the similarly mythic and no more explicitly Jewish problematic contained in the works of Kafka.[16]

Seghers has Grubetsch undergo his personal agony—his estrangement from the world and longing for community—not praying in a garden, but dreaming in the hollow of the stairway where he lies and sleeps: "Down there Grubetsch lay sleeping. Why should he hang around up above? Whether the twins had red or black hair, whether Paul's belly was fat or lean, what did he care? Grubetsch slept on" (69). But it is his desire to live among his fellows that seals his fate—as it was Jesus' decision to go to Jerusalem after all, and more recently Trotsky's decision to return to Moscow politics after his own illness following the civil war:

> Then all at once he longed for that smell of sweat and smoke, food and breath that permeated the cellar as the smell of straw and hide fills a sheep stall. He had such a longing for that smell that it was almost an agony.
>
> He longed also for the light of Munk's tavern, he feared that something might happen to that dim, burned-down yellow lantern before he could stick his head under it. He was afraid people would leave before he could push among them and feel their shoulders and hips to the right and left of him. For a moment he lay motionless, thinking that all this might come to him on its own.
>
> Then he jumped up and ran out. (71)

The last scene in the tavern is modeled on Rembrandt's three 1635 studies of Leonardo's *The Last Supper*. These do not stress the miraculous communal aspect, but the confused emotions of Jesus' intimates as they hear of a betrayal. Like Rembrandt, Seghers was not interested in the details of bread and wine, but in the grouping of the figures within the formal composition of the scene. Grubetsch himself is shown in a meditative sleep-dream, much like the Jesus figure in the Rembrandt study in pen and bistre—his upper body tilted forward, his head slightly bowed, his eyes cast down, his shoulders hunched, and his hands stretched out slightly. In Rembrandt's large red chalk study the disciples exhibit the various stages of shock and dismay. But in the pen and bistre version the agitation is heightened and the mood pitched in the direction of malicious, sneering contempt and outright gestures of violence. And here one disciple—who moves abruptly toward the center and, almost at Jesus' back, raises his hand with a long, extended finger to indicate his readiness to take up the sword—looks as if he were about to kill the master himself. This is of course the moment used by Seghers, who, after showing them in a near embrace, has Paul stab Grubetsch with Grubetsch's own knife:

> [Grubetsch] took one drink, pushed the glass aside and laid his head on the table. The warmth made him tired, as anyone who had been cold a long time. . . . They stared at Grubetsch's back, looked him meanly up and down. He hung around the courtyard the way an old stone lies in the road. Now, as if he were starting to crumble, his head slipped forward, his shoulders to the sides. They knew him well, hated him. He had spent time with them in his worn blue jacket, had walked ahead of them in the sun, had disappeared whenever he liked through the gateway. Now they had time to observe him close up. He hung tired and heavy over the table, the way any exhausted back and shoulders would.
>
> All of a sudden Sebald's wife said quietly: "Now we can be rid of him." The blond lad quickly slid out the tip of his tongue. The twins got up and sat down at the next table, across from Grubetsch.
>
> Somebody sat down next to Grubetsch, it was good to have someone next to him. This other one touched him. Grubetsch looked up, it was a face, it was sleepy. That was Paul's face, he looked at it more closely. It was not the real Paul, maybe just someone who looked like Paul. His face wasn't filled out and swollen, it was still broad and brown, but there wasn't enough flesh in it any longer to cover it up. The winter had eaten it away. Hunger and fear resided in it, naked and shameless. Grubetsch liked this face, he could get on with this Paul. Paul was excited, too, but Grubetsch was too sleepy to console him. He looked up, others had come to his table, a white band of faces wrapped around him. That was good, it wasn't enough, Paul knew that, pushed up close to Grubetsch, laid his head on his shoulder. Grubetsch pulled up his legs so he could cower right into Paul. Paul put his arm around Grubetsch's back. As far as Grubetsch was concerned he might have had twelve arms and put them all around Grubetsch's back. Paul's arm even stroked slowly down Grubetsch's back. His hand went quietly into Grubetsch's boot, pulled out the knife, pushed it under Grubetsch's shoulder blade, and rotated it around twice. The others bent over the table, dragged Grubetsch across it, and quickly stuffed him away somewhere. (71–73)

The theme of the passion found throughout Seghers's prose—even, in fact especially, when it pertains to contemporary political events, as it does in this work and all her works—is dually inspired by the history of European art and the history of Judaism and the Jews in the first century A.D. Whereas the expressionistic prose style of an early text like *Grubetsch* is characterized by thematic and stylistic compression, the narratives Seghers wrote after the victory of the National Socialists in January 1933, and after her own escape from Germany via Switzerland to France, exhibit the greater distantiation, scope, and more distinct story line of the extended historical view. In mythic terms this would be the view from the position of the Jewish apostles and other survivors of the catastrophes that marked Jewish history in Palestine and the diaspora during the first century A.D. Into this new framework that tends to look back rather than straight into the material, Seghers introduced a figure that was missing in her earlier stories—the witness, who will remember the event whichever way he or she knows how. The tenuous reliability of the witness is especially striking in the first work in which such a witness occurs, the short novel *Der Kopflohn* (1934, The Bounty), which Seghers began in late 1932 and completed in the first year of her exile in Paris. As in *Grubetsch,* the protagonist whose passion shows him isolated and alone is hardly a savior. Instead, we are presented from the start with a wanted man whose efforts to go underground in the countryside end abruptly when young Nazi thugs taunt and brutalize him, then turn him over to the police.

The narrative's final image shows the protagonist of *The Bounty* escorted by two gendarmes to an administrative hearing in the next town. The image evokes the mood of human exhaustion and suffering created by Rembrandt with a few simple strokes in his drawings devoted to the events surrounding similar moments in Jesus' life: the arrest in the garden, the walk to the hearing, the hearing before the high priest, the presentation by Pilate, the mocking at the column, the fall to the ground under the weight of the cross.[17] The taunting mob that includes children in the Seghers text quoted below is reminiscent of the small figures that crowd around the much taller figure of Jesus in Rembrandt's drawing of the arrest in the garden. The irritation of the gendarmes echoes the special attention given by Rembrandt to the administrative details and practical considerations of the events and physiognomies attached to Jesus' trials and his difficulties bearing the weight of the cross. And the hat that the unwitting witness quickly doffs at the end is a curious but perhaps historically appropriate substitute for the cloth with which Rembrandt's kneeling figure of Veronica wipes Jesus' sweaty brow. The end of Seghers's text makes clear in any case that her protagonist, significantly named Johann, is no mere anarchic vagrant like Grubetsch but, like the very Son of Man and his apostles, at once a martyr and a positive hero:

Many of them ran behind the gendarmes, who were dragging Johann more than they were leading him. They ran up ahead and once more, screaming and shouting at the outskirts of town, formed a narrow alley through which the three of them passed. The gendarmes took Johann under the arms, propped him up, and told him brusquely to step out: "Move it, damn you, march!" Johann came to for a moment. Instead of one burning body he could distinguish four or five different sharp pains, on his torso, on his back, and above his chest. He bored around in his mouth with his tongue and spit out a tooth. The one gendarme laughed: "Bitter candy?" The other, an older man with a pinched face, said gruffly: "Move, move!" and gestured threateningly at the children who were running along behind them. They stopped, took one last good look at Johann's back, then trotted on home. Johann tried to open his gummed-up eyes. He made out the edge of the wood that stretched like a solid black arch from the village to the river. The earth was an amber color, even the sky over the wood was about to turn yellow. Mixed with the rushing sound in his ears was the tinkling, tinny music of the carousel that was cranked up again in the sheep pasture behind him.

They walked on past the outermost fields belonging to Oberweilbach. A farmer came a few paces down the road to see why gendarmes would be escorting a man toward town. Algeier had begun to dig up turnips. He recognized Johann, understood at once, and started. His fidgety beard twitched, his jaw began to grind violently. He moved down to the edge of the road, his hoe in his hand. He quickly dropped the hoe and pulled off his hat, as if a dead man or a newborn just baptized were carried before him.[18]

CHAPTER 4

Island of Ignominy: Kierkegaard and the Budapest Sunday Circle

Fine, I said. The human race will find Heaven once you've redeemed
the world. But what of the other creatures, the plants and the animals.
You know I don't want to become blessed without them. To this
Lukács replied: Even the stones will be saved.
— Anna Lesznai, "Recollections," 1965[1]

The Hungarian pitcher has broken, its hundred shards have scattered
in a hundred directions, these few valuable people, this circle whose
members have the large measure of their knowledge from each other is
dispersed.
— Karl Mannheim, "Heidelberg Letter," 1921[2]

Georg Lukács was a great influence on me—long before I met him or
had read anything by him. . . . A sort of legend first attracted me to
him. It was the legend of his name and it was shaped by the stories I
heard about him from Hungarian émigrés who had fled the white terror. . . . At the centre of this legend stood a man who was brave and
clever. . . . An intellectual who protects our world of ideas by hazard-
ing his very existence.
— Anna Seghers, 1955[3]

The chiliastic thematic that is at the core of Anna Seghers's prose is
already evident in her first published work, a short narrative that appeared
in a special Christmas issue of the *Frankfurter Zeitung* on 25 December
1924. To her story's rather peculiar title, "Die Toten auf der Insel Djal"
(The Dead on the Island Djal), the author appended the no less curious
words "Eine Sage aus dem Holländischen, nacherzählt von Antje Seghers"
(A tale from the Dutch, retold by Antje Seghers). In so doing, she encoded
her authorial identity in the guise of a pseudonymous persona, indicating
that she was related in a familial way to her story's protagonist, the island
pastor Jan Seghers, who ministers to the shipwrecked dead and dying on

the rocky shores of Djal. As we eventually learn from his own tombstone in the cemetery of Djal, this island pastor, too, is a "dead" man. It is only his ecstatic physiognomy and bearing that testify to what from the start appears as a virtually resurrected life:

> A curious fellow, this pastor. He might have been the devil incarnate, had he not been just the pastor of Djal. His soul must have been thoroughly disheveled and perforated by all the confessions he'd listened to, those terrible, foaming, reeking-of-life-and-death confessions by the wretched and dying sailors from five continents. Stuck on a cliff, the house he inhabited was more like a fisherman's hut than a parsonage. He was nigh fifty years by this time, and his eyes glowed, his lips were raised, his skull still grew from year to year, his gown reeked of salt water. Such a one needed no children or siblings, no wife and no beloved. For such a one there were on Djal wilder, more magnificent delights, more surging passions. When the water boiled and the storm drove a hail shower of foundering ships against the shore and ripped the cliffs of Djal as if they were a silk fabric, then the parson took up the oars and rowed himself across the bay of foaming eddies so as to offer his last word to a dying man over there on the other side.[4]

Biographically, the figures in this narrative, as in many of Seghers's later narratives, are based on the life destinies of Hungarian-Jewish intellectuals who made up the Vasárnapi Kör, or Sunday Circle, in Budapest during World War One and the Hungarian revolutions of 1918–19. The intellectual leader and "philosopher-king" of this modern-day Socratic Circle was Georg Lukács, who after the defeat of the Hungarian Council Republic in 1919 lived more or less as a fugitive in Vienna. Here, from a relatively impoverished, semi-underground existence, not unlike that of the pastor Jan Seghers on the island of Djal, he ministered to his shipwrecked flock of philosophical and political rebels who had quickly fled after him to Vienna.

Lukács shocked not only his academic colleagues in Heidelberg, but also his fellow Hungarian Sundayers, as they called themselves, when in December of 1918 he suddenly and unexpectedly, just as "Saulus became Paulus,"[5] joined the Hungarian Communist Party. Lukács's decision to commit the philosophical question of ethics to the broader field of political action nevertheless set the tone for future discussions and activities within the circle. When in the spring of 1919 the reform-oriented Károlyi regime was succeeded by the Hungarian Council Republic, it was Lukács who took on a leadership position, first as Deputy Commissar and soon thereafter as Commissar of Education. As such, he appointed members of the Sunday Circle to a variety of cultural posts. Thus, within only a few months, the questions of ethics and aesthetics that had initially preoccupied the members of the Sunday Circle could no longer be kept separate from the more immediate existential and tactical issues of political commitment and action.[6]

After the defeat of the Commune, and in the everyday reality of exile—or, as the Sundayers experienced it, the diaspora—the once privileged circle of philosophers, who in fact were unable to reconcile ethics and politics in an absolute way, felt themselves dishonored and shamed, that is to say, utterly shipwrecked. What they all agreed on was that philosophy as they ideally once knew it was "dead," and that in this, not only neo-Platonic, sense they, too, as philosophers, were "dead."[7] To this extent they were indeed prototypes for the "dead" on the island Djal depicted only a few years later by Anna Seghers in her first published story.

The name *Djal* that Seghers chose for her mythical island is in fact the phonetic variant of the Hungarian root *gyal,* as in the verb *gyaláz,* meaning to abuse, revile, vilify, or in the noun *gyalázat,* meaning dishonor, ignominy, and shame. What is more, the combination of letters *gy,* which strikes speakers of most European languages as curious, is also found in the phonetic spelling *Djuri* of the nickname *Gyuri,* by which Georg, that is, György, Lukács was known to his Hungarian friends, and in time to Seghers as well. Certainly Seghers would have heard the name *Gyuri,* as in *Djuri,* uttered frequently in conversation among members of the Budapest Sunday Circle with whom she had regular and close contact during her years in Heidelberg from 1920 to 1924—Karl Mannheim, Júlia Láng, György Káldor, and of course her future husband László Radványi, whom she married in August of 1925, seven months after the publication of *The Dead on the Island Djal.*

The topical issues raised by Seghers's story can also be traced directly to the history of the Budapest Sunday Circle. In exile after 1919, its members became increasingly divided as to the possibilities of adhering to their collective revolutionary ideals within a larger European framework overshadowed by Bolshevism and Lenin's concept of an authoritarian Party elite. Lukács, Béla Fogarasi, and others held to their political convictions and continued in exile their now clandestine Party work, determined to defend the democratic Luxemburgian concept of spontaneous revolution within the Hungarian Communist Party headed by Béla Kun, and before the Comintern. Given the circumstances of the time, they opted in this way to remain, even within the Party, more or less permanently "underground." Other Sundayers, notably Arnold Hauser and Karl Mannheim, quickly became disillusioned with politics and chose to go "aboveground," as it were, as politically unaffiliated intellectuals in pursuit of an academic career.[8] This struggle between, on the one hand, remaining as "dead" philosophers "underground" to wait for the next historical chance, or "coming," and, on the other hand, maintaining an "aboveground" and, as Jewish intellectuals, more or less *assimilated* existence is depicted at the very beginning of Seghers's story, which renders the existential and philosophical parameters of the struggle in terms of spiritual, if not physical, death:

> The dead in the graveyard of Djal are a peculiar lot. Sometimes their bones twitch so fiercely that the wooden crosses and gravestones begin to skip. Especially in the spring and fall when the moaning and whistling starts before dawn they can't hold themselves back. That's because the whole lot of them were seafarers who traversed all the waters until they shipwrecked on the rocky shores of Djal. Now they have to lie still and listen as the sea roars and hisses behind the churchyard wall—and that's too much to bear even for one who is dead. (7)

Lukács's legendary "saintly" or "angelic" demeanor[9] in adhering to his ethical principles in matters of politics and Party discipline commanded the respect and admiration even of those who, like Mannheim, openly disagreed with him.[10] Thus, even in exile Lukács maintained, albeit no longer merely as philosopher-king, his exceptional status as the ultimate authority and soulful caretaker of the now dispersed. Accordingly, in Seghers's story it is the pastor of Djal, himself "dead," whose strength of faith and conviction allows him to rise beyond the grave, while below, the wretched "dead" carry on with their incessant moaning and wailing. And like Lukács in Vienna, who in addition to writing assumed the more menial duties of personal, political, Party, and family life, the pastor in Seghers's story is forced to maintain order among the "dead" in a manner that goes beyond the soulful example of prayer:

> Sometimes, when they simply wouldn't calm down, the pastor of Djal led a procession of parishioners singing around the churchyard and thus in wind and rain—for his reformed heart despises holy water and sacred things—had a circle of psalms placed soothingly around the restless sites. Now and then he even went straight along and in between the graves, and when there was quavering to the right and left of him he stomped on the ground and shouted: "Quiet down there." And at the sound of his voice those limbs settled down. (7)

The pictorial and topographic setting, anticipating *The Revolt of the Fishermen* of 1928, is evocative of the Atlantic seacoast. The author's pseudonymous Dutch first name, Antje, which later became Anna, underscores the Netherlandish aspect of the "tale," as does the patronym Seghers, taken from Rembrandt's elder contemporary, the Dutch landscape painter and engraver Hercules Seghers. In the words of Jean Leymarie, Hercules Seghers was a painter of "singular, egocentric genius" whose "numinous awe inspired by thoughts of the infinite vastness of space or by the sight of fathomless precipices enabled him to impart to his depictions of nature a sense of man's insignificance and solitude when confronted by the terrifying indifference of nature."[11] The generally ruined atmosphere surrounding the overgrown, weed-infested cemetery of Djal, as well as descriptions of the craggy rocks against which the seamen shipwreck, is reminiscent of many such barren landscapes and ruins in Hercules Seghers's own etchings.[12]

But the placing of the "tale" in a Dutch cemetery dating back to the seventeenth century—replete with "thickets and weeds," dark paths "between the tombs," a "churchyard wall" in the "still of night," and "beyond the dunes" the "half-sleepy roaring of the surf"—leads one to suspect that the pictorial aspect was more specifically modeled on Jacob van Ruisdael's *The Jewish Cemetery at Ouderkerk* (1660–70). Of this painting there are two versions, one in Dresden, one in Detroit. Most likely Anna Seghers was thinking of the smaller, darker, gloomier, and at the time better-known Dresden painting, which lacks the vivid rainbow of the Detroit version, and which Goethe notably described in 1813 in his famous essay on Ruisdael.[13] As an art history student specializing in seventeenth-century Holland, she must also have known Ruisdael's chalk and pen drawings of the Portuguese-Jewish Cemetery at Ouderkerk on the Amstel, as well as similar views in drawings and engravings by Abraham Blooteling, Romeijn de Hooghe, and Dirk Dalens, which render St. Urban's Church at Ouderkerk in its actual form with prominent church steeple and spire.[14]

If the stormy atmosphere of Ruisdael's painting gives a "sense of the inexorable flight of time and that preoccupation with the Infinite" that he shared with both Spinoza and Goethe,[15] the storyteller Seghers seems to have been more interested, and not without a familial sense of humor, in the actual trials of her parson and his "peculiar lot" of seafarers who "traversed all the waters until they shipwrecked on the rocky shores of Djal" (7). Nevertheless, not only does the eerie "churchyard wall" echo Ruisdael's church ruin at Ouderkerk; even the coffer-like tombs resemble the sarcophagi in Ruisdael's painting. In his struggle with the inhabitant of a particularly restless tomb, the parson Jan Seghers "pushed the respective stone aright," then "sat right down on it with all his weight, as on the lid of a trunk or a coffer, and thus awaited morning" (9). The image of a grave-stone resembling "a trunk or a coffer" with a "lid" alerts us to the two large, white, moonlit sarcophagi in Ruisdael's painting that look just so. The white sarcophagus pictured on the far right of the painting was in fact the tomb of Israel Abraham Mendez, who is known to have died in 1627,[16] only two years after the death of "Antje" Seghers's own "ancestor" Jan Seghers, as indicated by the dates 1548–1625 on the pastor's tombstone located in a "quite forlorn place" of "thickets and weeds" in the cemetery of Djal (12).

Allusions to Judaism and to Christianity coexist in Ruisdael's painting as well as in Seghers's story. But whereas the painting foregrounds the Jew-ish thematic, without, however, making it explicit, as we know from Goethe's ability to leave it unmentioned, in Seghers's story Christian requi-sites—parson, churchyard, crosses, etc.—prevail. In this sense we can assume that Seghers deliberately "painted over" Jewish aspects in Ruis-dael's cemetery with Christian "colors" in order to minimize the exotic-romantic aspect of the Jewish thematic found in Ruisdael and thereby ren-der its greater historical complexity. Indeed, the pseudonymous storyteller's ancestor Jan Seghers, who is hardly the typical churchyard parson, seems to have less in common with the likes of a John Calvin than with the more philosemitic Mennonites of the time (with whom both Ruisdael and Rem-brandt also sympathized). He seems even to have aspects in common with those Sephardic Jews who professed Christianity during the Inquisition and were later known in Holland as Marranos. As the narrator reminds us, alluding to the coerced conversions of Jews, "he might have been the devil incarnate had he not been the pastor of Djal' (7). If he dutifully reads from the New Testament, "the Old is better suited to the minor chords of his heart" (9). And since his "reformed heart despises holy water and sacred things," this "strange fellow" prefers to offer "a circle of psalms" as he walks around the tombstones to calm the limbs of the departed (7).

The religious or spiritual life, conveyed in *The Jewish Cemetery at Ouderkerk* in pantheistic terms by the concentration of light on the white tombs, trickling water, and rainbow, thus manifests itself in Seghers's story as eschatological yearning in the form of human *action*. From this point of view—that man must participate actively in his own redemp-tion—we can begin to make more sense of the "dead" pastor Jan Seghers's ecstatic physiognomy and bearing, as well as his final words to an equally restless, if more cowardly, fellow deceased who has managed to push aside the stone lid and steal out of his tomb:

Such a common Christian as you are, Captain, needs to stay patiently underground after death till our Lord is ready to sound his trumpet for the resurrection. As for me, I wasn't content to stretch out a hand, topple a tombstone, and frighten a pastor. I pestered God for so long with such wild and furious prayers that on the intercession of his seven angels he *had* to let me back into this life in my former shape. For you should know, Captain, I am myself a dead man! (12)

That Seghers published her story only a few months after completing her Heidelberg dissertation *Jews and Judaism in the Works of Rembrandt* would further support the argument that the vaguely seventeenth-century Netherlandish locale is the setting for an implicitly Jewish "tale." The coexistence of Jewish and Christian aspects in the story is in keeping with the notion of "Jewish-Christian interrelations" that Seghers characterized in her dissertation as being typical of political, cultural, and religious life in seventeenth-century Amsterdam.[17] Like the dissertation, Seghers's story differentiates not only Jewish-Christian, but also Jewish-Jewish "interrelations." In his religious iconoclasm, as already suggested above, and concomitantly his patriarchal, at times even rabbinical demeanor, the pastor Jan Seghers can be said to resemble the privileged and assimilated Marranos who by intermarriage with Spaniards and Portuguese also belonged to the aristocratic class of Sephardic Jews who fled north to Holland.

But what of the "seafarers who traversed all the waters until they shipwrecked on the rocky shores of Djal"? Again, we find the answer prefigured in Seghers's dissertation, even with phrasing similar to that in her story. Describing the "other side of Jewish life" in seventeenth-century Holland, the dissertation refers to the Jews of the Amsterdam ghetto as "German and later Polish Jews who came in flocks by ship across the Baltic Sea after the Cossack uprisings of 1640. Ragged and cowering, they belonged to the unpropertied, the money changers, hustlers and peddlers, . . . were despised by the Sephardim as proletarians and for their part despised the Sephardim as in their sense uneducated half-Jews."[18] Surely the author of *The Dead on the Island Djal* also had these fugitives in mind when she described the "terrible, foaming confessions reeking of life and death" made by "wretched and dying sailors from five continents" to the pastor of Djal, his soul "thoroughly disheveled and perforated" by the "confessions" he hears (7).

But Seghers's technique of "overpainting," reminiscent of the "over-realism" she ascribed in her dissertation to Rembrandt's depictions of Jews,[19] appears to have been meant neither to reject nor prioritize the Jewish material, nor to Christianize it in any systematic way. Instead, the deliberate mingling of Jewish and Christian elements in a vaguely Netherlandish cemetery dating back to the sixteenth and seventeenth centuries suggests the coexistence of myriad religious and heretical movements and sects that flourished in Holland during the Reformation (Anabaptists, Mennonites, et al.) and as Judaism strove to renew itself in the wake of the Inquisition and the Jewish migrations (Kabbalists, Sabbatians, etc.). Historically, then, the "dead" parson Jan Seghers, whose life spanned the years 1548–1625, as well as the shipwrecked seafarers whose souls he tries to save, would have belonged to that great number of heretical intellectuals, mystics, and political zealots who made up the messianic and chiliastic movements of the sixteenth and seventeenth centuries.

Describing the "Messianic activism" of that time, Gershom Scholem has pointed to "that peculiar double line of mutual influence between Judaism and Christianity which goes hand in hand with inner tendencies of development in both religions."[20] Like the "Jewish-Christian interrelations" stressed by Anna Seghers in her dissertation of 1924, this "mutual influence" took various forms. Scholem reminds us that "the political and chiliastic Messianism of important religious movements within Christianity often appears as a reflection of what is really Jewish Messianism," and that "again and again, such chiliastic and revolutionary Messianism as emerges, for example, among the Taborites, the Anabaptists, or the radical wing of the Puritans, draws its inspiration mainly from the Old Testament and not from Christian sources." But at the same time, "parallel to this line, along which Judaism has again and again furnished Christianity with political chiliastic Messianism, runs the other one, along which Christianity, for its part, has bequeathed to Judaism or aroused within it the tendency to discover a mystical aspect of the interiorization of the Messianic idea."[21]

Anna Seghers's own interest in mysticism, revolutionary messianism, and chiliasm can be traced to her early involvement with the Budapest Sunday Circle, particularly her relationship to László Radványi, with whom she was in Heidelberg from 1920 to 1924 and whom she married in 1925. In early 1923, less than two years before the publication of *The Dead on the Island Djal,* László Radványi submitted to the University of Heidelberg his doctoral dissertation: *Der Chiliasmus: Ein Versuch zur Erkenntnis der chiliastischen Idee und des chiliastischen Handelns* (Chiliasm: An Essay toward the Understanding of the Chiliastic Idea and Chiliastic Action). Awarded the distinction *summa cum laude* by a committee headed by Karl Jaspers,[22] the dissertation was completed shortly after the appearance in January 1923 of Georg Lukács's "heretical" defense of orthodox Marxism in his *History and Class Consciousness.* In this definitive work, the Hungarian philosopher revisited the events of the Hungarian Commune and reasserted his distance from the Leninist conception of the Communist

Party in favor of the radical legacy of Rosa Luxemburg. Radványi's own analysis of chiliastic ideas and movements within and without the institutional framework of religion can be seen as his effort to do much the same.[23]

Chiliasm differs from other theories of redemption in that it "postulates an *empirical* realm," Radványi argued in his dissertation.[24] Its concept of redemption is "absolutely *radical,*" comprises "all moments and relations in the empirical world" and penetrates them completely (36). That this concept pertains to "*all* people" is the sign of its *universality*" (37). It retains its "essential, specific, chiliastic meaning" owing to the fact "that for the chiliast redemption is *near, in the process of becoming,* that for the chiliast redemption is *the present moment*" (37–38), "not in a vaguely defined utopian distance, but *near at hand in a burning-real way*" (38). Radványi located the beginnings of chiliasm within Jewish and Christian eschatology (41), then described how the chiliastic tradition became separated from official Christianity after Augustine's doctrine establishing the Church as God's realm on earth: "From that point on the chiliastic idea could only develop *outside* the Church and *against* the Church, . . . which henceforth defined chiliasm as heresy" (49). Here the implicit twentieth-century parallel becomes evident: chiliasm–Christianity–Church; communism–Bolshevism–Communist Party.

Similar to Lukács's unsuccessful attempts to justify the events of the Hungarian Commune before the Comintern in Moscow, Radványi defended the "failures" of the "Christian-communist" Taborites in Bohemia and the later Anabaptists because in these instances chiliasm "did not enter into compromises, did not escape by detours, but remained with its original idea of redemption and the will to redemption. Therefore the Church prevailed, and the chiliastic attempts were without consequence" (79). This was in fact the situation faced by the Hungarian exiles, whose intellectual and political lives after the fall of the Commune were also largely "without consequence." Exiled from Hungary, out of favor in Moscow, and lacking the privileges afforded by bourgeois institutions, they "slept with walking stick in hand and knapsack on their back."[25]

At the end of his dissertation Radványi considered the possibility that Bolshevism—incidentally, like some early Jewish-Christian sects in their day—might represent a "new formation, a new developmental stage in the chiliastic idea" (79). But he was quick to add that "*God* is lacking in it, and a chiliasm without God can no longer be termed chiliasm" (80). Then, in an abstract and less than convincing gesture, he reflected on whether one day chiliasm might "eliminate God from its emotional world, that is, in the process of its development will sublate itself, . . . [and whether] from this essential transformation entirely new and unexpected and meaningful possibilities will arise for the human spirit; in just the same way it is possible that Bolshevism will be the transition to this new epoch" (81). But he conceded nonetheless that this particular "development of the human spirit" will only be decided in the course of "centuries that are yet to come" (81).

If the political problematic that remained unresolved in László Radványi's dissertation was left to history, the existential and philosophical questions attending the "present moment" of communism preoccupied him and other members of the Budapest Sunday Circle in terms of the ethical principles posited by Kierkegaard, among others, for the modern age. In the words of György Káldor, who was, like Radványi, one of the youngest members of the circle and who also left Vienna to study in Heidelberg, he and his Hungarian generation were devoted to "the Bible-Ady-Dostoyevsky-Kierkegaard-Claudel."[26] Even though dispersed, the Sundayers often reconvened in Vienna, where they continued to struggle with issues that had already preoccupied them, albeit in loftier times, in Budapest. On 26 April 1921 Béla Balázs wrote in his diary:

> Radványi is in Vienna. The Mannheims . . . are in Vienna. . . . Right now we're having very good Sundays. (Gyuri [Georg Lukács], Káldor, Fogarasi, Révai, Tolnay, Lena, Maria Lazar.) Young Káldor and Radványi have developed very strongly. This is a brave and aggressive new generation. In these Sunday get-togethers there is only talk about the issue of communism anymore, that is, about the fate and significance of our ethical individualism and artistic-philosophical "Platonism" in that new world that we're longing to have (for it's coming in any case and will be better than the present one), but about which none of us can say what kind of intellectual and spiritual world it will in fact be.[27]

For Balázs, who formulated the problem more abstractly than Radványi and surely Lukács would have done, the basic contradiction in which the Sundayers found themselves expressed itself in "our other issue, . . . that of individual ethics (Kierkegaard); our line of development till now led us to devote ourselves to a movement that excludes this individual ethics. We are thus dealing with two lines of development in humanity. That of the evolution of the classes and that of the individual soul, developments that can also follow paths that are entirely separate from each other, and in us they have crossed."[28]

Balázs and Lukács were both well into their thirties when these two separate paths "crossed" in them with sudden and unexpected force during the Hungarian revolutions of 1918–19. László Radványi, who was born in December of 1900, was barely eighteen. That he continued to grapple with this problem in his ensuing exile is obvious from the topic he chose for his Heidelberg dissertation as well as from other evidence we have about his life during these years.[29] At the time of his return to the family fold of Sundayers in Vienna in April 1921, Radványi had only recently become acquainted in Heidelberg with the twenty-year-old student of art history and sinology in whose later prose narratives the separate paths that "crossed" in him and other members of the Budapest Sunday Circle would play no small part, indeed, would become the stuff and flesh of contemporary legend and myth.[30]

"Dear Little Sister Netty Reiling, May God grant that what we long for will be"—this was Radványi's evangelical greeting on the title page of the 1911 Diederichs edition of Kierkegaard's *Die Krankheit zum Tode* (*The Sickness unto Death*), which he presented on 1 March 1921 to the future author of *The Dead on the Island Djal.*[31] It was evidently his first gift to the woman who was to become his lifelong soulmate and wife. Radványi's choice of the early Christian form of address "Sister" and the text of his inscription suggest how quickly Netty Reiling seems to have been recruited into the close-knit community of Hungarian-Jewish intellectuals with whom László Radványi (who also went by the apostolic name Johann) had left Hungary in the fall of 1919 and with whom he continued to associate and identify in what for all of them henceforth signified a life in the diaspora.

The appellation "Sister" also suggests the aura of secrecy and confidentiality surrounding the largely insular existence led by the exiled Radványi and other members of the Sunday Circle. Whereas they "exuded confidence" in Budapest, "convinced that Heaven itself cheered their march to the kingdom of the soul," in exile they "stewed in the bitter, thick juice of *émigré* barracks," lived on "chattering teeth and an empty stomach," and "talked in whispers," in constant fear of immigration authorities and the police.[32] This more or less underground existence was to be thematized by Seghers only a few years later in the island cemetery locale of her story *The Dead on the Island Djal.* To be sure, the pastor Jan Seghers's furtive preoccupation one evening with a passage from the New Testament—"And a message was sent to the church at Laodicea" (9)—has all the elements of the evangelical coupled with the clandestine, reminiscent not only of the lives of the Jewish-Christian apostles, but of those members of the Sunday Circle who felt obliged to circumvent postal censorship by having their letters and other communiqués either delivered personally or coded.[33]

Toward the end of her life Anna Seghers still only hinted at the connection between her early relationship to the Sunday Circle and her beginnings as a writer. Asked in 1973 if her decision to write was influenced by others, and if she belonged to any literary circles or groups during her years in Heidelberg, she was typically elusive and avoided specifics. In keeping with the practice of confidentiality among the Sundayers (and the Jewish Christians many of them emulated), she seems already at the time of her university studies to have kept this connection under cover by a variety of means: "All my friends were very interested in literature and in the arts in general, but they didn't write in a literary way as I did now and then. No one coerced me, some didn't at all know that I experimented as a writer. I published my first pieces under a pseudonym, at first no one knew who was hiding behind it. Sometimes I would casually let manuscripts circulate just to see the reactions. I wasn't at all secure about what I was doing."[34]

That her assumed name Seghers was more than the conventional pen name, that it was also a kind of code name by which she could enter into the select philosophical discourse of the Sundayers, is suggested by her words in an interview of 1976. Dismissing her choice of Hercules Seghers's name as having been merely circumstantial, and calling it "the idea of a moment," she went on to note: "Actually, I also had something else up my sleeve. I thought this would be an appropriate way of making myself noticeable to my friends—but not directly. This name is so unusual, and it would surely attract attention if it suddenly appeared above the title of a story in a newspaper. On the other hand I could also hide behind it."[35]

In the 1976 interview Seghers seems deliberately to have left out the most important element that would have made her "noticeable" to her "friends." More than the author's "unusual" name, it was the island named "Djal" in the title that would have particularly struck the Sunday Circle reader of the *Frankfurter Zeitung,* who would have recognized it at once as a code word, that is, as already mentioned, as the phonetic spelling of the root *gyal* in the Hungarian verb *gyaláz,* meaning to abuse, revile, vilify, and the noun *gyalázat,* meaning dishonor and shame. As to the "Kalomistic faith" ("dem kalomistischen Glauben") in which the pastor Jan Seghers, as inscribed on his tombstone, "lived and was born" (12), the author invented the word "kalomistisch" as well. Basing it on the Hungarian noun *kaland* (adventure, escapade) or *kalamajka* (rumpus) combined with *misztikus* (mystical), she created the composite "kalomistisch," which in combination with the notion of conviction or faith implies a belief in "mystical adventure."[36]

The Dead on the Island Djal of 1924 can thus be read as the author's fanciful testimonial response to László Radványi's gift of Kierkegaard's *The Sickness unto Death* to his "Little Sister Netty Reiling" three years earlier. Whatever Netty Reiling's actual reasons may have been for ascribing the authorship of *The Dead on the Island Djal* to "Antje Seghers," and it appears they were complex, her story's thematization of despair was inspired at least figuratively by her reading of Kierkegaard's *The Sickness unto Death* that Radványi presented to her in early 1921. That the Danish author himself signed his treatise with the pseudonymous name "Anti-Climacus" while crediting "Kierkegaard" with the editing of the text would only lend further credence to this assumption. His own splitting off of his authorial identity allowed Kierkegaard, as "editor," to suggest that Anti-Climacus only "has himself to blame for conflating himself with ideality (this is the demonic element in him), but his account of the ideality can be quite true, and I bow to it."[37] Netty Reiling's pseudonymous claim to the even more fantastic "ideality" thematized in *The Dead on the Island Djal,* "a tale from the Dutch, retold by Antje Seghers," may not have had altogether different motivations.

Kierkegaard's introduction to his treatise tells us that the words spoken by Jesus at Lazarus's tomb—"This sickness is not unto death" (John 11:4)—led to the disciples' misunderstanding, which Jesus clarified by assuring them that indeed "Lazarus is dead" (John 11:14). Thus, Kierkegaard argued, it is not because Lazarus has not died, but because "Christ exists"—"that is why this sickness is not unto death." The "sickness unto death," on the other hand, is resistance to this belief and manifests itself as the various forms of human despair: "Despair is a sickness of the spirit, of the self, and so can have three forms: being unconscious in despair of having a self (inauthentic despair), not wanting in despair to be oneself, and wanting in despair to be oneself."[38]

In the island cemetery of Djal there is far more "authentic" than "inauthentic" despair. It belongs to those who once had a more or less "authentic" self as seafarers, that is, as philosophers who "traversed all the waters" until they "shipwrecked" on the rocky shores of dishonor and shame. That they now "have to lie still and listen as the sea roars and hisses behind the churchyard wall" (7) is at once their "not wanting in despair to be oneself" and their "wanting in despair to be oneself." Like the dead Lazarus, who was prepared "for the glory of God" to respond to the cry "Lazarus, come forth,"[39] their bones "twitch so fiercely that the wooden crosses and gravestones begin to skip." But they hear no Christ's call, only the voice of the parson aboveground shouting "Quiet down there" (7).

If the raising of Lazarus from the dead gives evidence that, in Kierkegaard's words, "Christ exists," the continuously thwarted resurrections in the island cemetery of Djal evoke the despair of the diasporic condition *after* the crucifixion, where the coming of the awaited kingdom is postponed indefinitely. The notion of being last rather than first is underscored in the scene showing the pastor of Djal reading the Bible in his study. The line he repeats three times to himself—"And a letter went out to the community of Laodicea"—is one "particularly pleasing to his ear" and seems to him "a credit to the New Testament, even if the Old is better suited to the minor chords of his heart" (9). An early seat of Christianity in Asia Minor, Laodicea is, notably, the last of the seven churches enumerated in the Book of Revelation, where it is rebuked for being "lukewarm, neither hot nor cold."[40]

This "lukewarm" condition, or what for Kierkegaard would have been the "sin" of "despair," is exemplified by a visitor from the cemetery who has stolen out of his tomb. His sudden and very noisy arrival one evening at the pastor's door seems to invoke the words of the militant risen Christ of the Book of Revelation to the community of Laodicea: "Be on your mettle therefore and repent. Here I stand knocking at the door; if anyone hears my voice and opens the door, I will come in and sit down to supper with him and he with me."[41] But when the door is flung open and the sea captain Morten Sise steps in, the pastor recognizes him as being merely one of many "dead" sailors whom he himself fished out of the sea and buried. And so for all his self-importance, this captain who once again must return underground reveals himself as only the shadow of the risen Christ, or, as it were, of the "dead" Lazarus, whose "sickness" was *not* "unto death."

The crux of Seghers's story revolves around the contest between the island pastor Jan Seghers and the restless sea captain Morten Sise. Whereas the pastor wants to minister to the "dying" and bury the "dead," the sea captain refuses to remain underground and even attempts to overthrow the pastor by having him take his, the sea captain's, place in the empty tomb. Implicit in this contest is the personally close yet ideologically ever more troubled relationship between the two dominant philosophical figures of the Budapest Sunday Circle—Georg Lukács and Karl Mannheim. Considered within the context of her discursive relations with the members of the Sunday Circle, the contest between the island pastor and the sea captain represents the author's attempt to lend mythic proportions to an intellectual debate about ethics, politics, and assimilation that not only was crucial to her own beginnings as an author, but became paradigmatic for the predicament of many a Central European intellectual in the first half of the twentieth century.

As is known, the exiled Georg Lukács lived a semi-underground existence in Vienna while he dedicated himself to strengthening the ethical, or Luxemburgian, faction within the leadership of the Hungarian Communist Party vis-à-vis the more bureaucratically inclined and not at all Kierkegaardian Béla Kun. From Béla Balázs's diary entry of 4 December 1919 we know how radically different was Lukács's bearing in Vienna— "the most heartrending sight; nervous and sad, his face deathly pale and sunken"—compared to the philosophical and political heights he had reached in his former life in Budapest. Not unlike the "dead" pastor of Djal, who was born and lived in the "Kalomistic" faith, that is, the belief in "mystical adventure," Lukács, according to Balázs, "was born to be a quiet scholar, a lonely sage, a visionary of eternal matters." And like the resurrected pastor, who with "no children or siblings, no wife and no beloved" (8) devotes himself without complaint to the shipwrecked, making sure that once buried they stay underground, the exiled Lukács described by Balázs was "performing hopeless conspiratorial Party work, looking for people who embezzled the Party's money, while his philosophical genius remains suppressed like a watercourse that burrows, loosens, and destroys the earth as it is forced underground. . . . And he says he can't leave his post now, and 'out of a feeling of honor' must remain."[42]

In Balázs's view, at least at this point in time, Lukács in effect personified Kierkegaard's notion of "not wanting in despair to be oneself." Indeed, Balázs's somewhat quick judgment has an unmistakably Kierkegaardian ring: "In the case of Lukács the mask of the conspiratorial, active politician and revolutionary is a lie, is not his metaphysically rooted mission. . . . Out of a feeling of honor he leads a deceptive life (not one appropriate to him); he is committing a metaphysical sin." Lukács suffers from a "terrible banishment," and "he is indeed homeless because he has lost his intellectual and spiritual home."[43] But as Balázs well knew, by 1919 Lukács no longer believed in the conventional notion of the uniquely individual self, be it as a "philosophical genius" or any other. In this respect we might say, along with Kierkegaard, that he was "forced to be 'self' in such a way that he doesn't want to be, that is his torment—not being able to be rid of himself."[44]

In the case of Karl Mannheim, who rejected his mentor's chiliastic messianism to pursue philosophy within an institutional academic setting, we might say that his particular "sickness" exemplified the condition of "wanting in despair to be oneself"—which Kierkegaard also characterized as "defiance."[45] Mannheim was evidently the only member of the Sunday Circle who did not bow to Lukács's authority, openly disagreed with him, and "despite all respect, opposed him with critique that tended to be rather malicious."[46] During the Hungarian Commune of 1919, Commissar of Education Georg Lukács appointed Mannheim, who had just received his doctorate, to a university professorship in Budapest, a post that Mannheim readily accepted. In his university lectures during the spring of 1919, Mannheim speculated, drawing on the language of Lukács's *Soul and Form* of 1910, about three possible "life forms," which nonetheless appeared to him as problematic from the "point of view of the current ethical problem: whether it is permitted to resort to evil means for the sake of a good end."[47] His distinctions elaborate on Dostoyevsky's rendering of the problem in *The Brothers Karamazov,* a favorite topic of discussion among the Sundayers: "The politician doesn't believe in God, he believes in history. The saint believes in God, but he says that his kingdom is not of this world. The pedagogue believes neither in God nor in history, but only in culture."[48]

If Mannheim wanted "none of them in theory," in the world—in this case the Hungarian Council Republic of 1919, which afforded him a professorship—he was obliged to choose at least one of these "life forms," and it was, predictably, the third: "The pedagogue is resigned, he cannot touch people with the directness of the saint, because he knows that his gesture would be false. However, he knows that art, high in value as it may be, doesn't do it better. And yet he still hopes that the music of the soul will somehow break through in this way. Only this is given to us all. And if the pedagogue is conscious of this as well, if he has come to terms also with this, that he cannot reach the eternal, then he does at least as much as Charon—he ferries across the black waters."[49] (The typically Sunday Circle imagery of traversing waters, if not the tone of resignation, reappears in Seghers's own prose starting with *The Dead on the Island Djal.*)

Other Sundayers characterized Mannheim's adopted "life form" differently. In her later autobiographical novel, the poet Anna Lesznai likened his finely drawn features, aristocratic bearing, and emotionally reserved demeanor to that of an "Indian prince."[50] In the spring of 1919 Lesznai noted in her journal: "My essential metaphysical pain is desire, the affirmation of life. Mannheim's essential pain is skepticism (the detour of the intellect); when he is content and contemplates the wall between himself and God and strokes it: that is frivolous estheticism."[51] Mannheim's liberal-democratic inclinations, coupled with his deep-seated fears about the realities of violent reaction to popular revolution, are suggested in Balázs's description of the Sundayers' participation in the mass demonstration of 28 October 1918 that was met by police violence: "On the banks of the Danube we encountered a terrible row of fire and the crowd started to draw back. We pressed forward. Mali [Anna Lesznai], who thought her husband [Oszkár Jászi] was at the front of the crowd, rushed ahead like a terrible Valkyrie, pulling people with her. Mannheim, pale and clutching on to me, proceeded with determination. The others got lost somewhere."[52] Edit Gyömröi, one of the younger members of the circle, later remembered Mannheim as "a very intelligent, very sensitive, and very charming person," yet "totally frightened" at the time of the revolution. Obsessed with the eventual vindictiveness of the counterrevolution, "in this condition he fantasized that his nails would be torn out."[53]

Mannheim escaped from Budapest to Vienna by Danube steamer relatively late, in December of 1919. His somewhat exceptional situation and figure upon his arrival in the shabby refugee barracks of Grinzing is echoed in *The Dead on the Island Djal* in the island fishermen's discovery of a "tall, gaunt corpse" lying in a "cavity in the rocks, where the water was a bit shallower and stiller," and where the "silver chain around its neck" had caught on a boulder (8). Mannheim's reluctance to participate for long in the hand-to-mouth, more or less underground life led by his fellow Sundayers must have met with the kind of discontent and controversy that mark the island fishermen's struggle to dislodge the dead sea captain from his watery bed: "The tall gaunt corpse was that of Morten Sise, the captain himself, and since he had been an odd fellow all his life, he wanted even now to remain in the sea, where he had always liked it best, and hard as they tugged away at him with rods and barbed hooks, he didn't give way" (8).

Whereas Lukács put aside pure philosophical speculation, or what in 1921 Balázs, well known for his quick changes of mood and opinion, patly dismissed as "anachronistic play" or "stamp collecting,"[54] Mannheim insisted all the more on what he would later publicly espouse as the stance of the *freischwebende Intelligenz,* that is, the "socially unattached intelligentsia."[55] Lukács's orthodox position in terms of both ethics and tactics is suggested in *The Dead on the Island Djal* by the pastor's insistence, despite the risk of capsizing their small boat, that the "dead" sea captain be pulled out of the water and buried:

> As the small boat, pushed high by each wave, crashed up against the rocks, the boatmen started to grumble. But the pastor was of the opinion that a genius, even if dead, shouldn't be allowed to hang around with fish and all sorts of carrion among algae and corals, but belongs underground with a cross on top, and at the last minute he devised a sort of wire sling with whose help the captain was finally pulled into the boat. And before long he even had a gravestone with an inscription just like in the churchyard of Dordrecht. (8–9)

Mannheim's ambivalence toward the Sunday Circle group in Vienna, his inhibitions, occasionally fluctuating loyalties, and persistent striving for academic legitimacy and assimilation are described in Seghers's story in terms of the Kierkegaardian "sickness" of "despair." It manifests itself in the sea captain's repeated efforts to crawl, uninvited, out of his tomb so as to resurrect on his own a life of seafaring, that is to say, philosophical speculation, on alien dry ground:

> But the new inhabitant of Djal soon proved to be a restless soul. One evening the gravedigger, whose hut was located in one of the remote

corners of the cemetery, came running bathed in sweat to the parsonage and reported that the captain had toppled his gravestone and was
already stretching out one hand. The pastor rose without a word,
went out into the dark night of the cemetery, pushed said gravestone
aright and sat down on top of it with all his weight . . . and thus
awaited the morning. From now on the captain kept quiet. (9)

After a semester in Freiburg, where he attended lectures by Husserl
and Heidegger, and another in Berlin, Mannheim settled in Heidelberg in
March of 1921. His reputation as Lukács's most brilliant protégé allowed
him entry into the Weber circle, whose members would henceforth
advance his university career as they had once helped and stood by
Lukács. It was in fact Mannheim who, as a Hungarian-Jewish foreigner,
was able to achieve the academic career in Germany that had been denied
Lukács a decade earlier on the basis of even more extraordinary cultural
and intellectual credentials. As is well known, Lukács made his decision to
join the Hungarian Communist Party in December 1918 only a few days
after learning that the University of Heidelberg had denied his candidacy
for habilitation. Whereas the official letter of rejection asserted that the
university could not "admit a foreigner, especially a Hungarian citizen, to
Habilitation,"[56] Max Weber's explanation in his personal letter of regret
to Lukács was more to the point: "If the young scholar is a Jew, of course
one says *lasciate ogni speranza.*"[57] Four months later, and already working
for the Hungarian Council Republic as Commissar of Education, Lukács
wrote to the German playwright Paul Ernst, who had informed him of the
possibility of a lectureship in Marburg, that the contents of Ernst's letter
had "meanwhile become null and void in more than one sense. To begin
with, as a leading member of the then persecuted Communist Party, I lost
my chances of ever attaining an academic post."[58]

Karl Mannheim's attempts in the 1920s to retain the respect and
friendship of his extraordinary mentor, to benefit from his academic connections and reputation in Germany prior to 1918, and at the same time to
distance himself from his subsequent legacy and writings are well known.
Yet in many respects they remained on common ground: as fellow exiled
Hungarians, as philosophers committed to the language of ethics and the
soul, and as sociologists, in their shared critique of capitalist rationaliza-
tion. As late as in 1927, when Lukács's standing within the Hungarian
Communist Party and the Comintern had reached its lowest point and, by
contrast, Mannheim was about to reach the height of his career, Anna
Lesznai described in her diary a conversation between them in Vienna that
continued the topic of their earlier discussions within the Budapest Sunday
Circle: "Mannheim and Lukács debate about communism. . . . L. is always

right in view of the larger course of things, yet M.'s objections are also true. Reality *up till now* perhaps has proven M. more right, that is, up till now."[59]

At the same time that he sought to maintain his relationship to Lukács, Mannheim pursued his academic career, gradually moving away from aesthetics, philosophy, and the essay form characteristic of Lukács and toward sociology and the more accepted forms of academic discourse. (Max Weber had earlier advised Lukács to follow the same course, but his advice went unheeded.)[60] In 1922 Mannheim received a second doctorate, from the University of Heidelberg. In 1926, with the help of Alfred Weber, Emil Lederer, and others who, along with Max Weber, had earlier backed Lukács for a university post, he was appointed *Privatdozent.* Soon there-after he applied for and was granted German citizenship. In 1929, follow-ing publication of his widely discussed book *Ideology and Utopia*—which minimized Lukács's contributions to the topic, acknowledging him in a mere four passing mentions of his name and one footnote—he was offered a chair at the University of Frankfurt, which he assumed in 1930.

In the spring of 1921, shortly after his move to Heidelberg and mar-riage to the young Sundayer and psychoanalyst Júlia Láng, Mannheim visited Vienna—"as if to Canossa," wrote Balázs[61]—to ask for Lukács's blessing and reconciliation with the Sunday Circle. The meeting is thema-tized in *The Dead on the Island Djal* in the scene of the sea captain Morten Sise's sudden appearance—fresh from his tomb and quite "run-down and shabby" except for his "shiny buttons" and "neck chain"—at the door of the parsonage. The "frowning" stranger's "hesitant" and in fact fabricated request to visit his "cousin" Morten Sise's "grave" is met with an enthusi-astic "So, you landed here just for the sake of a grave. . . . I like that!" And the pastor hurries to fetch brandy, a potion that would inspire soulful philosophical debate (10).

Meanwhile, his "skinny limbs shaking" as if from "some sort of *sick-ness*" (my emphasis), the visitor pages through the pastor's Bible "in a par-ticularly unbelieving manner with the tips of his thumb and forefinger" (10). Given the nature of the philosophical differences between Lukács and Mannheim at the time Seghers wrote her story, the ensuing discussion of the Bible between the captain and the pastor can be understood, aside from referring to the messianic aspects of the Bible itself, as making implicit reference to the Hegelian and Marxist literature that overflowed the cramped quarters of Lukács's Viennese study at the time he was preparing the essays for his "heretical" book *History and Class Conscious-ness.* Thus the captain laments in a "contemptuous" tone about the "Bible": "I just can't understand . . . how a reasonable person can find pleasure in this kind of thing. If one were to rely on this, one might believe that human beings are on this earth in order to experience inside and out-side the most wonderful things, which however are only a prelude to the miracle that comes at the end. And what's it like in reality? They travel the waters a bit, perish some place or another, and lie with a hollow stomach in the dirty ground for the rest of eternity" (10). The pastor responds with a "smile from the corners of his eyes": "I think it's a splendid book. I know it by heart from A to Z, and if I had to live one more time, I'd put it to memory all over again. You can find all kinds in it, dumb and smart, strong and weak, hard and soft, seafarers and men of prayer. As to the miraculous stuff, any one can take with him as much of it as he can bear" (11).

The pastor easily wins this philosophical dispute on a discursive level, while the sea captain's mood turns "poisonous" as he is left with "nothing special to say" (11). He reveals his malicious intent only a few hours later as the two of them make their way across the dunes to the cemetery "in the still night, in the thin-sleepy rush of the surf" (11). "My dear man," the pastor suddenly calls out. "I can sense it just so, you're only posing as if you were alive, in reality you're a *dead man*" (11). In response the visitor merely mumbles: "What nonsense!" (11). But when they reach the ceme-tery and the tower clock strikes the midnight hour, the stranger reveals himself: "Now, Pastor, you're in my power, now you must climb in my stead into the empty grave. It is I, Morten Sise, the Captain" (11).

At the time of their reunion in Vienna, Béla Balázs and other mem-bers of the Sunday Circle alleged that Mannheim (and Arnold Hauser, whose break with the Sunday Circle remained permanent) sought to be reconciled with their fellow Sundayers because as marginalized intellectu-als with no "connection to the movement," they had "missed the train at their provincial station" and been "swept to the side of the road."[62] Mannheim responded to this allegation in his "Heidelberg Letters," which appeared in 1921 and 1922 in the Hungarian journal *Tüz* (Fire), published in Bratislava (Hungarian: Pozsony; German: Pressburg). The first letter, dated October 1921, strikes up the theme of alienation, displacement, and loss of identity belonging to one who, like Ahasver, is doomed to wander and, like Kierkegaard's despairing Christian (and the sea captain Morten Sise on Djal), is "unable to die":[63]

We Hungarians live in the dispersion, one here, the other there, and every place in the world today is more distant from the other than it was previously, but still our curiosity craves more than it ever did. Here on foreign soil I feel as though I have been sent out ahead like a sentry. . . . I look into every opened window, divine the bearing of the gesticulating speakers and the silenced words of the mutes that hold themselves back. When people come together I am there, when they learn I learn with them, and I would also wish to live together with them, to settle down—and still I don't find my place.[64]

Mannheim's "Heidelberg Letters" of 1921 and 1922 reveal the extent to which he yearned for the kind of intellectual niveau and community he had known within the Sunday Circle in Budapest.[65] "We have brought to matters more love and above all more desire than can be fulfilled by today's world," he wrote mournfully at the close of his first "Heidelberg Letter" of 1921. "We have ripened toward something, and no one is here to gather the fruits, and our soul fears having ripened only to wither away uselessly" (81–82). In his second "Heidelberg Letter" of 1922 Mannheim renewed his plea for soulful association and community, noting such occasional traces in his meetings with younger members of the Sunday Circle in Heidelberg, which included his wife Júlia Láng, György Káldor, László Radványi, and surely by this time their "Little Sister Netty Reiling": "When I step into the room illumined by the yellow light, and around the table sit people, young people, their eyes glow and the talk is about new pains and new joys—then I know that we are alive, and the petrification that comes from abandonment falls away from me" (83–84).

Suggesting that already at this time she participated in such convocations in "the room illumined by the yellow light," the scene described by Mannheim is of a kind that we find repeatedly in Seghers's later narratives, beginning in 1927 with the Rembrandt-like interiors of *Grubetsch* informed by scenes from the lives of Jesus and the apostles.[66] In his "Heidelberg Letter" of 1922 Mannheim wrote about the necessity of community in terms of "charismatic" associations where the "seeds" of relationships move "from soul to soul": "And precisely because in our time such charismatically based associations are so rare, and because I believe that the new human being can find new shape neither in the family nor in school, nor in the life and politics of the external world, I consider it important that this kind of communal life exist in our time" (86–87). Mannheim's letter suggests further that "timeless examples of this kind of soulful bond are given by Jesus and his disciples," for whom "this unity of a new life spirit" first made it possible that teachings of various origins could blend into a "system" (86). For Mannheim, and undoubtedly for his entire circle of young Sundayers in Heidelberg, including Netty Reiling, this early Jewish-Christian example, not the Bolshevist example of the Hungarian and German Communist Parties, continued to be the standard for what they called soulful communal association, or simply communism.[67] "In such a communal existence there is not yet a dogmatic bond," wrote Mannheim, "and the criterion for heresy is not opposition to any kind of thesis, but the sinful act against the spirit of the interconnecting soul" (86).

But Mannheim's "Heidelberg Letters" also presented a more overt challenge to Lukács and the Sunday group in Vienna and in this sense prefigured Morten Sise's attempt to overthrow the pastor of Djal by having *him* climb into the empty grave. Arguing for intellectual castes or elites on the basis of the decentralized model of the German educational system, Mannheim rejected the urban avant-garde model of the Hungarian intelligentsia as outdated and no longer valid in the postwar, postrevolutionary era. It is not insignificant that the form of the "Heidelberg Letters" echoes that of the New Testament epistles. Whereas in Vienna the notably orthodox Lukács remained close to the original scene of events in Budapest, reminding us of the "rock" Peter, who held together the Christian community within Palestine, Mannheim, not unlike the apostle Paul, who reached out to the gentiles, emphasized the aspect of the dispersion. In this way he sought to create a new kind of community consisting of "dispersed" Hungarians in fellowship with that "thin layer" of the German intellectual elite where "what can someday become important is being prepared and shaped" (76). Thus Mannheim countered Balázs's humiliating allegation that he had "missed the train" in Heidelberg, which Balázs dismissively called a "provincial station." Indeed, Mannheim now maintained that "the province, the small town is not the last emanation or peripheral deposit of life in the cultural center, but the living source itself" (76–77).

According to Mannheim's increasingly liberal, albeit still aristocratic, notion of the new intellectual elite, only those were to "be included in this caste who dedicate themselves in such great measure to the service of the intellect that it in fact stands at the center of their life and makes its presence felt in all their life expressions" (75). Modeled on the sociologically oriented Weber Circle as well as the Stefan George Circle of artists and humanists with which Mannheim also associated in Heidelberg,[68] "this caste" would of course have rejected the kind of political activity in which many of the Vienna and other Sundayers were involved. And Mannheim did not refrain from reminding his exiled compatriots that now more than ever he "despised the lies of those who under national or racist slogans or the battle cry of class struggle want to realize the romantic fantasy that they are one with the race or class they programmatically represent" (75–76).

All the more devastating than his already well-known opinions about such "romantic fantasy" must have been Mannheim's slightly coded suggestion that "Tristan" (i.e., Lukács) and "Don Juan" (i.e., Balázs), that is, the most prominent members of the exiled Hungarian avant-garde, had become virtually impotent as writers since their departure from Budapest (74). To be sure, Balázs's writing style and output had quite obviously deteriorated since his last writings in Budapest, which included his libretti for Béla Bartók's *The Wooden Prince* and *Duke Bluebeard's Castle,* as well as his celebrated collections of poetry, fables, and stories of 1918 and 1919.[69] And of course Lukács's contributions in exile to such journals and newspapers as *Communismus* and *Die Rote Fahne* hardly ranked in quality with his celebrated essays of former times. Instead of simply "loving" like Tristan or "flirting" like Don Juan, Mannheim asked, implying that in both cases the emotional object was an abstract proletariat, "what might be the figure of Don Juan or of Tristan if they had described themselves?" This would be possible, he argued, if they "included in some form of the sketch the conversion table, the degree of the perspective, so that the reader can add to it or draw from it, expand it or narrow it—according to the key to his soul and his interest" (74–75). In other words, Mannheim wanted dialogue, even about politics, as long as his interlocutors engaged in philosophical discourse at its former level of refinement.

The "Indian prince" had thrown down the gauntlet, and for his part, "Tristan" quickly rose to the challenge. In late 1922, not long after Mannheim published his second "Heidelberg Letter," his onetime mentor Lukács completed *History and Class Consciousness,* a collection of essays published in January 1923 in the first of many editions that would go down in history as the greatest formulation of Marxist philosophy in its time. In his preface to the new edition of 1967, Lukács noted that *History and Class Consciousness* "was born in the midst of the crises of this transitional period," that is, during a time when he was grappling with the "intellectual passion of my revolutionary messianism," and at the same time with "certain decisions relating to the organizational development of the communist movement in Hungary."[70] His attempt to give philosophical definition to the "orthodox" revolutionary-messianic dimensions of Marxism is encapsulated in the famous passage at the start of the first essay: "Orthodox Marxism, therefore, does not imply the uncritical acceptance of the results of Marx's investigations. It is not the 'belief' in this or that thesis, nor the exegesis of a 'sacred' book. On the contrary, orthodoxy refers exclusively to *method.*"[71]

As is well known, Lukács argued on two fronts, on the one hand against the scientific-positivistic approaches of traditional Marxism, and on the other against the neo-Kantian framework of bourgeois philosophy to which he had belonged, and Karl Mannheim still belonged. As Lukács wrote in 1967:

Above all I was absolutely convinced of one thing: that the purely contemplative nature of bourgeois thought had to be radically over-come. . . . Comprehensibly enough in the context of the period, I attacked the bourgeois and opportunistic currents in the workers' movement that glorified a conception of knowledge which was osten-sibly objective but was in fact isolated from any sort of praxis; with considerable justice I directed my polemics against the over-extension and over-valuation of contemplation.[72]

Among the members of the Budapest Sunday Circle the realm of the "over-valuation of contemplation" belonged quintessentially to Mannheim, while the theoretical impulse of praxis, which in 1922 still included the "intellectual passion of my revolutionary messianism," was Lukács's domain. This very distinction is played out in *The Dead on the Island Djal* as charismatic gesture versus eschatological exultation, or, in the more familial language of the Sunday Circle, philosophical skepticism versus the ethics of self-sacrifice toward a higher goal. On the mythical island Djal the "sickness" of skepticism is the greater, the "sickness" of activism the lesser shame and dishonor, and so it is, as already quoted above, that the "dead" pastor has the last word: "Such a common Christ-ian as you are, Captain, needs to stay patiently underground after death, till our Lord is ready to sound his trumpet for the resurrection. As for me, I wasn't content to stretch out a hand, topple a tombstone, and frighten a pastor. I pestered God for so long with such wild and furious prayers that on the intercession of his seven angels he *had* to let me back into this life in my former shape. For you should know, Captain, I am myself a dead man!" (12).

The identity of this particular "dead man" is rooted in the material evidence of history, represented in this case by the words inscribed on a "hunk of rock" that turns out to be the "dead man's" own tombstone lying under "thicket and weeds" in a "totally neglected place" in the cemetery of Djal (12). Seghers's painstaking emphasis on the utter shabbiness of this particular gravesite seems to have been inspired by one of the more pointed phrasings in the 1922 preface to *History and Class Consciousness*. Here Lukács argued that the time had come to resurrect Hegel from obliv-ion—that young "Old Man" who was a "heretical" theologian in his own day. If Hegel meanwhile had "once again become *persona grata*," indeed "even fashionable" in university circles, Lukács wrote with no little irony, nonetheless the great philosopher—incidentally not unlike Lukács during his inglorious subterranean years in Vienna—was "still treated as a 'dead dog.'"[73]

The banality of the metaphor finds its mythic equivalent in Anna

Seghers's story as the pastor Jan Seghers and the captain Morten Sise trudge across the dunes to the graveyard of Djal. Here the captain finally reveals his intention of having the pastor take his place underground. Seemingly unperturbed at the prospect of being, in Lukács's words, a "dead dog," the pastor Jan Seghers only laughs in the captain's face: "What a grandiose revenge you've thought up, wait, I'm coming. But first I want to show you something" (11–12). Thereupon the pastor kicks "thicket and weeds away from a hunk of rock" and says: "Can you read? Yes? Then read!" And the captain "stutter[s]" the words inscribed on the resurrected pastor's own gravestone: "Here rests / JAN SEGHERS / who died on Djal / in the year of the Lord 1625 / in the Kalomistic faith / in which he lived and was born / in Altmark / in 1548" (12).

Replete with coded allusions and innuendo, *The Dead on the Island Djal* was hardly intended for public consumption as fiction in the modern sense. Rather, it was written as the more or less internal chronicle of a contemporary Hungarian-Jewish journey, or passion, by which the author might contribute to and participate in its continuing saga. By the time she published her story at the end of 1924, "Antje" Seghers had spent five years in Heidelberg and was well acquainted with the person, ideas, and reputation of the man Karl Mannheim, on whom she modeled the figure of her sea captain Morten Sise. However, the man who informed the figure of her island pastor, Georg Lukács, or Gyuri, as he would later also be known to her, was still "a sort of legend . . . shaped by the stories I heard about him from Hungarian émigrés who had fled the white terror."[74] As a chronicler who seems to have empathized with both sides of a humorously rendered but potentially tragic conflict, she hardly came to a final judgment about a controversy that would continue within the Sunday Circle—and within an entire generation, not only of Hungarian intellectuals—for decades to come. Nonetheless, by signing this "tale" told anew as Antje Seghers, thus linking her authorial persona to the lineage of the resurrected pastor Jan Seghers, she clearly expressed her allegiance to the chiliastic-messianic striving of Georg Lukács and the legacy of the "dead dog."

The struggle depicted in *The Dead on the Island Djal* had a more intimate personal dimension. When it appeared in the *Frankfurter Zeitung* (25 December 1924), its author was unofficially engaged to László Radványi, whom she married in Mainz on 10 August 1925.[75] It was of course the man László Radványi, whose "Little Sister Netty Reiling" and "motherchild"[76] she was before becoming his fiancée, who was the dominant presence in her intellectual and personal life at this time. It was he who first introduced her to the Budapest Sunday Circle and in the course of their more intimate relationship remained the exegete of its history and its ideas. Thus it was through the perspective of Radványi's own experience and views during his years in Heidelberg that she gained her first and, from the evidence we have, her definitive impression of an essentially Hungarian-Jewish "tale" or "saga" whose subsequent historical twists and turns she would render in mythic form again and again in her literary work.[77] If László Radványi saw himself as the philosopher who both took part in and interpreted this "saga," Netty Reiling-Radványi, later known as Anna Seghers, became its chronicler. The arrangement appears to have been as permanent as their marriage, which lasted until Radványi's death in 1978.[78] Indeed, the stories in *Drei Frauen von Haiti* (1980, Three Women from Haiti), written after his death, attest to common themes in their relationship and to the extent of his widow's grief. The arrangement was hardly as one-sided as it might first appear. If Radványi found in his future wife a woman who gave written testimony of his own trials and tribulations, she found in him the "saga" of a lifetime, that is, from the point of view of an author, the rare kind of "story" that can bear lifelong fruit. In this sense the more conventional gender roles were reversed: he was the actor and critic who, as it were, rehearsed and interpreted the role; she was the chronicler who ultimately had the last word and wrote the final script—not for the stage in this case, but for history.

Radványi's Hungarian correspondence from the mid-1920s suggests that the struggles depicted in *The Dead on the Island Djal* were not only informed by the Sunday Circle debate represented at this time by Lukács and Mannheim, but pertained in a more immediate way to an existential crisis faced at the time by Radványi and, by implication, the author who was soon to be his wife. Like Mannheim, to whom he was particularly close during his years in Heidelberg, Radványi wanted desperately to pursue an academic career as a philosopher. "I actually wanted to become a teacher," he lamented in a letter to Hungary at the end of 1926, when he was already otherwise employed in Berlin.[79] He had, after all, completed his dissertation on chiliasm under Karl Jaspers in March of 1923 and been awarded the distinction *summa cum laude.* His main interests continued to be "ethics and metaphysics" and "theology and the history of religion," he wrote to the literary scholar Gyula Földessy, his former teacher and mentor in Budapest.[80] Albeit against great odds and with no little demand for accommodation and compromise, the elder, more experienced and accomplished, and perhaps simply more fortunate Mannheim was able to make the career in Heidelberg that led to his appointment as *Privatdozent* in 1926. Radványi, meanwhile, who tended toward theology while Mannheim espoused the sociological method of the Weber Circle, saw his chances for academic or comparable employment in Germany all the more limited owing to both his "Hungarianness and Jewishness," as he characterized his situation in a letter to Földessy in July of 1924.[81]

Not insignificantly, the publication of *The Dead on the Island Djal* on 25 December 1924 coincided with Radványi's decision to give up his unsuccessful search for academic employment in Heidelberg and Frankfurt.[82] On 10 January 1925, only two weeks after the story appeared in the *Frankfurter Zeitung,* he accepted a position in Berlin that he later described in a letter to Gyula Földessy as an "economic position," but thankfully "not in business." Of the "available economic means of earning one's bread" it was "perhaps the one most suited" to him, but the "economic issues" the job entailed were unfortunately still "quite far removed" from his "true philosophical interests."[83] Despite increasing time constraints, he continued to work on a book on ethics.[84] He had also completed a translation of 175 of Endre Ady's poems, which he wanted to publish in Germany.[85] Moreover, he had only recently taught himself Hebrew so as to read the Old Testament in the original, especially "the prophets, psalmists, and historical Books (Samuel, etc.)," which gave him "great pleasure."[86] The "economic position" in Berlin nonetheless allowed him, a more or less penniless Jewish refugee from East Central Europe, a relatively secure standing in Germany so that he might marry a woman who for all her unconventional views came from one of the oldest and most distinguished Jewish families in the Rhineland.[87] At the time of his marriage in Mainz on 10 August 1925 the city registry listed his profession as *Privatgelehrter* (independent scholar).[88]

Radványi was already involved at this time in the organization of the Marxistische Arbeiter-Schule (Marxist Workers' School) in Berlin, which came into being under the auspices of the Greater Berlin branch of the German Communist Party in the fall/winter of 1925–26, and he soon became the school's director.[89] As such he would call himself Johann-Lorenz Schmidt, having "forged"—as in "smithy" or "smith": Schmied, or Schmidt—his evangelical German pseudonym Johann and his Hungarian name László to represent his new identity. Although it was officially sponsored by the Communist Party, the MASCH, as it was popularly known, reached across a wide left internationalist spectrum of teachers and students. This was due largely to Radványi's own efforts. Indeed, as director of the MASCH Radványi was able to create, albeit under changed circumstances and with a decidedly working-class focus, the kind of alternative or free school and university that members of the Sunday Circle— and the Galileo Circle with its radical social-democratic orientation, to which many of the same belonged—established in Budapest shortly before the revolutions of 1918–19.[90]

As a *Gymnasium* student in Budapest Radványi had himself been a member of the politically active Galileo Circle and attended the lectures at the Free School of the Humanities before being invited by Béla Balázs to join the elite group of intellectuals that made up the Sunday Circle. Tibor

Gergely, the young Radványi's *Gymnasium* classmate and friend, was also involved in both groups and later remembered his and Radványi's first encounter with the members of the Sunday Circle. It can be assumed that the no less precocious Radványi was equally well read:

> In 1917 I was seventeen years old and had already read Nietzsche, Schopenhauer, and Stirner. Then I happened on real philosophy after seeing a notice in the Galileo Circle about the Free School of the Humanities. I already knew [Béla] Balázs's poetry by heart, and I had also read Lukács's *Soul and Form.* So off I went to hear the presentations in the public school on Papnövelde Street. László Radványi, who had been my classmate for eight years, had the same idea without my knowing it, and was there, too. Together we edited the *Pupils' News,* the student newspaper at the Barscay Street *Gymnasium.* At that time we were already both fervent Galileo Circle members. . . . The format of the presentations [in the Free School of the Humanities] was question and answer; on the basis of our answers the speakers took notice of us—me, Radványi, György Káldor, and Károly [Charles de] Tolnay—and invited us to their reserved table in the Café Modern. And so we went, and soon thereafter we were invited to the Sunday afternoon get-togethers in Béla Balázs's villa on Naphegy Street. Our discussions never ended, and these afternoons usually lasted till dawn.[91]

Thus it was hardly coincidence that some of the teachers and lecturers whose names appeared on the rosters of the MASCH had earlier been members of the Galileo or Sunday Circles in Budapest, among them Georg Lukács (pseud. Hans Keller), his wife Gertrud Bortstieber, Béla Fogarasi, Andor Gábor, Béla Balázs, and of course Radványi, who regularly taught courses on topics in Marxist theory, sociology, and economics.[92] Other notables of the time who lectured regularly or intermittently at the MASCH included the philosopher Karl Korsch, the psychoanalyst Wilhelm Reich, the theatre director Erwin Piscator, the writers Egon Erwin Kisch and Ludwig Renn, the composer Hanns Eisler, the montage artist John Heartfield, and the architect Walter Gropius and other Bauhaus members, who supplied the MASCH with ample donations of office furniture and chairs.[93] One of the most memorable public lectures sponsored by the MASCH occurred on 28 October 1931 in a North Berlin working-class district school where Albert Einstein spoke on the topic "What a Worker Must Know about the Theory of Relativity."[94] The invitation to Einstein, perhaps even the title of the lecture, came from Anna Seghers, who managed to persuade the renowned physicist to speak on this particular topic during a personal visit to his house outside Berlin.[95] It is to be assumed that the creative writing assignments Seghers gave to aspiring writers who came to her apartment for this purpose were also undertaken in connection with the MASCH.[96] Bertolt Brecht, whom she probably first met at the MASCH, as well as his wife Helene Weigel, who taught acting there, is known to have eagerly attended classes and lectures, especially those of the "heretical" Marxist Karl Korsch.[97]

Radványi's success as director of the MASCH was remarkable. By the time the school was forced to close its doors in early 1933 he had turned it into the most successful European venture of its kind. The Berlin MASCH served as the model for thirty more such schools established by 1931 in other parts of Germany,[98] as well as for similar schools founded in Zurich, Vienna, and Amsterdam.[99] Unfortunately, the official records of the MASCH were destroyed by the National Socialists. According to a study by Gabriele Gerhard-Sonnenberg, whose research included extensive interviews with Radványi in 1974, the number of adult students attending courses at the Berlin MASCH in the early 1930s was somewhere between twenty thousand and twenty-five thousand per year.[100] In the fall of 1932, that is, in its seventh year of operation, the Berlin MASCH offered as many as 210 courses in roughly twenty-six disciplines, most of them evening courses attended by employed and unemployed workers. Among these were forty-three courses in Marxist theory; thirty-seven language courses; twenty courses in health, hygiene, and sexuality; twelve courses in the visual arts; eleven courses in stenography, typing, and bookkeeping; ten courses in imperialism, reformism, militarism, and fascism; eight courses in German economics and politics; seven courses in the history of the working-class movement, revolutionary history, and general history; seven courses in capitalist economics; six courses in sports and gymnastics; five courses in social and communal politics; five courses on the Soviet Union; four courses in each of such areas as the natural sciences, law, journalism, and youth as well as theatre, film, music, radio, and photography; and two courses each in such areas as women, public speaking, literature, and organization and statistics.[101]

The Berlin police began patrolling the MASCH classrooms in 1930, and by 1931 the school was officially subject to police controls. Due to ever larger numbers of unemployed worker-students, classes were also held in the back rooms of taverns, where the price of a glass of beer served as tuition and where SA gangs frequently disrupted classes. Under the guise of checking the papers of foreigners, the police ransacked the MASCH offices on the evening of 25 November 1932, arrested eleven people who were unable to produce the required papers, and confiscated the faculty directory. This action signified the virtual end of the MASCH, although some classes were still offered in early 1933.[102] László Radványi, alias Johann-Lorenz Schmidt, fled Berlin, and thereupon Germany, shortly before the SA entered his house on the day following the burning of the Reichstag. Anna Seghers, née Netty Reiling, soon followed.[103]

"Innerly I sense no change in myself, and I have the same questions about life that I had 1–2 years ago," Radványi wrote to Gyula Földessy in December of 1925 after having occupied his "economic position" in Berlin for almost a year.[104] But if his correspondence with his former teacher and mentor admits how "envious" he was of academicians, it also reveals the sober realization on his part of why this life was not to be for a man burdened by less than upper-class "Hungarianness and Jewishness," at least not in the increasingly reactionary academic culture of late Weimar. As Radványi wrote in December 1926:

> Unfortunately it is still the case today that really sound and thorough work in the humanistic sciences, especially philosophy, can be afforded only by those who are rich. This is very sad, not only from the perspective of those who for financial reasons don't have the time for philosophical pursuit, but also from the standpoint of philosophy. For as the current trend in philosophy makes obvious, it is largely a preoccupation of the upper class.[105]

As director of the MASCH in the late 1920s, Radványi became an inspired educator and administrator who used his talents on behalf of an even less fortunate class than the increasingly disenfranchised intellectuals and *Privatgelehrten* among whom he belonged. Thus we might say, relying on the language of *The Dead on the Island Djal* and Kierkegaard's *The Sickness unto Death,* that Radványi left behind him the restless life of a sea captain "wanting in despair to be himself" to assume the more or less "resurrected" form of a charismatic pastor, much like Lukács in Vienna, whom Balázs described at the end of 1919 in terms of suffering from "not wanting in despair to be himself."[106] That this particular version of "despair" plagued Radványi in no small way in Berlin is indicated not only in his private Hungarian correspondence, but also in Anna Seghers's subsequent narratives such as *Die Wellblech-Hütte* (1929, The Corrugated Iron Shack), which remained a fragment,[107] and in her first novel, *Die Gefährten* (1932, The Wayfarers), in which the continued trials and tribulations of Lukács, Mannheim, Radványi, and other Sundayers figure more explicitly.[108] Siegfried Kracauer's perceptive review of *Die Gefährten* in the *Frankfurter Zeitung* on 13 November 1932 characterized the novel as "a martyr chronicle of today."[109] Only a few months later Anna Seghers would embark on her first, her husband László Radványi, Karl Mannheim, and other members of the Budapest Sunday Circle on their second, voyage toward the island "Djal."[110]

CHAPTER 5

The Archetypal Map: Georg Lukács and the Way of the Soul

A free and faithful ocean was my soul.
> —Endre Ady, "The Last Ships," 1918[1]

We have been twelve fishermen all this time, and now we shall soon become a church.
> —Lajos Fülep to Béla Balázs, 1918[2]

On a sinking ship is a man whose destiny it is to disembark on the opposite shore and there experience martyrdom for a higher goal. . . . What is the pure moral duty of this man if only one seat remains in the rescue boat?
> —Anna Lesznai, Sunday Circle diary, 1918[3]

The Revolt of the Fishermen (1928) is Anna Seghers's attempt to give epic form to that "archetypal map" and "transcendental *locus*" of the soul pursued by Georg Lukács in his early theoretical writings on art and aesthetics culminating in *The Theory of the Novel*.[4] "For what is the task of true philosophy if not to draw that archetypal map?" Lukács asked in the famous opening chapter of *The Theory of the Novel* that reflects on the "age of the epic" belonging to the "integrated civilization" of the Greeks. Here philosophy is described as the virtual soulmate of the epic, "as a form of life or as that which determines the form and supplies the content of literary creation" (*TN,* 29). "What is the problem of the transcendental *locus,*" Lukács continued, "if not to determine how every impulse which springs from the innermost depths is co-ordinated with a form that it is ignorant of, but that has been assigned to it from eternity and that must envelop it in liberating symbols? When this is so, passion is the way, predetermined by reason, towards complete self-being and from madness come enigmatic yet decipherable messages of a transcendental power, otherwise condemned to silence" (*TN,* 29–30).

The philosophical or, better, aesthetic challenge posed by *The Theory of the Novel* is already taken up in the opening scenes of Seghers's novella. Here, guided by what Lukács called "enigmatic yet decipherable messages of a transcendental power," we observe how "one morning, at dawn, early in October," a lone male figure stands on board a "small, rusty coastline steamer" headed for the fishing village of St. Barbara. The crossing to St. Barbara, with its "odour of salty air, of animals and of machine oil blended together into the sweet smell of a sea voyage," evokes the very atmosphere of a continuing passion as the man aboard the rusty steamer follows with his eyes "the white scar which the ship was ripping into the sea; the scar was healed and then torn open again; was healed; and again reopened."[5]

"The soul goes out to seek adventure," Lukács wrote in the opening chapter of *The Theory of the Novel;* "it lives through adventures, but it does not know the real torment of seeking and the real danger of finding; such a soul never stakes itself; it does not yet know that it can lose itself, it never thinks of having to look for itself. Such an age is the age of the epic" (*TN,* 30). As if in presentiment of the more tarnished modern soul as figured in Seghers's narrative, Lukács continued: "It is not absence of suffering, not security of being, which in such an age encloses men and deeds in contours that are both joyful and severe . . . : it is the adequacy of the deeds to the soul's inner demand for greatness, for unfolding, for wholeness. . . . For the question which engenders the formal answers of the epic is: how can life become essence" (*TN,* 29–30).

Seghers's protagonist Johann Hull is a man in whom integrity and insecurity, joy and suffering, coexist. Reminiscent of Joseph Conrad's restless seafarers who traverse the waters of the colonial empires,[6] he is a man with a past who lives on the brink of the moment, on the precipitous edge between life and death, adventure and catastrophe. Moving from one landscape, one seascape, to the next, he is mindful of a past to which he cannot return, reluctant to take on the uncertain, ominous future toward which he is propelled. We see in him what Lukács called "the soul's inner demand for greatness, for unfolding, for wholeness," despite his awareness not only of external dangers, but also of the inglorious, ultimately doomed aspects of his particular adventure. We learn already in the first paragraph of the novella that a warrant is out for the arrest of this man who was shot during an uprising in Port Sebastian, that he spent the summer nursing his foot in a harbor tavern on Margaret's Island. We are told that the revolt he is about to incite with his presence in the fishing village of St. Barbara will end badly, that a boy named Andreas will perish in the attempt to flee across the cliffs, and that the instigator of the rebellion will be arrested and transported back to Port Sebastian.

Instead of "psychology, whether of empathy or of mere understanding," which according to Lukács lies outside the world of the epic and is "a complete reversal of the transcendental topography of the mind" (*TN,* 31), Seghers's prose charts that "transcendental *locus*" that can "determine how every impulse which springs from the innermost depths is co-ordinated with a form that it is ignorant of, but that has been assigned to it from eternity and that must envelop it in liberating symbols" (*TN,* 30). Thus the narrative renders the profundity of the moment of Hull's arrival in St. Barbara not as emotional or epistemological, but *navigational* experience: "Noon came. He was frightened. The brown strip was no longer merely a vague distant object, it had actually become land. A circle of coast emerged in the field glasses; there, along the cliffs, were the huts, looking like heaps of stone; masts, piercing the living air, were visible; and slowly, like a crossbar in front of a door, the pier seemed, through the glasses, to be pushed back from the narrow, deeply indented harbour" (*RF,* 11–12).

If the "archetypal map" in the opening chapter of *The Theory of the Novel* is conceived according to the wider compass of earlier, happier ages "when the starry sky is the map of all possible paths" (*TN,* 29), it also informs Seghers's more troubled "transcendental *locus*" where, in a more beleaguered historical time and place, "rain stood in the air" (*RF,* 10). For, as Lukács wrote in the first paragraph of his opening chapter:

> Everything in such ages is new and yet familiar, full of adventure and yet their own. The world is wide and yet it is like a home, for the fire that burns in the soul is of the same essential nature as the stars; the world and the self, the light and the fire, are sharply distinct, yet they never become permanent strangers to one another, for fire is the soul of all light and all fire clothes itself in light. Thus each action of the soul becomes meaningful and rounded in this duality: complete in meaning—in *sense*—and complete for the senses; rounded because the soul rests within itself even while it acts; rounded because its action separates itself from it and, having become itself, finds a centre of its own and draws a closed circumference round itself. 'Philosophy is really homesickness,' says Novalis: 'it is the urge to be at home everywhere.' (*TN,* 29)

This "urge to be at home everywhere" accompanies Seghers's protagonist Johann Hull even after he reaches land, albeit still with no direct view of the "stars." At a window in the harbor tavern he looks out and sees only how "dull and immovable, blue-grey and heavy with rain, heaven and earth glared at each other like the two plates of a huge hydraulic press"

(*RF,* 13). The subsequently introduced sweeping light of a beacon is another modern industrial requisite, yet it nonetheless evokes Lukács's description of the "meaningful and rounded" duality that is "the world and the self," and implies a similar, if more tentative, congruence between the world outside and "the fire that burns in the soul." Thus, as he sits at nightfall in the harbor tavern, Johann Hull longs for a lost security, for escape into "the warm cosy little nooks in the world" signaled by the beacon light of Margaret's Island as it "swept round its appointed circle of sea and sky like the forefinger of an outstretched hand; first there was one brief breathing spell between the flares of light, then two longer intervals. Somewhere, far, far away, a steamer sobbed like a child which has recognized its mother in the dark"[7] (*RF,* 14).

The soul's expanse reaches into an even more remote and vaguely remembered, almost mythic, time and place as a daydream momentarily crowds out the no less tenuous reality setting of the narrative:

> The landlord scrambled onto the bar and lit the ceiling light. The men did not move. The lamp light, which usually makes people look softer and melts them together in a curious way, did not even make them blink.
>
> Hull turned his head towards the window. But behind the window there was just nothingness. It was now completely dark. Only the rain drew stripes across the window pane. Hull suddenly remembered the window of a public-house in some harbour town far away. This window had been smeary; behind the pane there was a pile of melons: one of them had been cut open, the juice had hardened into beads of sugar; the mosquitoes had been dancing about on the cut slice. The alley was narrow, the houses pressed close together, but the fiery heat had been so potent that it seemed to eat away one's skull. . . . From time to time the door had opened, then he had heard thin small tones coming from some wooden instrument—the tune was so damnably black, no white man could have played it.
>
> Silence. The beacon light continued to draw its circles at regular intervals; it touched the dark wall, the faces in the shadow. The public-house and everything that was in it seemed to be afloat and far out in the darkness of the sea like other boats in distress. The fishermen stared into space.[8] (*RF,* 15–16)

Even as he sits and drinks amidst the fishermen, Johann Hull imagines he might still escape the revolt he is about to unleash. Typically, the sequence presents the movement of thoughts and emotions as if they were *navigational* problems and actions:

How simple everything was, after all! Even now he could still leave. No one had recognized him. So far not a single soul knew that he was Hull from Sebastian. . . .

He jumped up, threw down a coin and ran out, slamming the door behind him. He ran down the hill, sprang across the pier, and crawled into the cabin. There he hid himself waiting desperately for the ship's bell to announce their departure. At last they were moving. He went up on deck. There lay Saint Barbara and it was just as uncanny to watch the town grow smaller and smaller before his eyes as it had been to see it grow larger and larger the day before.

Hull came to himself again; he was startled. The glass on the table before him was empty, there was a circle from his breath upon it, otherwise there was nothing. Now he rested his hands on his knees as the others were doing. He looked round, began to distinguish the men and to impress some of their faces upon his memory. (*RF,* 16–17)

The opening scenes of *The Revolt of the Fishermen* thus *picture* the world in terms of a visually conceived *navigational* schema. In this sense they represent the attempt to draw, in the modern era, the "archetypal map" of "such an age" as *The Theory of the Novel* terms the "age of the epic" (*TN,* 30). Conceived "in a mood of permanent despair" after the outbreak of World War One, the subsequent chapters of *The Theory of the Novel* present a philosophical meditation on the European novel of "romanticism and resignation" since *Don Quixote* and the dualism of the unhappy ages it represents (*TN,* 12). At the conclusion of *The Theory of the Novel,* written in what he called an "age of absolute sinfulness," Lukács found "no other herald but our hopes," the only "signs of a world to come, still so weak that it can easily be crushed by the sterile power of the merely existent" (*TN,* 153). In so doing he could refer only sparingly, if with great feeling, to Dostoyevsky, who "did not write novels" but belonged unequivocally to a "new world" requiring "a new form of artistic creation: the form of the renewed epic" (*TN,* 152). In Dostoyevsky this "new world, remote from any struggle against what actually exists," was "drawn for the first time simply as a *seen reality.*"[9] Hence the "form he created" had to lie "outside the scope of this book" (*TN,* 152). When she conceived her own prose "form" a decade later, Seghers must have felt that the "renewed epic" had found, no matter how tentatively, at least the possibility of realization in a new time and place.[10]

In 1910, four years before he began writing *The Theory of the Novel* in German, Lukács published his influential Hungarian essay "Esztétikai kultúra" (Aesthetic Culture), which ends with a similarly fervent yet hesitatingly expressed apotheosis of Dostoyevsky: "And in fear and trembling,

I write down here—as the only possible final chords after what has been said—the name of the greatest one of all, who was in my mind while I wrote this, our most sublime epic poet, the sacred name of Dostoyevsky."[11] Like the famous essays in *Soul and Form*,[12] "Aesthetic Culture" also articulates what Michael Löwy has called the young Lukács's tragic conception of modern man's "nostalgia for an authentic life incapable of realization in the concrete life of society."[13] The seemingly endless landscapes and seascapes traversed by Seghers's melancholy protagonist Johann Hull as well as the living "signposts" he encounters on his way recapitulate Lukács's depiction of the soul's journey in his "Aesthetic Culture" of 1910. As Lukács wrote in that essay:

> The soul is the road, not the result, an endless road where fully formed lives serve as signposts. How is the soul formed? The soul lies dormant in that chaos we usually associate with the spiritual life of man, that we casually refer to as the soul. The dormant soul is real and always alive, but only for those with discerning vision. The soul has to be divined and brought to life, in the same way as Michelangelo divined his statues in the block of marble that entombed them. . . . The soul of man, not unlike Michelangelo's statue, can be discerned and brought to life only through interminable struggle and suffering. . . .
>
> This kind of life is a symbolic life in a profound and true sense, it is a genuinely individual life. It is the soul in the marble which turns into a statue. Although in the process the soul parts with its marble brothers, it finds its brothers in other statues. This then is the soul's road: to chip away all that is not truly its own; this is the forming of the soul, making it genuinely individualistic, though what has been formed transcends the purely individual. This is why this kind of life is exemplary. It is exemplary because the realization of one man's life signifies the same possibility for others.[14]

If Lukács began his essay "Aesthetic Culture" with the sardonic lines of the poet Béla Balázs—"The world is full of armies, / But that is not what will kill us"[15]—in the course of his rather lofty conclusion he turned to the medieval mystic Meister Eckhart: "Where a clod falls, there falls a piece of the earth; thus we see that the earth is the resting place of all earth. When a spark flies upward, it means that heaven is its true resting place. Now we have such a spark sent to us in Jesus Christ's soul. The soul shows that our resting place is in heaven and nowhere else."[16]

Like the opening chapter of *The Theory of the Novel*, "Aesthetic Culture" posits the bygone ideal of an "integrated" culture in which the soul can find its true and most appropriate form when art is not alienated from experience. In *The Theory of the Novel,* written in German under the influence of German philosophical tradition in Berlin and Heidelberg, this bygone ideal belongs to the Greeks. "Aesthetic Culture," by contrast, was written in Hungarian at a time when Lukács was actively involved in the avant-garde cultural life of Budapest, a city in which Jews made up more than 20 percent of the population and a significant number among the intelligentsia.[17] Accordingly, the bygone ideal in "Aesthetic Culture" belongs not to the Greeks, but to the first-century Jewish Christians and the mystical legacy of the Judeo-Christian tradition. Just as Lukács would argue on two fronts in *History and Class Consciousness,* that is, against both neo-Kantian philosophy and the scientific positivism of Marxism, in "Aesthetic Culture" he aimed his critique not only at the bankruptcy of bourgeois aesthetic culture, but also at the spiritual impoverishment of socialism as reflected in the largely political-economic discourse of the social democratic parties:

> It appears that socialism does not possess the soul-expanding, religious strength of early primitive Christianity. It took early Christianity's anti-artistic stand to give birth to the art of Giotto and Dante, of Meister Eckhart and Wolfram von Eschenbach. Christianity produced the Bible whose rich offerings inspired art and artists throughout the centuries. Being a true religion, whose power created the Bible, Christianity had no need for art; it neither desired nor tolerated it. Christianity aspired to the absolute mastery of man's soul for it possessed the power to reign supreme. Socialism lacks this power and consequently it cannot become the real adversary of bourgeois aestheticism, as it wants to be and knows it ought to be.[18]

The aesthetic conception reflected in this passage, as well as in other passages from Lukács's early Hungarian writings, is crucial to our understanding of why Anna Seghers's prose, even where it reveals an explicitly socialist content, is in its aesthetic form more deeply embedded in the topographies and language of early Judeo-Christian legend and myth. We can certainly assume that Seghers read those works by Lukács that were available in German in the 1920s, such as *Soul and Form, The Theory of the Novel,* and *History and Class Consciousness.* But through her husband László Radványi she was also apprised of the content of Lukács's earliest Hungarian essays on aesthetics, which had crucial influence on discussions within the Budapest Sunday Circle over the years. It can be taken for granted that she also knew about the tenor of these discussions, particularly the aesthetic conceptions developed by Lukács and others. Interestingly, whereas Lukács himself eventually rejected the writings of his youth, Anna Seghers's prose, even as late as the 1960s and 1970s, remained indebted to the aesthetics of the young Lukács, especially in regard to the "anti-artistic" primacy of storytelling, legend, and myth. That Seghers relied on some of the theories of the young Lukács to argue against his later insistence on realism is evident from their public exchange of letters during the expressionism debates of the 1930s.[19]

Seghers would also have been familiar with the works of the Hungarian avant-garde poet Endre Ady, whose symbolist poetry, dually inspired by his socialist-pacifist and ecstatic-chiliastic leanings, was widely celebrated among the Sundayers and other sectors of the Hungarian intelligentsia. László Radványi was particularly devoted to him. In 1916, not long after a personal meeting with Ady, Radványi published at the mere age of fifteen a small volume of poetry, *Fekete Könyv* (Black Book), written in the style of Ady and with an introduction by the well-known Hungarian writer Frigyes Karinthy.[20] While in Heidelberg in the early 1920s, Radványi rendered no less than 175 of Ady's poems in German translation.[21] Certainly the ship and water imagery that abounds in Anna Seghers's prose, not only in *The Revolt of the Fishermen,* is indebted to such poem cycles by Ady as *Onward, My Ship* in *Leading the Dead* (1918) and *The Last Ships* (1923). Compare, for example, the symbolism in the last verse and coda of Ady's poem "Onward, My Ship":

And when that which is to pass has passed,
Tomorrow, time, eternal life-ocean,
Then let the ship go on to sway and rock—
This fragile, miraculous, life-ship of blood.[22]

As a socialist Ady was an effective and highly regarded political writer and journalist. As a poet he was unabashedly mystical and chiliastic, his voice resounding with the words of the Old Testament prophets and invoking the future as the coming of the kingdom of God. Within the Budapest Sunday Circle, whose members idolized him, Ady had the reputation of being the only Hungarian writer who found an adequate means to express the revolutionary consciousness of his age. Ady's socialism, Lukács wrote in 1908 in his famous homage to Ady, was "religion (for the lesser a mere opiate), the voice of a preacher in the desert, a drowning man's call for help, a convulsive clutching at the only possibility that still exists, worshiping it (at times blaspheming), sensing it as unknown, mysterious yet near, and nevertheless as being the only thing that is truly real."[23]

Like the Old Testament prophets whose words often went unheeded, Endre Ady was fated to come both too early and too late. Confronted with a "mournfully grotesque public" that awaits help "only from the revolution," he was compelled to remain "the poet of the Hungarian revolutionaries without a revolution."[24] Thus, according to Lukács, Ady's struggle with the all too secular world in which he lived was that of the "soul" in search of "form." Whereas the medieval mystics relied on the "forms given by the church, official religion, and the Bible," the "contemporary mystic can find these forms nowhere," wrote Lukács, "and has to produce everything out of himself: God and the devil, earth and eternity, Savior and Antichrist, saints and the damned; he is the one forced to write the Bible, and everything that one would want to read."[25] Indeed, Lukács found in Ady's poetry the very kind of mythic trajectory that would later, albeit in less ecstatic terms, inform Anna Seghers's own work. "These are religious verses," Lukács wrote in praise of Ady, "a great mystical, religious feeling flooding any and all banks. There is such a powerfully religious potentiality here, faith has such an infinitely passionate desire, that everything in the world of this poetry turns into myth, every manifestation of life into God or devil, every verse written about them into a psalm. In Ady's verses all life unfolds as myth."[26]

More than half a century later Hans Mayer used similar words to describe Seghers's prose: "All the world in Anna Seghers is at once *mythic world.*"[27] This "mythic world" is all too evident in *The Revolt of the Fishermen*—the title more literally "Uprising of the Fishers of St. Barbara" (*Aufstand der Fischer von St. Barbara*). Not surprisingly, the novella has long defied attempts by scholars to situate the village of St. Barbara historically and geographically. When asked about its whereabouts in 1963, Seghers responded with the dismissive remark that her fishing village "'swims' somewhere between Brittany and Holland," that she "didn't give much thought to an actual place" when she wrote her narrative, and "after all, it is a 'tale.'"[28] Seghers's mention of Brittany and Holland was evidently in reference to the narrative's vaguely Atlantic setting, that is, seascapes, landscapes, and interiors inspired by Dutch painting from Rembrandt to Jozef Israëls.[29] As a "tale," however, the narrative is also embedded in a more ancient mythic topography. This aspect has also eluded scholars, who for the most part either equate Seghers's work with, or, inversely, measure it against, a brand of socialist history and literature that, in the words of Lukács quoted above, "does not possess the soul-expanding, religious strength of early primitive Christianity."[30] Indeed, the story of Johann Hull and the failed uprising of his fishermen is the kind of biblical legend or "tale" that, in Lukács's words, has "no need for art."[31] Thematically, too, this "tale" echoes in many respects the trials of the first-century messianic movements in Palestine, notably around the Nazarene preacher Jesus and his community of followers.

Like the legendary, often reluctant liberator who traveled among the fisherfolk living along the shores of Lake Galilee, Johann Hull is, as it were, a fisher of men. His initial gesture is to offer his first drink, "according to the custom of the country" (*RF,* 13), to the boatswain Kedennek sitting opposite him in the harbor tavern. After Hull's speech that same evening to the fishermen assembled in the tavern, the generally uncommunicative Kedennek seems suddenly transformed as he arrives at his fishing boat in the harbor. The scene, reminiscent of the Dutch landscape painters, is set in a night darkness pierced by shades of light—the glow of a small lantern, a shiny patch of oil in the water, a remote warehouse light, houselights twinkling in the distance (*RF,* 24). In the foreground, reminiscent of Rembrandt's drawings of the vaguely first-century figures gathered around Jesus, we find Kedennek and his orphaned nephew Andreas, one sitting upright, one reclining, as Andreas learns the news of "his"— Hull's—arrival in St. Barbara, as if this "he" were a modern-day prophet, apostle, or even messiah:

> Andreas blinked. Kedennek sat bolt upright and looked down indifferently at Andreas' face. Though Kedennek looked exactly as he always looked, Andreas knew that something in Kedennek had altered. Though he did not know why this was so, it seemed strange to him that something about Kedennek should have changed. He raised himself slightly, resting on one of his elbows.
>
> "Some of them said that he would be coming," Kedennek said, "while others have been saying that he would not come; now he has come." "Yes," Andreas answered, "he has come." Kedennek continued: "Now they will at last stop making plans, that is good. Now things will become serious; one can tell that by the fact that he has come."[32] (*RF,* 25–26)

Evocative of a messianic time frame in which past and future converge, Kedennek's laconic sense of expectation uncovers a past waiting to be redeemed, exemplified in the form of a story told to his nephew, that is, a parable or tale within a tale:

> "This revolt in Port Sebastian"—Kedennek half closed his eyes—"we had already started for Newfoundland. . . . Things used to be bad too, but now they are worse; now there is only one Company; it lives in Port Sebastian but one cannot find it. . . . When I was as old as my youngest boy there was a shipowner called Lukedek; he made the whole village dance according to his tune. But then there was a fellow in our village, Kerdhuys he was called, who got sick of it all. He went

to the house where Lukedek lived, went up the steps and into the room where he was sitting, and asked: 'Will you give me my share of fish or will you not?' Lukedek said: 'No.' Then Kerdhuys stuck his knife into him, just there"—Kedennek touched a certain place on Andreas' jacket with his finger. "For a while he hid among the cliffs— the villagers helped him—but finally he was caught and hanged. But this Kerdhuys knew, at least, where to stick his knife." Kedennek stopped suddenly and remained silent. His face showed that he had nothing more to add, that he was pushing speech away, just as a man who has eaten his fill pushes away his plate. (*RF,* 27–28)

Like the legend of the so-called forerunner John the Baptist, who preached the kingdom of God as a day of judgment for the wicked, the story of Kerdhuys is presented as if he, too, were in anticipation of greater things to come.[33] For his part, Kedennek appears to be modeled on the fisherman Simon, a follower of John the Baptist until he was called by Jesus, who then named him Peter. Indeed, Kedennek's plodding strength, pride, and determination during the later uprising are reminiscent of the "rock" on whose shoulders the Jewish-Christian community in Palestine was built. At the same time Kedennek seems, like Lazarus, to awaken to a new life when Hull comes to stay in the cramped quarters of his family cottage. Among other characters loosely modeled on the early followers of Jesus are the prostitute Marie, eventually raped and killed by soldiers in revenge for her participation in the uprising; Marie Kedennek, an embittered, overworked woman, reminiscent of Lazarus's sister Martha, whose contempt for Hull is brought on by years of numbing poverty and oppression; and her neighbor Katharina Nehr, who, like Lazarus's sister Mary, is persistently "curious," becoming ever stronger and more courageous in the course of the uprising.

Finally there is Kedennek's orphaned nephew Andreas, who, like the "beloved" disciple, finds in the stranger the longed-for elder brother and teacher. Their physicalized relationship echoes images of the disciple John sitting next to Jesus in renderings of the Last Supper by Rembrandt and other masters: "Andreas's shoulder was touching Hull. Andreas had gone to sleep standing up. He slipped down easily beside Hull. Hull put his arm round him and went to sleep too" (*RF,* 73). Or, in another example: "Later, when most of the men had gone—only a few, who could not make up their minds to go back on land, stayed and leaned across the tables— Hull put his arm round Andreas's shoulders. They sat crouched together as they had during the winter" (*RF,* 135). It is at this point that Hull, despite the warnings of the men at the table that he should flee—"this time the revolt had been lost"; "it was a miracle that he had not yet been arrested" (*RF,* 135)—discloses to Andreas and those close enough to hear him his greater vision. His final words appear as little understood as Jesus' farewell to his disciples while he talked about bread and wine: "Hull talked to the boy earnestly. He did not talk about putting out to sea or about Santa Barbara, he talked about foreign countries; they were sailing together into a distant harbour compared with which Sebastian was small and paltry. Hull talked quickly and violently, as one repeats a phrase again and again so as not to forget it. He was perfectly aware that Andreas was too tired to listen but he went on talking just the same" (*RF,* 135–36).

Like several of Jesus' disciples, both Andreas and the elder Kedennek eventually suffer violent deaths at the hands of soldiers and police, a fate that appears prefigured when Kedennek, while telling the Kerdhuys story, touches "a certain place on Andreas' jacket with his finger" (*RF,* 28). Kedennek's own death occurs during the strike when a crowd of fisherfolk tries to prevent a company ship from putting out to sea. His unpremeditated and politically quite senseless action contradicts in one moment an extended life of quietude and submission:

> Kedennek was in the centre of the crowd. He had looked fixedly at the soldier standing at the gang-plank, the one who was just aiming his gun. . . . Kedennek moved on farther than had been agreed; he did not move too slowly but walked in unusually small, light steps. He had a curious bald feeling in his back, he realized that the others had stayed behind. He knew that he was moving forward alone; he knew, too, that the soldier would shoot him. He fell over in the space between the fishermen and the soldiers, about eight metres from where the former stood. All his life Kedennek had thought only of sails and of motors, of catching fish and of wage agreements; but as he moved across these eight metres of space there had finally been time for him to think about all sorts of things. All those thoughts, for which the heads of human beings have really been created, had entered his head. He thought, too, about God: not as one thinks about something which does not exist. No, he thought about God as something which had deserted him. (*RF,* 123–24)

Whereas Kedennek takes on the burdens of the strike, young Andreas experiences an entire lifetime of freedom in the few short months of the St. Barbara uprising. The spirit of revolt seems to find its highest expression in this young boy, even though the final sabotage he undertakes is a futile action and comes far too late. Hiding at first in a cave at the edge of the sea (like Kerdhuys before him), the boy runs across the cliffs and dies from the shots of soldiers' rifles as if he were running toward eternity:

. . . now, as he ran, he remembered everything. Hull had been wrong: Andreas was not so very young: after all he had already known everything: his mother's death, Kedennek's death, the sea and comradeship, [Marie's] brown arms round his body; what else could life hold for him, what was there left for him to expect, to look forward to?

They were already calling "Stop" and again "Stop." Kedennek had faced the shots, Andreas faced cragged cliffs and moving air. Andreas heard "Stop" again. He ran even more quickly, he heard a shot, it sounded as though someone had clapped their hands: he must run on—he ran . . . Even after he had fallen, after he had turned over and over on the cliffs and had remained hanging in them so that his face was bruised beyond recognition, something within him went on running and running. And finally this something, which had run on and on, was dispersed into every direction in the air and was filled with indescribable joy and lightness. (*RF,* 169)

Seghers's narrative depicts life as a series of interrupted, incomplete, but interrelated actions relayed individually and as a loosely interconnected whole toward future redemption. The revolt, or, better, *Aufstand* (literally, a "standing up"), is thus composed of a wide-ranging compass of "souls" that are more or less "set free": the boatswain Kedennek, whose long-impoverished life is redeemed in one great moment of courage and understanding; the prostitute Marie, modeled on Dostoyevsky's Sonya, whose bright and unmarred spirit is symbolized by the yellow scarf to which she holds fast to the end; Katharina Nehr, whose stubborn persistence, echoing that of her early martyred namesake, reveals itself in the physiognomy of her "young, white, and curious face" as she stands "in the first row" with the fishermen in their last confrontation with the soldiers (*RF,* 163); and young Andreas, whose short life culminates in a mystical-chiliastic moment of "indescribable joy and lightness" reminiscent of Meister Eckhart's description of the soul's "sparks" flying "upward to heaven,"[34] or, in the words of Walter Benjamin, in a "time of the now" that is "shot through with chips of Messianic time."[35]

It is significant that Hull, who puts himself in the greatest danger, finds neither a courageous nor reckless death. Instead, he appears doomed to a life of repeated failure and suffering without any visible sign that this life, too, might one day be redeemed. In this respect he lives the life of the Son of Man—the passion—as it was experienced, and written down in the Gospel of Mark, *before* the prevalence of the Pauline myth of the resurrection. Seghers's fundamentally pre-Pauline interpretation also allows us to consider Hull as an embodiment of the Wandering Jew or Ahasver figure—in some modern renderings closely related to the passion of Christ—who takes on the sins and sufferings of the world without the explicitly Pauline promise of salvation.[36]

In sum, the passion of Johann Hull leads not to the cross, but to the prolonged trials of the desert. This aspect is stressed in the rendering of Hull's final arrest and transport to prison, a fate he might have escaped had he not, after the brief temptation of flight, returned to St. Barbara to remain with the already failed revolt. Like Jesus in Jerusalem, Hull is arrested in the company of his followers who had just "moved closer to him and listened intently," and "for a few moments everything was as it had always been" (*RF,* 157). Also reminiscent of Jesus' arrest, soldiers take Hull to a local "prefect" sent from the capital. Thereupon he is transported overland to Port Sebastian on a "sand road between the dunes" that "stretched before them endlessly" (*RF,* 169) and is thus denied his last wish—"just once more, to see a small strip of sea" (*RF,* 170). The enforced separation from the sea appears to seal the fate of this particular fisher of men, as he "expected this sight of the sea would be quite close, at his left-hand side. But the flat wavy backs of the dunes followed one another with such incessant swiftness and persistency that his wish was not fulfilled" (*RF,* 170).

As in her first published narrative, *The Dead on the Island Djal,* the mythic or legendary aspect of *The Revolt of the Fishermen* also has a concrete, albeit even more encoded, contemporary dimension. The name of the protagonist Johann Hull, one of many political fugitives found throughout Seghers's oeuvre, provides the first clue. His given name Johann, like the names of Marie, Andreas, Marie Kedennek, and Katharina Nehr, is in keeping with the author's habit of assigning to her characters the names of Jewish apostles and other early martyred Christians in their Germanic variants.[37] His surname Hull, on the other hand, has a decidedly foreign ring to the ear of the German speaker. That it sounds vaguely Nordic, or indeed English, has been noted by scholars who tend to place the narrative in an Atlantic setting, spurred on by Seghers's not entirely reliable remark that the village of St. Barbara " 'swims' somewhere between Brittany and Holland."[38] That the name of this reluctant and ultimately unsuccessful revolutionary rings far more authentically Hungarian has gone entirely unnoticed, at least in the critical literature, since the narrative was first written more than seventy years ago.

The Hungarian verb *hullik,* or its poetic form *hull,* pronounced as in English *full,* means to fall, to drop, to shed tears or leaves, an appropriate characterization for Seghers's protagonist, who is from the start a melancholy figure, and by the end doomed. The Hungarian noun *hulla,* moreover, signifies a dead body or corpse, a no less appropriate signification for the ascetic Hull's temporal condition, and for his almost certain fate at the end. A slight alteration from *hull* to *hal* yields the verb "to die" as well as the noun "fish," significations that fit easily into the mythic framework of Seghers' narrative, as do the more uplifting variations of the root *hull:* the noun *hullám,* meaning wave; the adjective *hullámos,* meaning surging or undulating—both, incidentally, recurring in Endre Ady's poetry—and the noun *hullócsillag,* meaning shooting star. Thus the man whose name Hull signifies a shedding or dying is enacting "the soul's road," which in his "Aesthetic Culture" of 1910 Georg Lukács described as the necessity "to chip away all that is not truly its own; this is the forming of the soul, making it genuinely individualistic, though what has been formed transcends the purely individual. This is why this kind of life is exemplary. It is exemplary because the realization of one man's life signifies the same possibility for others."[39]

The name of the mild-mannered yet tenacious boatswain Kedennek, which strikes both the German and English speaker as foreign and strange, has as its last three letters the frequently occurring *nek* of the Hungarian dative pronoun: *nekem* (to me), *neked* (to you, sing.), *neki* (to her/him), *nekünk* (to us), *nektek* (to you, pl.), *nekik* (to them). The letters are also added to the end of a noun suggesting a directional dative, as in *Nettynek* (to Netty), which is how Anna Seghers would often have heard herself referred to in Hungarian conversation ("mond Nettynek": say it to, or tell, Netty). Also found in *The Revolt of the Fishermen* is the variation *ek* in the name of the shipowner Lukedek, and the variation *ak* in the name of the tavern proprietor Desak. *Kedély* means mood, humor, or spirit; *jó kedélyü*—virtually impossible for the non-native to pronounce, let alone guess at its spelling when heard—means good-humored or jolly; and *jó kedélyünknek* can mean "to our good spirits" (as, for example, in a toast among downhearted émigrés). Thus the name Kedennek might also be the German speaker Anna Seghers's version of "to his good humor" or "to our good spirits," sentiments that would seem appropriate when applied to the mild-mannered but tenacious Simon/Peter-like figure of Kedennek. The first three letters of his name, *ked,* also occur in the frequently used word *kedves,* meaning "nice" or "kind," as well as "dear," as in polite address in a letter or conversation; and in *kedvesem,* meaning the more intimate "my dear" or "dearest" when applied to a spouse or a child.

Seghers had been married for three years to László Radványi and was about to give birth to their second child when she completed *The Revolt of the Fishermen.* That the Hungarian language had personal meaning for her is indicated by the fact that she called her husband Rodi, her phonetic variation of the first syllable in Radványi, and was known in a familial way to him and their children as Tschibi, a Germanic variant of the common Hungarian nickname Csibi.[40] Even though Anna Seghers evidently never tried to master the language, she was of course intimately familiar with the intonation and cadences of Hungarian through her husband, whose closest friends and associates were Hungarians. That the peculiar intonation of this non-Indo-European language that she heard almost daily must have fascinated the young German writer (and had no insignificant impact on her own prose) has, strangely, not been taken into consideration by Seghers scholars. Be that as it may, the peculiar sounds and rhythms of Hungarian, whether uttered in the native tongue or in accented form in German, must have rung continuously in her ear at the time she was composing her first narratives, among them *The Revolt of the Fishermen.*

It was the Hungarians she knew most intimately who seem to have inspired the contemporary aspect of her narrative—László Radványi and other members of the Budapest Sunday Circle who were forced into exile after the defeat of the Hungarian Council Republic in the late summer of 1919. The particular impact of the failed revolution on the younger members of the circle was summarized by the writer Ervin Sinkó, who was only twenty-one years old, three years older than László Radványi, in 1919: "All the illusions and hopes of a feverishly chiliastic revolutionary generation—my generation—searching for more open and humane ways of life fell at a fantastic speed from the acme of this generation's development into a darkness from where not a single member of this generation could find the way back to its first ecstatic beliefs."[41] Or, as Béla Balázs wrote in his exile diary about a conversation with Georg Lukács in Vienna: "Our inner débâcle is that we live in two presents. We cannot translate our intellectual experience into ethics and actions because it lacks form. According to Lukács, our ethical present belongs to an intellectual past. Our intellectual experience protects us like a leafy tree. But the ground we stand on is covered with fallen leaves."[42]

Bearing a name that itself suggests the falling or shedding of leaves, Seghers's melancholy protagonist Johann Hull seems to be modeled above all on the figure of Georg Lukács, the Sunday Circle's intellectual, political, spiritual, and in some respects prophetic leader. As already noted in the previous chapter, in December of 1918 Lukács underwent what has been described as his conversion from "Saulus to Paulus" when, in the interval between two Sunday meetings of the circle, he joined the Hungarian Communist Party.[43] Only a few weeks earlier he had written the essay "Bolshevism as a Moral Problem," which made a sharp distinction between the ethical position of philosophy and the sociopolitical reasoning inherent in the demands of class struggle, thus summarizing his and the other Sundayers' views up to that point:

Bolshevism relies on the metaphysical assumption that good can come from evil, that it is possible—as Razumikhin says in "Crime and Punishment"—to lie our way through to the truth. The writer of these lines is not able to share this belief, and therefore sees an insoluble moral dilemma at the root of the Bolshevik stand, while democracy—in his belief—only demands superhuman resignation and self-sacrifice from those who want to carry it through consciously and honestly. But this, even though perhaps it demands superhuman strength, is not an essentially insoluble question, as is the moral problem of Bolshevism.[44]

In "Tactics and Ethics," which he wrote only weeks later, Lukács reasserted his insistence on an ethical view but now extended it to the communist struggle: "Everyone who at the present time opts for communism is therefore obliged to bear the same *individual* responsibility for each and every human being who dies for him in the struggle, as if he himself had killed them all."[45] Toward the end of the essay Lukács placed this notion of responsibility within the tragic framework of sacrifice and guilt, thus asserting the position that would henceforth characterize him. It was a position that would continue to haunt and be debated by the Sundayers during the months of the Council Republic and their subsequent exile—and find repeated exemplification in Anna Seghers's prose:

It is not the task of ethics to invent prescriptions for correct action, nor to iron out or deny the insuperable, tragic conflicts of human destiny. On the contrary: ethical self-awareness makes it quite clear that there are situations—tragic situations—in which it is impossible to act without burdening oneself with guilt. But at the same time it teaches us that, even faced with the choice of two ways of incurring guilt, we should still find that there is a standard attached to correct and incorrect action. This standard we call sacrifice.[46]

In Ervin Sinkó's novel *Optimisták* (1953/55, Optimists), which is generally thought to be one of the most reliable accounts of the Hungarian Commune,[47] the figure of Comrade Vértes, modeled directly on Georg Lukács, articulates this problem from a perspective that reflects Lukács's views at the time:

But faith—is not class consciousness, not even scientific conviction, because all this is rational. Believing differs from knowing; to believe means in fact that one assumes a consciously irrational attitude towards one's own personal life. For let us be clear about it: there is no rational tragedy; all heroism is irrational just like Shakespeare's plays. . . . One arrives at action personally *despite* one's knowledge; for knowing also means that one is clear about not being able to know all the possible consequences. This is why Hamlet is unable to act, because he only knows and doesn't believe. . . . All knowledge makes one skeptical; on the basis of knowledge alone no one would dare to stand at the head of a people or a revolution; for someone to be able to take the lead in a revolution, despite everything about which he knows he cannot know anything in advance—for this one needs that in which I believe: the strength of faith.[48]

Similar to Seghers's depiction of Johann Hull, Sinkó's rendering of Lukács in the figure of Vértes presents a complex, meditative intellectual whose involvement in extraordinary circumstances causes him not to suspend knowledge and reason when faced with a tragic *situation,* but to rely on "the strength of faith." In Thomas Mann's *The Magic Mountain,* by comparison, the portrait of Lukács in the figure of Leo Naphta renders the *character* itself as being tragic, not without an ironically charged comical aspect, for Mann ultimately has Naphta shoot himself in the head in a fit of "hysterica passio" during his pistol duel with Settembrini. Based on his admiration for Lukács's essayistic writings and a brief meeting with him in Vienna in 1922, Mann personified Lukács with no little irony as a brilliant Jewish Jesuit, an ideological, ultimately self-destructive demagogue straight from the pages of Dostoyevsky's novels. In 1922, at the urging of Lukács's father József von Lukács, president of the Hungarian National Bank, Thomas Mann received the younger Lukács in his stately rooms in Vienna's Hotel Imperial. As later described by his widow Katja Mann, the celebrated author of *Buddenbrooks* and *Death in Venice* listened bemused as the philosopher-turned-revolutionary-turned-exile, dressed in the one worn suit of clothes he still owned, held forth for an hour on the philosophical foundations of orthodox Marxism and the inevitability of revolutionary messianism in the spirit of Rosa Luxemburg.[49] Or, as rendered from a somewhat different perspective in *The Magic Mountain:* "Like many gifted people of his race, Naphta was both natural aristocrat and natural revolutionary; a socialist, yet possessed by the dream of shining in the proudest, finest, most exclusive and conventional sphere of life."[50]

In *The Revolt of the Fishermen,* by contrast, the physiognomy of Johann Hull is never described. We have no idea of how he *appears* physically. In other words, informed by the writings of the early Lukács (and by the pre-Pauline tradition of messianism), the author wants us to see not the physical human image, but the active *forms* taken by the soul. The lonely, brooding figure of Hull created by Seghers only a few years after the 1924 publication of *The Magic Mountain,* perhaps even as a deliberate counterfigure to Naphta,[51] takes into account the fragmented, semi-underground existence of the veterans of the Hungarian Commune in the 1920s and, more importantly, the alienation of the Lukács faction from Béla Kun and his group as well as from the Communist Party leadership in Moscow, which had already distanced itself from the Hungarian Commune in 1919. Thus, whereas Thomas Mann's "warped" and "ugly" Leo Naphta argues from the high ground of theory with untiring conviction and little regard for the patience of his listeners, the often taciturn Hull, who spends most of his time waiting out the winter amidst the impoverished fisherfolk, is more reminiscent of the politically isolated, beleaguered, and repudiated Lukács of the twenties who struggled against what he called the "bureaucratic utopias" of the Béla Kun faction at the same time that he was also a fugitive from the Hungarian police.[52] The description of Hull's yearning for a solid place in the world where "every day would shower him with comrades, with food and drink, and with someone to love" (*RF,* 149) recalls the extent of Lukács's alienation at the time, reaching as far as Moscow, where even Lenin scolded him for suffering all too obviously from the "infantile disease" of left-radicalism.[53] Added to these early humiliations were the graver political setbacks of the mid-1920s: Lenin's death in 1924; the renewed attacks on intellectuals led by Zinoviev's scourging of "professors" like Lukács and Karl Korsch; the mounting Stalinist course in Moscow, its victory over the Left Opposition, and Trotsky's abduction and banishment on 17 January 1928.[54]

Like Lukács in his repeatedly frustrated attempts to chart an independent radical course for the Hungarian Communist Party in the mid-1920s, Hull is a political activist who already has at least one failed uprising behind him when we first encounter him on the crossing to St. Barbara. One is struck by the fact that he is absolutely alone, a man with apparently no comrades and only vague memories of an earlier, happier, now distant and irrevocable past. As the mere ghost of the man who had once been so "different" and "still happy" (*RF,* 32), he tries to "concentrate on his favourite thought: those April days in Port Sebastian" (*RF,* 31)—clearly an allusion to the high point of the Hungarian Commune in April 1919—when he "would have needed only to clap his hands and the revolt would have risen out of himself into the town, out of the town into the towns on the coast; and from there, perhaps, away over the frontier" (*RF,* 32).

Other characters are also reminiscent of certain individuals or types. The hardworking Kedennek, who thought all his life "of sails and of motors, of catching fish and of wage agreements" (*RF,* 124), embodies an older tradition of working-class politics, as represented by Lukács's political mentor, the Marxist syndicalist Ervin Szabó,[55] or the left social democrat Jenö Landler, with whom Lukács attempted in the 1920s to move the Hungarian Communist Party in a direction that opposed the Béla Kun group. After the military defeat in St. Barbara, young Andreas alone insists on continuing the strike and engages in sabotage, reminiscent of the twenty-five-year-old Ottó Korvín, who, in the words of Lukács, remained in Budapest "to build up an illegal, underground organization for the coming era of the white terror."[56] Korvín was soon captured and publicly executed by the Horthy regime and became the Council Republic's most famous martyr. The staunch figure of Katharina Nehr is Seghers's tribute to the many courageous, emancipated women (notably within the Sunday Circle Balázs's first wife Edit Hajós) who were politically active throughout the Hungarian Revolution of 1918–19 and afterward continued their activities within the internationalist movement.[57]

Whereas Béla Kun and other leaders arrived in Vienna already on 2 August 1919 on a special train given diplomatic immunity, Lukács remained in hiding, like Korvín and others, to maintain the Party's presence in Budapest. Hull's continuous attempts in *The Revolt of the Fishermen* to evade the police, who have long had a warrant out for his arrest, are in many ways reminiscent of Lukács's own dangerous underground existence in Budapest in August of 1919. The parallel is most obvious in the raids on the tavern, where Hull's whereabouts are kept from the police by, among others, Marie, reminiscent in this instance of the artist Olga Matern, in whose studio Lukács as well as Balázs and others were able to survive at least one police raid. When Lukács learned of Ottó Korvín's capture and impending execution, he allegedly contemplated suicide, then made plans to flee.[58] With the help of his father József von Lukács, who paid a large sum for the service, Lukács was smuggled to Vienna in an official military car driven by an English officer serving in Sir George Clerk's British delegation in Budapest. The political and psychological irony of the situation was unique to Lukács in its details but could also be applied to the relatively fortunate circumstances of most members of the Sunday Circle who were able to escape the terror, while others, notably Ottó Korvín, paid a significantly higher price. That Lukács was fully aware of this contradiction is indicated by the deliberate modesty and impoverishment of his existence in Vienna and, as often noted, his uncomplaining dedication to his journalistic writing and political work.[59] It is this historical-biographical context that ultimately lends credibility to the somewhat obscure references in *The Revolt of the Fishermen* to Hull's lingering sense of doubt and shame in having abandoned the initial revolt in Port Sebastian and, when pursued by the police, having gone underground.

Seghers's depiction of Hull's final arrest and transport to Port Sebastian under military escort appears to have been influenced by a more contemporary, and politically far more consequential, event: Stalin's arrest and banishment of Leon Trotsky in January of 1928, signaling the defeat of the Left Opposition. That Lukács, and presumably his closest Hungarian associates, knew of the sordid circumstances of Trotsky's abduction by the GPU on 17 January 1928 is indicated by a confidential letter Lukács wrote at the time:

> Very likely you are well informed in party affairs. If not, let me report that Trotsky's departure was set for Monday. A huge crowd, estimated at five to six thousand people, gathered at the station, many carrying his picture. Consequently, the deportation was postponed until the next evening. At 2 p.m. the next day, they broke into his house and ordered him to get into a car for immediate departure. He refused, saying that only force could move him. Then they forced Trotsky into a police car and drove him to the railway station. He was dragged into a carriage that waited at a shunting yard and was bound for Turkistan.[60]

Seghers's deliberate effort to stress the solitary, seemingly endless aspect of Hull's transport to Port Sebastian—his tedious overland journey in a "reeling" tilt-wagon by military escort and with no "sight of the sea"—seems as if to recapitulate, with appropriate changes in topography and imagery, the macabre tale of Trotsky's secret police abduction (out of the sight of waiting crowds of supporters) and his long, solitary rail journey to Alma-Ata—a "town of earthquakes and floods, at the foot of the Tyan-Shan range on the borders of China, 250 kilometres from the railway and 4,000 from Moscow," as he quoted his wife's description one year later in his autobiography.[61] Seghers's rendering of Hull's "abduction" is as follows:

> That same day Hull was taken to Port Sebastian by several soldiers. They did not go back by boat but went overland in a small tilt-wagon. The rest of that day, throughout the night and for a part of the next day, the sand road between the dunes stretched before them endlessly. The little wagon reeled about in the sand. Everything was tired: Hull, the wagon, the soldiers, and the horses.
>
> At first Hull thought about all kinds of things. Perhaps his mind dwelt on days which had passed, on other roads and other coasts, on the sea, on comrades, on the sun; perhaps he thought about Saint Barbara, to which he had come from so far away and to which he had held tight until now when he was rolling along the beach in this little cart. The soft, persistent jolts which one feels from driving in the

sand, gradually slackened the vitality of his body and his mind. Finally Hull felt only one wish: he wanted, just once more, to see a small strip of sea, he expected this sight of the sea would be quite close, at his lefthand side. But the flat wavy backs of the dunes followed one another with such incessant swiftness and persistency that his wish was not fulfilled. (*RF*, 169–70)

Yet despite all historical and biographical parallels, *The Revolt of the Fishermen* hardly lends itself to interpretation as a roman à clef. Modeled on older epic traditions of storytelling and legend, Seghers's prose style deliberately avoids individual psychological portraiture and physiognomic verisimilitude as found in, for instance, Thomas Mann's *The Magic Mountain.* Moreover, Seghers was much more inclined to create composite characters. Nor are there attempts to communicate events or ideologies in any discursive or explanatory way. Siegfried Kracauer's perceptive remarks about Seghers's 1932 novel *Die Gefährten* (The Wayfarers), wherein Georg Lukács, László Radványi, and other members of the Budapest Sunday Circle are more readily recognizable, can apply just as well to the author's earlier work:

The attempt to find in this book any words about the goals of the struggle or any discussions of content will prove futile. But it must be so. For Anna Seghers does not describe the movement from the outside, but from the reality that belongs to the revolutionaries. I can imagine a documentary account that might do justice to the events more objectively and completely; at the same time I don't know of a book that renders the revolutionary events so entirely out of the constitutional makeup of those by whom they were enacted. What has been given shape here is not so much revolutionary consciousness per se as the consciousness of the revolutionaries themselves.[62]

Seghers's tendency to write not "from the outside" but from the "inside," to render characters in a more or less composite rather than psychologically individualized way, indeed to create parabolic rather than historically specific events, indicates that she was inspired not only by the mythic content found in the first-century narratives of the Jewish-Christian chroniclers, but by the very forms and styles of their storytelling. Béla Balázs's lament in his diary soon after the Sundayers' flight to Vienna brings together notions of witnessing and documentation for posterity in a way that would have been obvious to each and every member of the Sunday Circle, where Jewish traditions of revolt and storytelling had been important topics over the years: "What a sin that our Sundays didn't have a real chronicler! Then at least there would be an authentic record of what those beasts drove out of Hungary, and why."[63] Only a few months later Balázs recorded in his diary Anna Lesznai's suggestion that "we must found the new religion. Because certainly by now all of us have become St. Johns. . . . Let us become witnesses and documents. What has lit up our souls should not be lost, for we are the air in which the new prophet can breathe."[64]

László Radványi was undoubtedly the primary impetus behind Seghers's decision to become a more or less "real chronicler" of events for which he and others around him seem to have been ready and willing "witnesses and documents."[65] Known in the first years of his exile as Ladislaus or Wlass Radványi, he also went simply by Johann, which he later incorporated into his Germanicized pseudonym Johann-Lorenz Schmidt. Thus Seghers was introduced to the essayistic philosophical writings of Georg Lukács and other members of the Sunday Circle through the filter of László Radványi's own chiliastic, or at the very least transformative, experience—which in turn lent the discursive momentum within her narrative work the mythic topographies and altogether human "face" for which it is well known. In other words, philosophy as well as politics were experienced as part of a larger passion, as belonging to an extraordinary moment in history, as being legendary, grounded in the aspect of concrete, lived experience, and mediated in the oral history form of stories, chronicles, and tales.

The chiliastic *fishers* in *The Revolt of the Fisherman*—Hull, Kedennek, Marie, Andreas, Marie Kedennek, Katharina Nehr—are indeed, as Lukács wrote in 1910 in his essay "Aesthetic Culture," individuals who "create no culture, but live a life as if they lived in culture. They create no culture, but lead a life that would merit it." As Lukács observed in the same essay: "It is irrelevant whether the example is followed by others, or who they are and how many there are. For man can achieve salvation only for himself, and nothing can intensify the grace of the one who is saved. Even if one's triumphant struggle to attain salvation clears the road for others in the jungle of life, man must journey alone, and hope for deliverance only at the end of his road."[66]

As if to convey this very thought to her readers almost twenty years later, Seghers's novella opens with the acknowledgment that in a pragmatic sense, the outcome of the uprising whose story is about to be related was more or less futile: "The only result of their revolt was that the fishermen of Saint Barbara put out to sea later than usual: the agreement with their employers remained what it had been for the last four years. The revolt was really finished before Hull was turned over to the police in Port Sebastian and before Andreas was killed on his flight in the cliffs. The prefect of police departed after reporting to the capital that peace had once more been restored in the harbour" (*RF,* 9). But the same opening paragraph ends with the kind of "triumphant struggle" referred to by Lukács in his aforementioned essay: "And Saint Barbara looked just as it did every summer. But long after the militia had left, long after the fishermen were back at sea, the insurrection hung, brooding, over the empty white marketplace which had a deserted, almost bald look in the summer time; here the revolt remained, thinking quietly of its own, of the men it had borne, reared, nursed and protected in preparation for that which was best for them" (*RF,* 9).

In a Hungarian essay of 1907 devoted to the painter Paul Gauguin, Lukács contrasted the desperate search of the modern artist's "soul" for adequate "form" to the comparatively ideal situation of the medieval artist: "For the medieval painter, the Madonna was not a conceptual problem for she was already conceptualized and she therefore presented only an artistic problem. But any artist who wanted to paint the Madonna today would have to conceptualize—for himself—his own relationship to the Bible; and this relationship would constitute the substance of his artistic process."[67]

For the narrative at hand, we can easily substitute Seghers's *fishers* for the medieval painter's "Madonna." Here indeed there seems to have been no especial "conceptual problem," since the philosophical landscape of Seghers's narrative—clearly articulated in the figure of Hull—relies almost entirely on the young Lukács's conception of modern man's continuing nostalgia for an authentic life. Similarly, the plot of this particular chronicle is not at all "invented" in the modern sense of fiction. It is, rather, more a retelling of the events of a great passion, the story of a momentous revolt or uprising that was experienced by Seghers's own contemporaries and passed on to her in oral form. Moreover, this passion, this (hi)story, was itself experienced by those who enacted it, and as such narrated by them, as having had an even greater mythic precedent in the Gospel narratives of the first century. Thus Anna Seghers would happily *not* find herself in the situation of having to "conceptualize" for herself her "own relationship to the Bible," or be "forced to write the Bible" herself. Instead, the great communal revolt or uprising of 1919, which the poet Endre Ady, who died in 1918, had only been able to predict with the ecstatic voice of the prophets and psalmists, could now be looked back upon with the more sober, nostalgic, and ultimately elegiacal voice of the storyteller and chronicler who relies on the mythic timelessness and utopian potential of the epic form. Like the New Testament chroniclers, and as noted by Siegfried Kracauer in 1932, Seghers did not narrate "the movement from the outside, but from the reality that belongs to the revolutionaries."[68] In this sense the position from which she wrote was indeed closer to that of Lukács's "medieval painter" for whom "the Madonna was not a conceptual problem for she was already conceptualized and she therefore presented only an artistic problem."[69]

How, then, did Seghers solve the "artistic problem" in an era of mass culture that increasingly demanded new proletarian-revolutionary "forms," or at least those of the "New Objectivity"? Like Lukács, who in 1926 still claimed that "the great revolutionary transformation we experience has less impact on the creative imagination, the form and content of poetry, than is generally assumed,"[70] Seghers held fast to the "value of imaginative literature," which Lukács continued to defend in the 1920s against the more "superficial" currents in both bourgeois and socialist art. As he wrote in *Die Rote Fahne* in 1926: "A vital content can be expressed in different forms. . . . But from a particular situation in life may be drawn those deepest human emotions and thoughts which re-create the situation in terms of pleasure and sorrow, despair and ecstasy even for people who lack any understanding of the situation itself. For people change more slowly in their basic emotions than in their social life-forms."[71]

And so it is on this note, where a "vital content" can be drawn "even for people who lack any understanding of the situation itself," that *The Revolt of the Fishermen* ends, not with Hull's last, lonely journey of banishment into the "desert," but with the expansive image of the Atlantic fishing ship *Marie Farère* as it moves, despite the fishermen's previous attempts to change its course, toward the open sea:

> The *Marie Farère* had hardly left the harbour, when the wish, which she had secretly suppressed for weeks, became apparent: she moved forward with incredible swiftness. Now the children could still recognize the Bredel Shipping Company's numbers painted on the sails of the ship, then the sails looked like shining red leaves. The ship moved more and more swiftly towards that visible line which separates what is near from what is far away. The ship had already forgotten the harbour; and the grief which she had felt at leaving the land had passed away. (*RF,* 171–72)

To underscore nonetheless the poignant reality of the moment, since, in Lukács's words, "people change more slowly in their basic emotions than in their social life-forms," Seghers added a final coda: "The women on the pier began to realize that they were wet to the skin" (*RF,* 172). Or, as Lukács, according to Béla Balázs, already observed in 1921: "The protagonist . . . will sink back into the chorus just as he emerged from it."[72]

The Revolt of the Fishermen "is after all a 'tale.'"[73] Its consolation comes not by way of the content, but by the imaginative gesture of wholeness created by an author for whom the depiction of the world was not "a conceptual problem," but ultimately "only an artistic problem." And so *The Revolt of the Fishermen* does in fact resurrect the memory of those "happy ages" described in the first chapter of Lukács's *The Theory of the Novel,* "when the starry sky is the map of all possible paths," when "everything in such ages is new and yet familiar, full of adventure and yet their own," when "the world is wide and yet it is like a home, for the fire that burns in the soul is of the same essential nature as the stars," when "the world and the self, the light and the fire, are sharply distinct, yet they never become permanent strangers to one another" (*TN,* 29).

"For what is the task of true philosophy if not to draw that archetypal map?" Lukács asked at the beginning of *The Theory of the Novel* (*TN,* 29). As an epic writer and chronicler, Anna Seghers responded to Lukács by charting the archetypal topography of "happy ages" that "have no philosophy" in terms of the "aesthetic problem." In so doing she may have struck him as being not altogether different from his beloved Greeks (and in earlier essays, the Jewish Christians and medieval mystics), who "knew only answers but no questions, only solutions (even if enigmatic ones) but no riddles, only forms but no chaos" (*TN,* 31). In this spirit she, too, as Lukács described the Greeks, wanted to draw "the creative circle of forms this side of paradox." And, to borrow from Lukács one last time, "everything which, in our time of paradox, is bound to lead to triviality" led her to seek "perfection" in the epic "form" (*TN,* 31).

CHAPTER 6

Legends from the Carpathians,
Tales of the Purges

The legend is the myth of the calling. In it the original personality of
myth is divided. In pure myth there is no division of essential being. It
knows multiplicity but not duality.

—Martin Buber, 1907[1]

When the world is not visible, audible, in a word, sensible enough to
us, the artist overstates the faculty of sensation and throws it into
relief.

—Georg Lukács, 1925[2]

One has to immerse oneself completely in Anna Seghers's oeuvre, its
theses and its anti-theses. The author does not concede to the reader
the tools needed to interpret meaning. This is perhaps not only because
Anna Seghers was averse to literary colloquy. It may be that the forces
she depicted could only be named in this way.

—Hans Mayer, 1983[3]

During her exile from Germany in the 1930s and 1940s, Anna Seghers
wrote the novels for which she is best known: *Der Kopflohn* (1934, The
Bounty), *Der Weg durch den Februar* (1935, The Way of February), *Die
Rettung* (1937, The Rescue), *The Seventh Cross* (1942), *Transit* (1944), and
The Dead Stay Young (1949). These for the most part antifascist resistance
novels constitute a body of work fundamentally, if not programmatically,
political and ethical in nature, a body of work that, in the words of the
writer Walter Jens, "makes plain that Goethe's Germany was not preserved in the *Reichskanzlei,* but in the barracks of Buchenwald."[4] To the
extent that they are directly concerned with German history, these works
are also known as Seghers's *Deutschlandromane* and in this respect include
the novels *Die Entscheidung* (1959, The Decision) and *Das Vertrauen*
(1968, Trust), which she later wrote in the GDR. Notwithstanding formal

122

and stylistic differences, these works exhibit novelistic epic structures that respond at least in part to the political-ideological framework of the historical struggle against fascism. Thus, with significant exceptions, as in the short novels of the early 1930s as well as *Die Rettung* (The Rescue) and *Transit,* these works are informed by a more or less idealistic conception that, according to Lukács's *The Theory of the Novel,* indicates the divide between the protagonist of the European novel and a largely indifferent, even hostile world. Or, phrased in the language of the realism debates of the 1930s, these works increasingly reveal the historical scope and, as it were, objective totality of the nineteenth-century novel in the tradition of Stendhal, Balzac, and Tolstoy.

This was of course the very concept of the European novel that the young Anna Seghers, inspired by Lukács and the discussions within the Budapest Sunday Circle, had bypassed in her narratives of the 1920s. Her gradual turn to the more traditional form of the modern novel was influenced by the political exigency of historical events and her effort to support the popular front strategies advocating a united political and artistic stand in the struggle against fascism. Lukács, notably, stood at the forefront of this trend, rejecting his earlier avant-gardism and insisting henceforth on realism in the arts. In her public exchange of letters with Lukács during the expressionism debates of the 1930s Seghers took a more or less intermediary position. Whereas she supported Lukács's advocacy of objective criteria in the process of artistic creation, or *Gestaltung,* she argued in defense of avant-garde art along similar lines as represented at that time by Ernst Bloch, Walter Benjamin, and Bertolt Brecht.[5] The use of montage structure, subjective narration, and other modernist techniques within a more or less overarching novelistic form and through-composed plot structure revolving around a protagonist is evident in *The Seventh Cross,* on which she was at work at the time. *The Dead Stay Young,* which she wrote at the end of the war under increasing pressure resulting from struggles within the Communist Party in Mexico, relinquishes a good portion of modernist abstraction in favor of realism.

But Seghers's antifascist novels represent only one aspect of her productivity during these years. The other, less accessible but in some respects even more significant aspect of her creative work is better found in the underlying topography of her shorter and to a large extent "mythic" narratives—stories, chronicles, tales, and novellas that she wrote at critical times during her years in exile and continued to write after her return to Germany in 1947. Indeed, throughout her life Seghers saw herself primarily as an *Erzählerin,* that is to say, a writer of epic prose who was by inclination much more of a storyteller than a novelist.[6] Nothing was more foreign to her than the notion of the isolated reader who, in Walter

Benjamin's words, turns to the novel "in the hope of warming his shivering life with a death he reads about."[7] For Seghers, writing as storytelling was not merely about survival but was itself a form of survival, as in the legendary tradition of Scheherazade herself. Indeed, the fate of many a writer in the 1930s and in the years that followed proved once again that storytelling could still proceed at the risk of one's neck.[8] It is hardly coincidental that at the very time Seghers focused on her "mythic" tales in the mid-1930s Walter Benjamin also perceived the need for the "good counsel" of the folk or fairy tale, as he wrote in 1936 in his essay "The Storyteller": "The first true storyteller is, and will continue to be, the teller of fairy tales. Whenever good counsel was at a premium, the fairy tale had it, and where the need was greatest, its aid was nearest. This need was the need created by the myth. The fairy tale tells us of the earliest arrangements that mankind made to shake off the nightmare which the myth had placed upon its chest."[9]

The urgency to pass on the "good counsel" of the folk or fairy tale came at four crucial points in Seghers's politically eventful life: at the time of the Moscow trials and purges of the late 1930s while she was in France; upon her return to Germany in the 1940s at the onset of the cold war; in the years after the defeat of the Hungarian Revolution of 1956; and in the late 1960s and the 1970s, following the invasion of Czechoslovakia and the end of the Prague Spring. That she wanted to include in a larger cyclical concept of storytelling her tales and novellas about times that are at once ordinary and extraordinary, at once dangerous and commonplace, is revealed by her letters in exile, which often refer to the example of the *Thousand and One Nights* and Boccaccio's *Decameron.* Seghers evidently considered the cyclical concept of storytelling not only as a complement, but as a possible alternative, to the kind of focused and to some extent prescriptive thematic inherent in the antifascist novels she understandably felt compelled to write. As she wrote in a letter at the time she was working on *The Seventh Cross:*

> I'd like to put together a book that resembles the great and genuine old novella collections, that is, a book of about forty novellas from all sectors of life, political narratives, love stories, detective stories, historical themes, tales, legends, stories about trees, plants, etc. In other words, a book meant for all kinds of people and all kinds of conditions. Alternating austere and saucy stories, tragic and funny stories. I feel very attached to the book, first of all because I now feel capable of doing a really decent job with this kind of book, and secondly because I would bring to it so to speak all aspects of my writing and not be fixated on one specific topic.[10]

The outbreak of the war, followed by her perilous escape from France to Mexico in 1941, prevented further publication of her work in Europe. But as the war was reaching its end and she was at work on her next *Deutschlandroman,* namely, *The Dead Stay Young,* she once again proposed an alternative plan to her German publisher in New York, Wieland Herzfelde:

> Besides the novel I'm working on now . . . I'd like to put together a major book, something like the *Decameron* or the *Thousand and One Nights,* not just an arbitrary collection of novellas pieced together as an experiment. It would need an overarching title, I'd like to have, say, five strictly political novellas, five tales, five histories, five love stories, five detective stories, five landscapes, etc. etc. They don't have to be exactly five, but I'd like to render in stories a segment of all conceivable sectors of life. While even a first-class novel can only relate to one area of interest, in a novella collection like this I'd like to offer, aside from the variety, an artistic answer to the complaints of people for whom one story isn't artistic, another not political enough, this one too erotic, that one ascetic. I hope you'll get the gist of this letter that I've knocked off in great haste.[11]

Seghers continued to nurture this plan after her return to Europe in 1947. As reported by Brecht after their meeting in Paris in November of that year, he and Seghers talked about the threatening atmosphere of political intrigues in postwar Berlin, about her wish to have her work published in all four occupation zones, and about her plan "to write the 100 novellas" she had promised to write "12 years ago."[12] Six months later she wrote to Georg Lukács of her desire to visit him in Budapest in order to talk over the current political situation and the devastating effect the escalation of the cold war was having on her own plans and the publication of her work. Once again she drew a distinct line between her novels and her continuing work on novellas and tales:

> I would like to talk with you about my work. I had already finished a long novel [*The Dead Stay Young*] before I returned [from exile in Mexico]. I revised it over here. It's already translated into English and my publisher there will probably bring it out this year. If the situation isn't such [the escalating cold war climate in the U.S.] that they'll be prevented from doing so, which they don't believe. . . . The novel will also appear in the USSR, where I've just turned it in, but first they'll publish *The Seventh Cross.* All this publishing business is amusing. Aside from this I want to put together a fat volume of novellas, many

novellas, all possible topics, situations, and historical subject matter, and a very short frame as in the *Thousand and One Nights* or the *Decameron,* but in my case maybe as a loosely composed theoretical debate concerning the novellas and whether the listeners like or dislike them, depending on whether they are—applied—art or—pure—art or are seen as such. For these and other plans, dear Lukács, I very much need your advice.[13]

This letter of 28 June 1948 was written at the time of the Berlin blockade, that is, at a crucial moment in the cold war when Seghers's chances to continue publishing and thus living in the West were rapidly diminishing, and when purges against writers and intellectuals were accelerating in the East.[14] Another passage in the same letter to Lukács refers to her isolation and despair at this time:

Sometimes I have the feeling that I'm going to freeze up. I feel as though I've come into the ice age, that's how cold everything appears to me. Not because I'm no longer in the tropics, but because so many things around me are altogether oppressive and so incredibly frosty, no matter if it's work or friends, or political or personal things. In short, I have a terrible yearning for your warm stove.[15]

Seghers and Lukács were both practiced in the communicative art of allusion and innuendo. Thus Seghers did not need to spell out to Lukács that her plans for a theoretical debate about "applied" and "pure" art modeled on the dialogues in Boccaccio's *Decameron* had more fundamentally to do with their shared experience of the "plagues" of modern times. Nor did she have to make plain to him that storytelling in the tradition of the *Thousand and One Nights* could proceed under the knife, as exemplified in the Arabian tales. Seghers's letter to Lukács also fails to mention a bit of information that would have been obvious to both of them, namely, that the original idea for a book written in a time of crisis and modeled on Boccaccio's *Decameron* had in fact come, forty years earlier, from Lukács himself. That Seghers wrote to Lukács as late as 1948 about her continued interest in what she first described in 1936 as "an old *Lieblingsplan*"[16] shows that even after the war the ideas of the young Lukács continued to influence her literary development in a significant way.

Seghers must already have learned in the 1920s from the members of the Sunday Circle what Lukács revealed to the public many years later in his 1963 preface to a new edition of *The Theory of the Novel.* In this preface Lukács recalled that he had conceived his treatise in 1914 in a "mood of permanent despair over the state of the world" as the prospect of Germany's victory appeared "nightmarish."[17] No doubt modeled on the conversations within the Sunday Circle, he first wanted to write the text in dialogue form: "a group of young people withdraw from the war psychosis of their environment, just as the story-tellers of the *Decameron* had withdrawn from the plague; they try to understand themselves and one another by means of conversations which gradually lead to the problems discussed in the book—the outlook on a Dostoevskian world. On closer consideration I dropped this plan and wrote the book as it stands today."[18]

Evidently encouraged by members of the Sunday Circle, Seghers saw herself as a storyteller who in later "nightmarish" times would carry out an "old *Lieblingsplan*" that the Hungarian philosopher and essayist had conceived but put aside in the years 1914 and 1915.[19] Aside from Lukács's original plan for the larger conception, his discussion of shorter prose forms in the actual text of *The Theory of the Novel* appears also to have influenced Seghers in a significant way. Indeed, Lukács's special praise for the novella form in the tradition of Boccaccio allows us to better understand why Seghers herself often relied on this form, notably in her Caribbean novellas (1948–60), which thematize, among other things, the tragic fate of Jewish participation in the history of modern revolution, and by implication, Lukács's and Imre Nagy's involvement in the Hungarian Revolution of 1956.[20] As Lukács wrote in *The Theory of the Novel:* "The novella, the narrative form which pin-points the strangeness and ambiguity of life, . . . is the most purely artistic form. . . . It sees absurdity in all its undisguised and unadorned nakedness, and the exorcising power of this view, without fear or hope, gives it the consecration of form; meaninglessness *as meaninglessness* becomes form; it becomes eternal because it is affirmed, transcended and redeemed by form."[21]

The less "pure" and decidedly variegated "minor epic forms" that Seghers seems to have preferred in the early 1930s in such narratives of diverse thematic and length as *Bauern von Hruschowo* (Woodcutters of Hrushovo), *Der sogenannte Rendel* (Alias Rendel), *Marie geht in die Versammlung* (Marie Goes to a Meeting), *Der Führerschein* (The Driver's Permit), and so forth are also, if only vaguely, defined in *The Theory of the Novel.* Here the *Erzähler,* that is, the storyteller of the "minor epic forms," is described as "the chronicler who observes the strange workings of coincidence as it plays with the destinies of men, meaningless and destructive to them, revealing and instructive to us; or he may see a small corner of the world as an ordered flower-garden in the midst of the boundless chaotic waste-lands of life, and, moved by his vision, elevate it to the status of the sole reality; or he may be moved and impressed by the strange, profound experiences of an individual and pour them into the mould of an objectivised destiny."[22] When in the course of the 1930s the very truth of such "strange workings" and "chaotic waste-lands" was put to the test, Seghers began to work with forms of tale and legend from older folk traditions, as in *Die schönsten Sagen vom Räuber Woynok* (1938, The Most Splendid Tales of Woynok the Brigand), *Sagen von Artemis* (1938, Tales of Artemis), and *Die drei Bäume* (1940/46, The Three Trees).

To be sure, even Seghers's reliance on these older forms of storytelling can be traced to the writings of the young Lukács and ongoing discussions within the Budapest Sunday Circle.[23] Lukács's enthusiasm for the Hassidic legends rendered anew by Martin Buber is well known. His discussion of Buber's *The Legend of the Baalshem* and *The Tales of Rabbi Nachmann* in a 1911 review entitled "Zsidó miszticizmus" (Jewish Mysticism) compares the Baalshem's loose symbolic reinterpretation of the Old Testament to Meister Eckhart's mystical reading of the New Testament.[24] The writer Anna Lesznai's diary of her conversations with Lukács notes as early as 1912 a discussion about the *Märchen,* or folk/fairy tale, during a visit in Budapest by Ernst Bloch. Bloch's concept of the tale is described as an *"Urmythos* having religious value," Lesznai's own as "religious," and Lukács's as "a momentary return to paradise, but without the permanence of redemption," that is, as more differentiated: "Gyuri [Georg Lukács] says the tale redeems (offers the appearance of redemption) in that it brings everything to one level and refashions it as nature. The objects redeemed thus become equal before God. The art of the redeemed objects is the ornamental tale. It is delight in God (a unity without boundaries)."[25] Or, as Béla Balázs, wondering in 1921 about his political correctness and whether he should write a "utopian novel" or another "tale," wrote with apparent relief in his diary: "Gyuri said it's the very tone of the *Märchen* that 'saves him.'"[26]

That this redemptive aspect was not only a private matter to Lukács, but consistent with his larger social and political conceptions, is indicated by the cultural policies he promoted during the Hungarian Council Republic of 1919. As People's Commissar of Education, Lukács decreed that storytelling be officially introduced as a daily part of the curriculum at the preschool, elementary, and early secondary levels. To this end he even persuaded Anna Lesznai, hardly a supporter of the Communist Party, to head a specially established Commission for Storytelling within the republic's Division of Literature and Theatre. He had already appointed Béla Balázs, the Sunday Circle's outstanding poet, playwright, and fabulist, as director of the Division of Literature and Theatre. Seghers's later husband László Radványi, from whom she would first have learned about these events, worked as Balázs's secretary in the division.[27] According to an official newspaper report on 15 April 1919, the implementation of storytelling as an integral part of the educational system was meant to "further the aim of making school instruction a more pleasant experience and improving and refining the raising and education of schoolchildren under the age of fourteen, who are known to be receptive to the vivid presentation of fables and tales."[28]

Lesznai and Balázs were among Lukács's oldest friends and the two artists within the Sunday Circle on whose work he relied as he developed his aesthetic theories in the course of his early writings. Both were poets, though Lesznai was also a talented artist whose works were frequently exhibited, and Balázs also wrote short plays in an impressionist vein comparable to some early works by Schnitzler and Hofmannsthal. Both shied away from the novel form, and their short prose consists of fables, legends, and fairy tales. Like Béla Bartók and Zoltán Kodály, who occasionally participated in the meetings of the Sunday Circle, Lesznai and Balázs belonged to the Hungarian avant-garde movement devoted to the revival of peasant music and folk arts. Balázs, who accompanied Bartók and Kodály on their treks through the countryside in pursuit of Hungarian folk language and song, is well known for his collaboration with Bartók as the librettist for *Bluebeard's Castle* and *The Wooden Prince*. Lesznai, a Jewish convert to Catholicism who embraced elements of anthropomorphism and theosophy, wove the rhythms of Hungarian peasant music into her poetry and the patterns of Hungarian folk art into her artwork and her fables and tales.

The legacies of folk art in the works of Lesznai and Balázs stand in stark contrast to the rapidly accelerating modernity of bourgeois life in which the Sundayers found themselves in the first decades of the century. Whereas Lukács was thoroughly urbane, a product of patrician Budapest Jewry living in the elegant district of the Andrássy út, Balázs spent his formative years in an old Slovakian fortress town, where his parents Simon and Eugenie Levy Bauer were schoolteachers, and in the southern Hungarian city of Szeged on the Tisza River, an old center of Jewish life and tradition. Szeged's thriving community of rabbinical scholars and traders produced a large part of what by the turn of the century had become the wealthy assimilated class of Budapest Jews, including, among other progenitors of the Sunday Circle, Lukács's father József von Lukács, born József Löwinger, the son of a Szeged quiltmaker.[29] For her part, Lesznai was the daughter of a wealthy Jewish landowner whose close ties to the Hungarian aristocracy and political support of the interests of the Austro-Hungarian empire were rewarded with a barony. The vivid nature imagery in Lesznai's work is informed by fond memories of a childhood on the family estate in the largely Slovak-speaking territory of pre-1919 Hungary. In this multilingual, multiethnic, and by her own description magical world, Hungarians, Slovaks, Moravians, and Jews; genteel and peasant classes; poets, storytellers, and craftspeople; man, animal, mineral, and plant life existed side by side in what to Lesznai remained throughout her life the image of a balanced, unified world.[30]

The mythic topography in several of Anna Seghers's narratives of the 1930s and 1940s—from *Woodcutters of Hrushovo* (1930) to *The Ship of the Argonauts* (1949)—draws on the wide geographic arc created by the Carpathian Mountains as they stretch across the northern borders of pre-1919 Hungary, then along its eastern frontier where the Tisza River has its source and meanders before flowing southward to Szeged and later merging with the Danube on its way to the Black Sea. This wide-ranging topography—from jagged cliffs, deep ravines, and snowcapped mountains to lush woodlands bordering on grazing meadows and farmland—recalls in Jewish lore, via the tales of Martin Buber, which Anna Seghers knew well, the Ashkenazic travels of the Baalshem between Podolia and Volhynia along the eastern range of the Carpathian Mountains. It also recalls pogroms across the centuries that penetrated into the most remote mountain villages. Superimposed on this Ashkenazic topography and history are the shifting borders of modern nation-states, which after World War One formed a multicultural, multinational corner of the Carpathian Mountains that included sections of Hungary, Czechoslovakia, Romania, Carpatho-Russia, and the Ukraine, and within each of them, a diverse multitude of linguistic and ethnic populations.

Written at the time of Stalin's purges of kulaks and peasants during the collectivization program in the countryside, Seghers's *Woodcutters of Hrushovo* is set on the western slope of the Carpathians in eastern Moravia, belonging to Hungary until 1919, near the city of Uzhgorod across the Ukrainian border. The narrative is introduced in the epic-chronicle style of the legend or folktale and enumerates struggles that over the centuries preceded the allotment of land to peasants during the sweeping, if short-lived, land reform carried out by the Hungarian Council Republic in the spring and summer of 1919:

> In olden times the worth of a man in the Carpathians was measured by the heaves of an axe he needed to fell a tree so thick he could barely stretch his arms around it. How great was the passion in those who first left behind the orderly, yes, hallowed cities on the plain to press toward the woodland and deep into the forests. This passion that carries people beyond themselves to undertake the most fantastic and miraculous actions is—hunger. Once people wind up somewhere, that's what they cling to. The great roots of the trees plaited their way to their huts and into their living quarters.

> The woodcutters took their wood and wooden gadgets into the

cities. The wolves withdrew, less because of bullets than from the woodcutting and grating of saws and all the sounds of a human community. Only here and there did they rip apart a sheep and enter a yard in the winter. The people learned better to stick together and got the edge on them.

When the Rakoczi uprising broke out against the Crown in the eighteenth century the Carpathian woodcutters were strong and powerful enough that their following carried weight. The uprising failed. As punishment for their help the Crown took their woodland. It decreed that the forest belonged to the Crown and posted watchtowers on the Carpathian ridge. . . .

When fathers were killed or abducted, their children did not watch in vain. They resisted as well, but their resistance was only sporadic, something at which to marvel. These years brought the laws decreeing that poachers be hanged and the hands of those who felled trees be cut off and exhibited along with the axe in the village square. Many such hands were exhibited, but just as many hid axes in their barns.

The next generation of woodcutters lived in huts of clay and rotten wood and let the gaunt livestock graze on the village hillside. They were punctual in their payment for the lease of the land, for it was paid with their own blood. . . . The woodcutters forgot their origins, although they weren't more remote than those of others who remember their history. Their bodies had nothing left to prop them up and became weak, their thoughts idle.

In the First World War the men were sent as far away as possible as border patrols to the most distant theatres of war. The thin but tough threads of life flowed on. Some of the villages were blasted away with the hill they were stuck on. . . . The march of the armies across the mountain passes hammered into each and every sleep. Now and then in the middle of the night the women opened their doors and their skirts to the deserters from across the hills.[31]

The mingling of chronicle and legend reduces to a few short paragraphs a history that spans the centuries from the Christianization of Hungary in the tenth and eleventh centuries to the end of World War One. The more or less encoded references to those forced to flee the "orderly, yes, hallowed cities on the plain" for the woodland and forests, who "learned better to stick together" against "wolves," whose "woodland" was seized by "the Crown," whose petulant fathers were "killed or abducted" while those called poachers were "hanged," suggest that this history of dispersal and oppression alludes specifically, if not explicitly, to the experience of the Carpathian Jews. Here, as in many of her other narratives in which

Jewish experience is thematized *but left unnamed,* Seghers writes in a prose style punctuated by pauses, as Walter Benjamin already noted in 1938, a style to which "silence also belongs."[32]

The narrative's narrower focus is the story of the woodcutter Woytshuk, whose determination in the year of revolutions following the war turns around the history of generations that came before him. This story begins at the moment his wife gives birth in their village hut:

> The Woytshuk woman in Hrushovo was lying on her bed so she could give birth. One of the neighbors turned on the light, the other chased away the hens. Then they bent over the woman and urged her to scream. But she agonized in silence the way one agonizes about things that are all the same to one and have no use from the start. Her husband had been home nine months earlier, she hadn't heard a word since. Above her neighbor's face, far, far away in rings that were quickly fading, the tiny light circled in the endless, total darkness of the world. None of the women heard the steps of soldiers on the village street. Woytshuk appeared on the doorstep at the very moment a father in Hrushovo is supposed to enter the birthing room: when it's time to cut the umbilical cord. (156)

Woodcutters of Hrushovo employs some of the magical elements of the fairy tale: the thick forest setting where plant, animal, and human life are in balance so as to resemble and mirror each other; a series of small wonders, such as Woytshuk's timely appearance before the childbed, giving a semblance of unity between self and world and echoing the archaic origins of art when art was part of life and life had no greater need for art. But aside from the fairy-tale requisites and motifs, the overall aesthetic composition in this and other such narratives by Seghers has more in common with the traditional elements of the folk saga, folk legend, and folktale.[33]

Lukács articulated this very distinction in an essay of 1918 devoted to a collection of legends and tales by Béla Balázs. Here Lukács described the fairy tale as "par excellence a form that lacks problems, a homogeneous form without dissonances." The world of the fairy tale "has no reality"; its ultimate striving is "not toward metaphysical truth, but toward magic," and in this sense it "represents a transformed world." By contrast, the legend, so Lukács argued, is "radically different from the fairy tale" in that "its composition strives to clothe the represented transcendence in immanence. But the transcendent is thereby not brought down to the empirical level; indeed, the legend sharply accentuates all trans-empirical and miraculous nature. Yet it does not make the substance transparent with an equivalent meaning; indeed, the legend underscores and foregrounds the very miraculous reality that cannot be made transparent."[34]

This *intransparency* of a "substance" that defies "equivalent meaning" is fundamental to all of Seghers's legendary tales. Unlike the fairy tale, they clothe "the represented transcendence in immanence," even though the transcendent is "not brought down to the empirical level." Thus, whereas the fairy tale per se strives "toward magic," Seghers's legendary tales strive, however covertly and non-explicitly, toward "metaphysical truth." As is to be expected in such tales, the "truth" can contain both salvation and damnation. This is the case at the end of *Woodcutters of Hrushovo*. In a gesture that would henceforth be characteristic of Seghers's serial style of storytelling, the third-person narrator suddenly assumes the first person and ascribes the story just told to another: "I heard this story told by the Secretary of the Party in the district of Carpatho-Russia" (168). The narrator then continues with an addendum to the story just told:

> He also related that this same Woytshuk came to him one day to borrow twenty kronen so he could travel to Russia. "Even if I give you twenty kronen, Woytshuk, it won't do you any good, because Russia is wide and the trip costly." "Just give them and let me do it." Woytshuk was handed the kronen and bought himself a scythe.
>
> As autumn approached he hired himself out with his scythe as a fieldworker from one stretch of grain to the next. Behind him the naked brown earth, before him the harvest, he mowed his way toward Russia, where he wound up. (168–69)

If we read this ending from the top down, as it were, the story concludes with the kind of rounded, positive outlook on the future required by the tenets of socialist realism that were in the process of being defined at the very time of its writing. In this sense the metaphor of the scythe would pay homage to the Soviet emblem of hammer and sickle, the naked brown earth would recall the oppression of the past, the harvest the magnificence of the national Soviet future. In the Party Secretary we meet of course the obligatory figure whose role it is to correctly interpret events—including those in the tale the narrator has even just ascribed to him.

But we are also given small indicators by which we might read this ending more critically, or, as it were, from the bottom up. "Russia is wide," the Party Secretary warns Woytshuk, trying to dampen his enthusiasm for a trip that is "costly." Indeed, by the time the story was written down, the wide expanses of "Russia" suggested not only the largesse of possibilities, but also the "costly" travels of the members of the Left Opposition whom Stalin deported to the most remote corners of the Soviet Union—Trotsky, Rakovsky, Radek, and many others who were to be executed or clandestinely murdered in the course of time. Moreover, the final sentence of the German text, ending with the phrase "wo er hinkam," or "where he wound up" (wo ist er nur hingekommen?: what's become of him?), has the effect of an alienation device in the tradition of Kafka in that the more common expression with which the German reader is familiar and thus might have anticipated in such a linguistic context is "wo er umkam" (where he perished). This, so the text covertly implies, would be the alternative reading. And so we are left with the image of a hardworking Carpathian village woodcutter, turned idealistic fieldworker, who sees the communist harvest before him but at the same time mows his way forward under the darker shadow of the Grim Reaper.

The addendum to the story of Woytshuk, indeed his entire story, can be interpreted as yet another attempt by Seghers to thematize the continuing journeys of the soul of Georg Lukács, in the case of the addendum his repeated trips to Moscow during the 1920s, which were hopeful at first but ultimately unsuccessful and disappointing. Or we might also see in the last image the figure of Leon Trotsky, who himself originated from a region of "Jewish agricultural colonies"[35] in the southern Ukraine, not all that far from the locale of Seghers's story. It was Trotsky who enjoyed as no other the great heights of the Soviet "harvest" as well as its "costly," indeed *nightmarish* consequences under the shadow of Stalin. For all their differences, Trotsky and Lukács seem to have personified for Seghers the Jewish intellectual and revolutionary par excellence. Not least for this reason they figure implicitly in a number of her narratives, some set in the Carpathian mountains and forests of Jewish history and Jewish lore.[36]

Seghers wrote two of her most *intransparent* narratives—*Tales of Artemis* and *The Most Splendid Tales of Woynok the Brigand*—in the wake of the first two major show trials in Moscow: the trial of Zinoviev, Kamenev, and co-defendants in August 1936, and the trial of the "last internationalist" Karl Radek and co-defendants in January 1937. The most important man standing trial, whom Stalin in fact was unable to place in the dock, was Leon Trotsky. Stalin's most hated, most dangerous enemy had distinguished himself, even in the eyes of Lenin, as an exceptional revolutionary, political leader, and military strategist. Trotsky also surpassed Stalin by far as a brilliant thinker and writer who was internationally celebrated among intellectual and literary circles, not least by the surrealists and other avant-gardists who congregated in France and Spain at the time of the Spanish Civil War. And of course Trotsky was a Jewish cosmopolitan and internationalist.

Just before Seghers was to write *Tales of Artemis* and *Tales of Woynok,* Trotsky had completed, together with his family and closest supporters, a two-year sojourn in France between July 1933 and June 1935. After having been banned to more remote points of the world, first to Alma-Ata on the Chinese border and thereafter to Turkey, in France Trotsky was able to consolidate his forces within the international working-class movement, whose headquarters were established in Paris in 1933. For half a year Trotsky and his family lived only thirty miles from Paris, in a villa in Barbizon, from where he made frequent clandestine trips to his international secretariat in Paris. His discovery in Barbizon in April of 1934 attracted press attention and busloads of tourists. Thereafter he lived in Domène outside Grenoble under close surveillance by the French authorities and under false papers, his identity photograph showing him with closely cropped hair, his face clean-shaven and without the characteristic pince-nez or rimmed spectacles. His later whereabouts in France were carefully kept secret from the public but were a source of constant speculation, anxiety, and rumor, especially among the exiled antifascist community, for whom the increasingly violent rift between Stalin and Trotsky occasioned the purges of many actual and so-called Trotskyists in France and Spain during the years of the Spanish Civil War.[37]

By the mid-1930s not only Hitler's but also Stalin's agents roamed the streets and environs of Paris. The threatening atmosphere in which Seghers and other political exiles in Paris lived at this time may well have resembled the mood of tension and confinement depicted in *Tales of Artemis.* Here, in the tightly enclosed, smoke-filled quarters of a forest inn, a band of hunters, their dogs lying restlessly at their feet, waits out the inclement weather outside. Just as the antifascist exile community trapped in Paris exchanged the latest news about Stalin's purges and Trotsky's most recent whereabouts, the hunters pass the time telling stories of just when, where, and how one of them, or someone he knew, once caught sight of the goddess of the hunt—Artemis. Just as Trotsky in France seemed to be everywhere but was rarely seen, let alone recognized, the hunters meanwhile are barely aware of the new maidservant who moves quickly and easily among them. Once her chores are completed she draws nearer to the raging fire. There, in a gesture evocative of the statue *Artemis dit Diane de Versailles* in the Louvre, she leans back casually against the wall, "one arm pushed back behind her head" and "her knee cast slightly forward."[38] With her body positioned in such a way as to appear both seductive and threatening, she listens bemused—as Trotsky's face often appears in photographs—while the hunters exchange ever more intriguing tales about Artemis. They vaguely sense the disturbance in their midst but fail to recognize it in the elusive figure of the maidservant who stands among them. Finally, at the innkeeper's order that she resume her chores, she interrupts her reverie and takes the empty pail from the hook over the fire to draw water outside. When the door reopens an older woman stands in her place, dressed in "rough clothes and shoes, with rough, hard, though not evil features" (73). She stands at the threshold eager to begin her work as the official, if somewhat tardy, new maidservant. Reminiscent of work in the devil's kitchen, she arrives one day later than agreed because her previous employers required her services as a midwife one last time (73). The hunters rush to the door and peer into the darkness into which the young maidservant has disappeared—a darkness whose suddenly bare spruce branch harks back to the desolate seventeenth-century landscapes of Hercules Seghers:

> The outlines of the well appeared faint in the dark, rainy night. The filled pail of water stood on the threshold next to the door post. But no tracks led from the threshold to the well and from the well back to the threshold. And why did no branch beat against the house wall, and why did no spruce needles ripple, even though the clouds were racing between the roof and the timber? All of a sudden deep in the forest, probably hours away, two thin, long-drawn-out whistles sounded so as to make one's heart quake. A spruce branch brushed against the wall and shook off its needles. The whole forest roared. (74)

Like the changing of the guard from Lenin to Stalin that allowed Stalin to appear ever stronger the more Trotsky was pushed to the side, the solid, "rough" woman who takes the place of the elusive young maidservant makes the most of her situation and her talents. Strong and able, she is all too ready to be of use and displays a "fearlessness of the kind that emanates from sad hearts; for what is most important is long lost, and there's no need to tremble for it anymore" (74). Although the hunters avoid her gaze, she soon makes herself indispensable by claiming the work begun by her predecessor as her own: "Now the maid also looked out through the open door. She caught sight of the full pail of water. She picked it up before anyone ordered her to do so, and hung it on the hook over the fire. That was her first labor in this house" (75).

Tales of Artemis employs traditional requisites of the folk and fairy tale: a house deep in the forest; the allegorical use of the four elements earth, air, fire, and water; a reliance on archetypal figures to represent human emotions and actions—innkeeper and wife, hunters, dogs, and maidservants, or, as it were, maiden and witch. The approach in *The Most Splendid Tales of Woynok the Brigand* is much the same. But whereas *Tales of Artemis,* suggestive of Trotsky's virtual imprisonment in France, restricts the setting to a smoke-filled forest inn, with only the hunters' tales to bring memories of forested mountains into view, *Tales of Woynok* opens onto the wide expanse of Carpathian forests, mountains, and deep river valleys. In this seemingly endless wilderness human figures even assume the physical bearing and behavior of animals in the wild, evidently on the model of Rudyard Kipling's stories in *The Jungle Book*.[39] And in this wilderness robbers roam and plunder, one of its leaders together with his pack, the other and most "splendid" one of them all, "always alone."[40] There are no idle hunters, no legends of an elusive goddess in this narrative, only the tales of the notorious Woynok, who grows ever more isolated and pensive, unable to stay with the pack and unable to survive alone, thus finally reaching a bad, if memorable, end.

If *Tales of Artemis* concerns the magic of chance encounters with immortality, *Tales of Woynok* revolves around the consequences of idealism gone awry. We hear "splendid tales" about the reckless, melancholy rogue Woynok, whose characteristics are taken from Trotsky's physiognomy and biography. Reminiscent of Trotsky, who in the years of exile before 1917 first worked with Lenin and the Bolsheviks, then joined the Mensheviks in opposing him, Woynok's restlessness causes him at every turn to go beyond the confines of the pack and its leader Gruschek. Gruschek, who knows the benefits of moving with the pack and building a strong camp so as to survive the winter—a reference to Lenin's stabilization of the Party—invites Woynok to join him in his camp over the winter. Their first encounter, at which they "sat down on the earth, face to face, and devoured their bread together" (26), recalls the famous first meeting in the fall of 1902 between Lenin and the barely twenty-three-year-old Trotsky. After an adventurous escape from imprisonment in Siberia and a hasty trip across Europe via Zurich and Paris, the ebullient Trotsky knocked one early morning at the door of Lenin's London apartment and, after Lenin's wife Krupskaya opened the door, was taken in to meet the great man, who was still in bed.[41] Seghers's physiognomic references also recall the younger of the two Russian revolutionaries: "Gruschek carefully observed Woynok. Woynok still looked a lot younger than had been reported to him; his eyes were so clear, as if their blue transparency had never been clouded by the scum of even the unfulfilled remainder of an unfulfillable desire" (26).

But other than being robbers, Gruschek and Woynok have little in common. Indeed, like Lenin, whom Trotsky described in his autobiography as having "a peculiar capacity for attention, watching the speech of his interlocutor for the exact thing he wanted, and meanwhile looking past him into space,"[42] Gruschek sees in the "blue transparency" of Woynok's eyes only the reflection "of his own shaggy old face and what looked over his shoulders at mountain peaks and clouds" (26–27). Nonetheless, after the summer of Woynok's most glorious plunders, recalling the notoriety of Trotsky's military victories during the Civil War, Woynok is unable to weather the winter storms on his own and returns half-dead to Gruschek's camp. Here the figure of Woynok again recalls Trotsky, who was physically weakened after the Civil War and frequently ill, while Stalin rose to power during Lenin's own illness and following his death in 1924. The more the robbers celebrate, the more violent the fire in the camp, the more troubled Woynok becomes. Indeed, it is at this point that the pack leader Gruschek begins to take on the characteristics of Stalin, reveling as he does in glories that bring back memories of Cossack pogroms and other such earlier Russian victories:

> [Woynok] had never seen a fire burn so high. . . . The intermittent, pitiful i-i-i-i of an accordion drowned out the noise of the camp. All of a sudden Gruschek got his little dog hopping, put his arms to his hips, and swayed his upper body to and fro. The sight filled Woynok with horror, and he lowered his eyes in shame. Gruschek let out a piercing scream and bounded up in the air and snapped back his knees. The robbers screamed and clapped. Gruschek sprang up and down as if his years were a fraud, his white hair a deceit, his dignity as chieftain a swindle. The robbers went crazy for joy because Gruschek let falsehood and trickery have their way. . . . I want to get away from here, Woynok thought desperately to himself, but why should I leave so soon? I haven't been caught by soldiers. After all, I'm among robbers. I want to leave as long as there's still time. But why should I leave? It's not as if I'm in Doboroth. I'm in Gruschek's camp, after all. (30–31)

The same campfire that "made all of them happy" only "produced grief" in Woynok, and soon he "climbed out of the ravine into the deathly loneliness of the Prutka that had meanwhile become silent and covered by ice" (33). At one point Woynok is rumored to have come to a "miserable end" when peasants who find him half-frozen in the snow with his foot caught in a hunter's trap beat him to a pulp with their sticks (43). And so once again, like Trotsky, Rakovsky, Radek, and others whose banishment in the late 1920s allowed Stalin to destroy the Left Opposition, an extremely weakened Woynok seeks the winter warmth of the campfire, although he remains outside the pack: "A rush of icy cold air flew from him and fluttered around the foreheads of the robbers. . . . He sat down on the earth, beyond those circled around the fire. He resembled the Woynok of before as much as the dead can resemble the living" (44).

Like Brecht's *The Measures Taken* (1930), in which the young comrade's idealism is sacrificed for the sake of the survival of the whole, Seghers's narrative thematizes the philosophical contradiction inherent in the political-historical moment: "Woynok was much too weak to move nearer to the fire. Who should have thought of drawing him closer in?" (45). His growing isolation and ambivalence—"Why did I come back here? Why did I make my way back on the terrible road across the mountains? . . . I could have had my peace long ago, I could have been snowed under long ago" (45)—takes him away from the camp one last time. By the time Gruschek and his robbers find him, "he had burrowed himself headfirst into the snow" (46). "Should he be buried in the camp?" (46) the robbers ask in a tone reminiscent of Pilate's rather indifferent question as he presents Jesus to the crowd. Gruschek's laconic response—"That goes too far"—is followed by the no less shattering narrative gesture that concludes the tale: "So then they simply laid Woynok down flat with his face up and covered him with snow. That was quickly done" (46).

Seghers published *Tales from Artemis* and *Tales of Woynok* in 1938, that is to say, at the very time she contributed to the ongoing debates on expressionism, which in her case took the form of an open exchange of letters with Georg Lukács, published in *Internationale Literatur* in 1939 after *Das Wort* ceased publication. These letters contain her critique of Lukács's ever more adamant defense of realism against modernism. They also reveal her frustration with the vicious tenor of the debates among Stalinists who jumped on the bandwagon of realism with facile and even frightening versions of Lukács's basic argument that expressionism, or modernism, potentially had more to do with fascism than with progressive culture.[43] Privately, Seghers would have had legitimate fears about Lukács's safety in Moscow, where many of his neighbors in the international community had already been arrested and deported. By this time even Bukharin, a longtime defender of the Hungarian Council Republic, had been publicly condemned and executed in the spring of 1938, and Béla Kun, tried in 1937, was to be purged in 1939. As it turned out, Lukács was one of the few leading internationalists and members of the communard generation of 1919 who survived the purges of the thirties and forties.[44]

Nineteen thirty-eight was also the year when Seghers first mentioned in private letters her desire to carry out an "old *Lieblingsplan*" for a collection of stories in the style of the *Thousand and One Nights* and Boccaccio's *Decameron*.[45] Its connection to Lukács has already been noted. Seghers's particular interest in this plan in 1938 would have concerned the consolation of the *Märchen* in times of trial, a form of consolation that had long been close to Lukács's own heart.[46] The few words with which she prefaced her *Most Splendid Tales of Woynok the Brigand* must have been meant especially for Lukács in Moscow, a fantastic appeal to the private sentiments of a man who, as he would demonstrate once again in the years leading up to 1956, was never entirely able to trade the longings of the soul for the objective totality of history and its all too realistic manifestations. Thus Seghers wrote in her preface to *Tales of Woynok:* "And don't you ever have any dreams, wild ones and tender ones, in a sleep 'twixt one hard day and the next? and do you know why sometimes an old tale, a little song, yes, even the beat of a song, easily pierces the hearts against which we beat our fists bloody? Yes, the whistle of a bird tugs easily at the bottom of the heart and so, too, at the roots of all actions" (26). Not only in this sense, the tale of the idealistic, melancholy rogue Woynok, who "plundered alone" and eventually "burrowed himself headfirst into the snow," is also the story of the fate under Stalinism of the once illustrious "philosopher-king."

While we do not have Lukács's reaction to Seghers's *Tales of Woynok,* we do have Brecht's, thanks to Walter Benjamin's notes on his conversations with him in Svendborg in the summer of 1938. It was in fact Brecht who as one of the editors of *Das Wort* was responsible for the publication of Seghers's story in the journal's June 1938 issue, that is, directly following the third Moscow show trial, of Bukharin and co-defendants. According to Benjamin's notes on his conversations with Brecht, Brecht valued Seghers's narrative for the very reason that the central character in its "tales" is "a rebellious, solitary figure."[47] In the same conversation on 25 July 1938, Brecht addressed a point that preoccupied him as a writer who, like Seghers, was sympathetic to international communism and at the same time was disturbed by events in the Soviet Union and developments within the official Parties. In Benjamin's words: "Brecht praised Seghers's 'The Most Splendid Tales of Woynok the Brigand' because they reveal that Seghers is no longer writing to order." Thereupon Brecht added a perception that appears even more intriguing: "Seghers can't produce to order, just as, without an order, I wouldn't even know how to start writing."[48]

Whereas the general reader knows Seghers primarily as the author of antifascist novels, the members of the Budapest Sunday Circle and her German contemporaries in political exile such as Benjamin and Brecht were more interested in those aspects of her work exemplified in her shorter, highly poeticized narratives such as *Tales of Woynok.* In these narratives Seghers was able to probe the internal, in many respects obfuscated and obfuscating political issues pertaining to the complex and increasingly frightening developments within the dominant stream of communism in her time, that is to say, Stalinism. Like Brecht, and in contrast to essayists like Lukács and Benjamin, Seghers was an avant-gardist who developed her most refined theoretical positions within the very aesthetics of her creative work. The interpretive challenge posed by the intransparency of Seghers's "mythic" tales is analogous to a problem of exegesis that critics have already identified in Brecht's work, namely, the inconsistency between the "Grand Pedagogy" of his learning plays and the "Small Pedagogy" of the largely parable and chronicle plays.[49] The dialectic of fascism/antifascism fundamental to Seghers's novels is in this respect comparable to the anticapitalist critique, or "Small Pedagogy," that characterizes many of Brecht's best-known plays, from *The Threepenny Opera* to *Mother Courage*. Her shorter "mythic" narratives, on the other hand, have more in common with the experimental theatre form and internal critique of revolutionary history and method inherent in the "Grand Pedagogy" of the learning plays, which toward the end of his life Brecht called the "theatre of the future."[50] The comparison with Brecht also helps explain why the later East German playwright Heiner Müller, who returned again and again to the model of the "Grand Pedagogy" of the learning play, also relied repeatedly and throughout his writing career on the poetic models found in Anna Seghers's "mythic" tales.[51]

In a speech shortly after Seghers's death in 1983 the critic Hans Mayer pursued a "mythic" thread in Seghers's work leading from her early narrative *Grubetsch* to *Tales of Artemis* and to her postwar narrative *The Ship of the Argonauts*.[52] This thread can be extended to include more narratives, not only those of the 1930s already discussed, but also *Die drei Bäume* (1940/46, The Three Trees) and the Caribbean novellas written after the war: *Die Hochzeit von Haiti* (1949, Wedding in Haiti), *Wiedereinführung der Sklaverei in Guadeloupe* (1949, Reinstatement of Slavery in Guadeloupe), and *Das Licht auf dem Galgen* (1948/60, The Light on the Gallows). What do these narratives have in common? They revolve around the journeys of loners, heretics, or martyrs who cannot be integrated into the collective and because of this ultimately perish or disappear. In the final analysis these texts revolve around the tragedy of a philosophical or utopian striving that fails in the face of the contradiction inherent in the given political-historical moment. Here death does not offer an escape into a metaphysical realm of freedom as, for example, in the plays of Schiller. On the contrary, as indicated by the title of her postwar novel of 1949, it is precisely "the dead" who are obliged to "stay young" in Seghers's works, who as witnesses of their time offer an example to posterity to be tried over and over again by generations to come. It was of course this redemptive aspect of memory that first gave rise, not only in the Greek and Judeo-Christian traditions, to the narrative forms of saga, legend, chronicle, and folk and fairy tale—in short, the narrative topographies of myth.

When in 1948 Seghers expressed to Lukács her renewed interest in a collection of tales in the style of the *Thousand and One Nights* and the *Decameron,* she had just learned about the latest purges in the Soviet Union and was at work on several more of her "mythic" narratives.[53] One of them was *The Ship of the Argonauts,* which she published in 1949, shortly before the show trial and execution of László Rajk in Budapest. *The Ship of the Argonauts* revolves around the theme of the doomed revolutionary in the figure of the mythical Jason, who after innumerable voyages returns alone and unrecognized to his homeland. Seghers's own disillusionment at the time is evident in the lines: "Once he understood that fate had left him to himself, like the Argo that had sailed on without him, he stopped believing in fate. He didn't believe in the gods anymore either. And in humans, now less than ever."[54] The mood of despair culminates in the tragic irony of Jason's death as he lies down to rest under a great tree, swarming with birds, whose branches hold the remains of his own ship: "The storm broke. It burst the last cords with one blow. The entire ship's hull crashed down on Jason. He perished with his ship, as was told long ago in legends and songs" (139–40).

The protagonist Jason calls to mind any number of exiled antifascists and internationalists, who like Seghers herself, tried to return "home" from all corners of the world after the war. Informed by the various legends of Jason's travels from the Black Sea far up the Danube River,[55] *The Ship of the Argonauts* is once again situated in the vicinity of the mountain and forest topography of the Carpathian Mountains, in this case the southernmost reach of the Carpathians in Romania north of the Danube Delta. Seghers's Jason approaches but in fact never actually reaches this area as he moves across the range of hills above the Danube Delta to where he has climbed from a harbor in the Black Sea. Written in the wake of Nazi death camps such as Belzec and Sobibor, where Seghers's own mother may have perished after being deported to the ghetto of Piaski near Lublin,[56] *The Ship of the Argonauts* evokes a topography, indeed a topographic yearning, that took on even greater significance after the events of the war. From this point of view *The Ship of the Argonauts* presents us with a protagonist who is attempting to reach, at least in spirit if not in actual fact, a land that has been obliterated. That he is prevented from reaching it, is in fact killed unawares by his own ship, has to do not only with the narrative's adherence to the original Greek myth. It also reveals the author's awareness that the Ashkenazic topography of the Carpathians has been lost—to history, and to the utopian moment inherent in myth. Seghers never again returned to this topography as a writer.

By means of a typically rendered land-, cloud-, and seascape the text is able to evoke the existential and political conflicts surrounding the main figure. The passage also makes subtle reference to the vocabulary of *Arbeit* and *Ordnung,* suggesting that the earth, once magical and grand, has been carved up and administered to the most trivial detail. Only the sea and sky remain as pathways for the soul. Thus the wide ocean waterways of the past and the transparent clarity of the sky above are thrown into sharp relief against the cultivated fields below and the threatening forest where Jason will be killed by the hull of his own ship:

> Jason had already climbed so high that he saw the sea once more as it shimmered through a chink in the mountain. It was lonely on the ridge. The next bay was much wider. It tore deeper into the land. It was full of ships as if of flocks of birds picking up cargo and baled freight out of warehouses like feed out of a basin. He still had a long way before him, down into the swarm. The hillsides were planted with corn and grain and vineyards.
> A forest lay between the mountain ridge and the fields.
> The wind smelled of the sea and of trees. How miserly, how petty was the arrangement of the earth compared to the sky that stretched over it. The clouds never complied for a minute, they never fell into line, they never confined themselves to a single image, they transformed themselves much faster than anyone could think, into a range of mountains, and just as soon into fantastic beasts; here they grew god-like, over there like plants. Their shadows raced across the neatly ordered trifles. (131)

In Seghers's Caribbean novellas, also written at this time, the significance of forest and wood imagery is maintained. But what was earlier a Carpathian topography is transformed into a series of tropical jungle landscapes. In *Reinstatement of Slavery in Guadeloupe* we find again the enmeshments of forest, body, and beast that characterize *Tales of Woynok,* where the figures are represented in such a way as to resemble the movements and mannerisms of beasts stalking their prey in the Carpathian forests. Compare the first encounter between Gruschek and Woynok; as if in a scene from Kipling's *The Jungle Book,* they meet like two panthers who cautiously sense and inspect each other before they agree to share their booty:

> Gruschek followed the track for half a day before he spotted Woynok on the next to highest falls of the Prutka, on a rock in the sun. Woynok reached for his shotgun; then he recognized Gruschek by all the signs by which a bandit recognizes another. He climbed down from his rock and greeted Gruschek as the elder. They sat down on the ground, face to face, and devoured their bread together. . . .

They took leave of each other. Woynok climbed back onto his rock. Gruschek climbed carefully down the incline. Now it looked as if his small, gristly body wasn't bent with age, but so that he could better adapt himself to the curvatures of the steep mountain slopes. (26–27)

Like Gruschek, whose body shape adjusts to the "curvatures of the steep mountain slopes," Woynok is described at one point as virtually becoming one with the forest, an enmeshment preventing him from ever reaching the envisioned world that would lie on a horizon on the other side of the forests:

In the night, as the bandits slept, Woynok left the camp so that he might finally carry out his plan. He climbed down the rock face and tried to break into the forest alone. The fragrance and the darkness dazed him. Every movement of his body seemed to propagate itself into the endlessness, as if the forest were twitching convulsively over the splinter that had penetrated it. Woynok climbed a tree in order to check his course. He had scarcely moved away from the rock face. He had claimed as little of the endlessness of the forests as of the star-studded sky. (39)

In *Reinstatement of Slavery in Guadeloupe* the enmeshment is more explicit. Jean Rohan, a former slave emancipated by the French Revolution, flees from a government patrol as Napoleon's troops reinstate slavery in Guadeloupe. In the course of his flight he succumbs to the forest's "embrace":

He had penetrated the forest. Its roots twisted out of the earth like gristly hexes up into the branches. The branches grew back down into the forest ground, and everything was matted and mossy and entwined in liana. He didn't need to crawl any longer. The earth sucked him in. Its small animals whirred toward him, stared, tickled him. He was so alone that he no longer felt alone. He gave up feeling alone in the swarm. In the midst of so much life he gave up feeling like a special life that feared something. If any thoughts had still come to him in the hot, whistling darkness, then he might have thought that he would rather die a thousand ways than be destroyed by what he was fleeing.[57]

When the hounds running ahead of the patrol have caught his scent and are about to reach him, Jean Rohan climbs up into a tree. The notion of enmeshment with the forest suddenly turns into the possibility of a metamorphosis—self = body = forest = beast—as Rohan tries to endure within the already betrayed revolution as the one free soul that does not betray itself: "Jean Rohan knew it was the end. It would have been better to perish in the clench of a snake. Better a scorpion, even better a jaguar. Better to be a jaguar than a bloodhound. Was it better to be a slave than a dog? For a Negro it was only possible to live as a slave, or not at all" (112). The subsequent description of the hounds at the foot of the tree is reminiscent of a passage in *Tales of Woynok* wherein Woynok is roused from his treetop slumber by the nasty dog Gruschek has sent out in pursuit. The passage in *Tales of Woynok* is as follows:

> One night Woynok woke up in his treetop. He didn't know what could have wakened him. He crawled into another crotch, but right away he was wakened again. Far down below him something was scratching at the tree trunk and whining. Woynok wrapped his arms and legs more tightly around the branch. In these forests he knew of no animals that could whine so pitifully. For this reason he leaned his head down over one more time. This bristly, tiny beast meant nothing, if something so pitiful even existed in reality. And even as a dream it was bothersome and pitiful. Woynok slept on; now he dreamt that Gruschek's little dog was running so fast around the tree that its eyes described light circles. . . . There it was again sliding on its belly and forepaws and grumbling. Then it went vaulting at the tree. That made Woynok laugh in his sleep. Woynok had scarcely realized that these frantic vaults didn't at all slacken, but grew higher each time, when he already felt the teeth of Gruschek's little dog on his foot. (35)

The analogous passage in *Reinstatement of Slavery in Guadeloupe* presents the scene of Jean Rohan's discovery by the hounds of the government patrol as he cowers in a treetop. It is significant that the members of the patrol are collectively represented in the singular as "it" (incidentally, like Gruschek's "pack" in *Tales of Woynok*), that is, as one administrative-militarized body devoid of individual human aspect, whereas Rohan is shown "in gliding flight," indicating the release of his eternally free soul. If the characterization of Woynok in the passage quoted above evokes the image of a wildcat slumbering in a tree, the depiction of what in effect is Rohan's "death and transfiguration" in the passage that follows presents the enmeshment with the forest as no longer merely imagined by him, as in another passage quoted above, but in actual terms of his physical metamorphosis and reintegration into the life of the forest and the earth:

The hounds once again went into a raving frenzy. The patrol otherwise could not have distinguished the dark from the dark, nor have spotted the two white points that belonged to it. The patrol laid back its heads and yelled and whistled and screamed. Then it pointed and shot. The dead man first tumbled, then came down in gliding flight. The patrol left by the path the Negroes had cut with their machetes after it tore the ravenous hounds—for the hunting season was short—from the booty. In its back a migration of insects hurled itself onto the remaining flesh; then came small rodents with teeth and snouts. At the end, shooing away what had arrived first, came a large, bushy beast of prey with its cub, imperturbable and heavy, the mother hungry, her young one hungry. (112)

In Anna Seghers's mythic conception the reunion with the sea represents the final liberation. Already in her first published story, *The Dead on the Island Djal,* it is on the high seas that her sailors find the fulfillment of adventure before they shipwreck on the rocky shores of Djal. It is by way of a Rhine freighter headed for the Netherlands that the protagonist of her best-known novel, *The Seventh Cross,* can finally escape his pursuers. And it is from his small craft in the Caribbean Sea that the survivor of the failed revolution on Jamaica in *The Light on the Gallows* can glimpse the light that appears to shine from the gallows; and from there he steers his way to Cuba, where he passes to another a secret message that eventually finds its away across the Atlantic to France.

The examples are multiple and extend as far as Seghers's last collection of stories, *Three Women from Haiti* (1980), published two years after the death of her husband László Radványi and shortly before her own. All three stories revolve around Haitian women who remain alone after leading eventful and dangerous lives. *Das Versteck* (The Hideout) is set in the Napoleonic era after the defeat of the Haitian revolution led by Toussaint L'Ouverture. It relates the story of a Haitian girl who dives off a ship bound for France to escape the enslaved life of a concubine in the white courts of Europe. In the years that follow she survives among coastal cliffs and caves where she provides refuge for generations of Haitians, including her husband and children, who rebel against a series of repressive regimes empowered by European colonialism. As the "storms" of repression become ever more furious, she remains alone with only the sea to console her and finally take her back into itself:

One day, as she was lying in her cave, a raging storm broke. The ocean ripped away pieces of the coast. Trees were uprooted. The walls of the cave gave way. Toaliina crawled through the entry at the back, which was already partially blocked. She clung fast to the rock to catch her breath. Her face was soon bitten through by the salt air. Where are my children? In the mine pit? Fettered? Imprisoned? At sea? At any moment the surf could carry her away. With her last strength she clung to a boulder, feeling that no matter the danger, the sea she had known intimately since childhood would come to her aid.

She knew, her flight had succeeded.[58]

CHAPTER 7

Myth and Redemption: At the Roman *Limes* with Walter Benjamin

Redemption is the *limes* of progress.
——Walter Benjamin, 1939/40[1]

Fascism has devastated this country horribly, internally and externally, internally above all. . . . The few decent people I met alive (some I looked for I didn't find at all, or only [their names] on a death warrant) stick out from the rest like the early Christians from the spectators in a Roman arena.
——Anna Seghers, 1947[2]

There is a remarkable affinity in the writings of Seghers and Benjamin from their last years of exile in Paris in the 1930s. Curiously, this affinity has aroused no interest in the secondary literature, a state of affairs that surely has more to do with the respective intellectual formations and cold-war histories of Seghers and Benjamin scholarship in the second half of the twentieth century than with their own understanding of their times and their individual and common place therein. Although the intensity of their relationship as intellectuals can hardly be compared with that of Seghers and Lukács or Seghers and Brecht, or, conversely, with that of Benjamin and Scholem or Benjamin and Brecht, there is nonetheless evidence of a trajectory that passes through multiple layers of artistic, political, and theoretical intersection, especially as in the later 1930s that trajectory moved ever more precipitously toward the final impasse of the Hitler-Stalin pact, the war, and the Holocaust.

Biographically we know relatively little, given Seghers's well-known reticence regarding her personal affairs and the infrequent acknowledgment of Seghers in Benjamin's own work. However, the recent publication of Benjamin's letters from the mid-1930s corroborates my long-held suspicion that these two writers were far more aware of each other's significance, and communicated accordingly. On a card from Nice dated

23 July 1937, Walter Benjamin asked Alfred Cohn if he had received his essay "The Storyteller," which he had sent him two weeks before. The same card mentions Anna Seghers—"I heard from Anna Seghers that Fritz lost his job"[3]—who likely would also have been sent the essay and was evidently more prompt in acknowledging its receipt. The issues addressed in Benjamin's essay, whose publication he had eagerly awaited for many months, are frequently mentioned in his correspondence from the mid-1930s. In this regard we find occasional reference to Anna Seghers, as in a letter of 20 December 1937 to Karl Thieme, who in one of his Basel lectures read aloud section 15 of "The Storyteller" to inform his students "of my own position on the novel, yet without offending them with a formulation of my own."[4] Benjamin was delighted: "Might you not send me one or more excerpts from your lectures along with the much desired samples of the Bible selections? You don't have to worry about their prompt return. The issues you touch upon in your letter once again came into full swing just recently in some conversations I have had with Anna Seghers about the situation of the novelist ["Romancier"]."[5]

At this time of the expressionism debates and the Soviet trials and purges Seghers was no less aware of "the situation of the novelist" from her own perspective as a creative writer. As discussed in chapter 6, at this very point in time she began writing tales in the vein of the *Decameron* and the *Thousand and One Nights,* notably *The Most Splendid Tales of Woynok the Brigand,* published in the June 1938 issue of *Das Wort,* and *Tales of Artemis,* published in the same year in the September issue of *Internationale Literatur.* We can assume that Benjamin's essay "The Storyteller" reaffirmed her move in this direction. At the same time Seghers seems to have had a significant impact on Benjamin, an intellectual whose fascination with creative artists and writers, as for example Brecht, had a reciprocal effect in terms of his own work. On 26 April 1937 he wrote to Brecht's assistant and collaborator Margarete Steffin: "Last week Seghers spoke in commemoration of Büchner. Once again I was struck by how much better she is speaking than writing [for such occasions]. Her suggestion, about which I wrote to Brecht in my last letter, also belongs to the realm of the spoken word. I would be very interested to hear something about this."[6]

Among his contemporaries Benjamin was hardly alone in his impression of Seghers's remarkable style and manner of oral presentation. When speaking before what is usually described as a riveted audience, she had the ability to take up her subject matter *in medias res* in a tone and manner of voice that seemed to emanate from the deepest recesses of her psyche. Without reliance on notes she wove her way in and out of multiple themes, images, topographies, and discourses, flitting back and forth between cultures and across the centuries, all the while never losing her train of thought as she moved with a mingling of ease and determination toward her final point.[7] If there was anyone in Paris who both as a speaker and an author of prose, especially in the "darkest" of times, could vie with Leskov as the quintessential storyteller, it was undoubtedly Seghers. Indeed, reading "The Storyteller" today with Seghers's style and manner in mind, one could imagine that Benjamin might just as well have written his famous essay about her.

Such speculation appears more warranted when we consider that during the months following the publication of "The Storyteller" in *Orient und Okzident* in June 1937,[8] Benjamin expressed his admiration for Seghers's work in an extensive review of her novel *Die Rettung* (1937, The Rescue). Entitled "Eine Chronik der deutschen Arbeitslosen" (A Chronicle of the German Unemployed), the review appeared on 12 May 1938 in *Die neue Weltbühne.*[9] The plot line of Seghers's novel concerns the hardships of daily life among unemployed Silesian miners during the Depression, that is, on the eve of fascism, which would "rescue" them from their plight. As Benjamin noted in his review: "One of the conditions for the growth of fascism was the destruction of class consciousness, a danger to which the proletariat was exposed by unemployment. The new book by Anna Seghers is concerned with how that process worked."[10] (The novel also thematizes the exile experience of passing time aimlessly, and it addresses the futility, even before the German invasion of France, of waiting in dark times for what Samuel Beckett later called Godot.)[11]

Some years earlier Benjamin had written a scathing review of Alfred Döblin's *Berlin Alexanderplatz,* faulting the novel for what he considered to be a superficial use of epic and montage technique and thus consigning it to the dustheap of the idealistic tradition of the *Bildungsroman.*[12] By contrast, his review of Seghers's *The Rescue* commends its narrative depiction for its "rootwork" (*CA,* 531). Benjamin's commentary focuses on the epic-chronicle aspects of the narrative, suggesting that the novel "is not organized according to a main action and smaller episodes. It wants to get closer to older epic forms, to the chronicle or the chapbook" (*CA,* 537). Benjamin found in this work "no evidence of *Schicksal,*" only a few "witnesses" of history: "They are martyrs in the very sense of the word (martyr, in Greek: the witness). The report about them is a chronicle. Anna Seghers is the chronicler of the German unemployed" (*CA,* 533). Aside from these "witnesses" and "martyrs" of history there remains an elusive "Volk" that, according to Benjamin, communicates only in "whispers":

> Her awareness of this does not leave the storyteller for a moment. She relates her tales in pauses like someone who waits in silence for those who have been called to hear the news, and in order to gain time stops

for a breath now and again. "The later the evening, the better the guests." This tension pervades the book. It is far removed from the quick immediacy of reportage, which doesn't much ask to whom it speaks. It is just as far removed from the novel, which basically thinks only of the *reader*. The voice of this storyteller has not abdicated. Many stories are scattered throughout this book, wherein they await those that will *hear* them. (*CA*, 533)

Seghers's epic-chronicle style of narration, the review continues, "recalls the true folk art" that "once was invoked by *der blaue Reiter*" (*CA*, 535). Thus very much in support of expressionism, which was hotly debated among émigrés at the time, and reminiscent of the young Lukács, whose aesthetic theories still influenced Seghers (and Benjamin) in the mid-1930s, Benjamin pointed to examples of Gothic art and the chiliastic spirit of its time:

The chronicle can be distinguished from modern representations of history by its lack of temporal perspective. Its depictions come closest to approximating those forms of painting that preceded the discovery of perspective. When the figures in miniatures or early altar paintings approach the viewer on a gold surface, their features make no less of an impression on him than if the painter had placed them in a nature setting or housed them in an enclosure. They border on a transfigured realm without forfeiting accuracy. Thus the characters of the medieval chronicler verge on a transfigured time that suddenly inter-rupts their lives. The Kingdom of God overtakes them as catastro-phe. It is certainly not this catastrophe that awaits the unemployed whose chronicle is *The Rescue*. But it is something like its counterim-age, the coming of the Antichrist. He is well known to ape the bless-ing that was promised to be more messianic. In this way the Third Reich apes socialism. Unemployment can end because forced labor has become legal. (*CA*, 534–35)

Benjamin's perception of Seghers's indebtedness to chiliastic-mes-sianic traditions brought him close to her in a way that would have medi-ated between the world of Judaism represented by the Zionist Gershom Scholem and the world of dialectical materialism represented by the Marx-ist Bertolt Brecht. Perhaps for this reason he felt obliged to point to Seghers's "masculine" abilities: "The storyteller has dared to look in the eyes of the failure of the revolution in Germany—a masculine capability more urgently needed than it is widespread. This attitude also character-izes her other work" (*CA*, 135). The question raised by Benjamin at the

end of his review—"Will these people be able to *liberate* themselves?"—
pertains not simply to the characters in Seghers's novel, but to all those
affected by the "failure of the revolution in Germany." The novel itself
ends on a bleak note, leaving the answer to this question, typically for
Seghers, to the children of the Silesian miners, that is to say, to a fragile,
indefinite future. Summarizing the underlying theme of the novel, Benjamin's answer to his own question is unequivocal: "One is caught off
guard by the feeling that, like any poor souls, they can only hope for
redemption" (*CA,* 537–38).

During their exile years in Paris Seghers and Benjamin held comparable views in respect to politics and the arts, and it is well known that at the
time of the expressionism debates they were both defenders of modernism.[13] Indeed, as early as 1927 they had already voiced remarkably similar opinions in their respective reviews of the Soviet writer F. V. Gladkov's novel *Cement.* Seghers's review appeared on 22 May 1927 in the
Frankfurter Zeitung, Benjamin's review only two weeks later, on 10 June
1927, in *Die literarische Welt.* Whereas both reviewers lauded Gladkov for
the "realism" of his portrayal of the complexities within the Russian Revolution on the home front following the Civil War, they also faulted the
novel for its romantic tendencies, Benjamin rather neutrally comparing
Cement to the novels of Pilniak and Fedin,[14] Seghers arguing more deliberately that the novel fails to meet the standards of the "steeled and hammered rhythms" of Larissa Reissner's and Isaac Babel's prose—"by which
the future will remember the present."[15]

We can take for granted that the voracious reader Benjamin was
familiar with Seghers's novels and stories of the 1930s that appeared in the
leading exile presses and periodicals. We can also assume that he had read
the early prose of this well-known German-Jewish woman writer who
received the Kleist Prize in 1928 and whose work had been published since
1924 in the literary section of the *Frankfurter Zeitung.* Seghers was probably less familiar with Benjamin's own writings, at least before the mid-
1930s. As a wife and the mother of two young children she ran a household
in the Paris suburb of Bellevue and was rarely seen among artists and intellectuals who were more dependent on Paris café life.[16] Moreover, in contrast to a writer like Brecht, who delighted in theoretical banter, whether
passing the time playing chess or in intellectual debate, Seghers tended to
shun theory and literary conversation for their own sake, an indication
that her above-mentioned "conversations" with Benjamin about "the situation of the novelist" in late 1937 would have been especially significant to
her. Aside from their attendance at writers' congresses and similar events,
Seghers and Benjamin may also have had contact because of Benjamin's
involvement since the beginning of 1936 in the Freie Deutsche Hochschule

(Free German University) run by Seghers's husband László Radványi, who in this way wanted to continue the kinds of public lectures he had organized at the Berlin MASCH in the late 1920s.[17] As yet we have no evidence of further personal contact between Seghers and Benjamin during this time. We only know that during Benjamin's visit to Svendborg in the summer of 1938 he and Brecht discussed Seghers's *The Most Splendid Tales of Woynok the Brigand,* which had just appeared in *Das Wort,* and that Benjamin considered this particular conversation significant enough to record in his own notes.[18]

By this time Seghers was at work on *The Seventh Cross,* a novel about the underground resistance in Germany. On 23 September 1938 she wrote to Ivan I. Anissimov, director of the Gorky Institute for World Literature in Moscow, describing her novel in terms of the more or less acceptable tenets of realism: "I'm going to finish a small novel of about 200 or 300 pages based on a circumstance that took place in Germany a short time ago. In other words, a plot that allows one to become familiar with many strata within fascist Germany by way of events surrounding a single individual."[19] Her attempts to have the novel published in an exile press failed due to the rapidly changing circumstances in Europe, and by the beginning of 1940 she had sent copies of the manuscript overseas in hope of publication in the United States. On 25 January 1940, that is, several months after the Hitler-Stalin pact and the invasion of Poland, she wrote the publisher Wieland Herzfelde, who had escaped from Prague to New York (where he traded in stamps before he could establish the German-language Aurora Verlag): "I implore you, do your best for the novel. I would be very glad if the first chapter could be published in a newspaper or journal."[20] On 9 May 1940 she wrote again to Herzfelde: "As you know, I've still had no luck with the 'Seventh Cross.' . . . I don't need to tell you why of all my books I'm so attached to the topic and work involved in this one, because I want it to show . . . this particular phase of our story."[21] In another passage in the same letter she described, in a deliberately casual, encoded epistolary style, her ever more critical personal situation as she and her children awaited the German invasion of Paris:

> I've wanted to write you for a long time but found neither the outer nor the so-called inner peace. As you know, with us [like Seghers, Herzfelde was a communist and a Jew] there is always something new, and I tend to alleviate only half of all the confusion by writing; the other half I keep to myself in order not to drive our friends [the Communist Party] to sheer madness. For example, I recently got the small piece of news that since the death of my father [March 1940] there has been pressure on my mother to move from where she is [in a Mainz

Judenhaus] to Shanghai, only because a quota happened not to have been filled there—I'm still trying to crack this strange nut. About my husband you know [interned in the French concentration camp at Le Vernet].[22]

Benjamin was also trapped in Paris in the winter of 1939–40 and during this time wrote his last major work, "Über den Begriff der Geschichte" (On the Concept of History), also known as "Theses on the Philosophy of History." Its decidedly tongue-in-cheek equivalent, written in chronicle form and authored by the inveterate storyteller Seghers, is "Reise ins elfte Reich" (Journey into the Eleventh Realm). Suggestive of Dante and Kafka, the narrative is a satirical commentary on the diminishing possibilities of escape from the current inferno of history. It can be assumed that Benjamin read Seghers's text when it appeared in early 1939 in *Die neue Weltbühne,* the same journal in which one year earlier Benjamin had published his review of her novel *The Rescue.*

More importantly, I am persuaded that Benjamin read the first chapters of *The Seventh Cross,* which would have been available to him in their serial publication in the summer of 1939 in the June, July, and August issues of *Internationale Literatur.*[23] Further serial publication of this antifascist novel was terminated in the wake of the Hitler-Stalin pact and dual invasion of Poland. As indicated by Seghers in a letter of 1 September 1939 to Wieland Herzfelde—"I've had very good responses from all sides"[24]—these first chapters of her novel found resonance within the exile community. Benjamin in particular would have been interested in the mythic dimension that dominates the novel's beginning: the introductory frame, informed by Jewish mysticism, where concentration camp prisoners huddle around the "blue flames" and "sparks" of a fire in which the wood from "seven crosses" burns; and the first chapter's famous opening scene, where the shepherd stands on the Taunus northwest of Frankfurt marking the site of the Roman *limes,* while myth and history unfold in the Rhine valley that lies before him. Not insignificantly, both Seghers and Benjamin had their ancestral roots in this area rich in Jewish tradition.

These scenes, then, drawn by a chronicler and storyteller and evoking both personal and historical images of an at once remote and immediate past, offered Benjamin a vivid prose tapestry upon and against which to write his own philosophical-allegorical meditations in the winter of 1939–40. A comparison between the first chapter of Seghers's *The Seventh Cross* and Benjamin's "On the Concept of History" suggests myriad possibilities of intertextual interpretation. Particularly striking, as if written in direct response to the relevant passage in Seghers's chapter, is a note by Benjamin from this time that is not incorporated into the standard editions of "On the Concept of History": "Redemption is the *limes* of progress."[25]

Indicating an awareness of history as domination and oppression, the memory of the Roman *limes* dominates the pictorial sweep of Seghers's narration as the panorama of the Rhineland unfolds in the first chapter of *The Seventh Cross.* In the tradition of expressionist prose, time is suspended as the eye of the moment holds the turbulent legacies of past and present generations. The moment is announced by the lone figure of a worker cycling at dawn on the lower Taunus range as he begins his long ride down to the factory in Hoechst outside Frankfurt. This image is held in check by the gaze of a young shepherd who stands on his high place with a fiery red cloth tied round his neck, surveying the hills around him "as if he were watching an army, not merely a flock of sheep."[26] The shepherd's gaze brings to view, as if through the eye of a painter's memory, the vestiges of the past embedded in the surrounding terrain:

> This is the land of which it is said that the last war's projectiles plow from the ground the projectiles of the war before the last. These hills are no chains of mountains. A child can have coffee and cake with relatives on the farther side and be back home when the evening bells toll. For a long time, though, this chain of hills meant the edge of the world; beyond them lay the wilderness, the unknown country. Along them the Romans drew their *limes.* So many races had perished here since they burned the Celts' sun altars, so many battles had been fought, that the hills themselves might have thought that what was conquerable had finally been fenced and made arable. It was not the eagle, however, nor the cross that the town down below retained in its escutcheon, but the Celtic sunwheel—the sun that ripens Marnet's apples. Here camped the legions, and with them all the gods of the world; city gods and peasant gods, the gods of Jew and Gentile, Astarte and Isis, Mithras and Orpheus.
>
> Here, where now Ernst Schmiedtheim stands by his sheep, one leg forward, one hand on his hip, one end of his shawl sticking straight out as if a little wind were blowing constantly—here the wilderness called. In the valley at his back, in the soft and vaporous sun, stood the peoples' cauldron. North and south, east and west, were brewed together, and while the country as a whole remained unaffected by it all, yet it retained a vestige of everything. Like colored bubbles, empires rose up from that country, rose up and as soon burst again. They left behind no *limes,* no triumphal arches, no military highways; only a few fragments of their women's golden anklets. But they were as hardy and imperishable as dreams. So proudly does the shepherd

stand there and with such complete placidity that one might well think him aware of all that glorious past; or perhaps, though he may be unaware of it, it is because of it all that he stands thus. There, where the main road joins the motor highway, the armies of the Franks were assembled when a crossing of the Main was attempted. Here the monk came riding up, between the Mangold and Marnet farms, proceeding into the utter wilderness which from here no one had entered before—a slender man on a little donkey, his chest protected by the armor of Faith, his loins girded with the sword of Salvation. He was the bearer of the Gospels—and of the art of inoculating apples. (*SC,* 6–7)

Through the mythic eye of the shepherd we are shown the place at which past and present, archaic time and memory, converge. The writer Carl Zuckmayer, who, like Seghers, was a native of Mainz, wrote of this scene: "Here the Rhine valley, the undulating land between Worms and Mainz, unveils a landscape imbued by history and a European worldview. . . . Here stands the shepherd at the edge of the Taunus range, as if drawn by Dürer."[27] But this first section of the novel's first chapter also bears vestiges of a more deeply buried and, at the time of its writing, more urgent history. For meanwhile the sun is up, and Ernst the shepherd tears the hot red cloth from his neck, throwing it on the stubble field where it lies "like a battle pennant" (*SC,* 7). Thereupon the account of the past resumes with a review of those in Mainz who partook of its wine in the years of the Holy Roman Empire: bishops and landowners who elected the emperor; monks and knights who founded their respective orders; returning crusaders who burned Jews in the town square—"four hundred of them at one time in the square of Mainz which to this day is called the *Brand*" (*SC,* 7). And only a few days before the shepherd Ernst had seen in the distance the fireworks that turned Mainz into a "burning and roaring city beyond the river! Thousands of little swastikas twistedly reflected in the water. Watch the little flames whisk across!" (*SC,* 8).

If the initial image of the worker cycling down to the factory in Hoechst embodies the temporality of the narrative, the shepherd standing at the edge of the Taunus represents the dreamer before whom history unfolds and whose witness he is. The view from this place on high near the Roman *limes* takes us beyond the fortifications of empires, beyond the boundaries of republics and nations, beyond even the "thousand-year Reich." If Seghers's shepherd appeared to Zuckmayer "as if drawn by Dürer," he also recalls the young shepherds of the Old Testament: David the singer-storyteller, whose faith in creation endures, be it in the presence of the giant Goliath or the mad King Saul; or Joseph the dreamer, whose bright coat soaked with animal blood remains as the only visible sign of him after his transport into exile in Egypt. Like the legends of young David and Joseph, Seghers's epic sweep ends abruptly in the perilous immediacy of the present: "Ernst whistled to his little dog which brought him his neckcloth in its teeth. We have now arrived. What happens now is happening to us" (*SC,* 8).

The movement of the narrative takes its cue from the position incorporated by the shepherd: from the place on high where the bold figure surveys the landscape, "one leg forward, one hand on his hip," his fiery neckscarf blowing in the wind, to the final image of a common mortal who whistles to his dog and watches it run toward him with the red scarf clenched between its teeth. Here his, the shepherd's, place is taken by *us.* This place of vulnerability between flesh and blood, life and death, is the *conditio exemplaris* of the storyteller, the locus of immediate danger from which the great stories have always been told, at risk. It is the place of peril from where the vizier's daughter Scheherazade wove her tales of love, adventure, and death, passing narrative responsibility from one teller of tales to the next, as night after night she postponed the displeasure of the king and kept the morrow's executioner at bay. It is a topos of temporary safety and suspended time, the position from which the stories in Boccaccio's *Decameron* are told to pass away the time of waiting, to dispel one's fears so as to make room for tomorrow. And it is the point of experience from where the prophets and chroniclers of old passed on their legends and tales, whether from Baghdad, Jerusalem, Antioch, or Rome. From this position of urgency the subsequent chapters of *The Seventh Cross* concentrate on events in the valley below: the escape of seven inmates from a concentration camp, the recapture and "crucifixion" of six, and the survival of the seventh, who escapes on a Rhine freighter headed for Holland. His "cross" in the camp courtyard remains empty, reminding the witnesses of the continuity of life after all.

The initial scenic presentation of the Rhine valley is also inherently dramatic. Considered in this light, the topographic structuring of the narrative in this part of the novel resembles Nietzsche's description of the scene that lies at the heart of the birth of tragedy: "The form of the Greek theater recalls a lonely valley in the mountains. The architecture of the scene appears like a luminous cloud formation that the Bacchants swarming over the mountains behold from a height."[28] As we first look from on high with the shepherd, we experience what Nietzsche described as "the metaphysical comfort . . . that life is at the bottom of things, despite all the changes of appearances, indestructibly powerful and pleasurable—this comfort appears in incarnate clarity in the chorus of satyrs, a chorus of natural beings who live ineradicably, as it were, behind all civilization and remain eternally the same, despite the changes of generations and of the history of nations" (*BT*, 59). Like Nietzsche's "idyllic shepherd of more recent times," Seghers's shepherd Ernst, too, appears as the "offspring of a longing for the primitive and the natural" (*BT*, 61). This "bold and unshepherd-like rascal," who at night lures "compassionate farmers' daughters" to his hut (*SC*, 6), also incorporates the "*lethargic* element" belonging to the "rapture of the Dionysian state" in which "all personal experiences of the past become immersed" (*BT*, 59). As we look with him into the valley we ourselves become like Nietzsche's "profound Hellene, . . . uniquely susceptible to the tenderest and deepest suffering," who with the chorus of satyrs "comforts himself, having looked boldly right into the terrible destructiveness of so-called world history as well as the cruelty of nature" (*BT*, 59).

But as we approach the end of this first section, the novel retracts its wide-angle lens, and the metaphysically comforting vision of the "satyr chorus" quickly recedes from view. Hurled into the actuality of the present by the piercing whistle of the shepherd and the disturbing image of the little dog carrying the shepherd's red neckcloth in its teeth,[29] we are alerted to the moment's urgency and the mortality of all the players. Here we are no mere spectators gazing at events across the ages, but historical subjects thrust helplessly, as it were, onto the "world of the stage" below. "We have now arrived," we are told abruptly. "What happens now is happening to us." In thus announcing the story that is about to unfold in the valley before us, the narrator offers the reader the very gift the Greek tragedian gave to Nietzsche's "profound Hellene": "Art saves him, and through art—life" (*BT*, 59), albeit the novel is concerned not with catharsis, but redemption.

"Redemption is the *limes* of progress," Benjamin wrote, as already noted, not long after the first chapter of *The Seventh Cross* appeared in print in the summer of 1939.[30] A further echo of Seghers's first chapter with its dual image of the contemporary worker cycling to the factory (Benjamin: to "keep pace with" his own time) and the mythic shepherd surveying the past from on high can be found in another note by Benjamin from this time: "The historian turns his back to his own time, and his prophetic sight is fired by the heights of earlier generations that recede ever more into the past. It is this seer's eye to which one's own time is present far more clearly than it is to those contemporaries who 'keep pace with it' ['mit ihr Schritt halten']."[31] Benjamin's apparent fascination with the uniquely scenic-topographic configurations that characterize the beginning of Seghers's novel gives even stronger evidence of intertextuality. It is evidently the positioning of the narrative perspective alongside the shepherd, or "seer's eye," that allowed Benjamin to identify the historian who "turns his back to his own time" and allows his "prophetic sight" to be "fired by the heights of earlier generations that recede ever more into the past."

Moreover, Benjamin draws attention to the very lines of intersection between past and present around which the external events in the first chapter of Seghers's novel revolve—the "seer's eye" of the shepherd and "those contemporaries who 'keep pace' with" their own time. To be sure, Seghers's chapter opens not with "prophetic sight," but with the image of a young worker cycling down the slopes of the Taunus to the factory below in Hoechst: "Early in October, a few minutes before his usual time, Franz Marnet started on his bicycle from his uncle's farm in the township of Schmiedtheim in the Lower Taunus" (*SC,* 4). In spatial terms, the cyclist comes into view at several points as the shepherd surveys the landscape from his own high place. In temporal terms, the cyclist's downhill journey lasts about as long as it takes the shepherd's "prophetic eye" to summon the images of the past. We can assume that the cyclist has reached his destination at the factory in Hoechst at the same time that the text segment concludes with the words: "We have now arrived. What happens now is happening to us" (*SC,* 8). In juxtaposing the moving figure of the worker and the stationary shepherd on his high place, Seghers's narrative exemplifies the distinction between, as well as the intersection of, the making of history, that is, the trajectory of *homo faber* who in Benjamin's words "keeps pace with" his time, and by contrast the "seer's eye" of the historian or chronicler whose "prophetic sight is fired by the heights of earlier generations."

The posthumously published version of Benjamin's "On the Concept of History," to which the working notes cited above belong, bears further evidence of intertextualities. Like the author Seghers writing *The Seventh Cross,* Benjamin wrote from the point of view of one banished and exiled: "The true picture of the past flits by. The past can be seized only as an image which flashes up at the instant when it can be recognized and is never seen again."[32] As if in reference to the historical survey in Seghers's first chapter, which ends abruptly in the subjective immediacy of the present with the lines "We have now arrived. What happens now is happening to us" (*SC,* 8), Benjamin's sixteenth thesis contends: "A historical materialist cannot do without the notion of a present which is not a transition, but in which time stands still and has come to a stop. For this notion defines the present in which he himself is writing history. Historicism gives the 'eternal' image of the past; historical materialism supplies a unique experience with the past" (*CH,* 262). Reminding us of Seghers's account of empires that "rose up" like "colored bubbles" and "as soon burst again," leaving behind "no *limes,* no triumphal arches, no military highways; only a few fragments of their women's golden anklets" (*SC*, 7), Benjamin's third thesis suggests that "a chronicler who recites events without distinguishing between major and minor ones acts in accordance with the following truth: nothing that has ever happened should be regarded as lost for history" (*CH*, 254).

Benjamin's seventh thesis articulates in discursive form what Seghers's text expresses in the sequencing of images, among them "the monk proceeding into the utter wilderness" ("he was the bearer of the Gospels—and of the art of inoculating apples") and the four hundred Jews burned by crusaders "at one time in the square of Mainz which to this day is called the *Brand*" (*SC*, 7). In Benjamin's words: "Whoever has emerged victorious participates to this day in the triumphal procession in which the present rulers step over those who are lying prostrate. . . . There is no document of civilization which is not at the same time a document of barbarism" (*CH*, 256). The account of the past in Seghers's text is cut off by the realization: "We have now arrived. What happens now is happening to us" (*SC*, 8). Again, as if in response, Benjamin observes in his sixth thesis: "To articulate the past historically . . . means to seize hold of a memory as it flashes up at a moment of danger" (*CH*, 255). The subsequent sections of Seghers's novel belonging to its first two chapters, which Benjamin must also have read, give ample evidence of his argument in his eighth thesis that "the 'state of emergency' in which we live is not the exception but the rule" (*CH*, 257).

The shepherd Ernst's confident stance—"one leg forward, one hand on his hip" (*SC*, 6)—seems to disguise this "state of emergency." Yet Seghers's narrator alerts us to the fiery red cloth that is first tied around the shepherd's neck, then thrown on the ground like a "battle pennant" (*SC*, 7), and finally returned to him in the "teeth" of his "little dog" (*SC*, 8). This visual sign evoking what Benjamin preferred to call "shock" (*CH*, 262) counterpoints images of "little flames whisk[ing] across" the Rhine, of a once "burning and roaring city," of Jews burned by Christians—"four hundred of them at one time in the square of Mainz which to this day is called the *Brand*" (*SC*, 7). As to the mythic shepherd standing on high, Benjamin found an analogous figure in Paul Klee's painting *Angelus Novus*. Klee's angel also has his face "turned toward the past," which piles "wreckage upon wreckage and hurls it in front of his feet" (*CH*, 257). Seghers's shepherd is too "proud," too "placid" to appear as if he "would like to stay, awaken the dead, and make whole what has been smashed" (*CH*, 257). Yet as we look over his shoulder across the ages we, too, sense what Benjamin calls a storm "blowing from Paradise . . . while the pile of debris before him grows skyward" (*CH*, 258–59).

The storyteller and chronicler Seghers, like Benjamin's "historian," does not convey "the sequence of events like the beads of a rosary" but "establishes a conception of the present as the 'time of the now' which is shot through with chips of Messianic time" (*CH,* 263). Whereas the beginning of the first chapter of Seghers's novel establishes the intersections of time and space, present moment and mythic past (the worker cycling downhill past the shepherd rooted on his high place), the "chips of Messianic time" belong to a separate narrative thread that frames the novel at its beginning and end—the subterranean knowledge and memory of concentration camp prisoners huddled in a barrack around a fire. These prisoners are the witnesses who will remember the escape of their seven comrades, the recapture and "crucifixion" of six, and the successful flight of one whose "cross" remains empty.

If the scene on the Taunus where the Romans built their *limes* surveys what Benjamin's essay calls the "wreckage" of the past, the narrative frame at the beginning of the novel presents the very ground of immediate danger imbued by an eschatological dimension, or, in Benjamin's words, the "'time of the now' . . . shot through with chips of Messianic time." Suggestive of ancient caves in which succeeding generations of rebels tried to survive foreign armies, the dark barrack housing the prisoners is warmed by a fire made from seven "crosses" cut up into kindling wood. This "small triumph" belongs to those who witness events invisible to the ordinary world outside the camp. It is the mystical triumph of light and the myth of redemption assuring that, in Benjamin's words, "nothing that has ever happened should be regarded as lost for history" (*CH,* 254). Or, in the words used by Seghers at the beginning of the narrative frame that introduces her novel:

> Never perhaps in man's memory were stranger trees felled than the seven plane trees growing the length of Barrack III. Their tops had been clipped before, for a reason that will be explained later. Crossboards had been nailed to the trunks at the height of a man's shoulder, so that at a distance the trees resembled seven crosses. The camp's new commander, Sommerfeld by name, immediately ordered everything to be cut up into kindling wood. . . . A small triumph . . . which suddenly made us conscious of our own power, that power we had for a long time permitted ourselves to regard as being merely one of the earth's common forces, reckoned in measures and numbers, though it is the only force able suddenly to grow immeasurable and incalculable. . . . The billets crackled. Two little flames appeared—the coal had caught fire. . . . We only thought of the wood burning before our eyes. Softly, with an oblique look toward the guard and without moving his lips, Hans said: "Crackling!" Erwin said: "The seventh

one!" On every face there was a faint strange smile, a mixture of heterogeneous elements, of hope and scorn, of helplessness and daring. We held our breaths. The rain beat fitfully against the boards and the tin roof. Erich, the youngest of us, glanced out of the corners of his eyes, in which were merged his own inmost thoughts as well as ours, and said: "Where is he now, I wonder!" (*SC,* 3–4)

The text brings to mind crucifixions over the centuries as well as the "sparks" and messianic longings of the Kabbalists. As Gershom Scholem wrote of "the great mythos of exile and redemption which is the Lurianic Kabbalah": "'Sparks' of the divine life and light were scattered in exile over the entire world, and they long through the actions of man to be 'lifted up' and restored to their original place in the divine harmony of all being."[33] Raised in the Jewish faith and acquainted with Kabbalist traditions, Seghers knew as well as Benjamin that, in his words, "the past carries with it a temporal index by which it is referred to redemption," that "a secret agreement" exists "between past generations and the present one," that "our coming was expected on earth," that "like every generation that preceded us, we have been endowed with a *weak* Messianic power, a power to which the past has a claim. That claim cannot be settled cheaply" (*CH,* 254). This "*weak* Messianic power" is embodied in *The Seventh Cross* by Ernst Wallau, leader of the group that attempts escape, after he is recaptured and returned to the camp. Tied to one of the hastily erected crosses in the courtyard as an example to his fellow prisoners, he awaits death at the hands of the camp's brutal SA troop leader. Seghers's portrait of Wallau in his last hour is informed by the iconography of the suffering Christ as well as by the Kabbalist myth of the "travail of the Messiah," or, in Scholem's words, "those disasters and frightful afflictions which would terminate history and usher in the redemption":[34]

> Covered with blood, Wallau was sitting propped against the wall. From the door, Zillich looked over at him calmly. A faint light over his shoulder, a tiny blue corner of autumn, told Wallau for the last time that the structure of the world held firm and would continue to hold firm regardless of what struggles might come. For a moment Zillich stood rigid. Never before had anybody awaited him with so much calm, with so much dignity. "This is death," thought Wallau. Slowly Zillich pulled the door shut behind him.[35] (*SC,* 288)

The cross in Seghers's novel is not a symbol of salvation, but a vehicle of administrative power, reminiscent of hastily erected tree-crosses used by the Romans, singly and in mass executions, over the centuries. Only the cross that remains empty, the seventh cross, gives hope to the survivors. The collective memory of this one *empty* cross represents the victory of life over death, however slight, among the witnesses huddled around the sparks of a fire. It is this mythic-redemptive frame to which the novel, after having erupted into the harsh light of the Rhineland countryside, returns at its end: "The last little spark in the stove had gone out. We had a foreboding of the nights that were in store for us. The damp autumn cold struck through our covers, our shirts, and our skin. All of us felt how ruthlessly and fearfully outward powers could strike to the very core of man, but at the same time we felt that at the very core there was something that was unassailable and inviolable" (*SC,* 338).

The main protagonist of *The Seventh Cross* escapes from Germany on a Rhine freighter bound for Holland. He is brought to this point by members of the organized resistance willing to risk their lives for this "small triumph," as well as by an entire palette of characters who unwittingly display the "unassailable and inviolable" qualities that abet his chances for survival—a young gardener's apprentice who surrenders his jacket; a Jewish physician who treats the wounded man despite the dangers of his action; a carnival seamstress who gives him a change of clothes and money; a cathedral priest who burns the evidence of the man's camp clothes rather than letting the sexton hand it to the police; a group of boys on an outing with whom he can cross the Rhine undetected on a ferry; a young waitress who takes him in for a night. The protagonist himself is less a determined hero than a channel through which the myriad fragments of humanity as yet unclaimed by National Socialism can assert themselves. On the day before his departure he stands on the right bank of the Rhine River where it is met by the Main. From this point he looks across at the city of Mainz, his eye guided by the memory of the author who already as a child was familiar with its architectural detail:

> The Rhine lay before him, and beyond it the city through which he had scurried a few days ago. Its streets and squares, witnesses of his agony, were fused into one great fortress that was reflected in the river. A flock of birds, flying in a sharply pointed black triangle, was etched into the reddish afternoon sky between the city's tallest spires, making a picture that resembled a city's seal. Presently, on the roof of the cathedral, between two of these spires, George made out the figure of Saint Martin bending down from his horse to share his cloak with the beggar who was to appear to him in a dream: "I am he whom thou pursuest." (*SC,* 331)

The next day Georg Heisler embarks on his voyage to Holland only a short distance upstream from where the street of the author's childhood home, the Kaiserstraße, meets the Rhine. From here she often traveled to Holland, whose waterways and crowded cities had long embraced refugees. The waters of the Rhine might one day meet the waters of the Styx. But the man who leaves behind one empty cross is greeted by a figure that gives only the hint of a resemblance with the ferryman of that legendary river:

> George reached the Kastella bridgehead. The guard challenged him, and he showed his passport. . . . Looking down, he saw his tugboat, the *Wilhelmine,* with her green load line mirrored in the water. She lay quite near the bridgehead, unfortunately not touching the bank but alongside another vessel. George was less concerned about the guard at the Mainz bridgehead than about how he would get across the strange boat. He need not have worried. He was still twenty paces away from the landing place when the globular, almost neckless head of a man popped over the *Wilhelmine's* gunwale. George had obviously been expected by the man with the round, fattish face, whose wide nostrils and deep-set eyes gave it a rather sinister look. It was precisely the right kind of face for an upright man who was willing to run considerable risk. (*SC,* 337)

❖

If one were to navigate through the mythic waters of Seghers's prose in terms of her biographical journey, one might begin by plotting a curve across Europe from west to east. Marking the early influence of Jewish history and the heritage of the Enlightenment, this curve would originate in the topography of the Rhineland and Seghers's native Mainz. From there it would move north down the Rhine to the expansive landscapes and seascapes of Holland, which Seghers knew from Dutch painting and from her travels as a child; and it would encircle the city of Amsterdam, safe harbor for refugees over the centuries. From here the curve would move southeastward to the Danube and Tisza Rivers and across the Carpathian Mountains of pre-1919 Hungary, which Seghers knew by way of her husband László Radványi and the Budapest Sunday Circle. Then, marking her escape from Germany in 1933, and in 1941 from the continent of Europe, the curve would turn westward across Europe to France and to the edge of the Mediterranean, from where it would reach across the Atlantic to the Caribbean Sea.

This final expanse, conjuring up the age-old image of the journey into the diaspora, informs the mythic trajectory underlying Seghers's novel *Transit*. She began writing the novel aboard the *Capitain Paul Lemerle,* one of the last transport ships to leave Marseille before the Germans closed the harbor. Departing in March of 1941, the ship carried refugees across the Mediterranean with stops in the ports of Oran and Casablanca. From there it crossed the Atlantic to Martinique, where passengers remained in detention camps until they could board a ship bound for a destination for which they held entry visas. Among the passengers of the *Capitain Paul Lemerle* was Claude Lévi-Strauss, who described the ship's departure from Marseille in his memoir *Tristes Tropiques:*

> We went on board between two rows of helmeted *gardes mobiles* with sten guns in their hands, who cordoned off the quayside, preventing all contact between the passengers and their relatives or friends who had come to say goodbye, and interrupting leave-taking with jostling and insults. Far from being a solitary adventure, it was more like the deportation of convicts. What amazed me even more than the way we were treated was the number of passengers. About 350 passengers were crammed on to a small steamer, . . . men, women and children, were herded into the hold, with neither air nor light, and where the ship's carpenters had hastily run up bunk beds with straw mattresses. . . . The riff-raff, as the gendarmes called them, included, among others, André Breton and Victor Serge.[36]

Whereas she also writes from the perspective of an anthropologist, Seghers's novel contextualizes the desperate flight of Europeans driven to the edge of the Mediterranean in 1940–41 in historic-mythic terms. Here the tedious searching and waiting for visas and transit permits is suspended in time as the first-person narrator contemplates the Old Harbor of Marseille:

> The part of the café where we were sitting was next to the Cannebière. I could look out over the Old Harbor. A small gunboat lay near the Quai des Belges. Its gray funnels, visible beyond the street between the masts of the fishing boats, towered over the heads of the people who filled the café with their smoke and gossip. Was the mistral blowing again? The women going by had pulled up their capotes. The faces of the men who came through the revolving doors were tense with the wind and their own restlessness. Not a soul paid any attention to the sun above us, to the pinnacles of St. Victor's Church,

or to the fishing nets spread out along the length of the mole to dry. Everybody rattled on and on about transit permits, invalidated pass-ports, the three-mile zone, dollar quotations, exit visas; they always came back to transit permits. I was on the point of getting out of the place. The talk made me sick at my stomach.

Suddenly my mood changed. Why? I never know what it is that makes me change so suddenly. All at once that chatter ceased to be nauseating; it filled me with wonder. It was age-old harbor gossip, as old as the Old Harbor itself, even older. Wonderful old harbor gossip that has gone on as long as there has been a Mediterranean Sea! Phoenician gossip, Candian gossip, Greek gossip, and Roman gossip. The place had never lacked gossipers, worrying about ship accommo-dations and funds, fleeing from every real and imagined terror in the world! Mothers who had lost their children, children who had lost their mothers. Remnants of armies that had been cut to pieces, fleeing slaves, hordes of people put out of their own countries who finally got to the harbor where they madly boarded ships that would take them to a new country which they'd be put out of again! Ships must always have lain at anchor here, in this harbor, because this was the edge of Europe and the beginning of the sea. A shelter for travelers must always have stood here, because a highroad ended at the shore. I felt a thousand years old because I'd lived through all this before; and I felt wonderfully young, eager for everything that would happen in the future—I felt immortal!

But my mood soon changed once more; it was too strong for any-one as weak as I. Despair swept over me—despair and homesickness. I grieved over the twenty-seven years that I'd frittered away in foreign countries. . . . O deadly gossip. . . . The sun was going down behind Fort Saint-Nicolas.[37]

The narrator's view of the Old Harbor from a window of one of Mar-seille's many harbor cafés recalls Seghers's own experience in the winter of 1940–41. Like thousands of other refugees in Marseille, she spent her days in the anxious pursuit of visas and transit permits for herself and her two children and, with greater difficulty, for her husband László Radványi, who was interned in the concentration camp at Le Vernet, and briefly at Les Milles, until the family's departure in March of 1941.[38] The numbers of suicides by those who feared being held in Le Vernet or similar camps, from where Jews without travel permits were increasingly handed over to the Germans and transported to camps in the east, include those of the writers Walter Hasenclever, Ernst Weiss, Carl Einstein, and, on 26 Sep-tember 1940, Walter Benjamin. In May of 1940 Benjamin had fled ahead of the German army from Paris to Lourdes, where he spent the summer.

In late August he traveled on to Marseille, where an entry visa for the United States awaited him at the U.S. consulate. In Marseille he tried to obtain the remaining papers required for his departure. When after several weeks this prospect seemed hopeless to him, he decided to cross illegally into Spain and flee across the Pyrenees to Lisbon. His Spanish transit visa was deemed invalid by the authorities, and he was forced to return to the border town of Port Bou on 26 September. That night he died from an overdose of the morphine tablets he had long carried with him.[39]

In the same month Seghers and her two children—Peter, fourteen, and Ruth, twelve—were able to slip illegally across the demarcation line that separated occupied France from the so-called free zone in the south. Their first attempt to flee to the south in June had been abortive, and they were forced to return to German-occupied Paris, where they remained in hiding throughout the summer.[40] It was during this time that Seghers learned of the suicide in June of Ernst Weiss, the writer on whom she modeled the figure of the dead author Weidel in *Transit*. The news of Benjamin's suicide reached her in October or November when she was living in Pamiers near Le Vernet, from where she traveled regularly to Marseille to obtain the required papers for her family's departure. On 23 November she wrote from Pamiers to F. C. Weiskopf in New York:

> I can't describe our life to you. Dante, Dostoyevsky, Kafka, those were bagatelles! Small inconveniences that soon passed. This is serious. And what's funniest is that one does everyday things. The children are in school, I'm concocting a strange soup for the three of us and 2 newcomers. For example, we've just learned that [Walter] Benjamin committed suicide at the border because he couldn't travel through Spain. When you think of what an odd bird ["kauzig"] he always was. What good fortune did he expect from a transit via Spain? In Paris I went to [Ernst] Weiss's hotel, asked if he was in, and was told he'd been evacuated. Later it turned out he'd committed suicide.[41]

Expanding on the theme of this letter of November 1940, her novel *Transit* alludes with even greater incredulity to the disappointed hopes of "good fortune" behind Benjamin's suicide in Port Bou:

> I sat down in the glass-enclosed veranda of the Café Rotonde on the other side of the Cours Belsunce. Involuntarily I overheard the conversation at the next table. A man had shot himself during the night at a hotel in Portbou, across the Spanish border, because the authorities were going to send him back to France the next morning. My neighbors, two middle-aged, sickly-looking women—one of them

had a little boy with her, probably her grandson, who was listening avidly—added details to the story in animated voices. The whole event was much clearer to them than it was to me, much more plausible. What boundless hopes had that man had for his goal, to make the return unbearable to him? The country in which we were all still marooned and to which he was to have been forcibly returned must have seemed hellishly uninhabitable to him. Occasionally you hear of people who prefer death to loss of liberty. But had that man actually gained liberty? If you could know the answer! A single shot, a single blow against the thin, narrow door above your eyes, and you'd be home and welcome forever.[42] (*T,* 217)

Transit both carries forward and recasts the thematic that informs the compositional structure of Seghers's earlier novel. Whereas *The Seventh Cross* posits its ideational thematic in terms of martyrdom and freedom— six "crucifixions" versus the seventh empty cross—the field of possibilities presented in *Transit* is reduced to a choice between suicide and a life without "liberty" informed by defeat. Within the parameters of this choice there is little sign even of that "*weak* Messianic power" noted by Benjamin in his "On the Concept of History" (*CH,* 254) and witnessed by camp prisoners around the sparks of a fire in the frame narrative of *The Seventh Cross.* Instead, *Transit* offers the hope of redemption in the active remembrance of the dead informed, in Benjamin's words, by the "secret agreement . . . between past generations and the present one" (*CH,* 254).

This "secret agreement" is embodied in the relationship between the first-person narrator, whose "real" name we never learn, and the dead writer Weidel, whose identity he assumes and gradually accepts as part of his own. The circumstances of the writer Weidel's suicide in the novel are based not on Benjamin's suicide in Port Bou, but on the second suicide mentioned by Seghers in her letter of November 1940 to F. C. Weiskopf in New York—that of the Prague writer Ernst Weiss. There are a number of reasons why Seghers would have modeled the figure of Weidel on Weiss instead of Benjamin, to whom she in fact was closer in terms of education and background. Like Seghers, Benjamin came from an upper-middle-class assimilated German-Jewish family whose familial roots were in the Rhineland.[43] By contrast, Ernst Weiss was culturally East Central European and would have represented for Seghers the legacy of East European Jewry that she first found in Rembrandt's depictions of Christ and in the "Carpathian" heritage of the Budapest Sunday Circle that she thematized in her work. Moreover, Weiss wrote fiction rather than essays and was a friend and contemporary of Franz Kafka, by whom Seghers was decisively influenced. The particular language, poetic intensity, and moral fervor of his writings must have struck her as being more vulnerable to the impact of fascism on European Jewry than the theoretical writings of Benjamin, whom she remembered as being "an odd bird." In basing the circumstances of Weidel's suicide in a Paris hotel room on that of Weiss, and describing the unfinished manuscript in his suitcase in terms of the themes and style of Weiss's own writing, Seghers evidently wanted to memorialize a larger Ashkenazic tradition of Jewish life and writing that was most urgently under the threat of extinction.[44]

The figure and significance of Weidel may also have had familial import. Seghers's father Isidor Reiling died in March of 1940 only days after being forced to relinquish the art and antiquities firm he and his brother Hermann had inherited from their own father and turned into one of the most successful art dealerships in the Rhineland. Meanwhile her mother, for whom she desperately tried to obtain visas from France, and later from Mexico, was forced to reside in several of Mainz's *Judenhäuser* until her deportation to the Piaski ghetto near Lublin in 1942.[45] In this respect the story of the writer Weidel, whose language and legacy the first-person narrator preserves, and of Weidel's widow Marie, who searches eternally for him, is not only the story of exiled writers and intellectuals like Weiss and Benjamin but suggests the larger, both personal and historical tragedy of European Jewry at this time.

In *The Seventh Cross* "this particular phase of our story," as Seghers phrased it in her letter to Wieland Herzfelde in May of 1940,[46] involves the escape of one, the martyrdom of six, and the subterranean survival of a few witnesses whose fate remains undecided. By May of 1940 the events of the war belonging to the next phase of "our story" had already begun, as later chronicled by the author in *Transit*. Here "our story" is more obviously, if not explicitly, a Jewish story. It relates tales of suicides, presages deaths in ghettos and concentration camps, records the desperate flight of survivors to safety across the seas in pursuit of a new life, and reminds us of those, exemplified by the first-person narrator, who opted to remain behind on the continent of Europe to continue the work of the resistance.[47]

The protagonist's perilous journey in *Transit* continues on another track the story of Georg Heisler's flight in *The Seventh Cross:* a young worker escapes from a German concentration camp in 1937, swims across the Rhine, escapes via the Saar to France, is interned in a French camp after the outbreak of the war, flees from there to occupied Paris and from there to the unoccupied south of France, and, upon finally obtaining transit papers in Marseille, decides to remain on the continent of Europe after all. The structuring of the mythic topography, however, is fundamentally different. Whereas *The Seventh Cross* only hints at the existence of a diasporic landscape stretching beneath and across the topographical layers of empires and nations, the definitive landscape in *Transit* is the threatening prospect of the diaspora itself. Or, put differently, the familiar undulating landscapes of the Rhineland give way to the topography of the unknown, and the limitless possibilities of death, at the edge of the Mediterranean Sea.

Here, as compared with the end of *The Seventh Cross,* there is no familiar medieval city and river, no comforting beacon or captain of a ship, no memory of home or promise of arrival on a welcoming shore. There are only the stark outlines of a Mediterranean harbor and the at once strange and familiar land- and seascapes signaling the diaspora. But *Transit* does provide the reader with an epistemological and ultimately active choice, as exemplified by the narrator's offer to his listener as he begins his story in the harbor café: "Which view do you prefer? The *pizza* baking over the open fire? Then you'll have to sit beside me. The Old Harbor? Then you'd better sit opposite. You can see the sun go down behind Fort Saint-Nicolas. That won't bore you, I'm sure" (*T,* 3). These two perspectives, the look inward toward the fire and the wide-ranging panoramic spectrum, are analogous to the mythic trajectories represented in *The Seventh Cross:* on the one hand the redemptive traditions of Jewish mysticism and messianism belonging to the prisoners huddled in a barrack around a fire in the novel's frame; on the other hand the epic-pictorial sweep before the "seer's eye" of the shepherd standing on the lower Taunus range. The first-person narrator's desire in *Transit* to look into the fire to the very end of his story ("All I can see is the open fire which I never grow tired of watching" [*T,* 312]) signifies his decision to remain on the continent of Europe to redeem the dead: "Grief for the dead man whom I'd never known swept over me. We were staying behind together, he and I. And there was nobody to mourn him in that country shaken by war and betrayal, nobody to do him the final honors, as they say, but myself, seated in a café, near the Old Harbor" (*T,* 304). In having her protagonist remain before the "open fire," Seghers had him assume the place of the rebels and prophets of antiquity—Isaiah, Jeremiah, the Maccabees, the Essenes, John the Baptist, Jesus the Nazarene and his disciples, and the participants in the rebellions leading up to the Roman destruction of the Temple in the year 70.

The author's own historical place as a chronicler would be a different one. Unlike Walter Benjamin and Ernst Weiss, Seghers survived the Holocaust by embarking on a voyage that took her far beyond even the second view from the Old Harbor at the edge of the Mediterranean. In this sense her novel *Transit,* which she began writing aboard ship and completed in Mexico, is a diasporic work. It is the work of a survivor who no longer looks into the "open fire" with her narrator, nor through the "seer's eye" as in *The Seventh Cross,* but as a chronicler writes testimony offered to the memory of the dead. The topographic situation from which Seghers wrote her novel thus calls to mind the writings of the controversial first-century chronicler Josephus Flavius, who was one of the more fortunate survivors of the rebellions of 66–69. As is well known, Josephus recorded the turbulent events of his time in *The Jewish War* (circa 75 A.D.) on the basis of his firsthand experience in Palestine, but from a privileged position of safety and security in Rome.

Josephus, who came from a distinguished priestly family, was born in Palestine in the year 37, attended a rabbinic school in Jerusalem, and after spending three years in the desert with the Essenes made the decision to become a Pharisee. As a young man he went on a diplomatic mission to Rome and gained the favor of, among others, Nero's wife the Empress Poppaea. On his return to Palestine he attempted to prevent the rebellion of 66, which he argued would be quickly crushed by the military superiority of Rome. Branded as a traitor, he allied himself with the moderate peace party and, when all parties became embroiled in the conflict, was assigned the position of military commander in the northern province of Galilee. During the first Roman attack his army abandoned him, and he retreated to a stronghold with forty remaining men. Wanting to prevent a mass suicide, Josephus tried to persuade his men to accept the terms of defeat, but when he understood "they had long ago devoted themselves to death,"[48] and he himself felt threatened by their swords, he persuaded them to draw lots and kill each other one by one. He himself was able to draw the last lot, so he tells us in his account, sparing the life of the man with the lot next to his. After his surrender he prophesied that Vespasian would become the next emperor and thereby gained the commander's favor. He spent the rest of the war with the Roman forces and thus became even more "an object of the gravest suspicion to his own people."[49] When Vespasian became emperor he liberated Josephus and awarded him his family name Flavius as well as an estate, Roman citizenship, and a lifelong pension. Josephus spent the remainder of his life in Rome, devoting himself to writing the chronicles that to this day represent some of the most valuable, if not altogether accurate, accounts of the history and lives of the Jewish people from their beginnings to the first century of the new era.[50]

There is just the hint of a reference to the legacy of Josephus at the beginning of *Transit* in the narrator's rather obscure acknowledgment of his sense of shame: "I used to get implicated in things which today I'm ashamed of. Just a little ashamed, you understand, for that's all past and gone. But it would bother me no end if I bored anyone. . . . All the same, I want to tell you my story" (*T,* 5). The story that he thereupon relates, and that constitutes virtually the entire novel, thus takes on the character of the testimony of a witness. The narrator's admission of his shame comes at the end of the novel's short introductory chapter and thus parallels the comments made by Josephus in his preface to *The Jewish War*. Here, telling his story in Greek to the gentile world, Josephus alluded to his dubious history as a survivor: "I myself, Josephus, son of Matthias, am a Hebrew by race, and a priest from Jerusalem; in the early stages I fought against the Romans, and of the later events I was an unwilling witness."[51] And, like the narrator of *Transit* in the passage quoted above, Josephus ended his prefatory remarks with an appeal to his audience: "To those who took part in the war or have ascertained the facts I have left no ground for complaint or criticism; it is for those who love the truth, not those who seek entertainment, that I have written. I will now begin my story where I began my summary."[52] Josephus's episodic style combines what later became the separate talents of the historian and the storyteller, ranging from blunt annalistic reporting to verbatim dialogue and often fantastic digressions into the realms of fable and legend. In *Transit* and elsewhere Seghers for her part also wrote in a deliberately episodic chronicle style that relates events as if to elaborate on aspects of a larger experience that is familiar to some but not all of her implied readers.

At the time of her flight to the "mysterious western hemisphere" in the spring of 1941,[53] Seghers was surely aware that the problematic of her situation, like that of other artists and intellectuals who escaped the Holocaust, came dangerously close to the legacy of Josephus. In this respect Josephus may not have been particularly close to Seghers's heart as she began working on *Transit* on board the *Capitain Paul Lemerle*. Yet he seems to have been on her mind. When her twelve-year-old daughter Ruth asked her to explain to her the meaning of the word *diaspora,* which seemed to be on all passengers' lips, Seghers quickly referred her to "*The Jewish War* by Josephus Flavius."[54] Indeed, the ghost of Josephus Flavius would continue to haunt her after her arrival in the "mysterious western hemisphere." Notwithstanding its tendency toward exaggeration and its meanwhile carefully documented inaccuracies, with *The Jewish War* Josephus "succeeded beyond his wildest dreams" in making "the tragedy of his people known to the gentile world."[55] If we keep this in mind, Seghers's subsequent success in the New World with the American publication of *The Seventh Cross* in 1942 can be seen as being fraught with its own set of contradictions. Published in slightly abridged English translation, the novel was marketed as an adventure thriller and, as a Book of the Month selection, quickly became a best-seller. Thereupon it was serialized nationwide as a comic strip, republished in a special armed forces edition, and turned into a successful Hollywood melodrama with Spencer Tracy, Hume Cronin, and Jessica Tandy in the starring roles. The introductory scene on the Taunus as well as many other scenes were excluded from the film and, needless to say, many more from the comic strip.[56]

But like *The Seventh Cross,* Seghers's *Transit* is undergirded by a mythic dimension that reaches beyond the perspective of historical immediacy represented in Josephus's *The Jewish War.* Containing an eschatological dimension that is also missing in Josephus's other great work, *The Jewish Antiquities,* the mythic aspect in *Transit* is most vividly personified in the figure of Marie, a woman who haunts the pages of the novel with her elusive presence as she becomes enmeshed in the lives of three of the novel's main figures: the writer Weidel, whose widow she is; the narrator, who falls in love with her; and the doctor, with whom she finally departs on the *Montréal.* Reminiscent of the *Capitain Paul Lemerle,* whose passengers included Seghers and Claude Lévi-Strauss, the *Montréal* is the next to last ship to leave Marseille and is headed for Martinique. The novel begins with the narrator's seemingly indifferent account of the news that the *Montréal* "struck a mine" and went down somewhere "between Dakar and Martinique" (*T,* 3). Compared with the fate of other ships, he soberly informs us, "the sinking of the *Montréal* in time of war is only a natural death for a ship" (*T,* 3). But by the time he finishes his story, the *Montréal* appears to the narrator as a ship that "must have sailed centuries ago, a legendary ship, always on her way, timelessly affected by cruising and foundering" (*T,* 311). Its equally legendary personification is the dead Weidel's widow Marie, a character reminiscent of the Trojan Hector's widow Andromache, and in Judeo-Christian tradition the legendary Maria Magdalene, who first discovered the empty tomb and whose soul, according to the legends of the medieval mystics, searches eternally to be reunited with her beloved.[57] Thus, in *Transit,* the narrator's reflections before the "open fire" end not with his own story or Weidel's, but with the restless mythic spirit of Marie:

> Marie—who knows?—may turn up again, just as a miraculous escape makes shipwrecked persons turn up on some coast, or sacrifice and fervent prayer call up the shades of the dead from the lower regions. . . . She is still roaming the streets and squares of the city, the stairways, hotels, cafés, and consulates, looking for her beloved. She is ceaselessly searching not only this city, but all the cities of Europe I know, even the phantasmal cities of foreign continents that have remained unknown to me. I shall sooner grow tired of waiting than she of searching for the undiscoverable dead. (*T,* 312)

Historically and biographically, it was of course Seghers's continued involvement in antifascist politics in Mexico as well as her decision to return to her homeland after the war that set her apart from the legacy of Josephus.[58] But whose memory would accompany her on her return? Her farewell speech in 1946 before the Heinrich Heine Club of Mexico, whose president she was, suggests it was that of her own literary predecessor from the Rhineland. As Seghers observed in her speech in Mexico City, Heine was "the guardian patron of our community in this strange land to which we were driven by our wanderings. . . . Whenever we were overcome by homesickness we let ourselves be comforted by his scoffing sorrow. It told us the same stars will hang suspended like death lanterns over our graves, be they along the Rhine or among palms, even if no one prays a Requiem and no Kadish is said."[59] Although Heine's legacy—incidentally, like that of Ernst Weiss and Walter Benjamin—is that of the émigré who remains forever far from home, in his case "far away in the cemetery of Montmartre in his beloved Paris,"[60] this generation of exiles would nonetheless return to Germany with "the determination to put an end to the *Wintermärchen*," for "the Barbarossa who established himself in the Kyffhäuser" had to be "stamped out," and with him "the goblins that meanwhile had settled in all kinds of brain matter."[61] Not by chance, Seghers carried with her through all the phases of her exile a handwritten letter sent by Heine from Paris to his mother Betty Heine, a letter that her own father, the antiquities dealer Isidor Reiling, gave her as a farewell gift when she fled Germany in 1933. She held on to the document even in 1940 and 1941 when her circumstances in Paris and Marseille led her to relinquish or leave behind other valuables. After her return to Berlin the letter and its original envelope hung in a frame on the wall behind her desk until her death in 1983.[62]

CHAPTER 8

The Show Trials and the Trial of Jeanne d'Arc: Collaboration with Brecht

With Anna you have to know that when you think she's talking to you she's knitting away at the novel she's got tucked away, and way in back in that place where nobody thinks anything's going on, she's working out something theoretical, that's Anna.

—Bertolt Brecht, 1952[1]

This is a deep gash that cuts right into our language, through all our work. I think of everything I still would have wanted to ask him, all the things, too, that I still wanted to tell him.

—Anna Seghers on Brecht's death, 1956[2]

A proof of the superiority of the system was its better literature, Brecht, Seghers, Sholokhov, Mayakovsky.

—Heiner Müller, 1992[3]

It is not uncommon to find the names of Seghers and Brecht listed side by side in reference to their shared dedication to socialist issues and active participation as writers in the international working-class movement. John Willett, writing on Brecht about this aspect of their political kinship, noted that "if there was a sister around, it was Anna Seghers."[4] The names of Brecht and Seghers are also linked by their political critics, who have faulted them over the years for what is seen as their failure to take public stands against Stalinism and the GDR state. The assessment of Manès Sperber, who was close to Seghers in Paris until he left the Communist Party at the time of the Moscow trials, is paradigmatic for the views of Central and East Europeans of his generation who espoused the general principles of Hannah Arendt's totalitarianism theory during the cold war:

Just like Brecht, Anna Seghers championed the working class, but she made common cause with the bureaucracy rather than the prole-

175

tariat—and this at a time when the leadership of the Communist parties became the more tyrannical the more spinelessly they [writers like Seghers and Brecht] subjected themselves to Stalin and his people. . . . Anna Seghers differed from Brecht in that she was in her youth a literary advocate of the exploited and the oppressed, the ordinary people who were invincible in their resistance. Her corruption probably began during the emigration, but it did not become complete until Anna Seghers had returned to Germany and become Ulbricht's poet.[5]

Although Seghers and Brecht are often linked as ideological kin or, as the case may be, political cohorts, there is little mention in the secondary literature of the extent of their personal and working relationship. On the basis of letters and other sources it can be documented as spanning almost three decades till the time of Brecht's death in 1956. Seghers's friendship with Brecht, and with his wife Helene Weigel, began in the early 1930s with their involvement in the Marxist Workers' School in Berlin, known as the MASCH. Weigel taught acting classes at the MASCH; Seghers taught creative writing; Brecht, as is well known, regularly attended MASCH lectures and the classes taught by Karl Korsch; and Seghers's husband László Radványi, alias Johann-Lorenz Schmidt, was director of the MASCH, which became a model for similar schools in other German and European cities.[6] Seghers and her husband are mentioned in the uncertainty of Brecht's first letters in exile as he searched for a place of residence for himself and his family. "I'd like to know how it is on Lake Zurich," he wrote in the spring of 1933 from Lugano, Switzerland, to Helene Weigel in Vienna, where she and the children were staying with her family. "Döblin and Seghers are there and besides it's a German city. Still, I think Lugano is cheaper than a few days in Zurich with a family and no flat, and later on we'd be able to take a trip there with this as a base. . . . Seghers would like to have you in Zurich. If only they at least would come here. Schmidt is no Marx, but even so . . ."[7]

In terms of friendship, Seghers and Weigel were on more intimate terms. In the spring of 1937 Brecht asked Walter Benjamin to see if it was feasible for his wife to stay with Seghers and her family in Bellevue outside Paris during the Paris run of *The Rifles of Señora Carrar,* in which Weigel played the lead.[8] Seghers herself reviewed the production enthusiastically in an essay entitled "Helene Weigel Onstage in Paris," which appeared in the April 1938 issue of *Internationale Literatur.*[9] That she focused her review on Weigel's talents as an actress suggests her efforts on behalf of a woman friend, like herself a thirty-seven-year-old wife and mother of two children. As Brecht scholarship has shown, at this time Weigel was not only undergoing professional hardships in exile but was also having to cope with the two women, Margarete Steffin and Ruth Berlau, that Brecht had brought into the intimate sphere of his personal and working life. Interestingly, Seghers wrote a second essay on Weigel's talents as an actress in 1952, at the very time Weigel and Brecht were again having serious marital difficulties, now because of Brecht's affair with the young Berliner Ensemble actress Käthe Reichel. The friendship and loyalty between Seghers and Weigel, who were born in the same year, 1900, and had similar upper-middle-class Jewish roots, persisted over the years until Weigel's death in 1971.[10]

Seghers's and Brecht's relationship also stood the test of time. Upon learning on 26 June 1943 of Seghers's near-fatal accident in Mexico, Brecht expressed what for his work journal was unusual personal concern: "half past nine in the morning: anna seghers is lying in a coma in a mexican hospital, having been found lying in the street yesterday after being run over, or, as the police are assuming, thrown from a car."[11] Werner Hecht's *Brecht-Chronik* enumerates letters exchanged by Brecht and Seghers during the war that were intercepted by the FBI.[12] On 23 October 1947, having returned to Germany six months earlier, Seghers wrote to Weigel thanking her for her "Wunderpaket," apparently a food parcel sent from California, and complained of how intellectually isolated she felt in Berlin. "The longer I'm here," she wrote, "the more often I've wished that you [Weigel and Brecht] were both here. . . . It is very difficult to find people with whom one can—not only work, I'm not even talking about that—but with whom one can speak normally about work."[13]

One week later, the day after his hearing in Washington before the House Committee on Un-American Activities, Brecht flew to Paris and extended his stay for several days so as to be able to meet with Seghers, who was arriving from Berlin, and to consult with her about the political situation in Germany (just as he was eager to talk with her when he first went into exile in 1933). On 4 November 1947 he recorded in his journal:

> anna seghers, white-haired, but her beautiful face fresh. [she says] berlin is a witches' sabbath where they already need more broomsticks. she is visiting her children who are studying in paris, and she also wants to recuperate. in order to safeguard her mexican passport she is not living in the russian sector, so she does not get the privileges without which it is impossible to work. she wants her books to be read in the non-russian zones too. she seems to be perturbed by the intrigues, suspicion and spying. i encourage her to complete the 100 novellas she promised me 12 years ago.[14]

Following their meeting Brecht wrote to Ruth Berlau that Seghers, who herself shuttled between Berlin and Paris, recommended that "definitely, one must have a place to live outside Germany," and that it was important to "build up a strong group. It's impossible to exist there alone or practically alone."[15]

That Seghers, Brecht, and Weigel also maintained "a strong group" in the GDR is suggested by evidence of their mutually supportive working relationship over the years. In 1950 Seghers lived for almost half a year with Brecht and Weigel in Berlin-Weißensee while waiting for a vacant apartment in Berlin-Adlershof, an outlying working-class district far removed from the city center and from Pankow-Niederschönhausen, where most Communist Party functionaries and leading writers were settled in villas.[16] The years surrounding the German division of 1949 were of course crucial for both Brecht and Seghers as creative writers as they struggled to maintain the integrity of their artistic projects while groping their way through the labyrinth of cold-war politics. Despite their international reputations and more or less privileged status in the GDR, both of them came under frequent attack by the SED (Sozialistische Einheitspartei) for their alleged "formalism," a common plight that seems to have cemented their relationship all the more.

At the time of the antisemitic purges of "cosmopolitans," Party functionaries in Moscow and Berlin questioned the political motives behind Seghers's postwar novel *The Dead Stay Young* (1949), which opens with the defeat of the revolutionary uprising of 1919 and the deaths of Rosa Luxemburg and Karl Liebknecht as symbolized by the clandestine murder of a young Spartakist by the Freikorps (reminiscent of the final scene in Kafka's *The Trial*). The novel barely makes reference to later developments in the Communist Party, and upon reading it no less a functionary than Walter Ulbricht was forced to wonder out loud: "What happened to the Party in Seghers's novel?"[17] In one of several quite revealing letters during this time to her Aufbau Verlag editor Erich Wendt (who spent several years of his exile in the Soviet Union in prison and a Siberian labor camp), Seghers referred with no little sarcasm to the threat of being perceived as "heretical and schismatic."[18] Evidently on the advice of her Czech publisher and Party members in France, at this time she even changed the title of a new collection of stories to "Die Linie"—and dedicated it to Stalin on his seventieth birthday.[19] She surely discussed the matter with Brecht and Weigel, with whom she was living at the time in Weißensee, and gave them, or at least Brecht, a copy of this collection of stories when it appeared. Several months later, on 11 July 1951, Brecht wrote in his work journal: "a valuable element in anna's beautiful stories in the little volume, DIE LINIE: the identification of what the party plans with what the proletarian does."[20] Brecht had only recently listened to SED criticism and changed the title of his opera libretto "The Trial of Lucullus" to "The Condemnation of Lucullus," for which a new premiere had been set at the Staatsoper for October. As he made marginal notes that summer in his copy of Seghers's *Die Linie,* using such phrasing as "würdig" (worthy, dignified),[21] Brecht was himself trying to write a contemporary piece about the German proletariat—his *Garbe* project, based on the GDR factory activist Hans Garbe. Like Seghers's three proletarian stories—albeit set in China!—in the slim volume she entitled "Die Linie," a successful *Garbe* play, which as we know he never finished, might have eased Brecht's troubles for a while.[22]

Officially, Seghers and Brecht collaborated only once, on the 1952 adaptation for the Berliner Ensemble of Seghers's radio play *Der Prozeß der Jeanne d'Arc zu Rouen 1431* (1937; The Trial of Jeanne d'Arc at Rouen, 1431). No records are available that might tell us just when and why Seghers and Brecht, and the Berliner Ensemble *Intendantin* Weigel, decided to create a theatre version of a radio play Seghers had written fifteen years earlier at the time of the Moscow show trials and the Spanish Civil War. We do know, however, that they worked on the production in the late summer and fall of 1952 (not long after Seghers's close friends Georg Lukács and his wife Gertrud Bortstieber made a personal visit to Brecht in his summer house in Buckow outside Berlin).[23] More importantly, we know that the premiere was set for Sunday, November 23 and coincided with the Slansky show trial in Prague, which was held between Friday, November 21 and the following Thursday, November 27, the day of the sentencing. We also know that after its premiere on November 23 *The Trial of Jeanne d'Arc* was regularly performed together with the one-act play *The Rifles of Señora Carrar.* Helene Weigel again played the title role as she had in 1937 in Paris, when Seghers herself reviewed that production. Brecht had also written his play fifteen years earlier at the time of the civil war in Spain.

The timing of the premiere and the linking of the subject matter and historical frame of reference seem to have been far more deliberate than coincidental. Rather than assume that Seghers, Brecht, and Weigel merely wanted to recycle old material for personal or any other reasons, I would argue that the collaboration of 1952 was informed by no less of a critical stand toward Stalinism than ideas voiced in the late 1930s by Brecht in *Me-ti* or by Seghers in *Tales of Artemis* and *The Most Splendid Tales of Woynok the Brigand.*[24] The concept of the dialectical cunning of reason is said to be the key to more than one such complexity in Brecht's oeuvre and legacy. By the same token, the notion of inspired heresy seems more appropriate in the case of Seghers, who as I have argued in previous chapters put greater trust in the example of the medieval mystics than the more rational legacies of a Bacon or Hegel. In this sense, of course, the "heretic" Leon Trotsky, whose ever more obdurate insistence on his convictions went far beyond what even many of his early supporters saw as the limits of reason, would have presented himself to Seghers as a far more fascinating historical and ultimately mythic figure than he ever was for Brecht.

On 15 August 1936 Radio Moscow announced the impending trial of Zinoviev, Kamenev, and fourteen other defendants charged with treason, conspiracy, and assassination attempts against Stalin. Trotsky, by now living in Norway, was of course Stalin's chief target. Accused of terrorism against the Soviet Union and even of being an agent of fascism, he was the focal point of this trial as well as the two subsequent show trials of January 1937 and March 1938. Accounts of the first Moscow trial, held between 19 and 24 August 1936, appeared on the front pages of the leading European newspapers and were broadcast by radio directly from Moscow. One is reminded of the famous photograph of Trotsky, "ears glued to the wireless set," as he listened to Radio Moscow's reports of the accusations hurled by the prosecutors at the "Trotskyite-Zinovievist conspirators."[25]

Trotsky's biographer Isaac Deutscher has compared the show trial confessions of former Bolshevik leaders of the revolution of 1917 to the medieval testimonies once forced on women who "had to relate to the Inquisition every act of their witchcraft and every detail of their debauchery with the Devil."[26] Zinoviev, a leading figure of the revolution, stunned the world with his masochistic summary of his case: "I am guilty of having been organizer, second only to Trotsky, of the Trotskyist-Zinovievist bloc, which set itself the aim of assassinating Stalin, Voroshilov, and other leaders. . . . I plead guilty to having been the principal organizer of the assassination of Kirov. We entered into an alliance with Trotsky. My defective Bolshevism became transformed into anti-Bolshevism and through Trotskyism I arrived at fascism. Trotskyism is a variety of fascism, and Zinovievism is a variety of Trotskyism."[27]

Only hours after he first heard the news of the trial Trotsky stood before international reporters to clear his name, accusing Stalin of "staging this trial in order to suppress discontent and opposition" and denouncing the charges as "the greatest forgery in the world's political history."[28] In order to prove his innocence and justify the claims of the international Left Opposition against Stalin, Trotsky proposed that his personal papers be put at the disposal of the Norwegian government and an impartial international Commission of Inquiry. The Norwegians placed him under house arrest and made arrangements to deport him. In December he was offered asylum by the government of Mexico, and he arrived there on 9 January 1937. In the fall of 1936 Trotsky's son Lyova published in Paris the *Livre Rouge sur le procès de Moscou* (Red Book on the Moscow Trial), the first detailed critique of the charges and procedures at the first Moscow trial in August 1936. In January 1937, shortly after Trotsky arrived in Mexico, the second trial, against Karl Radek, Pyatakov, and fifteen co-defendants took place in Moscow, once again amidst great publicity. Meanwhile Trotsky's American supporters put together the international Commission of Inquiry called for by Trotsky the previous August. In April the commission, headed by the American educator John Dewey, began its hearings for the countertrial in Mexico City. In September, one year and one month after the first Moscow trial, the Dewey Committee concluded its work and found the defendant Trotsky "not guilty."[29]

In the course of the very same year, Seghers completed, had broadcast, and published her first and only major radio play, *The Trial of Jeanne d'Arc at Rouen, 1431.* It is noteworthy that up to this point Seghers had authored only prose. Moreover, except for two short and comparatively insignificant pieces, she never again tried her hand at a dramatic work. The radio play was broadcast by Flemish Radio in early 1937, shortly after the second show trial in Moscow and the fifteen executions that followed it. The text itself appeared in the July 1937 issue of *Internationale Literatur* two months before the Dewey Commission concluded its countertrial in Mexico. Based on the original transcripts of the 1431 church trial, which Seghers examined in Paris archives, possibly also in the 1848 compilation by Joseph Fabre,[30] *The Trial of Jeanne d'Arc at Rouen, 1431* is for the most part a documentary dramatization of the trial proceedings to which the author added sequences containing "voices" of the "people," exchanges between Jeanne and her guards, and conversations among observers at the trial.

Seghers's artistic inspiration came from the expressionistic silent film *La Passion de Jeanne d'Arc* by the Danish filmmaker Carl Dreyer, which she saw in Paris in the mid-1930s.[31] She often mentioned her debt to Dreyer after the publication of the Berliner Ensemble adaptation in Brecht's works in 1959.[32] Like the radio play, the film is based on the proceedings of the historical trial of 1431 and focuses on the intensity of Jeanne's faith and suffering—the *passion* of Jeanne d'Arc. Thereby a show trial dominated by devilish intrigue is rendered as both a political Church trial and a trial of the individual and collective soul. When writing her play, Seghers must have had in mind a text that in the way of a film script would give voice to the silent images conveyed in Dreyer's film. Indeed, the development of the dialogue in the radio play, both in the trial and folk scenes, corresponds for the most part to the visual images in Dreyer's film.

In this respect Seghers's dramatization for radio was an attempt to lend words to the silent images of a moment in history that expressed both a deliberate political striving and the trials of a larger passion.

Carl Dreyer's starkly structured, profoundly emotional film is built on a series of close-ups that capture the unstudied immediacy of sudden frowns, grimaces, flashes of eyes, turns of the head, quick starts of the body. Given Seghers's particular interest since her studies in Heidelberg in physiognomy and traditions of East Asian and Gothic art, we have an idea of the extent to which Dreyer's film would have fascinated her. The film's expressionistic composition gives an overall impression as if its characters were at times hovering in rows over a Gothic cathedral portal, at other times emerging precariously from behind a large supporting pillar, and at yet others perched gargoyle-like atop a cathedral roof. The events in Dreyer's film are conditioned by the passions of good and evil, innocence and guilt. With her androgynous physiognomy and bearing suggestive of a quick-witted, courageous peasant girl, the actress Marie Falconetti seems to cite the youthful sweetness, simplicity, and serenity of both the smiling Gothic Madonnas and the "beloved" disciple John, at other times the startled yet always compassionate look of the Gothic angels. The Bishop Cauchon de Beauvais is modeled on church fathers carved in stone who rigidly stand guard in ornate dress at places of devotion and mourning, while the physiognomies of the ecclesiastics sitting in judgment remind us of repulsive devils and other beasts posing mockingly on Gothic cathedral pillars and rooftops. In 1928, shortly after the premiere of Dreyer's film, the poet and film critic Béla Balázs (who first brought Seghers's husband László Radványi into the Budapest Sunday Circle in 1918) wrote about the main courtroom scene:

> Fifty people sit for the entire time in one place. For a thousand meters only heads. Without a space. But we never even become aware of this space. Why should we? There are no races, there is no boxing match here. These raging passions, thoughts, convictions do not bounce against each other in a space. And yet there is breathtaking excitement in this dangerous duel in which glances are crossed instead of blades, for two hours long. For we are able to see each attack and each parry, every feint, every thrust of the mind, and we see each and every wound that the soul endures.[33]

Politically, Seghers evidently wanted to engage in the media discourse of the show trials by resorting to channels of communication that were being exploited so successfully in Moscow. Her documentary radio play about a fifteenth-century heretic and martyr who was officially rehabilitated twenty-five years after she was burned at the stake was clearly a provocation that called into question the legality of the show trials. The very form of the radio play, intended for broadcast within a public forum, responded in kind to media channels that, despite the irrationality and absurdity of the subject matter, were quite successful in confirming their particular logic and reality in the ears of the listeners. Not only in this sense did Seghers create her own version of the kind of countertrial that Trotsky had already called for in August 1936. In so doing she preempted by several months the Dewey Commission hearings, which like her play had no legal, only moral, jurisdiction. *The Trial of Jeanne d'Arc at Rouen, 1431* also allowed the radio listener (and later the reader of her text) to come to the same verdict of "not guilty" within a historically tested judicial context. As far as Seghers seems to have been concerned, the 1431 Church trial and execution of Jeanne d'Arc, her rehabilitation in 1456, and her elevation to sainthood in 1920 set a far better precedent for the case of a man like Trotsky than all the petty arguments and details he felt compelled to enlist, first in Norway, then before the Dewey Commission in Mexico, in order to wage his carefully researched point-by-point defense against indictments altogether monstrous and absurd.[34]

In this respect Seghers can be said to have preempted the position taken by the author of *Saint Joan* and longtime Trotsky admirer George Bernard Shaw. Questioning the viability of the countertrial in Mexico, Shaw wrote in the summer of 1937 to the British Committee for the Defence of Leon Trotsky: "I hope Trotsky will not allow himself to be brought before any narrower tribunal than his reading public where his accusers are at his mercy. . . . His pen is a terrific weapon. . . . The strength of Trotsky's case was the incredibility of the accusations against him. . . . But Trotsky spoils it all by making exactly the same sort of attacks on Stalin." Shaw finally succumbed to the kinds of equivocations heard from ever greater numbers of artists and intellectuals who felt torn between their support of the Soviet Union's (and Stalin's) socialist aims and, confronted with the spread of fascism across Europe, their exasperation with the ever more remote and narrowing scope of Trotsky's revolutionary battlegrounds and opinions. As Shaw went on to say: "Now I have spent nearly three hours in Stalin's presence and observed him with keen curiosity, and I find it just as hard to believe that he is a vulgar gangster as that Trotsky is an assassin."[35]

In retrospect it appears remarkable that of the prominent German writers exiled in France in the 1930s, it should have been Anna Seghers, a lifelong member of the Communist Party, who took the most deliberate, if not altogether explicit, stand against Stalin and on behalf of Trotsky at this time. This obtains for her radio play as well as her narratives *Tales of*

Artemis and *The Most Splendid Tales of Woynok the Brigand,* which thematize the figure of Trotsky and were also written at this time. The comparison is all the more intriguing if one takes into account the views represented in these years by such left-liberal authors as Lion Feuchtwanger and
Heinrich Mann. Mann's admiration for Stalin's policies and his concept of
building socialism in one country led him to draw a number of parallels
between Stalin's Five-Year Plan and the "Great Plan" devised for the
nation and its people by the popular French king Henri IV le Grand in
Mann's novel *Die Vollendung des Henri Quatre* (1938, The Fulfillment of
Henri Quatre). A more blatant example is Lion Feuchtwanger, who toured
the Soviet Union in late 1936 and early 1937, met personally with Stalin,
and even sat in as a guest on the second show trial in January 1937. Upon
returning to France, his reports about Stalin, the trials, and just about
everything else in the Soviet Union were unconditionally glowing. Against
the advice of friends and even his publisher he insisted on making available
to the public his enthusiastic *Moskau 1937,* which Querido Verlag in Amsterdam reluctantly published in the late spring of 1937, to its own and eventually Feuchtwanger's lifelong chagrin.[36] The egregious tone of Feuchtwanger's comparison of Stalin and Trotsky pervades his entire book:

> Trotsky strikes me as the typical revolutionary-only; very useful in
> times of pathos and struggle, but no longer useful when careful, con-
> stant planning and work are called for rather than pathetic excess. As
> soon as the heroic time of the revolution passed, Trotsky's world and
> its people became distorted, and he began to see everything falsely.
> . . . The man Stalin . . . worked and walked the right path. He put the
> peasants into cooperatives, industrialized, built socialism in the
> Soviet Union and organized it. His reality refuted Trotsky's irrefut-
> able theory. . . .
>
> Stalin's work prospered, promoting coals, promoting iron and
> ores, bringing electrical power plants into being. Heavy industry no
> longer lagged behind other countries, cities were built, real wages
> increased, the petty bourgeois revolts of the peasants were overcome,
> their cooperatives were rich in yield, pressing in ever greater masses
> into the collectivized farms. If Lenin was the Soviet Union's Caesar,
> Stalin became its Augustus, its "multiplier" in every sense. Stalin's
> building site grew and grew. But Stalin had to realize there were still
> people who didn't want to believe in this obvious, palpable work, who
> had more faith in Trotsky's theories than in what their own eyes could
> see. . . .
>
> What was the man Stalin forced to think, feel, when he learned that
> these his colleagues and friends still, in spite of the evident success of

his work, remained loyal to his foe Trotsky, how they surreptitiously warped information and sought to sabotage his own work, the "Stalin-State," in order to bring their old leader ["Führer"] back into the country?[37]

Feuchtwanger's book caused quite a stir, especially since it was the first major firsthand account of the Soviet Union since André Gide's sudden about-face rejection of the "Stalin-State" the previous year. Feuchtwanger's book was thus pitted against Gide's, and the critical responses and reviews reflected the growing uncertainties, shifts, and animosities within the exiled antifascist community. Leopold Schwarzschild, editor of *Das Neue Tage-Buch,* opened the debate with a single-handed attack on Feuchtwanger's "good news." Ernst Bloch's review in the July 1937 issue of *Die neue Weltbühne* argued with all earnestness in the book's defense. Arnold Zweig, whose views were shared by Franz Werfel and Bruno Frank, got a decidedly "sour" taste from reading it. Brecht, who had been especially close to Feuchtwanger ever since their Munich days, tactfully labeled it "Tacitus-like," notwithstanding the attendant irony.[38]

Seghers's radio play *The Trial of Jeanne d'Arc* appeared in the July 1937 issue of the widely read exile journal *Internationale Literatur,* that is, at the height of the controversy posed by Gide's and Feuchtwanger's books. Seghers restructured the terms of the debate in that her radio play focuses attention not so much on differing moral or ideological convictions—one man's personal experience and opinion versus another's—as on the underlying *political* struggle between Jeanne's resistance Party and the representatives of the ruling Church and State. On the one side stands the slight but heroic figure of a "heretic," an illiterate peasant girl whose cause is supported by the majority of the commoners who observe parts of the trial and witness her execution; on the other side stands the administrative power structure of Church and State, whose capacity for repression and violence expresses itself in an unbending, all-male alliance consisting of the Duke of Bedford, the Bishop Cauchon of Beauvais, and forty-two nobles, scholars, and priests, as well as armed soldiers and wanton prison guards.

In sharp contrast to the demeanor of the defendants at the Moscow trials, Seghers's Jeanne d'Arc asserts herself at the very start of her interrogation: "I'm willing to swear that I'll tell you about my people and my homeland and about everything before I came to France. But not anything about my voices and my revelations—you can even cut off my head, but you won't find out anything. . . . You can ask me what you want. I'll answer what I want. If you really knew how I am you'd breathe much easier if I were quite far away."[39] Before the torture instruments are brought in, the Bishop of Cauchon asks her, "For the last time I ask you, will you submit to the church?" to which she responds: "What *is* the church? No. I will not submit to you judges" (171). When the impending Council of Basel is mentioned, and described to her as "an assembly of the entire church" including "members of the English Party as well as your own" (171), she has a spark of hope and says: "Yes! that's what I want. I could much better submit to them" (75). The distinction between the church judges in occupied France and at the Council of Basel, where all parties, including those of the resistance, were assembled, calls to mind divisions in the 1930s between the ruling Communist Party in the Soviet Union and the international labor organizations to which Trotsky appealed in order to create an international court of justice for his countertrial in Mexico. The Council of Basel met from 1431 to 1448 and attempted to weaken the power of Rome by creating a more broadly based democratic governing body for the Church. On this count it ultimately failed, anticipating the repeatedly failed attempts to fundamentally reform the Soviet-style Communist Parties five centuries later.[40]

In the faint hope that with the Council of Basel her case may not be entirely lost, Jeanne regains for a moment her fighting spirit at the sight of the torture instruments: "If you break my bones with these instruments and squeeze my soul out of my poor body, I will not say anything different. And if I do say something different, I'll say afterwards that it was torn from me by force" (172). The possibility of recourse as well as her fear of the fire motivate her to sign the recantation that has been prepared for her. Her recantation does not free her from prison but only forces her again to "wear women's clothes" and puts her at the continual mercy of the prison guards who abuse her. Once she realizes that without the hope of recourse she has betrayed her "voices" and her cause, she is willing to prepare for her death. Her final words can be taken as Seghers's answer to the confessions elicited by psychological terror and force in Moscow: "I betrayed my cause. I only recanted out of fear of the fire. . . . I didn't at all know what a recantation means. . . . Now I would rather die at once than slowly in your hands. . . . Am I not released from the fear of death? Am I not released from the fear of those who wield power?" (102–3).

The seeming "otherness" of the peasant girl—with cropped hair, clad in men's clothes and boots, standing before rows of male inquisitors seated in long flowing robes—inverts not only the institutional conventions of gender. The judges' persistence in wanting to find out just why and on whose advice Jeanne first decided to put on men's clothes finally leads her to object: "Why do you keep asking about my clothes? The clothes don't mean anything, they're the least important of all" (38). The red thread of repeated questions about Jeanne's decision to trade women's clothes for the men's clothes with which she thenceforth covered a woman's body can be likened to the antisemitic lines of interrogation that characterized the Moscow trials. Here the systematic uncovering of the respective defendant's "concealed," or as it were "Jewish," identity lying somehow hidden beneath the outer layer of loyalty to the Soviet state led the prosecutors to unravel all the more quickly the knots in the larger conspiratorial web connecting the defendants to the archenemy of the Soviet state, Leon Trotsky.[41]

The radio play alludes more directly to Trotsky when Beaupère asks, "What do you know about the Duke of Orléans?" to which Jeanne quickly responds: "That God loves him" (30). The answer is met by "disturbance" among the judges, followed by the "rapid succession of question and counter-question, blow upon blow":

BEAUPÈRE: Why did you take off women's clothes?

JEANNE: Because I had to. And I was well advised!

BEAUPÈRE: How did you get to the man you call your King?

JEANNE: With no difficulty. I arrived in Chinon at noon, went to a shelter, went to the castle, went into a room, and recognized the King. I called out to him that I had come to fight the English.

BEAUPÈRE: Did the King hear voices too?

JEANNE: Ask him, maybe he'll tell you.

BEAUPÈRE: Why did the King receive you?

JEANNE: Those belonging to my Party knew exactly who I was, and recognized me.

BEAUPÈRE: Do you hear your voices often?

JEANNE: Always, when I need them.

BEAUPÈRE: What do you ask of them?

JEANNE: "Victory for my Party." (30–31)

The mere mention of the Duke of Orléans was meant as a trap for Jeanne. The duke was the nephew of King Charles VI and the father of the later King Louis XII. He was a prominent leader of the Armagnacs—the Party of Jeanne d'Arc—who bitterly opposed the alliance between the Burgundians and England. Wounded at the battle of Agincourt in 1415, he was captured by the English and taken to London, where he lived as a prisoner until 1439. It was during this time that he wrote, in French, English, and Latin, the chansons, ballads, and rondeaux for which he became famous as Charles d'Orléans and is still best known today. The obvious parallel to Trotsky, who was the renowned exiled leader of the Left Opposition and widely admired for his intellectual wit and talents as a writer, would have been even more striking to Seghers's contemporaries than it is today. The following conversation among trial observers draws an implicit connection between the medieval Church trials and Stalin's trials of the members of the Left Opposition:

> The report of the Paris faculty is in. Only fuel for the fire. Devastating for the accused. Schismatic and heretical on twelve counts.
>
> But it's said another report from old Gerson has also arrived, favorable to the accused.
>
> His word doesn't count for much anymore.
>
> Nonetheless, for decades this man was Europe's leading luminary. As Dean of the Paris faculty his opinion was the decisive one in all the ecclesiastical trials.
>
> He's loyal to Jeanne because he's in the same Party. The English drove him out of the University.
>
> What a fox he is. At the Council of Constance he had no misgivings about letting John Hus burn after he submitted his report. Yet the prosecution's charges were exactly the same as they are today.
>
> John Hus, however, was a learned man. He was up to dealing with the courts of law. He knew what was at stake and he risked his neck. The girl has no clue.
>
> Gerson likes that. She's just a poor girl, a child of the people. He always liked to needle those who were on top. He always preached against corruption and against the offices that were bought and the pomp of the bishops. He always had an eye out for the people, for the masses of the faithful.
>
> That's an old story. Then why did he let Hus burn?
>
> Gerson wanted to clean up shop. Hus wanted to wipe the entire enterprise off the map. (82–83)

The text invites us to draw parallels between Jan Hus's execution in 1415 and Trotsky's expulsion from the Party and banishment in 1927–28; between Jean Gerson's prosecution of Hus and Bukharin's betrayal of the Left Opposition at the time of his realliance with Stalin in the late 1920s; and between "old" Gerson's interest in Jeanne d'Arc (Jean Gerson in fact died in 1429, two years before Jeanne's trial) and an altogether weakened Bukharin's attempts to maintain his theoretical preeminence in the 1930s—until he himself was tried and executed in 1938, one year after Seghers completed her play. Seghers's radio play, however, is not structured along fixed allegorical lines, but according to the dramaturgical principle of the epic model that can be adjusted to the given historical situation—like the concept of the epic model Brecht himself favored. It was of course this very principle of the "model" that made possible Seghers's later collaboration with Brecht on the adaptation of the play for the Berliner Ensemble in 1952.

To be sure, we would be misguided if we were to interpret Seghers's radio play primarily in terms of Stalin's show trials. This documentary play about the political trial of a fifteenth-century heretic and martyr can just as well be seen as Seghers's effort to respond to the notorious German courtroom trials of the 1930s that allowed for the so-called legal eradication of the antifascist resistance within Germany. Between 1933 and 1935 alone there were in Germany 5,425 political trials and sixty executions.[42] Moreover, thousands more people were incarcerated in German prisons and concentration camps and either "accidentally" murdered or "legally" executed in the course of time. The case of Carl Ossietzky, who received the Nobel Peace Prize while in prison and was eventually murdered, is well known. One of many lesser known cases is that of Seghers's close friend the sinologist Philipp Schaeffer, with whom she studied in Heidelberg. A member of the underground resistance, Schaeffer was tried and sentenced to five years in prison in 1935, a conviction that would surely have been on Seghers's mind when she wrote her radio play about Jeanne d'Arc.[43]

It is well known that Seghers voiced her outrage at the brutality of the Nazi regime in speeches and essays as well as in her antifascist novels of this period. At the end of 1936, the very time she would have been working on her radio play, she was collecting materials for a book about Spain to be smuggled to members of the underground resistance incarcerated in German prisons and concentration camps. On 2 November 1936 she wrote to the Hungarian playwright Julius Hay, who had escaped from Dachau and thereupon joined the international brigades: "For our book about the antifascists killed in Spain I need from you a short trial scene. This could be a scene from the Fiete-Schulze trial or from any other you think appropriate."[44] Those who were sentenced to death at the Fiete-Schulze trial in Hamburg stood up for their cause in court with the very kind of defiance that Seghers would also have found in the transcripts of the 1431 court trial of Jeanne d'Arc at Rouen.[45]

The figure of the legendary Maid of Orléans who stormed the ramparts of more than one city to defeat the Burgundians and liberate France from foreign domination also brings to mind the many volunteers who traveled from all parts to join the Republican forces fighting in Spain. Reminiscent of the French Maid was the young German Hans Beimler, who died in the battle for Madrid after rescuing his comrades from the fire. Beimler was "always in the front lines," Seghers wrote in the essay she devoted to him.[46] Her review of the Paris production of Brecht's *The Rifles of Señora Carrar* in the fall of 1937 is written in a similar vein. In the role of Señora Carrar, Helene Weigel spoke her lines the way "one hammers in a little nail," Seghers wrote. When put to use, this voice "could be as valuable as multiple newspaper editions or many packages of political flyers or an entire railroad car filled with munitions. Because with this voice one can revive the apathetic and scare off the enemy and strengthen our own."[47]

Although we lack documented evidence, it is safe to say that Brecht was familiar with Seghers's radio play after, if not already before, it appeared in the July 1937 issue of *Internationale Literatur.* We can also assume that he talked with Seghers about the issues it raised during his visits to Paris in the summer and fall of 1937, when the Soviet purges and trials were on everyone's mind. I would even argue that Seghers had no little impact on the gradual shift in direction that we find in Brecht's own work in the late 1930s. First, Seghers's critical stand on the purges and trials, coming from a staunch, if critical, Communist Party member whose husband was more or less a functionary, must have encouraged Brecht to move beyond the kinds of equivocations we still find in his journal notes and papers during this time. And second, as indicated by her own shift toward the historic-parabolic theme of her *Trial of Jeanne D'Arc* and the allegorizing prose style of such narratives as *Tales of Artemis* and *The Most Splendid Tales of Woynok the Brigand,* all three originating before 1938, she was already experimenting in the mid-1930s with aesthetic forms that might encompass the dual impact of fascism and Stalin's purges and trials.

Brecht's own shift in this direction came a bit later and can be dated from the latter part of 1938, when he wrote the first draft of his *Life of Galileo,* which also thematizes the historical church trial of a "heretic." Galileo's famous speech at the end of the play (in this first November 1938 version) is modeled on the ingeniously structured speech made by Bukharin at his own trial in March 1938.[48] Structural and thematic parallels to Seghers's play can be found in *Life of Galileo* in scene 12 containing the discussion between the Pope and the Cardinal Inquisitor, and in scene 13 containing Galileo's recantation after he is shown the torture instruments (as also happens in the case of Jeanne's recantation in Seghers's play). The Pope's comment about Galileo in scene 12, for example, reveals the rhetorical pattern of a comment made by one of the observers about Jean Gerson in Seghers's play. Seghers: "Nonetheless, for decades this man was Europe's leading luminary. As Dean of the Paris faculty, his opinion was the decisive one in all the ecclesiastical trials." Brecht: "After all the man is the greatest physicist of our time, the light of Italy, and not just any old crank. He has friends. There is Versailles. There's the Viennese Court."[49] Moreover, Galileo's students react with the same kind of anxious small talk before, and the same kind of outrage after, his recantation as does the *Volk* in the corresponding recantation scene in Seghers's play.

The difference is that in the case of Galileo's students intellectual accusations are hurled at the once great national hero who can no longer be a hero, whereas in the case of Jeanne's recantation the *Volk* reacts with "angry, wild screams" and even "stones hurled" (94).

We know that in conversation with Walter Benjamin in the summer of 1938, Brecht showed particular interest in Seghers's narrative *The Most Splendid Tales of Woynok the Brigand* and the fact that Seghers "can't produce to order," just as "without an order" he, Brecht, "wouldn't even know how to start writing."[50] We also know that Brecht later made use of at least one text Seghers wrote while in Paris.[51] Indeed, we also find intertextualities in other examples of Brecht's work from the late 1930s. Anticipating the Stalin-Hitler pact, Seghers's satirical tale *Reise ins elfte Reich* (1939, Journey into the Eleventh Realm) takes the reader on a Dantesque-Kafkaesque journey of emigration and deportation as provided—albeit with no explicit references—by the "realms" of Hitler and Stalin. The story appeared in *Die neue Weltbühne* in March 1939 and is in many ways echoed in Brecht's *Flüchtlingsgespräche* (Conversations among Émigrés), which he first intended as "a small satirical novel with a contemporary subject."[52] Seghers's story anticipates not only the thematic content, but also the bizarre mingling of satirical styles—the ironically earnest and seriously tongue-in-cheek—characterizing Brecht's dialogues.

Brecht was already fascinated by the possibilities of radio in the last years of the Weimar Republic. His radio play of 1939, *Das Verhör des Lukullus* (The Trial of Lucullus), which he later turned into an opera libretto, bears a title reminiscent of Seghers's radio play *The Trial of Jeanne d'Arc at Rouen, 1431*. Like Seghers, who responded to the dual impact of the Nazi trials and the trials in Moscow with a historic-parabolic theme, Brecht wrote his radio play about the trial of the Roman military commander Lucullus in response to the Stalin-Hitler pact and the invasion of Poland, which in respect to the Soviet invasion from the East he called "curiously Napoleonic."[53] Brecht's purpose was to question the fame and glory of the conqueror. Having completed the play in the first week of November 1939, he wrote in his journal: "very quickly it more or less reaches the limit of what can still be said."[54] The November 1939 broadcast planned by Stockholm Radio did not come about, likely due to the volatile political content, and the play was first broadcast by Swiss Radio on 12 May 1940. Like Seghers, Brecht published his radio play in the journal *Internationale Literatur*.[55]

Brecht first mentioned his plans for *The Visions of Simone Marchard* in July 1940. In December of 1941, already in California, he wrote in his work journal: "now i am planning a JEANNE D'ARC 1940 for the stage."[56] The phrasing of the project echoes almost word for word the historically specific title of Seghers's 1937 radio play *The Trial of Jeanne d'Arc at Rouen, 1431.* Reminiscent of Seghers's play, and in sharp contrast to his *St. Joan of the Stockyards* of 1929, which parodies the idealism of Schiller's *The Maid of Orléans,* Brecht presented his main character as a positive model of resistance, albeit in the contemporary context of the German occupation of France. Like Seghers, Brecht foregrounded Jeanne's relationship to the people and what he called "the social material": "the 'voices' are the voices of the people, jeanne represents what the people say. la voix de dieu est la voix du peuple."[57] In this, his second Joan of Arc play Brecht drew a comparison between French collaboration with the English invaders in fifteenth-century France and the Vichy government's cooperation with the Germans in 1940: "our social circumstances are such that in wartime not only the ruled but also the rulers of the two hostile countries have common interests. the owners and the robbers stand shoulder to shoulder against those who do not recognise property.—the patriots. (this illuminates among other things the difficulties which a *scorched earth* policy must face in certain countries.)"[58] After the war Brecht saw these "common interests" shift from German-French collaboration in World War Two to Allied and later NATO collaboration in western Europe during the cold war. Thus it was that in the GDR he embarked on what was to become his third Joan of Arc project: the adaptation of Anna Seghers's radio play for the Berliner Ensemble.

Seghers first made public mention of her radio play in a discussion session at the congress of the German Writers Union in May 1950, at which time she was living with Brecht and Weigel in Weißensee. Seghers's reference to her radio play before the assembled congress of writers came as part of a "self-criticism" in response to charges of "formalism" leveled against her both before and during the congress. The Schweikean charm and seeming naïveté with which she presented her case belies the gravity of the concerns she wanted to address with the broadcast of her play and at the same time reflects the intricate situation in which she found herself as a writer at the height of the cold war and the antiformalist (and anticosmopolitan and antisemitic) campaign in the Eastern bloc. The historically vague, factually imprecise, slightly provocative, and generally equivocal tone with which she delivered her words would henceforth characterize all her future references to this radio play about a fifteenth-century heretic and martyr so that it might survive the times as best it could. It is noteworthy that she deliberately confused the issue as to when she wrote her play (e.g., "Long before Hitler"!), presented the work as though she had simply copied from the original 1431 transcripts, and omitted the fact that it had been published at all, namely, in the summer of 1937 at the height of Stalin's purges and between the second and third trials in Moscow:

Long before Hitler I wrote a radio play. . . . I think it was two or three years before the war. At one point I was working for Flemish Radio in Antwerp and adapted the trial of Jeanne d'Arc for radio. This is the same woman as the Maid of Orléans by Schiller, only after she was condemned to burn at the stake her trial was recorded word for word in Latin and is preserved up to this day in the Chamber of Deputies in Paris. This is an extraordinarily interesting trial, a great work that belongs so to speak to the national treasure, to the cultural heritage of French culture, studied and known by every French schoolchild and even worked through by the French Communist Party, and in this way it is brought to the people. At that time I adapted this trial for the city of Antwerp with some changes as is proper for radio, with many abbreviations, clarifications, and so forth, but rather word for word. Well, after the Americans came to Germany the thing somehow surfaced again. It got into my hands somehow. I first submitted it to Radio Berlin and then, after my Soviet friends read it, they rejected it and told me the maturity of German youth wasn't yet up to a presentation of this play. At that time I had just arrived in Berlin, and I didn't understand this. And so, like every one of you often does in life, I grumbled about it. It just didn't make sense to me. Then the Americans took an interest in it—at that time tension wasn't as high as now—and they wanted to broadcast it. They telephoned very fast: they couldn't broadcast the play knowing that in the minds of German youth the fact that a judge can be wrong will turn into the idea that the Nürnberg court might be wrong. Well, all right. After this the English took a look at the piece. They then said: we can't have this performed; it shows resistance against the English.[59]

The theatre adaptation for the Berliner Ensemble was undertaken in the late summer and fall of 1952. The material added to the original text was intended as a critique of the military acceleration of the cold war and the expansion of the NATO alliance, which threatened to make permanent the division of Europe. At issue was the impending remilitarization of West Germany, and thereupon the likelihood of the militarization of the GDR and the Eastern bloc. Brecht and Seghers hoped that a French plebiscite would reject participation in the Western alliance and thereby reverse the current trend. Whereas the original radio play focused on the enduring character and faith of a martyr within the framework of a political show trial, the expanded stage version was weighted toward the larger social and national issue and became a play advocating demilitarization and neutrality. The production specifically supported the Soviet Union's proposal of March 1952 for a neutral, demilitarized, unified Germany at the center of Europe to counter the United States' promotion of NATO. Drawing a direct parallel across the centuries, the theatre program included the historical Jeanne d'Arc's words challenging the English before she raised the siege of Orléans: "The Maid has come in the name of God. She is ready to conclude the peace if you will leave France and also pay for having been here. And you, all of you together, bowmen, soldiers, and so on, who find yourselves before our city of Orléans, by God, return to your land. If you do not, you can soon expect the Maid to pass among you, at your great peril."[60]

The adaptation retained for the most part the original text focusing on the trial proceedings and expanded those parts concerned with the military occupation of France by the English and the struggle for national liberation represented by Jeanne and her Party. Changes in 1952 also differentiated situations and characters in the folk scenes that were generalized in the original radio play: "a crowd of people being pushed back," "great unrest," and voices "among the people." Thus, in addition to expanded dialogue and folk milieu, characters came into being: "well-dressed gentleman," "fishwife," "peasant woman," "wine merchant," "loose woman," and so forth. The originally through-composed text was divided and expanded into fourteen scenes, each introduced by historical commentary used as stage projections. According to Benno Besson, Brecht's assistant responsible for directing the play, Seghers worked primarily on the folk scenes.[61] One recognizes her hand in the additions to scenes 1, 4, and 14, as well as in 7, 9, and 12, consistent with the pithy epic style of the original text. For example, the lines spoken in scene 1 by a woman who has brought her children to see the Maid pass by betray Seghers's keen ear for the discursive combinations and asides in the speech patterns of a harried mother: "Eugene, have you got the food parcel?—They say she's a real manwoman"; "Careful with the eggs, Eugene! And cross yourself."[62] In scene 4 the conversation among food vendors at the marketplace in Rouen is a typical Seghers rendering of "plebeian" everyday talk:

PEASANT WOMAN: People shouldn't joke about religion. The girl is a witch and that's that.
FIRST NIECE: That's right.
FISHWIFE: Too bad she's a witch if she's against the English.
PEASANT WOMAN: Her voices come from the devil.
FISHWIFE: Bah, her voices seem to say what we're all saying. I mean, that the English should get out of France.
SON: She's a saint.
PEASANT WOMAN: You shut up![63]

It is unlikely that Seghers, or for that matter Brecht, had anything to do with writing the prologue, the expansion of scene 12, and the entirely new scene 17 that were later added to give a loose epic frame to the final 1954 version. The additions were meant to counterbalance the trial scenes and make a full-length production for the Berliner Ensemble's move to the Theater am Schiffbauerdamm in 1954. The additions introduced elements of slapstick and farce in the tradition of *commedia dell'arte,* thus not only radically altering the intent of Seghers's original play, but also shifting the precarious balance achieved in the 1952 version. In the 1954 version of scene 12, for example, the "loose woman" finally confronts her "well-dressed gentleman": "You think going to bed with you is a pleasure? And listening to your hogwash day and night? Pay up and clear out. A peasant girl! What does that make me? A dockside whore, I suppose. Pay if you want to have fun, pay, pay, pay!" Then he rants: "That's the last straw. There's only one thing to be done with you scum, your Maid included: root out, burn to the ground, drown in blood, hang, crush underfoot, extermi-nate." Thereupon the "loose woman" slaps her man and he runs off.[64] At the end of the scene the peasant lad Eugene, wearing a dented English hel-met on his head, rides in on the shoulders of two Frenchmen. One of them offers the helmet to a child for use as a chamber pot: "Come on, Jean Marie, and pissypissy in your new pot." The fishwife adds: "Maybe they're only blisters, but on certain gentlemen you can find them right on top of the nose." At which point the lad Eugene starts up the song: "The Bishop Cau-chon of Beauvais / Is an Englishman now, I would say . . ."[65]

The tendency toward epic-comic heightening and slapstick was hardly consonant with the sustained drama of the courtroom scenes in which Jeanne was to appear in her passion as a martyr. The effort to bal-ance these two tracks—the loose epic-comic historical framework and the drama of the trial as both courtroom trial and trial of the soul—was already problematic in the 1952 version but failed altogether with the addi-tions of 1954, thus contributing to the play's reputation as one of Brecht's least successful adaptations. But this stylistic inconsistency with its dis-turbing effect on the aesthetic sense is all the more interesting politically. The 1952 version envisioned by Seghers and Brecht was apparently intended to proceed simultaneously on two levels: on the one hand the epic-comic additions allowing for the broader social perspective of the mil-itary occupation by the English; on the other the heightened drama of the trial scenes, which, though expanded, sought to retain the original tenor of the trial as political show trial and trial of the soul. Thus, consistent with the Brechtian concept of the "Small Pedagogy," the alienation and distan-tiation techniques employed in the epic-comic frame were meant to call attention to the *external* threat in contemporary times, that is, the political-economic "occupation" of West Germany and the military NATO alliance in western Europe. At the same time, corresponding to the notion of communist self-criticism represented by the "Grand Pedagogy," as in Brecht's *The Measures Taken* or Seghers's own "mythic" tales, the courtroom trial scenes were intended to pose the question of the *internal* threat represented by the continuation of the Stalinist purges and trials.[66]

The parabolic aspect of the original radio play is retained in the trial scenes of the Berliner Ensemble adaptation. This generalizing tendency allowing the play to simultaneously raise the issue of political trials in Germany and in the Soviet Union in the 1930s was preserved in the 1952 version in such a way as to potentially address a wide-ranging spectrum of political trials. Some of these would especially have concerned Seghers after the war. On the most personal level, she learned upon her return to Germany in 1947 that her close friend Philipp Schaeffer, who had first been tried and sentenced to a German prison in 1935, was arrested again in 1943 and executed, beheaded by axe, in Plötzensee.[67] As is evident from both personal letters and her published writings, Seghers was increasingly disturbed by the rising tide of antisemitism within and without Germany following the Holocaust in which she had lost family members and friends.[68] Given her close ties to Georg Lukács and his circle in Budapest, and her marriage to László Radványi, who for personal, professional, and no doubt also political reasons did not return from Mexico until 1952,[69] she would have been particularly concerned about the Rajk trial in Hungary in September of 1949, after which three of the defendants were hanged and four shot. László Rajk, who was officially rehabilitated in 1956 by the revolutionary Nagy government, in which Lukács also participated, is said to have approached the gallows in 1949 "with head held high" and to have "hailed the Party, Stalin and Rákosi"[70] one last time— an example in the spirit of Seghers's Jeanne d'Arc, who holds fast to her "voices" and her "Party" (incidentally, without condemning the Church and the Pope) to the end. As a German-Jewish exile who had spent six years in Mexico and during this time became a best-selling author in the United States, Seghers was equally alarmed at the succession of anticommunist witch-hunts in the United States, which culminated in the trial and conviction of Ethel and Julius Rosenberg. She and Brecht both protested the death sentences resulting from the Rosenbergs' conviction.[71]

But the trial that in 1952 would have been of greatest concern to Seghers—and that because of their connections in exile to at least two of the defendants also posed a danger to her and her husband László Radványi—was the Slansky trial scheduled to take place in Prague amid much bombast in November of 1952. As mentioned, the premiere of the Berliner

Ensemble production of *The Trial of Jeanne d'Arc* was set for November 23 and thus coincided with the trial of Rudolf Slansky and thirteen co-defendants conducted in Prague.[72] For this reason, and in light of other evidence, we have reason to believe that Brecht, Seghers, and Helene Weigel intended the production of *The Trial of Jeanne d'Arc in Rouen, 1431* to serve as a moral exemplum staged by artists, that is to say, as a countertrial in the very spirit and age-old tradition of political theatre.

The Berliner Ensemble production countered the proceedings in Prague in form as well as content. Whereas the trial scenes in Berlin were staged in a formal style befitting the dignity of a medieval martyr and mystic, the show trial in Prague, as Brecht and Seghers must have anticipated, was presented as nothing more, and nothing less, than a virtual experience. Artur London, sentenced to life imprisonment and released after Stalin's death, described the propaganda spectacle in his memoir of 1968: "I felt that I was on a stage, with my thirteen comrades and the members of the tribunal. Every one of us was ready to perform his part of the spectacle, which had been meticulously produced by the experts in Ruzyn. . . . There were microphones everywhere, and the lights and electric wires running across the floor heightened the effect of the première."[73] London recalled that while the indictment was read, "from time to time we were dazzled by the light of the reflectors. We were being filmed, and would soon be shown in dark cinemas before the main feature" (270).

The precautions undertaken by Seghers and Brecht give evidence of their awareness of the risks to which they exposed themselves. A statement by Seghers in the theatre program stressed the protocol character of her original play and blurred the date of the writing as having been "around 1935," that is, before the first Moscow trial in August 1936. The statement made no mention of the play's publication in the July 1937 issue of *Internationale Literatur*.[74] This evidence was even missing from the working copy of the radio play used by Brecht to make the changes for the adaptation. The relevant pages he needed were in fact torn out of a copy of the July 1937 issue of *Internationale Literatur,* evidently to conceal this information even within the Berliner Ensemble and thereby prevent speculation about the circumstances surrounding the origins of the radio play. On this working copy, which contains his characteristic markings, Brecht deleted the exchange between Jeanne and her interrogator that referred to the Duke of Orléans, and implicitly to Trotsky: Beaupère: "What do you know about the Duke of Orléans?" Jeanne: "That God loves him" (30).[75]

The lines referring to Trotsky were potentially harmful to Seghers in particular, and she was clearly aware that defendants in Prague who had spent their years in exile in France, Spain, and Mexico were being accused of "Trotskyist" leanings. In his 1968 memoir published in France, which Seghers kept in her library wrapped in brown paper,[76] London described the interrogations that preceded the trial:

> My three inquisitors shouted names of veterans from the Spanish Civil War—some of whom I had not seen since 1939—the names of volunteers of various nationalities, among others the Poles, Rwal and Winkler, who had disappeared in Moscow; the Hungarians Rajk and Baneth. . . . They questioned me about Anna Seghers, about Egon Erwin Kisch and his wife whom they accused of organizing Trotsky-ist meetings in Paris and Prague. . . . They screamed out names of towns—Paris, Marseilles, Barcelona, Albacete—they mentioned my meetings with so and so, but gave no details.[77] (51)

London's testimony in Prague on November 22, one day before the Berlin premiere of *The Trial of Jeanne d'Arc at Rouen, 1431,* was typical of the "confessions" forced on defendants and carefully rehearsed during the pretrial hearings:

> I admit that I am guilty of having actively participated, from 1948 to the day of my arrest, in the centre of conspiracy against the State of Czechoslovakia, formed and led by Rudolf Slansky. It was above all my eleven-year stay in the West which made me totally alien to Czechoslovakia. . . . During my stay in the West I became cosmopoli-tan and entered the bourgeois camp. This led me into the Trotskyist group from the International Brigades in Spain when I was in France in 1940. The group was centred at Marseilles and financed by the American organization, the YMCA, and . . . an organ of the Ameri-can intelligence services. (272)

During pretrial hearings interrogators repeatedly hurled antisemitic epithets at the eleven out of fourteen defendants officially labeled as hav-ing neither "Czech" nor "Slovak" but "Jewish origins" (50, 269–70, 283–85). Of the eleven defendants executed in December, all but Rudolf Slansky revoked their "confessions" shortly before they went to their deaths (315–16). As if to deliberately challenge the slander against so-called and actual Trotskyists who had fought in the international brigades during the Spanish Civil War, the 1952–53 Berliner Ensemble production of *The Trial of Jeanne d'Arc* was staged in tandem with a new postwar pro-duction of Brecht's one-act Spanish Civil War play *The Rifles of Señora Carrar,* first staged in Paris in 1937. Except for its premiere on 23 Novem-ber 1952, *The Trial of Jeanne d'Arc* was performed in each case before the intermission, followed after intermission by *The Rifles of Señora Carrar,* with Helene Weigel in the title role. This practice changed in 1954 when *The Trial of Jeanne d'Arc* was expanded into a full-length theatre production. By that time of course Stalin was dead, and the era of the show trials against "Trotskyist" internationalists and veterans of the Spanish Civil War had come to an end.

The extent to which Seghers was committed to the countertrial aspect of her collaboration with Brecht is evident in the letter she wrote to him on Thursday, 27 November 1952, the very day the Prague court pronounced eleven death sentences and three of life imprisonment (308–11). Seghers's letter, which came to light only recently,[78] revolves around the political issues raised by the production and addresses them in terms of the actual theatre work. The letter's tone of urgency suggests that its author had the greater political investment and was at greater risk. From the mode of argumentation we can surmise that Seghers relied on her own judgment to weigh the political risks and potential consequences of the production. Brecht's characteristic penciled arrows in the margins of the letter, as well as the stage script of 1953, show that he took her suggestions to heart, making the required changes on the stage script and for the production.[79]

Seghers's letter begins with the audience's emotional reaction to events onstage: "The people sitting around me were utterly devastated, and they were sobbing" (35). This response, evidently by first-generation Communist Party members seated around Seghers in the front rows, might have seemed inevitable at the end of the performance, as onstage fifteenth-century French citizens, including the executioner, voiced their dismay while Jeanne d'Arc burned at the stake. In light of this, Seghers's letter urges that the production put greater emphasis on moments of resistance, which would outlast the immediate reaction to an individual event and foreground what might appear as an "optimistic tragedy" (35). "What is most important," she implored, "is to make use of everything that more clearly points up the resistance rather than the terror of the invasion, the eventual consequences of the trial and the execution rather than the empathy with Jeanne" (35).

Seghers asked Brecht to make two adjustments that she considered "undebatable" (36). First, the shocking effect of the executioner's remorse (documented in 1431) should not take precedence over the political awareness among the people: "The most important thing is not his understanding of his guilt, but the people's understanding of Johanna" (35). Second, she suggested that the courtroom scenes put even greater emphasis on the court recorder writing the protocols—which in 1431 provided the necessary documentation for the arguments that secured Jeanne's rehabilitation two decades later. During the Berliner Ensemble performances the court recorder was very obviously seen and heard writing down the testimony in each courtroom scene. The foregrounding of the court recorder served to emphasize that Seghers's text drew on original documents, clearly also a ploy to keep the production from being censured, or prohibited altogether. At the same time the court recorder was permanently onstage in order to serve as a reminder that more recent show trials would also be subject one day to historical review. Along these lines Seghers also recommended, not without humor, that because the announcer's cap "came across like a Cossack's cap," it should be traded for another (36).

The remainder of the letter focuses on the figure of Jeanne as played by the actress Käthe Reichel. For Seghers, Jeanne d'Arc was the very personification of political resistance—tougher, cleverer, and more spirited than at first she might have seemed to Brecht. Seghers differed with Brecht's interpretation of the character of Jeanne during her recantation as "a completely destroyed girl, knock out" (37). She suggested instead that Jeanne's willingness to recant was not merely guided by suffering and fear, but by quick thinking and the hope of a resolution at the Council of Basel: "The moment she hears that people from her own Party will be there, too, she perks up, sees a chance, and signs the document" (37). Seghers recommended further that in the role of Jeanne d'Arc, Käthe Reichel be at times more audacious, more mocking, and that at other times she alternate between restraint and occasional demonstrations of emotion—demonstrations that Brecht must have feared would result in too much "pathos," since Seghers assured him more than once in her letter that they would not. In recommending that Reichel display such sudden changes and ranges of emotion, Seghers must have had in mind the remarkable physiognomy of the actress Marie Falconetti, who played the role of Jeanne d'Arc in Carl Dreyer's silent film of 1928 *La Passion de Jeanne d'Arc,* which had inspired her to write her radio play in the 1930s. The very phrasing in the following passage from Seghers's letter to Brecht invokes Falconetti's frequent physiognomic transformations as Jeanne recalls at various points during the trial how it was and how she was when she first entered France:

> For example: I think that twice or three times or even just once she could forget for a moment that she's a prisoner. When the Court asks her, and in the course of her answer she remembers her capture, and she says—"I came to France in men's clothes, bearing a sword"—there for a split second she must take command and stand poised just as she stood poised and took command when she came to France, for the first time, in men's clothes, bearing a sword. The ecclesiastics, yes, even the English on the scene, must freeze up with fear. They have to

get a taste of what it was that the people and the soldiers felt and sensed about her. (Without any pathos. But Katrin is talented and will get it right.) This kind of thing would heighten the atmosphere of the resistance struggle enormously.

The same thing could also occur when she says: "I had a banner, snow-white." (37)

With its appeal to the mysticism of the Gothic era, the expressionistic aesthetic of Dreyer's film differs radically from the epic-comic historicizing style of the Berliner Ensemble adaption of *The Trial of Jeanne d'Arc at Rouen, 1431*. Brecht's own pictorial conception envisioned a sweeping epic design in the manner of what he called the "narrative paintings" of his favorite "plebeian" painter Pieter Breughel the Elder. Brecht made the following comment during a rehearsal of scene 2, in which Jeanne, preceded by English lords and Church prelates, is brought to the trial in chains before a crowd of onlookers: "The crowd has arrived as if for a folk festival—this is the way Breughel portrays the crucifixion [in *The Procession to Calvary*]. The crowd enjoys the spectacle of a procession of (English) military men and (French) clerics, mocks the hats of the Paris scholars, begins to get bored, etc. The last point is important because it demonstrates that they are waiting for a show and that their interest is very superficial."[80]

The corresponding scene in Seghers's radio play (and in the Dreyer film) also includes the element of mindless curiosity. But more importantly, the scene foregrounds figures whose words (in Dreyer's film, faces) articulate the combined emotions of agony and hope, suggesting not merely historical immediacy, but also a larger transhistorical conception of redemption and continuity. This broader generalizing aspect, which in both the radio play and the film evokes the chiliastic moment of historical events surrounding the individual figure of Jeanne d'Arc, was significantly reduced in the Berliner Ensemble production of 1952–53 and became virtually eclipsed in the 1954 version. After Brecht's death Seghers was reserved yet candid in her efforts to distinguish her radio play from the Berliner Ensemble adaptation. As Elisabeth Hauptmann wrote to Peter Suhrkamp in 1959, when the 1954 version was to appear in volume 12 of Brecht's works: "It was important to her [Seghers] that she not be named as an adapter of her own radio play."[81]

The essential difference between the radio play by Seghers and the Berliner Ensemble adaptation revolves around the issue of chiliasm. To what extent Seghers—and her husband László Radványi, whose 1923 dissertation on chiliasm first influenced this aspect of her work—held fast to this concept against the grain of the ever more "really existing socialism" in the GDR cannot be satisfactorily documented. The letters in the Anna-

Seghers-Archiv in which there is mention of her radio play suggest she became more interested in its subject matter during the period of the Prague Spring in the 1960s when the victims of the Slansky trial of 1952 were officially rehabilitated. On the one hand she continued to withhold or blur information when responding to inquiries about the origins of the radio play.[82] She also appears to have prohibited circulation of her text when requests for the script were made to the few radio stations that broadcast it, as for example Norddeutscher Rundfunk in Hamburg in 1962.[83] On the other hand she evidently wanted her version to be known when, after the first performance of the Berliner Ensemble adaptation in West Germany, the inspired chiliastic trial scenes of the radio play that were retained in the adaptation were assumed to be entirely Brecht's work.[84]

Almost every one of her letters that makes mention of her radio play refers to the influence of Carl Dreyer's film. Clearly, Seghers had a say in the format of the small but exquisitely designed paperback edition of the play published in 1965 by Reclam Verlag in Leipzig. The text of the play was accompanied by no fewer than fifty-six stills from the Dreyer film, arranged in such a way as to have the text and the respective still correspond in each case. Thus the text, as Seghers surely intended already in 1937, serves to give voice to the silence of the visual images, while the stills are placed in such a way as to provide the text with the visualized physiognomic interactions to which it had responded in the first place. The Reclam edition, republished in 1975 and 1985, and currently out of print, also contains an appendix of excerpted documents from the 1431 trial of Jeanne d'Arc and the posthumous rehabilitation hearings conducted between 1450 and 1456, including the significant revelations of the court scribe and notary Guillaume Manchon. The back cover of the Leipzig Reclam edition highlights an excerpt from the testimony at the rehabilitation proceedings, thereby drawing an implicit parallel between the rehabilitation of Jeanne d'Arc in the 1450s and the efforts at rehabilitating the victims of the Slansky trial during the Prague Spring in Czechoslovakia: "It is apparent that the court recording of said trial was mendacious, distorted, corrupt, incomplete, and inaccurate and thus can claim no credibility. Even though Johanna . . . appeared to the judges to be a believing Christian . . . , this did not prevent them, out of fear of or compliance with the English, from unjustly condemning Johanna to death by fire."

In response to a request from the Piccolo Teatro di Milano for a statement in the theatre program of its spring 1968 production of the Berliner Ensemble adaptation of *The Trial of Jeanne d'Arc in Rouen, 1431,* Seghers wrote in a letter on 1 February 1968: "I wrote the radio play in Paris based on the original court protocols that I studied in the Bibliothèque Nationale. At the time I was very impressed by the silent film Dreyer had made about the trial of Jeanne d'Arc, with Falconetti. This film was surely one of the best films of that time. Bert Brecht was interested in my radio play. With some changes and additions he turned it into a theatre play."[85] The Milan production attempted visually to approximate the aesthetic of Dreyer's film based on still photographs in the Italian edition of the film, *La passione di Giovanna d'Arco.* Seghers's enthusiastic response on 23 April to photographs of the production sent to her concludes with the words: "As a young person I was very excited by this silent film and then again by the little book [*La passione di Giovanna d'Arco*]. Had we [Seghers and her husband Radványi] been able to attend your performance, we would surely have experienced the same excitement for the same cause."[86]

Whereas in spring 1968 the Eurocommunist landscape in Italy might have furthered that "same excitement for the same cause," within the Soviet bloc such hopes were soon dashed by the Warsaw Pact invasion of Czechoslovakia in August, and only a few years later by the events surrounding the expulsion of Wolf Biermann from the GDR in November 1976. In 1981, three years after László Radványi's death and two years before her own, Anna Seghers received a request from the Hungarian sociologist Éva Gábor for permission to publish in Hungary Radványi's dissertation of 1923 on chiliasm, which she had found in the University of Heidelberg archives.[87] According to Gábor, Radványi had said to her in 1978 that unfortunately the dissertation was "lost," but that he "still adhered to what he had written, even if today he saw the place and the role of chiliasm in human knowledge and action differently."[88] Typically cautious and unforthcoming, the author Seghers, who privately bemoaned but publicly supported the GDR Party's decisions in November 1976 and soon thereafter resigned as president of the Writers Union, suggested that her Hungarian colleague "could certainly judge better than I whether such a publication makes any sense at all right now" and decided better "to leave the decision to you people in Hungary."[89]

As Christa Wolf observed in 1992: "We don't know everything about her, not nearly everything about her hidden motives and actions, and we will never know it. All the witnesses are dead."[90] Or, as Hans Mayer suggested one year earlier: "Whoever wants to make a judgment about Anna Seghers has to accept her entirely, or reject her entirely. She never changed. . . . There was always an air of secrecy about her. [Even] the eighty-year-old woman loved this obscurity."[91]

Unlike those who faced their mortality in more favorable political climates and created autobiographies in dialogue with younger adherents— Georg Lukács in Kádár's Hungary in 1971, Heiner Müller in post-Wall Germany in 1992[92]—Anna Seghers left us no such accounting of her self and her times. But even if given the opportunity, she is unlikely to have revealed to us much more of her "true" self shortly before her death than she did in 1924, when under the cover of a pseudonymous persona she began writing about a mythic island "Djal" inhabited by the dead. She completed her mythic journey on a distant island across the seas in her last collection of stories, *Drei Frauen von Haiti* (1980, Three Women from Haiti). She had already visited there in her imagination in the late 1940s, in *Die Hochzeit von Haiti* (1949, Wedding in Haiti), long before most of her European contemporaries would have embarked on such a voyage, long before her critics might have considered topographies that pointed beyond racism and colonialism.

The "truth" about Anna Seghers, as I have tried to argue not only in this chapter, can best be found, at least for a start, in the shape her imagination took on the printed page. From the point of view of scholarship, it is unfortunate that along the often dangerous course of her life journey across national borders and ocean waterways she lost, was dispossessed of, or felt compelled to destroy most of her working papers and other documents that might have lent greater insight into specific circumstances informing her work. Had this not been the case, we might as critics more easily master our subject matter, as readers more easily consume it. But given the little we have accrued, the "meaning" of her work continues to elude us—or perhaps entices us all the more. In looking through the books in her library I was able to find that, whether deliberately or by chance, she did manage to leave some signposts along the way. To many of these I have alluded in earlier chapters. I will mention one more, a piece of blank notepaper stuck between the pages of the "Story of the Three Dervishes" in one of the worn volumes in her library containing stories from the *Thousand and One Nights.* It points us to the words with which the story ends: "Come along with me to my berth. From now on let us together be infidels."[93] The passage hardly strikes me as being conclusive in any way, only as another indication in favor of our further pursuit of the more "heretical" ingredients in her work.

Biographies

Anna Seghers (1900–1983)

Née Netty Reiling, Anna Seghers was born on 19 November 1900 in Mainz. Her mother Hedwig Fuld Reiling came from a prominent Frankfurt family of jewelers and was a founding member of the Jewish Women's League in Mainz. Her father Isidor Reiling, together with his brother Hermann, owned a successful art and antiquities firm whose regular clients included the Hessian court. An only child, Netty Reiling was raised in the religious traditions of Judaism and the Enlightenment as it developed over the centuries in Holland, Germany, and France. She completed her secondary education during the French occupation of Mainz and received her *Matura* in February 1920. Her studies at the University of Heidelberg from 1920 to 1924 included art history, philosophy, and sinology. Here, in the winter of 1920–21, she met her future husband László Radványi and other Hungarian political refugees whose destinies she later thematized in her writings. In November 1924 she received her doctorate with the dissertation *Jude und Judentum im Werke Rembrandts* (Jews and Judaism in the Works of Rembrandt). A month later she published her first story, *Die Toten auf der Insel Djal* (The Dead on the Island Djal). She never used her academic title and henceforth wrote under the pen name Seghers. In August 1925 she married László Radványi and moved to Berlin. Their son Peter was born in May 1926, their daughter Ruth in April 1928. In March 1927 she published *Grubetsch,* for which a year later, together with *The Revolt of the Fishermen,* she was awarded the coveted Kleist Prize. In 1928 she joined the German Communist Party and became active in its League of Proletarian-Revolutionary Writers. In 1929 she traveled to London and spoke at the PEN. The next year she participated in a conference of proletarian-revolutionary writers in Charkov. Her narratives appeared in liberal and left-wing publications, and by the time she was forced into exile in early 1933 she was known as one of Germany's leading avant-garde writers.

Seghers and her husband and children escaped to France via Switzerland and settled in the Paris suburb Bellevue. Her first novel, *Die Gefährten* (1932, The Wayfarers), was followed by publication in exile of *Der Kopflohn* (1934, The Bounty), *Der Weg durch den Februar* (1935, The Way of February), *Die Rettung* (1937, The Rescue), and *The Seventh Cross* (first book publication 1942, in English); shorter narratives and essays appeared in leading exile journals. Seghers was a prominent voice among political exiles and a frequent speaker on behalf of the antifascist movement at exiled writers' congresses and related events in France, in Spain during the Civil War, and later in Mexico. In June 1940, after an abortive attempt to flee south before the invading German army, Seghers and her children were forced back to Paris, where they remained in hiding. In September they managed to reach the unoccupied zone and spent the winter in Pamiers, near the French camp at Le Vernet where László Radványi was incarcerated. From Pamiers Seghers made frequent trips to Marseille in search of visas and transit permits, an experience hardly unique to her and one she memorialized in her novel *Transit* (1944). In March 1941 she and her family departed Marseille on the transport ship *Capitain Paul Lemerle.* With stops in Oran and Casablanca, and, across the Atlantic, detentions in Martinique, and New York's Ellis Island, they arrived on 30 June in Mexico, where they had been granted asylum.

In Mexico Seghers was president of the Heine Club and a regular contributor to the exile journal *Freies Deutschland.* She achieved considerable renown in the English-speaking world with the 1942 publication of *The Seventh Cross* by Little, Brown & Co. in Boston. The novel was a Book of the Month Club selection, quickly became a best-seller, was reissued in an armed forces edition, and was turned into a nationally syndicated comic strip as well as a successful Hollywood film directed by Fred Zinnemann and starring Spencer Tracy. In June 1943 Seghers was struck down by a hit-and-run driver on a busy thoroughfare near her apartment in Mexico City. For a time she lay in a coma and thereafter suffered from amnesia. During her recovery she wrote *The Excursion of the Dead Girls,* an autobiographical narrative in memory of her parents and childhood teachers and friends who became the victims of National Socialism. Residing in a series of *Judenhäuser* in Mainz since the pogroms that swept Germany in November 1938, Seghers's father Isidor Reiling died in March 1940, two days after having to relinquish all claims to the art and antiquities firm he and his brother Hermann inherited from their father. Her mother Hedwig Reiling, despite her daughter's attempts to secure visas for her from France and Mexico, was deported in March 1942 on a transport of one thousand Hessian Jews to the Piaski ghetto near Lublin. Johanna Sichel, Seghers's favorite teacher in high school, was on the same transport.

Seghers's uncle Hermann Reiling died two days later. In September his wife Flora Reiling was put on a transport to Theresienstadt. Sehers wrote two more Holocaust narratives at the end of the war: *Post ins gelobte Land* (Post to the Promised Land) and *Das Ende* (The End).

After the war Seghers sent her children to France to study at the Sorbonne. Pierre Radvanyi worked with Joliot-Curie and became a distinguished French physicist. Ruth Radvanyi later moved to East Berlin where she worked as a physician and director of a children's hospital and clinic. Seghers returned to Berlin in 1947 via New York and Stockholm. In interviews she gave at the time she said she wanted to be of help in her own language to reeducate younger generations and made reference to the Mexican government's literacy campaign as part of its own efforts to combat fascism (*Tägliche Rundschau,* 24 April 1947; *New York Times,* 25 April 1947). Similar to the work of the Mexican muralists and the musicological experiments of Zoltán Kodály in Hungary, Seghers's postwar prose was indeed a kind of literacy campaign for a young readership recovering from twelve years under National Socialism. Her productivity as a creative writer, speaker, and essayist was extraordinary in these and later years: countless speeches and essays; the novels *The Dead Stay Young* (1949), *Die Entscheidung* (1959, The Decision), *Das Vertrauen* (1968, Trust); and numerous prose collections devoted to working-class life, with an emphasis on the problems of women, indigenous peoples, and the emancipation struggles of African slaves and former slaves in the colonies, as exemplified by *Friedensgeschichten* (1950, Stories of Peace), *Karibische Geschichten* (1962, Caribbean Stories), *Die Kraft der Schwachen* (1965, The Power of the Weak), and her last work, *Drei Frauen von Haiti* (1980, Three Women from Haiti).

As a member of the executive board of the World Peace Council Seghers was a sought-after speaker at congresses in Vienna, Warsaw, Stockholm, and Paris. Reading tours and other travels took her throughout Europe and as far as China (1951) and Brazil (1961, 1963). As president of the East German Writers Union for twenty-five years (1952–78) she had an enormous impact on younger writers, an especially large number of them women. The wide-ranging spectrum and diversity of East German literature as well as the exceptionally high rate of public literacy in the GDR would have been unimaginable without her efforts and example. She was the recipient of numerous national and international prizes and honors. Her stories and novels have been read and studied by generations of German schoolchildren as well as around the world. *The Seventh Cross* alone has been read in over forty languages. Despite national and international fame Seghers stayed true to her beliefs, eschewing privilege and amassing no material wealth aside from her books. Until the end of her life she lived rather modestly in an apartment in the outlying working-class district Berlin-Adlershof. She died on 1 June 1983. She bequeathed her books and papers to the German Academy of the Arts. Her testament specifies that royalties from the sale of her books be distributed annually, in the form of literary prizes, to deserving young, especially Latin American writers.

Béla Balázs (pen name for Herbert Bauer; 1884–1949)

A poet, fabulist, storyteller, and playwright, Béla Balázs was one of the leading avant-garde writers of his generation. He was a close friend of Zoltán Kodály and wrote the libretti for Béla Bartók's operas *The Wooden Prince* and *Bluebeard's Castle.* In the Hungarian Council Republic of 1919 he was director of the Cultural Ministry Division of Literature and Theatre. In the 1920s he lived in Vienna and Berlin, where he achieved success as a film critic, theorist (*Visible Man,* 1924; *The Spirit of Film,* 1930), and scenarist (e.g., *Grand Hotel,* 1927; *The Threepenny Opera,* 1930; *The Blue Light,* 1931). From 1933 to 1945 he lived in the Soviet Union, where he continued to write plays and scenarios. After the war he was celebrated as a pioneering figure in cinema by the new realist school of Polish and Italian directors but failed to find official approval in his native Hungary, where he was prolific until his death. His revival began in Hungary in the 1970s, more recently among film scholars in the West.

Walter Benjamin (1892–1940)

Early studies by Walter Benjamin include *The Concept of Art Criticism in German Romanticism* (1920), "Goethe's *Elective Affinities*" (1924–25), and *The Origin of German Tragedy* (1928). Unable to secure a university position, Benjamin devoted himself to essays and aphoristic writings in the manner of *One-Way Street* (1928). His relationship to Siegfried Kracauer and Theodor Adorno began in 1923; in later years he published in the Frankfurt School's *Journal of Social Research.* Also close to Gershom Scholem and Brecht, he had an abiding interest in both Zionism and Marxism. He fled to France in March 1933, there published his famous essays on Kafka, Eduard Fuchs, "Art in the Age of Mechanical Reproduction," and "The Storyteller," and continued work on his larger projects on French surrealism and the Paris arcades. In June 1940 he fled to Lourdes and from there to Marseille, and after a failed attempt to cross the Pyrenees committed suicide on 27 September in Port Bou. Much of Benjamin's writing, including his last extraordinary work "On the Concept of History," remained fragmentary. The first posthumous publications were in New York (1942), France (1947), East Berlin (1949), and Frankfurt (1950).

Bertolt Brecht (1898–1956)

One of the great German poets, Bertolt Brecht is internationally renowned as the playwright who revolutionized modern drama and theatre. Major plays of the 1920s range from the lyrical *Baal* (1920) to *The Threepenny Opera* (1928) and *Rise and Fall of the City of Mahagonny* (1929). In the early 1930s he experimented with forms of the learning play, as in *The Measures Taken* (1930) and *The Mother* (1932). Brecht was quickly blacklisted by the National Socialists and fled to Denmark. Plays of the 1930s such as *Fear and Misery of the Third Reich,* as well as poetry and prose, are devoted to the fight against Hitler. With the onset of the war and his escape to Sweden, Finland, and the United States, he wrote his famous parable and chronicle plays: *Life of Galileo, Mother Courage, The Good Woman of Setzuan, The Caucasian Chalk Circle,* and others. After the war Brecht first spent a year in Zurich and thereafter settled in East Berlin, where he was assured his own company. His work as artistic director of the Berliner Ensemble together with his wife, the leading actress Helene Weigel, who continued to head the Ensemble after his death, soon reverberated throughout Germany and Europe.

Anna Lesznai (1885–1966)

Poet, fabulist, illustrator, and artist, Anna Lesznai was a key figure in the Hungarian avant-garde, an early contributor to the seminal journal *Nyugat* (West), and a member of the experimental group of artists Nyolcak (The Eight). During the war and revolutions she was married to the radical democrat Oszkár Jászi, a cabinet minister in the liberal Károlyi government of 1918–19 who broke with the supporters of the Council Republic and left Hungary in the spring of 1919. At that time Lesznai worked with Lukács in the Commissariat for Education to introduce folk and fairy tales into school curricula. In exile in Vienna she married the graphic artist Tibor Gergely, one of the youngest members of the Sunday Circle. They returned to Budapest in the 1930s and in 1939 emigrated to New York, where Lesznai continued to exhibit her work. Her autobiographical novel *Spätherbst in Eden* (1965, Late Autumn in Eden) contains reminiscences of her friendship with Balázs and Lukács and meetings of the Sunday Circle.

Georg Lukács (1885–1971)

Georg Lukács established his European reputation as a philosopher and aesthetician with *Soul and Form* (1910), *History of the Development of Drama* (1911), and *The Theory of the Novel* (1916). He studied in Budapest and Berlin, belonged to the Weber Circle in Heidelberg, and returned to Budapest in 1916 to become the driving force within the Sunday Circle and the Free School of the Humanities. He was Commissar of Education during the Hungarian Council Republic of 1919. Its theoretical justification, *History and Class Consciousness* (1923), became a classic document of critical Marxism for his own and future generations. Exiled in Vienna, Lukács continued clandestine work within the Hungarian Communist Party. Repeatedly criticized by the Comintern, he retreated from Party work in 1929 and turned to his writings on realism: 1930–31 in Moscow, 1931–33 in Berlin, and 1933–44 in Moscow. Under frequent attack by the Rákosi regime, after the war he nonetheless became a major intellectual force in Hungary. His exile and other writings appeared: *Balzac, Stendhal, Zola* (1945), *Essays on Thomas Mann* (1947), *The Historical Novel* (1947), *Goethe and His Age* (1947), *The Young Hegel* (1948), *Essays on Realism* (1948), *The Destruction of Reason* (1954). In 1956 he became the leading figure in the revolutionary Petöfi Circle and Minister for Public Education in the short-lived revolutionary government of Imre Nagy. Retired from public life after 1956, he devoted himself to his students, later known as the Budapest School, and his late writings: *Specificity of the Aesthetic* (1963), *Solzhenitsyn* (1969), *On the Ontology of Social Reality* (1970).

Karl Mannheim (1893–1947)

Influenced by Lukács and Béla Zalai, Karl Mannheim studied in Berlin and Budapest and received a doctorate in 1918 with the dissertation *A Structural Analysis of Epistemology.* He achieved renown with his brilliant lectures on epistemology and "soul and culture" at the Free School of the Humanities in 1918, and on aesthetics and culture at the University of Budapest in 1919. In exile in Heidelberg he joined the Weber Circle and was appointed *Privatdozent* in 1926. Like the art historian Arnold Hauser, whose later works include *The Social History of Art* (1953), *Philosophy of Art History* (1959), and *Mannerism* (1964), in the 1920s Mannheim distanced himself from the politics, if not all the ideas, of Lukács. His gradual shift from studies of aesthetics and philosophy to sociology and culture culminated in his major work *Ideology and Utopia* of 1929, whereupon he was appointed to a professorship in Frankfurt. In 1933 he was forced to resign his post and thereupon emigrated to England, where he taught at the London School of Economics and continued to write and publish. His wife Júlia Láng, a psychologist who first worked with Géza Révész on experiments with music, furthered Mannheim's own considerable interest in psychology and after his death worked as a psychoanalyst with Anna Freud.

László Radványi [Johann-Lorenz Schmidt] (1900–1978)

Inspired as a *Gymnasium* student by the poet Endre Ady's call for political reform and revolutions of the soul, during the war László Radványi was politically active in the radical democratic and pacifist Galileo Circle at the same time that he nurtured interests in poetry, aesthetics, and philosophy. Not yet sixteen, he published a book of poetry, *Fekete Könyv* (1916, Black Book), inspired by Ady and with a foreword by the writer Frigyes Karinthy. In 1918 he attended Lukács's, Balázs's, and Mannheim's lectures at the Free School of the Humanities, became one of the youngest members of the Budapest Sunday Circle, and during the Hungarian Council Republic of 1919 was politically active in the student movement and education reform. In exile he studied at the University of Heidelberg with Karl Rickert, Emil Lederer, and Karl Jaspers, and in March 1923 he was awarded a doctorate *summa cum laude* for a dissertation written for Jaspers, *Der Chiliasmus.* After his marriage in 1925 to Anna Seghers and their move to Berlin he was extraordinarily successful as the director of the Marxist Workers' School (MASCH), which became the model for comparable schools throughout Germany and abroad. In exile in Paris he established a similar school and in 1940–41, during his incarceration in the French camp at Le Vernet, taught classes on a daily basis to fellow prisoners. His reputation as an inspiring teacher and expert in multiple fields is widely documented. In 1943 he was appointed to a professorship in economics at the National University of Mexico, where he remained until 1952. Upon his return to East Berlin he assumed a chair in economics at the Humboldt Universität, which he held until his death. His journal and book publications in both Mexico and the GDR are devoted to his lifelong scholarly interest in the economic and sociological problems of developing nations. Radványi's sister Lilli, to whom he was close throughout his life, was married to the Hungarian psychoanalyst Leopold Szondi. Incarcerated with their two children in the German concentration camp Bergen-Belsen in 1944, they were freed on the intervention of an international group of psychoanalysts and emigrated to Switzerland. Their son Peter Szondi achieved renown as a critical theorist and Benjamin and Celan scholar.

Appendix

The Library of Young Anna Seghers

The twelve-volume Insel Verlag edition (1913) of the *Thousand and One Nights,* with an introduction by Hugo von Hofmannsthal, is the most obviously worn and frequently read of the titles in the Anna-Seghers-Archiv library that display the ex libris "Netty Reiling" (ASA lib. 4140). The six volumes of the 1923–27 Insel Verlag edition are equally worn (ASA lib. 4141–42). Furthermore, Seghers owned and, from the look of its wear and tear, often used the 1925 Insel Verlag edition *Tausend und ein Tag: Orientalische Erzählungen* (Thousand and One Day: Oriental Stories), with an introduction by Paul Ernst (ASA lib. 4112).

Displaying the ex libris "Netty Reiling," the books in her early library, in some cases in both German and the original language and in multiple editions, include the collected works of Shakespeare, Goethe, Schiller, Hölderlin, Kleist, Heine, Keller, Jacobsen, Ibsen, and Oscar Wilde (ASA lib. 2399, 2400–2401; 2641, 2646–49, 2575–76; 2603–10; 923; 2910, 1914, 2642–44; 3046–48; 2583–84; 4166–68; 4941; 2423, 2424–27). Other books displaying the ex libris indicate that she read Dickens, Andersen, Barrie, Defoe, Kipling, Hauff, Brentano, Eichendorff, Hebel, Turgenev, Dostoyevsky, and Strindberg (ASA lib. 2448; 4008; 3937; 3895; 2459/2545; 2996–98; 2974; 2999, 3000; 4999; 3656; 1808, 2312; 4193/4194/4235). The collection of philosophical writings from her later university years includes seven titles by Kierkegaard, two of them displaying the ex libris "Netty Reiling" (ASA lib. 232; 233; 234, 256; 235; 236; 237; 257). The library indicates a significant interest in legends and tales: stories from the Old Testament, Netherlandish and Scandinavian legends, volumes of the *Edda,* Balkan and Japanese tales, medieval French legends of the Virgin Mary (ASA lib. 4231; 4160; 4097, 4102; 4126; 4103; 2653–54). The library also contains pre-1920 editions without an ex libris "Netty Reiling" that include old French, African, Chinese, and Greek-Albanian tales (ASA lib. 2677; 4099; 4131; 4104–5).

Netty Reiling's reading fancy also drew her, probably with her mother's encouragement, to the romantic legacies of Napoleon. She owned his correspondence with Josephine and several memoirs, as well as histories of the time by Charles Laurent, Alexander Kielland, Alexandre Dumas, and Sir Walter Scott (ASA lib. 2371; 4485–88; 2381–82; 2397; 2369; 2395; 2386; 2398; 2383). She read Maria Teresia's letters as well as Voltaire's, and the memoirs of Catherine de Medici's daughter Margarethe de Valois, the wife of Henri of Navarre (ASA lib. 3756; 2699–700; 2725–26). She was also familiar at this time with Villon, Cervantes, Rousseau, Stendhal, Loti, de Musset, Flaubert, Fontane, and Schnitzler, and with translated selections of modern poetry by Rossetti, Swinburne, Verlaine, Mallarmé, and Rimbaud (ASA lib. 293; 387–88; 2708; 2703; 2705; 421; 5300; 3269; 2994; 5536; 2881–82). During the French occupation of the city at the end of World War One this well-educated daughter of Mainz acquainted herself with Caroline Schlegel-Schelling's eyewitness accounts of the Mainz Republic and Ricarda Huch's character study of Wallenstein during the Thirty Years' War (ASA lib. 1931–32; 2947). Moreover, she eagerly read *Le Matin* (instead of the usual *Frankfurter Zeitung*) and referred to herself—"Tiffel" was her family nickname—as "French-Tiffel" (see the excerpt from her mother's letter of 22 December 1918 to her own mother Helene Fuld in Frankfurt, in *Anna Seghers: Eine Biographie in Bildern,* ed. Frank Wagner, Ursula Emmerich, and Ruth Radvanyi [Berlin: Aufbau Verlag, 1994], 28).

Aside from direct access through her father to plates, prints, and original art objects as well as art books, while still in Mainz Netty Reiling had a number of books on art and art history in her own library, among them a life of Michelangelo and a collection of his writings, the lives of Leonardo da Vinci and Velázquez, Emile Verhaeren's life of Rembrandt, Rainer Maria Rilke on Rodin, and a book on Goethe's physiognomy (ASA lib. 3360–61; 3389; 3388; 3375; 3367; 4928; 4929). She also owned a book on modern women artists, from the Dutch artist Betzy Akersloot-Berg, whose intriguing depictions of working-class women may well have influenced Seghers's own narrative renderings, to the American Mary Cassatt: Anton Kirsch, *Die bildenden Künstlerinnen der Neuzeit* (Stuttgart: Verlag von Ferdinand Enke, 1905) (ASA lib. unnumbered).

Some of the distinctive images from Gothic architecture and sculpture that influenced topographic and physiognomic images in her later prose are found on large, finely produced plates contained in the following books in her library: *Maria im Rosenhag: Madonnen-Bilder alter deutscher und niederländischer Meister,* Die Blauen Bücher series (Königstein: Verlag Karl Robert Langewiesche, n.d.); *Deutsche Köpfe des Mittelalters,* ed. Richard Hamann (Marburg: Verlag des kunstgeschichtlichen Seminars,

1922); *Gotische Madonnenstatuen in Deutschland,* ed. Ad. Goldschmidt (Augsburg: Dr. Benno Filser Verlag, 1923); and *Die deutschen Dome des Mittelalters,* Die Blauen Bücher series (Königstein: Karl Robert Lange-wiesche Verlag, 1924) (ASA lib. unnumbered). Also significant would have been Max J. Friedländer's books on early Netherlandish and German painting: *Die altniederländische Malerei,* 3 vols. (Berlin: Paul Cassirer Verlag, 1924); and *Die Zeichnungen von Matthias Grünewald* (Berlin: Grote'sche Verlagsbuchhandlung, 1927) (ASA lib. unnumbered). Her Asian collection included the multivolume edition *Orbis-Pictus: Welt-kunstbücherei,* ed Paul Westheim (Berlin: Verlag Ernst Wasmuth, n.d.), with separate volumes of plates: *Indische Baukunst, Alt-Russische Kunst, Indische Miniaturen, Hethitische Kunst, Die chinesische Landschafts-malerei, Chinesische Kleinplastik, Asiatische Monumentalplastik* (ASA lib. unnumbered).

At the time of their marriage in August 1925 Isidor Lutz Reiling pre-sented his daughter Netty and her husband László Radványi with a revised and expanded Frankfurt edition of the *Israelitisches Gebetbuch: Hebräisch und Deutsch* (1885, Israelite Prayer Book: In Hebrew and German), with an extensive inscription by him (ASA lib. 4118). Perhaps from another source Netty Reiling Radványi received a book of recommenda-tions on the traditional behavior and practices of the Jewish wife (ASA lib. 1634). She herself opted to present her husband with a volume *Ostjüdische Liebeslieder* (Eastern [European] Jewish Love Songs), which she endowed with an unambiguous inscription in her own hand: "du tschibischer Genoss / du Ross, du Ross!" (you're chick's comrade and chum / you steed, you steed!) (ASA lib. 4096). (Radványi's pet name for his wife was "Csibi," a not uncommon Hungarian form of endearment meaning "chick," which in the phonetic German spelling became "Tschibi"; in the inscription the proper noun was turned into an adjective.)

Netty Reiling Radványi/Anna Seghers had in her possession several versions of the *Haggadah,* the Exodus narrative read at the Passover seder (ASA lib. 4108; 4121; 1642). Due to her husband's influence their com-bined collection of Jewish writings increased considerably during the 1920s. Aside from the works of widely known Central European Jewish authors such as Kafka (ASA lib. 96), Toller (2854), and Werfel (4124, 5463), it held Anski's *Dybuk* (ASA lib. 2868); several of bin Gorion's edi-tions of Jewish legends and stories, including the *Born Judas* (ASA lib. 4156; 4157; 4114–15); most of Martin Buber's early writings (ASA lib. 409; 410; 411; and more than ten unnumbered titles by Buber); and a set of the *Encyclopedia Judaica* (ASA lib. 2355–56), as well as numerous Hebrew editions of the Bible and editions of the Old and New Testament in several languages. From her penciled markings in the margins of the English-language editions of Sholem Asch's *The Nazarene* (1939) and *The Apostle* (1943), which were purchased in a Mexico City bookstore (ASA lib. 2411; 2422), it appears that Seghers read these novels in the early 1940s while she was finishing *Transit* and preparing her next novel, *The Dead Stay Young.*

At the time that she wrote *The Revolt of the Fishermen* in 1927–28, Anna Seghers had in her library three works by Joseph Conrad in German translation: *Chance, Typhoon,* and *Nostromo* (ASA lib. 2446; 2442; 2444). Also significant in this respect are the Scandinavian sea tales of August Strindberg (ASA lib. 4193; 4194) and Selma Lagerlöf (ASA lib. 4174; 4189). Seghers also owned German editions of Pierre Loti's *Pêcheur d'Islande* (ASA lib. 4211) and Jack London's *Sea Wolf* (ASA lib. 2477). She would also have been familiar with B. Traven's *The Death Ship,* which was widely reviewed when it first appeared in Germany in 1926. Later acquisitions of Joseph Conrad in German include a 1929 Berlin Fischer edition of *Freya of the Seven Islands* (ASA lib. 2443), a 1947 Berlin Suhrkamp edition of *Lord Jim* (ASA lib. 2445), a 1962 Leipzig Insel Verlag edition of *Tales* (ASA lib. 2447), and a 1971 Berlin Volk und Welt edition of *Almayer's Folly* (ASA lib. 4680). It was evidently Seghers who penciled the date "27.IV.27" (27 April 1927) at the top left-hand side of the first recto page of the 1927 Fischer edition of *Nostromo.* Next to it, clearly not in her handwriting, is written in red ink "Weihnachten 1927" (Christmas 1927). Generally, Anna Seghers made no marginal comments or other markings in her books. Yet the wear and tear on the 1927 edition of *Nostromo* (evidently read while she worked on *The Revolt of the Fishermen*) and on the 1947 edition of *Lord Jim* (evidently read while she worked on *Das Argonautenschiff* [The Ship of the Argonauts] and her Caribbean novellas about Haiti, Guadeloupe, and Jamaica) suggests that she probably read these novels more than once and at different times in her life.

The Library of Young László Radványi

The Hungarian and German books Radványi brought with him at the time of his emigration from Hungary in the fall of 1919 reveal the extent of his preoccupation with the ideas and writings of members of the Budapest Sunday Circle and the authors and topics they discussed in their weekly meetings in Budapest, and later in Vienna. Radványi's Hungarian library includes the most important titles by authors who up until 1919 constituted the Hungarian avant-garde: first editions of the poetry of Endre Ady (ASA lib. 6145; 6152; 6553; 6154), Anna Lesznai (ASA lib. 6131; 6141; 6142; 6177), and the plays and poetry of Béla Balázs (ASA lib. 6146; 6147; 6148; 6149; 6150); prose by Zsigmond Moricz (ASA lib. 6115) and Frigyes Karinthy (6233; 6136); issues of the leading cultural-literary journal *Nyugat* and other avant-garde journals and anthologies (ASA lib. unnumbered); and the volume of philosophical essays *Konzervativ és progressiv idealizmus* (1918, Conservative and Progressive Idealism) (ASA lib. 6140), documenting the important debates of the revolutionary period at the end of World War One between the radical and social democrats Oszkár Jászi, Ervin Szabó et al., and the Budapest Sunday Circle members Béla Fogarasi and Georg Lukács (with studious pencil markings by Radványi in the margins of Lukács's essay). Radványi also owned three books published by Lukács in Hungary prior to 1919: *A lélek és a formák* (1910, Soul and Form) (ASA lib. 6172), *A modern dráma fejlödésének története* (1911, History of the Development of Modern Drama) (ASA lib. 6108–9), and *Balázs Béla és akiknek nem kell: Összegyüjtött tanulmányok* (1918, Béla Balázs and Those Who Don't Want Him: Collected Essays) (ASA lib. 6134).

Radványi also collected Hungarian exile publications: *Március Tribün* (1922, March Tribune), an anthology of poetry written during the Commune of 1919, its cover designed by his close school friend and fellow Sundayer Tibor Gergely (ASA lib. 6223); *A fájdalmas Isten* (1923, The Suffering Christ), with an image of Christ with a large open wound on the book's cover, by the young Sundayer and revolutionary Ervin Sinkó, who after 1919 became a Tolstoyan (ASA lib. 6224); and several issues of Sinkó's exile journal *Testvér* (Brother/Sister) containing essays about the passion of Christ and the writings of Angelus Silesius, Matthias Claudius, Kierkegaard, Martin Buber, and André Gide, as well as the Sundayers Béla Balázs, Anna Lesznai, Sinkó, and other exiled Hungarian intellectuals (ASA lib. 6207–17).

Radványi's 1917 Budapest edition *Uj Testament és a Zsoltárok* (New Testament and the Psalms) contains a large number of underlinings and markings in his hand and presumably at the time of his death was left with a paper marker at the start of the Gospel of John (ASA lib. unnumbered). To friends and comrades in Heidelberg Radványi was known as Johann. After his move to Berlin he assumed the German name Johann-Lorenz Schmidt, Lorenz being the German equivalent of László. The poem "Min Jehann" by the Low German writer Klaus Groth was found among Anna Seghers's papers after her death and appears in *Anna Seghers: Eine Biographie in Bildern,* 231.

Other books acquired by Radványi in Budapest and during the first years of his exile include the Sunday Circle's—and, as we know from her own later essays, also some of Anna Seghers's—most favored authors: Dostoyevsky (multiple editions in several languages), Tolstoy (multiple editions of the best-known works as well as his folk legends), Goethe, Flaubert, and Claudel. Radványi also owned a 1922 edition of Solovjev's essays on Dostoyevsky in which he marked passages pertaining to the

prophetic aspects of Dostoyevsky's writings (ASA lib. 3660). From conversations within the Sunday Circle Radványi, and through him Anna
Seghers, would already have known at this time the young Lukács's more
extensive thoughts on Dostoyevsky, also informed by Solovjev, which
scholars only discovered decades later among the "Heidelberg Manuscripts" deposited by Lukács in a suitcase in Heidelberg upon his return to
Budapest in 1916. In his notes on Dostoyevsky Lukács was concerned
with intersections of mystical and revolutionary thought, not only in Dostoyevsky. On this topic in English, see Michael Löwy, *Georg Lukács: From
Romanticism to Bolshevism,* trans. Patrick Camiller (London: New Left
Books, 1979), 91–128; see also Lee Congdon, *The Young Lukács* (Chapel
Hill: University of North Carolina Press, 1983), 96–117.

Radványi's enthusiastic markings in his personal copy of the 1923
Malik Verlag edition of *History and Class Consciousness* (ASA lib. 6004),
especially in the first chapter, "Orthodox Marxism," reveal how great an
influence and inspiration Georg Lukács continued to be for him. This
work, as well as his heavily annotated Hungarian copy of the New Testament and the Psalms, seems to have preoccupied him above all during his
decisive Heidelberg years. In addition Radványi owned practically all the
writings of Martin Buber that appeared prior to his completion of his dissertation on chiliasm in March 1923. In September 1922 in Mainz, where
she must have introduced him to her parents, Netty Reiling presented Radványi with the 1920 Rütten & Loening edition of Buber's *Die Legende des
Baalschem,* with the inscription: "This book belongs / to Rodi / from his
child" (ASA lib. unnumbered). Eight months earlier, in February 1922,
Radványi had given her a Low German version of Philip Otto Runge's
fairy tale *The Fisherman and His Wife,* accompanied by a Low German
inscription in his hand: "Lütt Tschibe" (to little chick) (ASA lib. 4204).
This was a no less appropriate gift for a young woman with talents in storytelling than the gift of Kierkegaard's *The Sickness unto Death,* with which
Radványi had approached Netty Reiling one year earlier, along with the
inscription: "Dear Little Sister Netty Reiling, May God grant that what we
long for will be" (ASA lib. 234). The last record we have of such gifts
exchanged during their years in Heidelberg is a large Insel Verlag volume
inspired by chiliastic history and legend: *Der Heiligen Leben und Leiden aus
dem 15. Jahrhundert* (Lives and Sufferings of the Saints from the Fifteenth
Century). Radványi dedicated it to Netty Reiling with the words: "For his
motherchild at Christmas 1922, her Rod" (ASA lib. 3028).

Notes

Abbreviations

ASA Anna-Seghers-Archiv, Akademie der Künste, Berlin; holdings include manuscript and letter files in the Akademie der Künste am Robert-Koch-Platz, Berlin, and the author's personal library of over nine thousand titles located in her former apartment, now a museum, in Berlin-Adlershof.
BBA Bertolt-Brecht-Archiv, Akademie der Künste, Berlin
PIM Petőfi Irodalmi Múzeum, Budapest (Petőfi Literary Museum)
MTA Magyar Tudományos Akadémia—Kézirattár, Budapest (Hungarian Academy of Sciences—Manuscripts)

Introduction

1. Anna Seghers, "Illegales legal," *Über Kunstwerk und Wirklichkeit,* vol. 1, *Die Tendenz in der reinen Kunst,* ed. Sigrid Bock (Berlin: Akademie Verlag, 1970), 185.

2. Walter Benjamin, "Eine Chronik der deutschen Arbeitslosen: Zu Anna Seghers Roman 'Die Rettung,'" in *Gesammelte Schriften,* vol. 3, *Kritiken und Rezensionen,* ed. Hella Tiedemann-Bartels (Frankfurt am Main: Suhrkamp Verlag, 1972), 534–35.

3. Georg Lukács, *The Theory of the Novel: A Historico-Philosophical Essay on the Forms of Great Epic Literature,* trans. Anna Bostock (Cambridge, Mass.: MIT Press, 1971), 41.

4. Benjamin, "The Storyteller," in *Illuminations,* ed. Hannah Arendt, trans. Harry Zohn (New York: Schocken Books, 1969), 101.

5. This approach was first used in Martin Esslin, *Brecht: The Man and His Work* (Garden City, N.Y.: Anchor, 1971). See my reference in chapter 8, note 84, to the misinformed discussion of Brecht and Seghers's collaboration on *The Trial of Jeanne d'Arc at Rouen, 1431* by Hellmuth Karasek in 1960. For more on this and other misreadings, see Helen Fehervary, "Brecht, Seghers, and *The Trial of Jeanne d'Arc*—with a Previously Unpublished Letter of 1952 from Seghers to Brecht," *The Brecht Yearbook* 21 (1996): 20–47.

6. Joseph Conrad, *Lord Jim,* ed. Cedric Watts and Robert Hampton (London: Penguin Books, 1986), note 10, page 355.

7. Hans Mayer, *Der Widerruf: Über Deutsche und Juden* (Frankfurt am Main: Suhrkamp Verlag, 1994), 277–78, 283.

8. Anna Seghers, "Ansprache in Weimar: Rede auf dem Internationalen Schriftstellertreffen 1965," in *Über Kunstwerk und Wirklichkeit,* vol. 1, *Die Tendenz in der reinen Kunst,* ed. Sigrid Bock (Berlin: Akademie Verlag, 1970), 150. On some of the correspondences between Seghers's work and Kafka's, see Paul Rilla, "Die Erzählerin Anna Seghers," *Sinn und Form* 2 (1950): 83–113; and Kurt Batt, *Anna Seghers: Versuch über Entwicklung und Werke* (Leipzig: Reclam Verlag, 1973), 152–64.

9. See Netty Reiling (Anna Seghers), *Jude und Judentum im Werke Rembrandts* (Leipzig: Reclam Verlag, 1981); includes a foreword by Christa Wolf and 48 plates. The significance of the dissertation is acknowledged in the Rembrandt literature. See Christian Tümpel, *Rembrandt* (Reinbek bei Hamburg: Rowohlt Verlag, 1977), note 67, page 134.

10. See my discussion in chapter 2.

11. See Ladislaus Radványi, *Der Chiliasmus: Ein Versuch zur Erkenntnis der chiliastischen Idee und des chiliastischen Handelns,* ed. Éva Gábor (Budapest: MTA Filozófiai Intézet, 1985).

12. Friedrich Albrecht, *Die Erzählerin Anna Seghers, 1926–1932* (Berlin: Rütten & Loening, 1965); Inge Diersen, *Seghers-Studien: Interpretationen von Werken aus den Jahren 1926–1935* (Berlin: Rütten & Loening, 1965); Frank Wagner, ". . . der Kurs auf die Realität": Das epische Werk von Anna Seghers, 1935–1943* (Berlin: Akademie Verlag, 1975); Batt, *Anna Seghers: Versuch über Entwicklung und Werke;* Frank Wagner, *Anna Seghers* (Leipzig: Reclam Verlag, 1980).

13. E.g., Peter Beicken, Ute Brandes, Christa Degemann, Bernhard Greiner, Gertraud Gutzmann, Erika Haas, Sonja Hilzinger, Kathleen LaBahn, Peter Roos and Friderike J. Hassauer-Roos, Klaus Sauer, Alexander Stephan, Hans-Albert Walter, Christiane Zehl Romero.

14. Christa Wolf, "Ein Gespräch mit Anna Seghers," in *Die Dimension des Autors,* vol. 1 (Berlin: Aufbau Verlag, 1986), 286. See in the same volume Wolf's essays on Seghers (unfortunately not yet translated into English): "Das siebte Kreuz," 263–78; "Glauben an Irdisches," 293–320; "Anmerkungen zu Geschichten," 323–31; "Bei Anna Seghers," 332–38; "Fortgesetzter Versuch," 339–45; "Die Dissertation der Netty Reiling," 346–52; "Zeitschichten," 353–63; "Transit: Ortschaften," 364–77. See also her introductory essay "Die Gesichter der Anna Seghers," in *Anna Seghers: Eine Biographie in Bildern,* ed. Frank Wagner, Ursula Emmerich, and Ruth Radvanyi (Berlin: Aufbau Verlag, 1994; reprint, 2000), 6–9.

15. Notably Marcel Reich-Ranicki, e.g., "Nicht gedacht soll ihrer werden?" *Frankfurter Allgemeine Zeitung,* 21 July 1990; among younger critics, Andreas Schrade, *Anna Seghers* (Stuttgart and Weimar: Metzler Verlag, 1993); and Schrade, *Entwurf einer ungeteilten Gesellschaft: Anna Seghers' Weg zum Roman nach 1945* (Bielefeld: Aisthesis Verlag, 1994). (See my review of the latter in *Monatshefte* 90 [summer 1998]: 286–89.) A decidedly more differentiated interpretation of Seghers's work is found in Julia Hell, *Post-Fascist Fantasies: Psychoanalysis,*

History, and the Literature of East Germany (Durham, N.C.: Duke University Press, 1997).

16. Siegfried Kracauer, "Eine Märtyrer-Chronik von heute," *Frankfurter Zeitung,* 13 November 1932.

17. See Rosa Luxemburg, "Socialism and the Churches," in *Rosa Luxemburg Speaks,* ed. Mary-Alice Waters (New York: Pathfinder Press, 1970), 131–52; originally: Jósef Chmura [pseud.], *Kosciól a socjalizm* (Cracow, 1905).

18. Georg Lukács, *Soul and Form,* trans. Anna Bostock (Cambridge, Mass.: MIT Press, 1974), 1.

19. Hans Henny Jahnn, "Begründung für die Verleihung des Kleist-Preises," *Die Literatur* (Stuttgart, Berlin) 31, no. 5 (1928–29): 305; Jahnn, "Rechenschaft Kleistpreis 1928," *Der Kreis* (Hamburg) 6, no. 3 (1929): 137–41; Stephan Hermlin, "Das Werk der Anna Seghers," in Hermlin and Hans Mayer, *Ansichten über einige Bücher und Schriftsteller* (Berlin, 1947). Regarding Walter Benjamin, see note 1; Hans Mayer, note 6; Christa Wolf, note 13.

20. Erika Haas, *Ideologie und Mythos: Studien zur Erzählstruktur und Sprache im Werk von Anna Seghers,* Stuttgarter Arbeiten zur Germanistik, ed. Ulrich Müller, Franz Hundsnurscher, and Cornelius Sommer (Stuttgart: Akademischer Verlag Hans-Dieter Heinz, 1975).

21. The comprehensive bibliography by Rost and Weber for the years until 1974 is found in *Über Anna Seghers: Ein Almanach zum 75. Geburtstag,* ed. Kurt Batt (Berlin: Aufbau Verlag, 1975), 307–410; by Behn-Liebherz for 1974–81 in *text + kritik* 38 (1983): 129–47; and by Hilzinger for 1982–92 in *Argonautenschiff: Jahrbuch der Anna-Seghers-Gesellschaft* 1 (Berlin: Aufbau Verlag, 1992): 213–25. For the years 1992–97 see the bibliography compiled by Margrid Bircken and Thorid Rabe in *Argonautenschiff* 7 (1998): 339–49.

22. Ute Brandes, *Anna Seghers* (Berlin: Colloquium Verlag, 1992); Alexander Stephan, *Anna Seghers, "Das siebte Kreuz": Welt und Wirkung eines Romans* (Berlin: Aufbau Verlag, 1997); Christiane Zehl Romero, *Anna Seghers* (Reinbek bei Hamburg: Rowohlt Verlag, 1993). Regarding Schrade, see note 15. My own study was completed before the publication in late 2000 of Christiane Zehl Romero, *Anna Seghers: Eine Biographie, 1900–1947* (Berlin: Aufbau Verlag), and thus does not take this biography into account.

23. *Encyclopedia of German Literature* (Chicago: Fitzroy Dearborn, 2000).

24. *Argonautenschiff: Jahrbuch der Anna-Seghers-Gesellschaft* (Berlin: Aufbau Verlag, 1992–); eight volumes published to date.

25. *Anna Seghers: Eine Biographie in Bildern.*

26. *Anna Seghers in Perspective,* ed. Ian Wallace (Amsterdam and Atlanta: Editions Rodopi, 1998).

27. Anna Seghers, *Werkausgabe,* ed. Helen Fehervary and Bernhard Spies, 24 vols. (Berlin: Aufbau Verlag, 2000–).

28. "Translator's Note," in Seghers, *The Revolt of the Fishermen,* trans. Margaret Goldsmith (New York: Longmans, Green & Co., 1930), 5–6.

29. "Translator's Note," 5.

30. Seghers, *The Seventh Cross,* trans. James A. Galston (Boston: Little, Brown & Co., 1942). On the circumstances and reception of the novel, see Stephan, *Anna Seghers, "Das siebte Kreuz": Welt und Wirkung eines Romans.* The transla-

tion is reprinted in Seghers, *The Seventh Cross,* foreword by Kurt Vonnegut, afterword by Dorothy Rosenberg (New York: Monthly Review Press, 1987).

31. Seghers, *Transit,* trans. James A. Galston (Boston: Little, Brown & Co., 1944).

32. Seghers, *The Dead Stay Young* (Boston: Little, Brown & Co., 1950).

Chapter 1

1. Anna Seghers, "Die Tendenz in der reinen Kunst," in *Über Kunstwerk und Wirklichkeit,* vol. 1, *Die Tendenz in der reinen Kunst,* ed. Sigrid Bock (Berlin: Akademie Verlag, 1970), 211. In act 4 of *The Doctor's Dilemma,* the twenty-three-year-old tubercular painter Louis Dubedat says (incidentally, without being "asked what he believes"): "I believe in Michael Angelo, Velasquez, and Rembrandt; in the might of design, mystery of color, the redemption of all things by Beauty everlasting, and the message of Art that has made these hands blessed. Amen. Amen." (George) Bernard Shaw, *Complete Plays with Prefaces,* vol. 1 (New York: Dodd, Mead & Co., 1962), 173.

2. Anna Seghers, *The Seventh Cross,* trans. James A. Galston (Little, Brown & Co., 1942), 88–89.

3. Seghers, *The Seventh Cross,* 48–49.

4. Seghers, *The Seventh Cross,* 67. Translation modified.

5. Seghers, "Die Tiefe und Breite in der Literatur," in *Über Kunstwerk und Wirklichkeit,* 1:125. In her public exchange of letters with Georg Lukács during the expressionism debates of the 1930s, Seghers made frequent reference to the visual arts in order to support her arguments in defense of modernism. See "A Correspondence with Anna Seghers (1938/9)," in Georg Lukács, *Essays on Realism,* ed. Rodney Livingstone, trans. David Fernbach (London: Lawrence & Wishart, 1980), 167–97. The letters are dated as follows: Seghers, 28 June 1938; Lukács, 29 July 1938; Seghers, February 1939; Lukács, 2 March 1939. A very good analysis of this correspondence is found in Kurt Batt, "Erlebnis des Umbruchs und harmonische Gestalt: Der Dialog zwischen Anna Seghers und Georg Lukács," in *Dialog und Kontroverse mit Georg Lukács: Der Methodenstreit deutscher sozialistischer Schriftsteller,* ed. Werner Mittenzwei (Leipzig: Reclam Verlag, 1975), 204–48.

6. Seghers, "Glauben an Irdisches," in *Über Kunstwerk und Wirklichkeit,* vol. 3, *Für den Frieden der Welt,* ed. Sigrid Bock (Berlin: Akademie Verlag, 1971), 47.

7. Seghers, "Glauben an Irdisches," 51.

8. Achim Roscher, "Wirklichkeit und Phantasie: Fragen an Anna Seghers," in *Also fragen Sie mich! Gespräche* (Halle: Mitteldeutscher Verlag, 1983), 52–53.

9. Roscher, "Wirklichkeit und Phantasie: Fragen an Anna Seghers," 55. See also Seghers's essays "Die gemalte Zeit: Mexikanische Fresken" (1947) and "Diego Rivera" (1949), in *Über Kunstwerk und Wirklichkeit,* vol. 2, *Erlebnis und Gestaltung,* ed. Sigrid Bock (Berlin: Akademie Verlag, 1971), 69–73, 85–88.

10. Seghers, *Steinzeit: Erzählungen 1967–1980* (Berlin: Aufbau Verlag, 1994), 7. My translation differs from that in Anna Seghers, *Benito's Blue and Nine Other Stories,* trans. Joan Becker (Berlin: Seven Seas Publishers, 1973), 9.

11. See the text by Seghers's daughter Ruth Radvanyi in *Anna Seghers: Eine Biographie in Bildern,* ed. Frank Wagner, Ursula Emmerich, and Ruth Radvanyi (Berlin: Aufbau Verlag, 1994), 18–19; see also Friedrich Albrecht, "Gespräch mit Pierre Radvanyi," *Sinn und Form,* no. 3 (1990): 510, where Seghers's son Pierre Radvanyi suggests the name was to be "Annette." The statement by Seghers's daughter two years later, in 1992, was evidently a corrective.

12. Achim Roscher, "Wirkung des Geschriebenen: Gespräche mit Anna Seghers," *Neue Deutsche Literatur,* no. 10 (1983): 70.

13. Quoted in Friedrich Schütz, "Die Familie Seghers-Reiling und das jüdische Mainz," *Argonautenschiff: Jahrbuch der Anna-Seghers-Gesellschaft* 2 (Berlin: Aufbau Verlag, 1993): 158.

14. Schütz, "Die Familie Seghers-Reiling und das jüdische Mainz," 158.

15. Christa Wolf, "Fortgesetzter Versuch" (1974), in *Die Dimension des Autors: Essays und Aufsätze, Reden und Gespräche, 1959–1985,* vol. 1 (Berlin: Aufbau Verlag, 1986), 342.

16. See the appendix for a summary of Netty Reiling's library. On the later influence of the *Thousand and One Nights,* see my discussion in chapter 6. A brief account by Seghers of her early reading habits is found in *Erste Lese-Erlebnisse,* ed. Siegfried Unseld (Frankfurt am Main: Suhrkamp Verlag, 1975), 19–21. This text is not altogether reliable, however, since it is slanted toward her later preoccupation with Schiller and Dostoyevsky, as reflected in her essay of 1963 "Woher sie kommen, wohin sie gehen," in *Über Kunstwerk und Wirklichkeit,* 2:182–217.

17. See Sigrid Bock, "Die Last der Widersprüche: Erzählen für eine gerechtere, friedliche, menschenwürdige Welt—trotz alledem," *Weimarer Beiträge,* no. 10 (1990): 1554.

18. Schütz, "Die Familie Seghers-Reiling und das jüdische Mainz," 157.

19. See the excerpt from the Fuld family chronicle quoted in Sigrid Bock, "Die Last der Widersprüche," 1554; see also Frank Wagner, "Deportation nach Piaski: Letzte Stationen der Passion von Hedwig Reiling," *Argonautenschiff: Jahrbuch der Anna-Seghers-Gesellschaft* 3 (Berlin: Aufbau Verlag, 1994): 117–26.

20. Seghers, *Die Hochzeit von Haiti: Erzählungen 1948–1949* (Berlin: Aufbau Verlag, 1994), 12. Page references henceforth in the text. Written in 1948 at a critical point in the cold war, the novella draws an unmistakable parallel between the Napoleonic age and the stalemate of international revolutionary socialism under the hegemony of Stalinism. Seghers thematized the transition to the Napoleonic era in two other Caribbean novellas, *Wiedereinführung der Sklaverei in Guadeloupe* (1949, Reinstatement of Slavery in Guadeloupe) and *Das Licht auf dem Galgen* (1948/1960, The Light on the Gallows).

21. Schütz, "Die Familie Seghers-Reiling und das jüdische Mainz," 155–56.

22. Schütz, "Die Familie Seghers-Reiling und das jüdische Mainz," 165.

23. Johanna Sichel was on the same transport to Poland in March 1942 as was Hedwig Reiling. See Wagner, "Deportation nach Piaski: Letzte Stationen der Passion von Hedwig Reiling," 117; and *Anna Seghers: Eine Biographie in Bildern,* 23.

24. On Judaica in Seghers's library, see the appendix. See also the pertinent sections in Barbara Einhorn, "Anna Seghers Returns to Germany from Exile and

Makes her Home in East Berlin," in *Yale Companion to Jewish Writing and Thought in German Culture, 1096–1996,* ed. Sander L. Gilman and Jack Zipes (New Haven: Yale University Press, 1997), 662–70.

25. On her art history books when she was a child, see the appendix. On her familiarity with her father's art library, see *Anna Seghers: Eine Biographie in Bildern,* 37.

26. See Schütz, "Die Familie Seghers-Reiling und das jüdische Mainz," 158.

27. Regarding philosophical influences during her years in Heidelberg, see chapter 4.

28. ASA file 33.

29. *Anna Seghers: Eine Biographie in Bildern,* 37, 39.

30. Full-page color plate depicting treasures from the Königliches Museum zu Berlin, in *Geschichte des Orients: Die Kulturwelt des alten Orients, der Islam, die Reiche der Indogermanen in Asien und die Völker Zentralasiens, China, Japan,* ed. J. von Pflugk-Harttung (Berlin: Ullstein Verlag, 1910) (ASA lib. unnumbered).

31. The two sculptures are otherwise known as *Buddha in Nirvana* and *Heavenly King.* See *The Art Treasures of Dunhuang,* compiled by Dunhuang Institute of Cultural Relics (Hong Kong and New York: Joint Publishing Co. and Lee Publishers Group, 1981), plates 64, 72.

32. Manès Sperber, *Until My Eyes Are Closed with Shards,* trans. Harry Zohn (New York: Holmes & Meier Publishers, 1994), 66.

33. Pictured in *Anna Seghers: Eine Biographie in Bildern,* 40.

34. *Anna Seghers: Eine Biographie in Bildern,* 41.

35. Carl Zuckmayer, "Grußwort," in *Anna Seghers aus Mainz,* ed. Walter Heist (Mainz: Verlag Dr. Hanns Krach, 1973), 11.

36. The subject of Seghers's significant debt to East Asian art and philosophy unfortunately goes beyond the conception of the present book. The topic most certainly warrants an in-depth study of its own that might bring to Seghers scholarship the kind of methodological breakthrough that was realized some years ago in Brecht scholarship by Antony Tatlow with his book *The Mask of Evil* (Bern: Peter Lang Verlag, 1977).

37. *Die Bahn und der rechte Weg des Lao-tse,* German translation by Alexander Ular (Leipzig: Insel Verlag, 1917), 65 (ASA lib. 3198). I have made a literal translation from the German version so as to approximate the kind of wording Netty Reiling herself read. The relevant page from the 1917 Insel Verlag edition is pictured in *Anna Seghers: Eine Biographie in Bildern,* 41.

38. Karl With, *Java: Brahmanische, Buddhistische und eigenlebige Architektur und Plastik auf Java,* 165 illustrations and 13 diagrams (Hagen: Folkwang Verlag, 1920), 16 (ASA lib. unnumbered).

39. With, *Java: Brahmanische, Buddhistische und eigenlebige Architektur und Plastik auf Java,* 46. The first part of the paragraph reads: "The architectonic mass or substance resembles the earth mass insofar as it is peopled by the manifold life of sculptured forms. All architectonic form stands under the influence of infinite space and under the law of substance classification; all sculptured form—to make an analogy—stands under the influence of psychic space and under the laws of life

content, that is, interior events or processes dictate the formal composition, and human forms are the embodiment of psychic processes; movement, restriction, structure, and composition are interruptions of a psychic relationship to infinity" (46).

Netty Reiling also marked the following paragraph: "All earthly being is incorporated into the thematic of the expression of mass and developed therein—with all its passion and petrification, movement and limitation, its thousandfold multiplicity and containment. In keeping with the philosophical principles of matter and spirit, material and the divine All, the artistic principle of substance is contrasted with the immaterial principle of space. Thus the impenetrable substance, confined on every side, is confronted by the ungraspable whole of infinite space" (26).

40. Roscher, "Wirklichkeit und Phantasie: Fragen an Anna Seghers," 55.

41. See the list of Netty Reiling's art books at this time, in the appendix.

42. *Anna Seghers: Eine Biographie in Bildern,* 49.

43. See Zuckmayer, "Grußwort," 11; and *Anna Seghers: Eine Biographie in Bildern,* 49.

44. On the extent to which concepts put forth in her dissertation influenced the aesthetics of her own narrative prose, see chapter 3. For an analysis of *The Dead on the Island Djal,* see chapter 4.

Chapter 2

1. Anna Seghers, "Inneres und Äußeres Reich" (1946), in *Die Macht der Worte: Reden, Schriften, Briefe* (Leipzig and Weimar: Gustav Kiepenheuer Verlag, 1979), 62. The passage refers to "a novel by Tolstoy." The novel is *Anna Karenina,* the artist implied is Mikhaylov in part 5, chapters 9–13, who shows Anna and Vronsky his unfinished painting *Pilate's Admonition* during their stay in Italy. Vronsky's friend Golenishchev tells him it is "Christ before Pilate. Christ is pictured as a Jew with all the realism of the New School." Leo Tolstoy, *Anna Karenina,* trans. Louise and Aylmer Maude (Oxford: Oxford University Press, 1980), 464. Golenishchev disapproves of this just as he disapproves of the "new type of born free-thinkers" like Mikhaylov, who is "the son of a head footman" and with "no education." Tolstoy, *Anna Karenina,* 465. The passages to which Seghers's words refer are quoted below:

> About his picture—the one at present on the easel—he had at the bottom of his heart a firm opinion: that no one had ever painted anything like it. He did not consider his picture better than all Raphael's, but he knew that what he wanted to express in that picture had never yet been expressed by anyone. Of that he was firmly convinced, and had long been so—ever since he had begun painting it; yet the opinion of others, whoever they might be, seemed to him of great importance, and disturbed him to the depths of his soul. Every remark, even the most trivial, which showed that those who judged it saw even but a small part of what he himself saw in it, moved him deeply. He always attributed to those judges a better understanding than his own, and

always expected to hear from them something he had himself not noticed in his work, often fancying that in their criticism he had really found that something. (Tolstoy, *Anna Karenina,* 468)

In spite of his elation, this remark about technique grated painfully on Mikhaylov's heart, and, glancing angrily at Vronsky, he suddenly frowned. He often heard the word *technique* mentioned, and did not at all understand what was meant by it. He knew it meant a mechanical capacity to paint and draw, quite independent of the subject-matter. He had often noticed—as now when his picture was being praised—that technique was contrasted with inner quality, as if it were possible to paint well something that was bad. He knew that much attention and care were needed not to injure one's work when removing the wrappings that obscure the idea, and that all wrappings must be removed, but as to the art of painting, the technique, it did not exist. If the things he saw had been revealed to a little child, or to his cook, they would have been able to remove the outer shell from their idea. And the most experienced and technical painter could never paint anything by means of mechanical skill alone, if the outline of the subject-matter did not first reveal itself to his mind. Moreover, he saw that if technique were spoken of, then he could not be praised for it. In all he painted and ever had painted he saw defects that were an eyesore to him, the results of carelessness in removing the shell of the idea, which he could not now remedy without spoiling the work as a whole. And in almost all the figures and faces he saw traces of wrappings that had not been entirely removed and that spoilt the picture. (Tolstoy, *Anna Karenina,* 472)

2. Seghers, *The Revolt of the Fishermen,* trans. Margaret Goldsmith (New York: Longmans, Green & Co., 1930), 105–6. Page references henceforth in the text. Soon after its publication in Germany in 1928, the novella appeared in English, French, Dutch, and Russian translation. The English translation omits a taproom song sung by the prostitute Marie in a seaside tavern in the novella's first chapter because it "might offend English and American readers." Seghers, *The Revolt of the Fishermen,* 5. The song is quoted below in my translation:

On Captain Kedel's wife's backside
You'll find a great big shock and scandal,
'cause Count Vaubert and sons, they spend the winter
'n the underskirts of Captain Kedel's wife's.
And then there're those nice gentlemen von Godek,
And there's young Bredel from Port Sebastian,
And even old Herr Bredel gets a turn sometimes.
As for the Captain himself, well, now and then a spot's left over.

(Seghers, *Aufstand der Fischer von St. Barbara* [Berlin: Aufbau Verlag, 1994], 10–11)

3. In keeping with the German "ihre frischen Hauben," I have added the word "fresh" to Goldsmith's "their bonnets." See Seghers, *Aufstand der Fischer von St. Barbara*, 93.

4. Seghers, "Die Wellblech-Hütte," in *Der letzte Mann der Höhle: Erzählungen, 1924–1933* (Berlin: Aufbau Verlag, 1994), 129–30. Page references henceforth in the text.

5. Wilhelm Hausenstein, for instance, wrote in the *Frankfurter Zeitung* in January 1921: "This Herkules [Seghers], who cut his teeth on the earth between 1590 and 1640, climbed distended Baroque precipices till his soles bled, cast his desires onto the breakers as no painter before him ever saw them. . . . Unknown, undervalued, and much despised; two and a half centuries later he was resurrected in the genius of van Gogh." Quoted in Friedrich Albrecht, "Originaleindruck Hercules Seghers," in *Über Anna Seghers: Ein Almanach zum 75. Geburtstag,* ed. Kurt Batt (Berlin: Aufbau Verlag, 1975), 35.

6. See also the end of chapter 1.

7. Wilhelm Fraenger, *Die Radierungen des Hercules Seghers: Ein physiognomischer Versuch* (1922; reprint, Leipzig: Reclam Verlag, 1984), 56.

8. Fraenger, *Die Radierungen des Hercules Seghers,* 55. See also John Rowlands, *Hercules Segers* (New York: George Braziller, 1979).

9. Seghers, "Das Argonautenschiff," in *Die Hochzeit von Haiti: Erzählungen 1948–1949* (Berlin: Aufbau Verlag, 1994), 131. Page references henceforth in the text.

10. See Robert Graves, *The Greek Myths* (London: Penguin Books, 1992), 603–4. Seghers published her first narrative devoted to a Greek myth, *Sagen von Artemis* (Tales of Artemis), in 1938, at the time of the Moscow trials and the defeat of the Republican forces in Spain.

11. Seghers, "Das Licht auf dem Galgen," in *Das Schilfrohr: Erzählungen 1957–1965* (Berlin: Aufbau Verlag, 1994), 164–65.

12. Seghers, "Das Licht auf dem Galgen," 162–63. Sasportas's words "You Negroes, do it the way they're doing it in Haiti!" refer to the Haitian revolution under the leadership of the former slave Toussaint L'Ouverture. Seghers's 1949 novella *Wedding in Haiti* is concerned with those events. In the Jamaican revolt described in *Das Licht auf dem Galgen* (The Light on the Gallows) the three Jacobin leaders are white—one of them the son of a plantation owner; another, Sasportas, a Sephardic Jew.

13. Seghers, *The Dead Stay Young* (Boston: Little, Brown & Co., 1950), 397–98.

Chapter 3

1. Anna Seghers, "Die Toten auf der Insel Djal," in *Der letzte Mann der Höhle: Erzählungen, 1924–1933* (Berlin: Aufbau Verlag, 1994), 11.

2. Seghers, interview with Achim Roscher (1978), quoted in *Anna Seghers: Eine Biographie in Bildern,* ed. Frank Wagner, Ursula Emmerich, and Ruth Radvanyi (Berlin: Aufbau Verlag, 1994), 23.

3. Netty Reiling (Anna Seghers), *Jude und Judentum im Werke Rembrandts* (Leipzig: Reclam Verlag, 1981), 32–33. Page references henceforth in the text.

4. Seghers, *Die Rettung* (Berlin: Aufbau Verlag, 1995), 251.

5. Seghers, *Die Rettung,* 474.

6. Seghers, *Die Rettung,* 474–75.

7. Achim Roscher, "Wirklichkeit und Phantasie: Fragen an Anna Seghers," in *Also fragen Sie mich! Gespräche* (Halle: Mitteldeutscher Verlag, 1983), 53. Seghers's own interest in Rembrandt's mingling of democratic and religious principles is evident in her dissertation and in her subsequent prose fiction. Not only on this point do I disagree with Annette Dorgerloh, who claims that Seghers "put Neumann's views behind her." See Dorgerloh, "Der 'Schöpfer-Künstler' und sein Gegenstand: Anna Seghers' Dissertation im Kontext der Rembrandt-Rezeption nach 1900," *Argonautenschiff: Jahrbuch der Anna-Seghers-Gesellschaft* 5 (Berlin: Aufbau Verlag, 1996): 115.

8. Carl Neumann, *Rembrandt,* 2 vols. (Munich: F. Bruckmann, 1924), xi. Page references henceforth in the text.

9. *Rembrandt Handzeichnungen,* ed. Carl Neumann (Munich: R. Piper Verlag, 1923), 6. Page references henceforth in the text.

10. Seghers, "Grubetsch," in *Der letzte Mann der Höhle: Erzählungen, 1924–1933.* Page references henceforth in the text.

11. See my discussion of the MASCH at the end of chapter 4. The shabby settings and characters in *Grubetsch* were no doubt also influenced by cityscapes and interiors in the silent films Seghers was able to see in Berlin, and by the work of Käthe Kollwitz, whose prints she had in her library (ASA lib. 3796 and 2768). The influence of Dostoyevsky, in whom Seghers was especially interested at the time, is more obvious. For cursory discussions of his impact, see Friedrich Albrecht, *Die Erzählerin Anna Seghers, 1926–1932* (Berlin: Rütten & Loening, 1965), 16f.; and Kurt Batt, *Anna Seghers: Versuch über Entwicklung und Werke* (Leipzig: Reclam Verlag, 1973), 24ff. Seghers wrote about Dostoyevsky in a number of later essays, notably "Prince Andrei and Raskolnikov"(1944), "The Napoleonic Ideology of Power in the Works of Tolstoy and Dostoyevsky," and "Whence They Come, Whither They Go" (1963). *Grubetsch* is one of Seghers's most cryptic texts. Critics who have tried to decipher its meaning have focused by and large on character development based on action and dialogue—with limited success. As I try to show in my own analysis, the text cannot be understood in terms of its naturalism or social realism and must be read parabolically. For previous discussions, see Albrecht, *Die Erzählerin Anna Seghers, 1926–1932;* and Batt, *Anna Seghers: Versuch über Entwicklung und Werke;* see also Inge Diersen, *Seghers-Studien: Interpretationen von Werken aus den Jahren 1926–1935* (Berlin: Rütten & Loening, 1965).

12. *The Expulsion of Hagar,* etching, 1637; *The Return of the Prodigal Son,* etching, 1636. See also the pen and brush side view of the full-figured *A Woman Leaning out of a Window,* circa 1655; the pen and wash front view *Saskia Looking out of a Window,* circa 1633–34; the reed pen and bistre front view *Sleeping Woman at a Window,* 1655–57; the reed pen and bistre front view *Girl Leaning on a Window Frame,* 1651; and the black chalk front view *Girl Leaning on the Sill of*

a Window, 1645. See also *Drawings of Rembrandt,* ed. Seymour Slive, 2 vols. (New York: Dover, 1965); and *Rembrandt's Drawings and Etchings for the Bible,* ed. Hans-Martin Rotermund, trans. Shierry M. Weber (Philadelphia: Pilgrim Press, 1969).

13. This combined thematic can be traced to Seghers's study of sinology and art history at the University of Heidelberg in the early 1920s.

14. Seghers, "Selbstanzeige" (1931), in *Die Macht der Worte: Reden, Schriften, Briefe* (Leipzig and Weimar: Gustav Kiepenheuer Verlag, 1979), 7.

15. For more elaborate discussions of the significance of Trotsky in Seghers's works, see chapters 4–6 and 8.

16. Seghers's relationship to the work of Kafka was first noted by Paul Rilla, "Die Erzählerin Anna Seghers," in *Literatur: Kritik und Polemik* (Berlin: Henschelverlag, 1950), 199–240. See also Albrecht, *Die Erzählerin Anna Seghers, 1926–1932,* 16f.; and Batt, *Anna Seghers: Versuch über Entwicklung und Werke,* 24ff. The topic is intriguing and deserves an in-depth study of its own. (See a more recent attempt by Mary Lyons, "'Ein Urwald von Dossiers': Kafkaesque Imagery in *Transit,*" in *Anna Seghers in Perspective,* ed. Ian Wallace [Amsterdam/Atlanta: Editions Rodopi, 1998], 101–15.) The above-mentioned GDR studies still represent the most thoroughgoing attempts to come to an understanding of Seghers's early prose within the context of her work's development as a whole. See also Diersen, *Seghers-Studien: Interpretationen von Werken aus den Jahren 1926–1935;* Frank Wagner, ". . . *der Kurs auf die Realität": Das epische Werk von Anna Seghers, 1935–1943* (Berlin: Akademie Verlag, 1975); and Tamara Motylova, *Anna Zegers: Kritikobiografichesky ocherk* (Moscow: Gos. izd. khudozhestrennoy literatury, 1953). Motylova, who was Georg Lukács's Russian translator and close to both Lukács and Seghers, had access to biographical and other information that her German counterparts lacked.

17. See *Rembrandt's Drawings and Etchings for the Bible,* 274–81: *The Arrest of Jesus, Jesus Taken before Caiaphas, Peter Denies Christ, Jesus Taken before Caiaphas, Here Is the Man! (Ecce Homo), Jesus before Pilate, The Mocking, Jesus Carrying the Cross.*

18. Seghers, *Der Kopflohn* (Berlin: Aufbau Verlag, 1995), 181–82. The parallelism of "dead man" and "newborn just baptized" in the final sentence is accentuated by the alliteration of "Toten" and "Täufling" (preceded by "Hacke" and "Hut") in the German text: "Er ließ die Hacke fallen und zog hastig den Hut ab, als ob man einen Toten oder einen Täufling an ihm vorbeitrug." See Helen Fehervary, "'Die gotische Linie': Altdeutsche Landschaften und Physiognomien bei Seghers und Müller," in Jost Hermand and Helen Fehervary, *Mit den Toten reden: Fragen an Heiner Müller* (Cologne: Böhlau Verlag, 1999), 113–35.

Chapter 4

1. Anna Lesznai, "Erinnerungen," in *Georg Lukács, Karl Mannheim und der Sonntagskreis,* ed. Éva Karádi and Erzsébet Vezér (Frankfurt am Main: Sendler Verlag, 1985), 95.

2. Karl Mannheim, "Heidelberger Briefe," in *Georg Lukács, Karl Mannheim und der Sonntagskreis,* 73.

3. Anna Seghers, "Georg Lukács," in *Über Kunstwerk und Wirklichkeit,* vol. 3, *Für den Frieden der Welt,* ed. Sigrid Bock (Berlin: Akademie Verlag, 1971), 162–63; translation, modified by Helen Fehervary, from *György Lukács: His Life in Pictures and Documents,* comp. and ed. Éva Fekete and Éva Karádi, trans. Péter Balabán, trans. rev. Kenneth McRobbie (Budapest: Corvina Kiadó, 1981), 148.

4. Seghers, "Die Toten auf der Insel Djal," in *Der letzte Mann der Höhle: Erzählungen, 1924–1933* (Berlin: Aufbau Verlag, 1994), 7–8. Page references henceforth in the text.

5. Quoted in Éva Karádi, "Einleitung," in *Georg Lukács, Karl Mannheim und der Sonntagskreis,* 19. On some of the early Christian and Kierkegaardian aspects of Lukács's "conversion," see Arpad Kadarkay, *Georg Lukács: Life, Thought, and Politics* (Cambridge, Mass.: Basil Blackwell, 1991), 202ff.

6. See also my discussion of this issue in chapter 5.

7. Themes of death and dying were especially favored in Béla Balázs's writings. Through László Radványi Seghers would at least have been aware of those of his writings that were not available in German. The story by Béla Balázs that would have interested her in particular in 1924 would have been his short tale "Kisértetek Szigete" (Island of the Ghosts) (MTA), about a group of Europeans stranded on a tropical island. For more on Balázs's significance, see chapter 6. *The Dead on the Island Djal* also exhibits characteristics of the sea tale and seems to have been influenced by such stories as August Strindberg's "Die Insel der Seligen," based on the myth of Atlantis, and Selma Lagerlöf's "Herrn Arnes Schatz," both of which the young Anna Seghers had in her library (ASA lib. 4193 and 4189).

8. See Karádi, "Einleitung," 21–22; Béla Balázs, "Tagebuch, 1915–1922," 122–27; and Arnold Hauser, "Erinnerungen," 102–3, all in *Georg Lukács, Karl Mannheim und der Sonntagskreis.*

9. Tibor Gergely, one of the youngest members of the Sunday Circle, caricatured several of its members. His caricature of Lukács shows the elder Sundayer descending Jacob's ladder from heaven's door to the rung of "history-philosophy." Pictured in *György Lukács: His Life in Pictures and Documents;* and in Kadarkay, *Georg Lukács: Life, Thought, and Politics.*

10. See Karádi, "Einleitung," in *Georg Lukács, Karl Mannheim und der Sonntagskreis,* 11.

11. Jean Leymarie, *Dutch Painting,* trans. Stuart Gilbert (Lausanne: Éditions d'Art Albert Skira, 1956), 77–78.

12. See my discussion of Hercules Seghers's influence in chapter 2.

13. Johann Wolfgang von Goethe, "Ruysdael als Dichter," in *Schriften zur Kunst,* vol. 13 of *Gedenkausgabe,* ed. Christian Beutler (Zürich: Artemis Verlag, 1954), 670–76; English translation: "Ruisdael as Poet," in Goethe, *Essays on Art and Literature,* ed. John Gearey, trans. Ellen von Nardroff and Ernest H. von Nardroff (New York: Suhrkamp Publishers, 1986), 62–66. The essay in the Suhrkamp volume rather unfortunately includes a plate of the Detroit version of

The Jewish Cemetery rather than the Dresden version, with which Goethe, who lived in nearby Weimar, was familiar and which he described as "The Cemetery" in his essay.

14. See the commentaries in Seymour Slive and H. R. Hoetink, *Jacob van Ruisdael* (New York: Abbeville Press-Publishers, 1981), 67–77, 192–97.

15. Leymarie, *Dutch Painting,* 111.

16. On the historical Israel Abraham Mendez and others buried in the sarcophagi in the Portuguese-Jewish Cemetery at Ouderkerk on the Amstel, see Slive and Hoetink, *Jacob van Ruisdael,* 193–96. Seghers was familiar with the history of the Jews in the Rhineland and in Holland and must have known their artifacts and their cemeteries. The old Jewish cemetery in Mainz, dating back a thousand years, was surely well known to her, located within walking distance of the apartment on the Parcusstraße where she first lived as a child, and only a bit farther from her later residence on the Kaiserstraße to where the family moved when she was five. The name Mendez would need preoccupy us no longer had Seghers not assigned this very name to the Sephardic patriarch of the Jewish family of jewelers that moves its business to Haiti at the time of the French Revolution in her 1949 novella *Die Hochzeit von Haiti* (Wedding in Haiti). See my summary of this novella and reference to its family associations in chapter 1. On Seghers's maternal Frankfurt lineage, see Friedrich Schütz, "Die Familie Seghers-Reiling und das jüdische Mainz," *Argonautenschiff: Jahrbuch der Anna-Seghers-Gesellschaft* 2 (Berlin: Aufbau Verlag, 1993): 151–73.

17. Netty Reiling (Anna Seghers), *Jude und Judentum im Werke Rembrandts* (Leipzig: Reclam Verlag, 1981), 22.

18. Reiling, *Jude und Judentum im Werke Rembrandts,* 24–25.

19. See the chapter "Die Gestaltung des überwirklichen Juden im biblischen Bilde," in Reiling, *Jude und Judentum im Werke Rembrandts,* 36–55.

20. Gershom Scholem, *The Messianic Idea in Judaism* (New York: Schocken Books, 1971), 15.

21. Scholem, *The Messianic Idea in Judaism,* 15–16.

22. Éva Gábor, "Vorwort," in Ladislaus Radványi, *Der Chiliasmus: Ein Versuch zur Erkenntnis der chiliastischen Idee und des chiliastischen Handelns,* ed. Éva Gábor (Budapest: MTA Filozófiai Intézet, 1985), 5.

23. Books by Lukács in Radványi's library at this time are listed in the appendix. See also Radványi's personal recollections of Lukács in *A Vasárnapi Kör: Dokumentumok,* ed. Éva Karádi and Erzsébet Vezér (Budapest: Gondolat, 1980), 67–68; and the introductory text and correspondence with Radványi in Éva Gábor, "Egy 'elfelejtett' vasárnapos emlékeiböl," *Világosság,* no. 7 (1980): 449–52.

24. Radványi, *Der Chiliasmus: Ein Versuch zur Erkenntnis der chiliastischen Idee und des chiliastischen Handelns,* 40. Page references henceforth in the text. As indicated by its title, Radványi's dissertation focuses not only on philosophical principles, but on historical models of theory and practice, that is, *lived* experience. Thus the first chapter, introducing the "significance and role of empiricism in the conceptual and emotional world of the religious individual," is followed by a second on its various human "types": the hermit and mystic "disinterested in the

world," and those who "turn toward the world" (the mystic in the world, the Calvinist, the individual concerned with works, and the chiliastic individual). The third chapter presents a theoretical discussion of chiliasm, followed by another providing historical illustration. Here Radványi distinguished between forms of chiliasm that grew out of Judaic apocalyptic eschatology: "passive" chiliasm (as in the Book of Daniel, Jewish messianism, early Christianity, the Montanist movement, medieval mysticism) and what he called the "active" period (Taborites, Münsterites, etc.). The final chapter focuses on ethical questions of "chiliastic action," echoing issues raised in the Sunday Circle during the Hungarian Commune of 1919.

25. Balázs, entry January–May 1920, "Tagebuch," 122–23.

26. György Káldor, "Über Bücher," in *Georg Lukács, Karl Mannheim und der Sonntagskreis,* 68.

27. Balázs, entry 26 April 1921, "Tagebuch," 125.

28. Balázs, entry 26 April 1921, "Tagebuch," 126.

29. See the appendix.

30. During her years in Heidelberg Netty Reiling enrolled in almost as many courses in philosophy, sociology, and history as she did in art history or sinology. In her first semester, in spring and summer of 1920, she attended lectures in nineteenth-century history and in the social theory of Marxism, the latter delivered by Emil Lederer, Lukács's close friend and supporter during his Heidelberg years. For the winter semester of 1920–21 she enrolled in, in addition to courses in ancient history and sinology, a lecture and seminar on nineteenth-century French history taught by Windelband, an introduction to philosophical interpretation, a survey of Russian literature, and two more courses taught by Emil Lederer: sociopolitical and social movements, and the theory of socialism. László Radványi, who in the winter of 1920–21 was in his first semester in Heidelberg, enrolled almost exclusively in courses in philosophy, one taught by Friedrich Gundolf, two by Karl Jaspers. He also attended lectures on Russian literature and Emil Lederer's two lecture courses in which Netty Reiling was enrolled; it was during this time that they first met. During her years in Heidelberg Netty Reiling enrolled in two courses taught by Karl Jaspers: logic and philosophical methods in the winter semester of 1922, and ethics in the winter semester of 1923–24. Aside from major courses, she attended lectures on Buddhism, Indian philosophy, and the history of Christianity. ASA file 33.

31. ASA lib. 234. Radványi's inscription in German reveals a small but interesting orthographical error: "Liebes Schwesterlein Netty Reiling, Gott gebe, das [*sic*] es so werde, wie wir es wollen." From his use of "das" instead of "daß" (perhaps a hasty oversight, but nonetheless a quite elementary, and for more advanced learners inexcusable, error), we can assume that although he was able to read philosophical texts in German, his written command of the language, and especially his spoken German, undoubtedly with a heavily accented Hungarian intonation, made him appear all the more distinctive and foreign, not only when he first met Netty Reiling in winter 1920–21. Radványi's reference to Netty Reiling as his "Schwesterlein," or "little sister," was not capricious but rather his effort to

continue the Budapest Sunday Circle custom of referring to its youngest initiates, among whom Radványi and apparently now also Netty Reiling were included, as "kis" (little) or as "gyermekek" (children). Arnold Hauser, Karl Mannheim, and others who belonged to the so-called second generation were dubbed "knábák" (boys), while those of the "third generation"—Radványi, György Káldor, Tibor Gergely, Károly Tolnay—were called "unokák" (grandchildren), even "bambinos." Radványi described this practice of assigning familial ranking within the Sunday Circle in an interview he gave in 1977, summarized in Gábor, "Egy 'elfelejtett' vasárnapos emlékeiböl," 450; see also Anna Lesznai's recollections in Karádi and Vezér, *A Vasárnapi Kör: Dokumentumok,* 54–55. Some more examples are listed in the section on Radvány's library in the appendix.

32. See Kadarkay, *Georg Lukács: Life, Thought, and Politics,* 239, 242.

33. See Balázs, entry 4 December 1919, "Tagebuch," 120–21.

34. *Anna Seghers: Eine Biographie in Bildern,* ed. Frank Wagner, Ursula Emmerich, and Ruth Radvanyi (Berlin: Aufbau Verlag, 1994), 39. On Seghers's lifelong inclination to elusiveness and obscurity, see Hans Mayer, *Der Turm von Babel: Erinnerung an eine Deutsche Demokratische Republik* (Frankfurt am Main: Suhrkamp Verlag, 1991), 202–3.

35. *Anna Seghers: Eine Biographie in Bildern,* 49. The newspaper mentioned by Seghers would have been the left-liberal *Frankfurter Zeitung,* known for its excellent literary and cultural section and for such reviewers as Alfred Kerr, Siegfried Kracauer, and on occasion Walter Benjamin.

36. Interestingly, Emma Ritoók entitled her 1922 memoir of the Budapest Sunday Circle "A szellem kalandorai" (The Adventures of the Soul). A philosopher and writer, Emma Ritoók broke with the Sunday Circle at the time of the revolutions of 1918–19 when she became politically reactionary. She later became an ardent supporter of the Horthy regime. Her memoir is not only extremely critical of her former friend Georg Lukács and other Sunday Circle members but also accuses them, including those Sundayers who never joined the Communist Party, of being "Communist terrorists."

37. Søren Kierkegaard, *The Sickness unto Death: A Christian Psychological Exposition for Edification and Awakening by Anti-Climacus, edited by S. Kierkegaard,* ed. and trans. Alastair Hannay (London: Penguin Books, 1989), 15.

38. Kierkegaard, *The Sickness unto Death,* 37, 43.

39. Kierkegaard, *The Sickness unto Death,* 37 (John 11:43).

40. *The New English Bible with the Apocrypha* (Oxford and Cambridge: Oxford University Press/Cambridge University Press, 1970), 320 (NT).

41. *The New English Bible with the Apocrypha,* 320 (NT).

42. Balázs, "Tagebuch," 121.

43. Balázs, "Tagebuch," 121–22.

44. Kierkegaard, *The Sickness unto Death,* 50.

45. Kierkegaard, *The Sickness unto Death,* 98.

46. Karádi, "Einleitung," in *Georg Lukács, Karl Mannheim und der Sonntagskreis,* 11.

47. Karl Mannheim, "Die Grundprobleme der Kulturphilosophie," in *Georg Lukács, Karl Mannheim und der Sonntagskreis,* 230.

48. Mannheim, "Die Grundprobleme der Kulturphilosophie," 230–31.

49. Mannheim, "Die Grundprobleme der Kulturphilosophie," 231.

50. See Anna Lesznai, *Spätherbst in Eden* (Karlsruhe: Stahlberg, 1965), 608–11.

51. Lesznai, "Erinnerungen," in *Georg Lukács, Karl Mannheim und der Sonntagskreis,* 136.

52. Balázs, diary entry 29 November 1918, trans. Mary Gluck, in Mary Gluck, *Georg Lukács and His Generation, 1900–1918* (Cambridge, Mass.: Harvard University Press, 1985), 198. Balázs was as much a free-spirited artist as Mannheim was a self-conscious intellectual. "How I envy your courage to commit errors!" Mannheim apparently said to Balázs after their first Sunday Circle meeting in 1915. "At times I dare not make one move for fear of taking a wrong step." To this Balázs evidently replied: "I'm not afraid, because it's not I who commits the error, but at best am *myself* an error." Balázs, diary entry December 1915, "Tagebuch," 109. On 4 August 1917 Balázs compared the emotionally distant Mannheim to the more soulful Lukács: "Vegetative warmth is lacking [in Mannheim], and the pathos of that great fellowship of destiny isn't there either, as it is with Gyuri [Georg Lukács]." Balázs, "Tagebuch," 116. And on 27 September 1918, after having vacationed with him, Balázs lamented Mannheim's "weakness and pettiness, and bloodlessness: cowardice and continuously distrustful control. He can't 'let go.' He's always pleasant, but he can never touch and electrify me." Balázs, "Tagebuch," 118.

53. Edit Gyömröi, "Erinnerungen," in *Georg Lukács, Karl Mannheim und der Sonntagskreis,* 106. Compare the eyewitness account of Lukács's voluntary service on the front with the Red Army's fifth division in June of 1919:

> This frail, bespectacled figure, dressed in plus fours, green stockings and heavy walking-shoes, struck the war weary, lice-ridden soldiers as something unreal. Lukács was the very picture of a German professor taking his Sunday stroll. As Lukács clambered up an embankment one day, a machine-gun started to bark from the Czech trenches. Oblivious to the hail of bullets, Lukács calmly walked along the top of one of the trenches manned by the Red Army soldiers. Suddenly a hand reached out and pulled him into the trench. A soldier stood over Lukács shouting in anger, "You green-legged monkey. Who let you loose from your cage?" Wiping clean his glasses with a handkerchief, Lukács said, "I only did what duty demanded. And I can assure you that my presence here ensures victory." (József Lengyel, as paraphrased in Kadarkay, *Georg Lukács: Life, Thought, and Politics,* 222)

54. Balázs, entry 12 July 1921, "Tagebuch," 126.

55. See Mannheim, *Ideology and Utopia: An Introduction to the Sociology of Knowledge* (New York and London: Harcourt, Brace and Routledge & Kegan Paul, 1949), 136–46.

56. Quoted in Kadarkay, *Georg Lukács: Life, Thought, and Politics,* 193.

57. Quoted in Kadarkay, *Georg Lukács: Life, Thought, and Politics,* 193. Weber was referring to the phrase from Dante's *Inferno:* "Lasciate ogni speranza, voi ch' entrate!" (Abandon hope, all ye who enter here).

58. Lukács, letter to Paul Ernst, 5 April 1919, in Lukács, *Selected Correspondence, 1902–1920,* ed. and trans. Judith Marcus and Zoltán Tar (New York: Columbia University Press, 1986), 280.

59. Lesznai, "Tagebuch, 1912–1927," in *Georg Lukács, Karl Mannheim und der Sonntagskreis,* 139. The poet Anna Lesznai (1885–1966), whose journal recordings of her conversations with Georg Lukács go back as far as 1912, was a lifelong friend of both Lukács and Balázs. At the time of the Hungarian Revolution she was married to the radical democratic leader Oszkár Jászi, who was in the cabinet of the Károlyi government and was strongly opposed to Béla Kun and the politics of the Council Republic. Jászi already left Hungary in the spring of 1919 and later emigrated to the United States. After 1919 Lesznai married László Radványi's classmate and friend Tibor Gergely, with whom she lived in Vienna in the 1920s and in Hungary in the 1930s. In 1939 they emigrated to the United States.

60. See Kadarkay, *Georg Lukács: Life, Thought, and Politics,* 191.

61. Balázs, entry 12 July 1921, "Tagebuch," 126.

62. Balázs, entry 12 July 1921, "Tagebuch," 126. According to Balázs, Mannheim and Hauser

> distanced themselves from Sunday when it committed itself to the communist revolution. They are nervous and cowardly, hesitaters, types of a transitional generation. Typically, one and a half years later they have converted at about the same time, as if to Canossa. But the conversion was not to communism. Instead they say they are the homeless and banished outside Sunday, cannot find their place intellectually and cannot live. That they returned is probably because the world revolution is keeping us waiting ever longer. For the time being there is no way Sunday can commit itself to any serious action; as a result it is much less dangerous for them to be around us right now. (Balázs, entry 12 July 1921, "Tagebuch," 126–27)

Balázs also sought another explanation: "Today every intellectual activity that doesn't have some sort of connection to the movement takes on the character of anachronistic play, of stamp collecting. They sense that. That they missed the train at their provincial station. That they've been swept to the side of the road." Finally, Balázs commented that "Mannheim was able to return to us, but nobody wants Hauser. He is sick and miserable, and no one knows at what moment he'll abandon us again out of cowardice. . . . Right now it's not possible to have human relationships that aren't alliances." Balázs, entry 12 July 1921, "Tagebuch," 126–27. For Arnold Hauser's much later assessment, see his "Erinnerungen," in *Georg Lukács, Karl Mannheim und der Sonntagskreis,* 97–103.

63. Kierkegaard, *The Sickness unto Death,* 48.

64. Mannheim, "Heidelberger Briefe," in *Georg Lukács, Karl Mannheim und der Sonntagskreis,* 13. Page references henceforth in the text.

65. When he visited Hungary in the 1930s, Mannheim apparently told a fellow Sundayer, the art historian Lajos Fülep, "that he had found never and nowhere the equivalent of what the Sundays had been." Quoted in Karádi, "Einleitung," in *Georg Lukács, Karl Mannheim und der Sonntagskreis,* 10.

66. See my discussion in chapter 3.

67. Rosa Luxemburg referred in 1905 already to the communal example of the early Christians. See Luxemberg, "Socialism and the Churches," in *Rosa Luxemburg Speaks,* ed. Mary-Alice Waters (New York: Pathfinder Press, 1970), 131–52; first published in Cracow in 1905 as "Kósciól a socjalizm" under the pseudonym Jósef Chmura. J. P. Nettl, *Rosa Luxemburg* (London: Oxford University Press, 1969), 221.

68. Albeit Mannheim also criticized the George Circle as an "exclusive intellectual-aristocratic community that closes itself off from any happenings in the external world." Mannheim, "Heidelberger Briefe," in *Georg Lukács, Karl Mannheim und der Sonntagskreis,* 88.

69. See Joseph Zsuffa, *Béla Balázs: The Man and the Artist* (Berkeley: University of California Press, 1987).

70. Lukács, *History and Class Consciousness: Studies in Marxist Dialectics,* trans. Rodney Livingstone (Cambridge, Mass.: MIT Press, 1972), xvi, xiv.

71. Lukács, *History and Class Consciousness,* 1.

72. Lukács, *History and Class Consciousness,* xviii.

73. Lukács, *History and Class Consciousness,* xliv.

74. Seghers, "Georg Lukács" (1955), in *Über Kunstwerk und Wirklichkeit,* 3:162; translation, modified by Helen Fehervary, from *György Lukács: His Life in Pictures and Documents,* 148.

75. See Schütz, "Die Familie Seghers-Reiling und das jüdische Mainz," 165.

76. See note 31 to this chapter.

77. See the pertinent discussions in chapters 5 and 6.

78. Unlike writers who in the interest of posterity retain early drafts, notes, and other documents pertaining to their creative work, Seghers was in the habit of destroying her files once she finished a project. Thanks to her last secretary Ruth Hildebrandt, who in some cases did not follow her orders, the document files for the novels *Die Entscheidung* (1959, The Decision) and *Das Vertrauen* (1968, Trust) are more or less complete. They include a substantial number of notes and letters containing László Radványi's detailed comments, criticisms, and suggestions for changes on various drafts (suggestions she mostly, if not always, followed), as well as his and Seghers's written exchanges of opinion pertaining to these two novels as they were being written. Although we have such documented evidence only from the postwar period, we can assume that Radványi had no less, indeed possibly even more, influence on her earlier works.

79. Budapest, Petöfi Irodalmi Múzeum (henceforth PIM), letter of 17 December 1926 from Radványi to Gyula Földessy in Budapest, page 1.

80. PIM, letter of 3 October 1924 to Földessy, page 4.

81. PIM, letter of 8 July 1924 to Földessy, page 5. As philosophers, Radványi and Mannheim had similar interests. Mannheim's earlier interest in sociology is already evident as an influence in Radványi's 1923 dissertation on chiliasm. In 1929 Mannheim acknowledged Radványi's dissertation in his own discussion of chiliasm in *Ideology and Utopia.* See Mannheim, *Ideology and Utopia,* 195. According to the interview Radványi gave to Éva Gábor in 1977, in Heidelberg he and Seghers "visited regularly" with Mannheim and his wife Júlia Láng ("rendszeres kapcsolatot tartottunk a Mannheim-házaspárral"). Radványi last saw Mannheim in the mid-1930s when Mannheim visited him in Paris. As Radványi later recalled: "I can still picture him before me, gesticulating in a lively manner and explaining: 'Try to understand, I am not a communist. I am a liberal bourgeois thinker. This is how you have to accept me and judge me.'" In 1940, when the Radványis and their children were trapped in France, Mannheim appealed from London to President Cárdenas of Mexico on their behalf. See the summary of the 1977 interview with Radványi in Gábor, "Egy 'elfelejtett' vasárnapos emlékeiböl," 450–51.

82. PIM, letter of 17 December 1925 to Földessy, pages 1–2.

83. PIM, letter of 17 December 1925 to Földessy, pages 2–3.

84. PIM, letters to Földessy, 3 October 1924, page 4, and 17 December 1926, page 3.

85. PIM, letters of 8 July 1924 and 3 October 1924 to Földessy. On Radványi's book of poetry in Hungarian and his relationship to Ady, see chapter 5 and its note 20.

86. PIM, letter of 3 October 1924 to Földessy, page 4.

87. See Schütz, "Die Familie Seghers-Reiling und das jüdische Mainz," 151–73; and Sigrid Bock, "Die Last der Widersprüche: Erzählen für eine gerechtere, friedliche, menschenwürdige Welt—trotz alledem," *Weimarer Beiträge,* no. 10 (1990): 1554–55.

88. See Schütz, "Die Familie Seghers-Reiling und das jüdische Mainz," 165; and *Anna Seghers: Eine Biographie in Bildern,* 52.

89. See Gabriele Gerhard-Sonnenberg, *Marxistische Arbeiterbildung in der Weimarer Zeit (MASCH)* (Cologne: Pahl-Rugenstein Verlag, 1976), 72; and *Anna Seghers: Eine Biographie in Bildern,* 61.

90. To my knowledge this influence has not yet been explored. In 1974 Radványi himself described the teachers and students in the MASCH as "convinced democrats, socialist and communists"; quoted in Gerhard-Sonnenberg, *Marxistische Arbeiterbildung in der Weimarer Zeit,* 142. See also the 1976 radio interview with Johann-Lorenz Schmidt (László Radványi) (ASA lib. audio-visual collection). On the Free School of the Humanities in Budapest, which its organizers saw as a "counter-university," see *Georg Lukács, Karl Mannheim und der Sonntagskreis,* 11–18.

91. *A Vasárnapi Kör: Dokumentumok,* 58. At this point in time Balázs still wanted to preserve a tradition of Platonic elitism within the Free School of the Humanities. He described the encounter with the already politically active young men in his diary:

Met the youngest members attending our school, boys who just graduated: Radványi, Gergely, Tolnay, Káldor, etc. A philosophically and ethically new and serious generation. They will surely belong to us. We have to gather them around us and spend time with them. Thursday afternoons in the Café Modern (where I've seldom been). . . . I am deeply moved to observe that our eighteen-year-olds are mindful of the need to uphold the intimate refinement of our earlier lectures and adherence to a unified worldview, so that the purpose of our school not be threatened by any practical success or usefulness. (Balázs, entry 15 July 1918, "Tagebuch," 118–19)

92. See Gábor, "Egy 'elfelejtett' vasárnapos emlékeiből," 449–52.

93. Gerhard-Sonnenberg, *Marxistische Arbeiterbildung in der Weimarer Zeit,* 74, 78ff.

94. Gerhard-Sonnenberg, *Marxistische Arbeiterbildung in der Weimarer Zeit,* 124.

95. See Seghers's lively account of her visit with Albert Einstein and his wife, "Einstein in der MASCH" (1974), in *Anna Seghers: Eine Biographie in Bildern,* 61–62.

96. See Seghers, "Kleiner Bericht aus meiner Werkstatt," in *Über Kunstwerk und Wirklichkeit,* vol. 2, *Erlebnis und Gestaltung,* ed. Sigrid Bock (Berlin: Akademie Verlag, 1971), 11–15.

97. See Werner Hecht, *Brecht Chronik, 1898–1956* (Frankfurt am Main: Suhrkamp Verlag, 1997), 296.

98. Gerhard-Sonnenberg, *Marxistische Arbeiterbildung in der Weimarer Zeit,* 94–95.

99. Johann-Lorenz Schmidt, "Vorwort," in Gerhard-Sonnenberg, *Marxistische Arbeiterbildung in der Weimarer Zeit,* 9.

100. Gerhard-Sonnenberg, *Marxistische Arbeiterbildung in der Weimarer Zeit,* 129.

101. Gerhard-Sonnenberg, *Marxistische Arbeiterbildung in der Weimarer Zeit,* 136–37.

102. Gerhard-Sonnenberg, *Marxistische Arbeiterbildung in der Weimarer Zeit,* 141–42.

103. See *Anna Seghers: Eine Biographie in Bildern,* 72.

104. PIM, letter of 17 December 1925 to Földessy, page 4.

105. PIM, letter of 17 December 1926 to Földessy, page 4.

106. For the Balázs diary entries that gave rise to this sentiment, see notes 42 and 43 to this chapter.

107. See my discussion of this narrative in chapter 2.

108. The most prominent and deeply troubled Hungarian figures in *Die Gefährten* are Böhm, modeled on László Radványi; Bató, on Georg Lukács; and Steiner, on Karl Mannheim.

109. Siegfried Kracauer, "Eine Märtyrer-Chronik von heute," *Frankfurter Zeitung,* 13 November 1932.

110. On the antisemitic attacks on Mannheim by Ernst Robert Curtius and oth-

ers while Mannheim was still in Heidelberg, the difficulties surrounding the professorship finally offered to him by the University of Frankfurt in late 1929, and his enforced "leave of absence" and "retirement" in early 1933, followed by his hasty departure from Germany, see Éva Gábor, "Karl Mannheim: Zweifacher Emigrant im Spiegel seiner eigenen Philosophie und Soziologie," *Society and Economy in Central and Eastern Europe* 19, no. 1 (1995): 124–46; see also Henk E. S. Woldring, *Karl Mannheim: The Development of His Thought* (New York: St. Martin's Press, 1987), 32–37.

Chapter 5

1. Endre Ady, "Az utolsó Hajók," in *Összes Versei* (Budapest: Athenaeum Kiadása, n.d.), 479.

2. Béla Balázs, entry 15 July 1918, "Tagebuch, 1915–1922," in *Georg Lukács, Karl Mannheim und der Sonntagskreis,* ed. Éva Karádi and Erzsébet Vezér (Frankfurt am Main: Sendler Verlag, 1985), 19. Together with Georg Lukács, Fülep founded the philosophical journal *A Szellem* (The Soul) in 1911. As an art historian he was especially interested in the national element in Hungarian art. Lukács appointed him to a post as university professor during the Council Republic of 1919. After its overthrow Fülep was one of the few members of the Sunday Circle who remained in Hungary, and, in a form of inner emigration, he worked from 1919 to 1947 as a village pastor in southern Hungary. In 1948 he received an appointment as professor of art history and was made a member of the Academy of Arts and Sciences. At the time of their conversation in 1918 he was the only gentile in the Sunday Circle, and Balázs followed up his citation of Fülep's "twelve fishermen" with a typically histrionic aside to his diary: "If only he didn't still have in him a certain tinge of Judas" (19). See also László Radványi's somewhat critical remarks about Fülep in Éva Gábor, "Egy 'elfelejtett' vasárnapos emlékeiböl," *Világosság,* no. 7 (1980): 450.

3. Anna Lesznai, entry 1918, "Tagebuch 1912–1927," in *Georg Lukács, Karl Mannheim und der Sonntagskreis,* 131.

4. Georg Lukács, *The Theory of the Novel: A Historico-Philosophical Essay on the Forms of Great Epic Literature,* trans. Anna Bostock (Cambridge, Mass.: MIT Press, 1971), 29. Page references henceforth in the text, preceded by *TN.*

5. Anna Seghers, The *Revolt of the Fishermen,* trans. Margaret Goldsmith (New York: Longmans, Green & Co., 1930). Page references henceforth in the text, preceded by *RF.*

6. On works by Conrad in Seghers's library, see the appendix. An in-depth study of Seghers's indebtedness to Conrad would surely yield fascinating results. See already Frank Wagner's suggestions of Conrad's influence on the novels *Die Rettung* (The Rescue) and *The Seventh Cross* in Wagner, *". . . der Kurs auf die Realität": Das epische Werk von Anna Seghers, 1935–1943* (Berlin: Akademie-Verlag, 1975), 157, 283 note 132.

7. In the original German text the island is Margareteninsel (Margaret Island). The images created in this passage as well as others in which this island is

mentioned suggest that Seghers was thinking of the Margitsziget (Margaret Island) in Budapest, which stretches in the middle of the Danube for several kilometers in a north-south direction, its southern end connected to the Margaret Bridge spanning the Danube from Buda to Pest, its northern tip marked by a beacon, alerting approaching steamers to pass southward on the Buda side alongside a series of docking sites for small river craft. With its grand hotel, public baths, and public gardens, Budapest's Margaret Island has been described as "the best-known island along the entire 2,000-mile length of the Danube," more poetically as "pearl of the Danube, nest of flowers, sweet odours, and cool air, whence and whither the white steamers go." See John Lukacs, *Budapest 1900: A Historical Portrait of a City and Its Culture* (New York: Grove Press, 1988), 39. More importantly in this case, the island is within easy reach by public transportation to Budapest citizens, and one might easily spend a summer there "nursing one's foot"—out of the sight of local district police, as did Johann Hull before he made the crossing to St. Barbara. The encoded references to this and other Hungarian sites in this novella suggest that here, as in her first published story, *The Dead on the Island Djal,* Seghers had in mind the political events of the Hungarian revolutions of 1918–19, and in the case of Hull's pursuit by the police, the "white terror," as Seghers called it, that came in the wake of the Hungarian Council Republic in August 1919 after its defeat by the white troops of Miklós Horthy.

8. Translation modified. Here again Seghers seems to have had a Hungarian locale in mind, in this case the local taverns along the Tisza River in southern Hungary, where temperatures soar during the summer months and melons are abundant, where "thin, small tones coming from some wooden instrument" would have been those of a *cimbalom,* and where a tune "so damnably black, no white man could have played it" would have been played by a Gypsy. The Tisza River, which has its source in the Carpathian Mountains, was for centuries the main route for the delivery of timber to towns and cities on the Hungarian plains, an important trading center being Szeged, a city with a significant Jewish population. Seghers could have heard about this area not only from her husband László Radványi, but also from Béla Balázs, who was Radványi's first mentor in the Sunday Circle and lived in Berlin as a film critic and scriptwriter in the late 1920s. Balázs spent his boyhood in Szeged along the Tisza River and brought these topographies into his poetry and short prose. See his memoir *Álmodó ifjúság* (Dreaming Youth) (Budapest: Athenaeum, 1946); German: *Die Jugend eines Träumers* (Vienna: Globus-Verlag, 1948). On the significance of the Carpathians for Seghers's work, see my discussion of *Bauern von Hruschowo* (1930, Woodcutters of Hrushovo) and other narratives in chapter 6.

9. My emphasis.

10. See the discussions of Dostoyevsky's influence on Seghers's early prose in Friedrich Albrecht, *Die Erzählerin Anna Seghers, 1926–1932* (Berlin: Rütten & Loening, 1965); and Kurt Batt, *Anna Seghers: Versuch über Entwicklung und Werke* (Leipzig: Reclam Verlag, 1973).

11. *The Lukács Reader,* ed. and trans. Arpad Kadarkay (Oxford: Blackwell Publishers, 1995), 158. "Aesthetic Culture" first appeared in the journal *Renais-*

sance in May 1910 and was republished in 1913 in a small book edition, *Esztétikai kultúra* (Aesthetic Culture). See *The Lukács Reader,* 143.

12. *Soul and Form* was published in Hungarian as *A lélek és a formák: Kisérletek* (Budapest: Franklin Társulat Nyomda, 1910). Several of the essays first appeared in Hungarian journals as early as 1908. The German edition, in a translation rendered by Lukács himself, did not include all the original essays and appeared as *Die Seele und die Formen: Essays* (Berlin: Egon Fleischel & Co., 1911). This edition is found in Anna Seghers's library. ASA lib. 1280. A postcard from France, dated 28 May 1981, was found in this volume at the time of Seghers's death, suggesting that this study continued to hold significance for her, seventy years after it first appeared and sixty years after she would have first read it. The English edition, *Soul and Form,* trans. Anna Bostock (London: Merlin Press; Cambridge, Mass.: MIT Press, 1974), follows the standard German Luchterhand edition of 1971. On the essays in *Soul and Form* and other seminal writings by the young Lukács, see the essays by his students Ferenc Fehér, Ágnes Heller, György Márkus, Sándor Radnóti, and Mihály Vajda in *Lukács Revalued,* ed. Ágnes Heller (Oxford: Basil Blackwell, 1983).

13. Michael Löwy, *Georg Lukács: From Romanticism to Bolshevism,* trans. Patrick Camiller (London: NLB, 1979), 100. On the young Lukács's tragic conception, see also *Lukács Revalued;* and Lee Congdon, *The Young Lukács* (Chapel Hill: University of North Carolina Press, 1983). On Lukács's relationship to messianic thought, see Löwy, *Redemption and Utopia: Jewish Libertarian Thought in Central Europe,* trans. Hope Heaney (London: Athlone Press, 1992).

14. *The Lukács Reader,* 157–58.

15. *The Lukács Reader,* 146. Lukács used these lines as the motto for his essay.

16. *The Lukács Reader,* 158.

17. See John Lukacs, *Budapest 1900: A Historical Portrait of a City and Its Culture,* 187–96. As Mary Gluck writes: "By the late nineteenth century, Jews made up 5 percent of the total population of Hungary but supplied 12.5 percent of the industrialists, 54 percent of the businessmen, 43 percent of the bankers and moneylenders, 45 percent of the lawyers, and 49 percent of the doctors." Gluck, *Georg Lukács and His Generation, 1900–1918* (Cambridge, Mass.: Harvard University Press, 1985), 58. Or, as Arpad Kadarkay summarizes: "For all practical purposes, capitalism, culture, and finance were preponderantly Jewish." Kadarkay, *Georg Lukács: Life, Thought, and Politics* (Cambridge, Mass.: Basil Blackwell, 1991), 9. For a detailed historical study of the time, see *Magyarország története, 1890–1918,* 2 vols., ed. Péter Hanák (Budapest: Akadémiai Kiadó, 1978).

18. *The Lukács Reader,* 151. Lukács did not read Martin Buber's Hassidic stories until the summer of 1911 when he spent time with Buber in Florence. Thereupon he wrote "Zsidó miszticizmus" (Jewish Mysticism), an enthusiastic review of *Die Legende des Baalschem* and *Die Geschichten des Rabbi Nachmann* published in the December 1911 issue of *A Szellem,* edited by Lukács and Lajos Fülep.

19. Seghers and Lukács exchanged a total of four open letters published in *Internationale Literatur* in 1939 in issue 5, 97ff. The essays are available in English

in Georg Lukács, *Essays on Realism,* ed. Rodney Livingstone, trans. David Fern-bach (London: Lawrence & Wishart, 1980), 167–97. An excellent assessment of this debate is provided in Kurt Batt, "Erlebnis des Umbruchs und harmonische Gestalt: Der Dialog zwischen Anna Seghers und Georg Lukács," in *Dialog und Kontroverse mit Georg Lukács: Der Methodenstreit deutscher sozialistischer Schriftsteller,* ed. Werner Mittenzwei (Leipzig: Reclam Verlag, 1975), 204–48.

20. The titles of the poems in *Fekete Könyv* indicate what must have been the fifteen-year-old *Gymnasium* student Radványi's rather turbulent feelings in respect to his own adolescence and to the war that was raging around him at the time: "Ének a fekete tüzröl" (Song of the Black Fire); "Fekete szimfonia" (Black Symphony); "Fekete madarak" (Black Birds); "Én vagyok a fekete lovag" (I Am the Black Horse); "Sohasem fogok már szeretni" (I Will Never Love Again); "Fekete fogadás" (Black Prison); "Halál" (Death); "Ifjúság" (Youth). ASA lib. unnumbered.

21. The translated poems belong to Radványi's unpublished correspondence with Gyula Földessy (PIM) and were sent by Radványi to Földessy for evaluation in the fall of 1924. In an accompanying letter dated 3 October 1924 Radványi wrote that he had shown the translations to several German friends. One of them was surely Netty Reiling, that is, Anna Seghers, whom he married the following year. See my discussion of this correspondence at the end of chapter 4.

22. From Endre Ady, "Tovább a Hajóval," in *Összes Versei,* 432. The library holdings of the Anna-Seghers-Archiv include two Hungarian editions of Ady's poetry (1906 and 1923) and one German edition: *Auf neuen Gewässern* (On New Waters) (Leipzig, Wien, Zürich, 1921) (ASA lib. 5430, 5431, 5426). On Hungarian editions of Ady and other avant-garde Hungarian writers belonging to the young László Radványi, see the appendix.

23. Lukács György, "Uj magyar líra," in Lukács, *Ifjúkori müvek, 1902–1918,* ed. Árpád Tímár (Budapest: Magvetö Kiadó, 1977), 249. Ady's prophetic style made its personal imprint on Lukács. Karl Jaspers attributed to the philosopher Emil Lask the saying that circulated in Heidelberg when Lukács and Ernst Bloch were there together after 1911: "What are the names of the four evangelists? Matthew, Mark, Lukács, and Bloch." Karl Jaspers, "Heidelberger Erinnerungen," *Heidelberger Jahrbücher,* 1961, 5; quoted in Löwy, *Georg Lukács: From Romanticism to Bolshevism,* 93.

24. Lukács, "Uj magyar líra," 248.

25. Lukács, "Uj magyar líra," 251.

26. Lukács, "Uj magyar líra," 250.

27. Hans Mayer, *Der Widerruf: Über Deutsche und Juden* (Frankfurt am Main: Suhrkamp Verlag, 1994), 278.

28. See Inge Diersen, *Seghers-Studien: Interpretationen von Werken aus den Jahren 1926–1935* (Berlin: Rütten & Loening, 1965), 316.

29. See my discussion in chapter 2.

30. *The Lukács Reader,* 151.

31. *The Lukács Reader,* 151.

32. A similar mood of messianic expectation is created when large crowds of

men, women, and children from neighboring villages converge in St. Barbara to hear Hull speak. The following crowd scene, its constructive setting reminiscent of Rembrandt's depictions of Jesus speaking in semi-open spaces among crowds, precedes Hull's arrival:

> They all met in the fish-market. Towards the sea the market-place was unprotected but the stone walls on the other sides made it as safe as a room. "So he has come."—"You don't say so!"—"Yes, he is here."—"Well, I never, so he has actually come!"—"It is good that he has come."—"Yes, that is good."—"Really, here in Saint Barbara?"—"Yes, here with us."—"A three-fifths share and new agreements."—"So he has actually come."—"Yes, really, three-fifths share, seven pfennig per kilo."—"And new agreements and a three-fifths share." (*RF,* 51)

33. In more contemporary terms the figure of Kerdhuys suggests the tradition of nineteenth-century Russian anarchism and its literary mediation in the novels of Dostoyevsky.

34. *The Lukács Reader,* 158.

35. Walter Benjamin, "Theses on the Philosophy of History," in *Illuminations,* ed. Hannah Arendt, trans. Harry Zohn (New York: Schocken Books, 1969), 257.

36. Compare, for example, August Strindberg's poem "Ahasver" (1905), Josef Winckler's *Der Irrgarten Gottes* (1922), and Paul Mühsam's *Der ewige Jude* (1925).

37. Main characters in *Grubetsch* (1927) are named Anna, Marie, Martin, Paul; in *Die Ziegler* (1930) Anna, Marie, Matthäus; in *Der Kopflohn* (1934) Johann and Marie; in "Der Vertrauensposten" (1933), expanded version "Der sogenannte Rendel" (1940), Katharina and Marie; and so forth.

38. Diersen, *Seghers-Studien: Interpretationen von Werken aus den Jahren 1926–1935,* 316.

39. *The Lukács Reader,* 158.

40. See also chapter 4, note 31.

41. Quoted in Éva Karádi, "Einleitung," in *Georg Lukács, Karl Mannheim und der Sonntagskreis,* 22.

42. Quoted in English translation in Kadarkay, *Georg Lukács: Life, Thought, and Politics,* 275.

43. Quoted in Karádi, "Einleitung," in *Georg Lukács, Karl Mannheim und der Sonntagskreis,* 19.

44. Lukács, "A bolsevizmus mint erkölcsi probléma," quoted in English translation in Béla Köpeczi, "Lukács in 1919," *New Hungarian Quarterly,* no. 2 (1975): 68–69.

45. Lukács, "Tactics and Ethics," in *Tactics and Ethics: Political Essays, 1919–1929,* ed. Rodney Livingstone, trans. Michael McColgan (New York: Harper & Row Publishers, 1972), 8.

46. Lukács, "Tactics and Ethics," 10.

47. At the end of his life Lukács praised this novel as "a fairly accurate docu-

mentary reminder of the period." See Lukács, *Record of a Life: An Autobiographical Sketch,* ed. István Eörsi, trans. Rodney Livingstone (London: Verso, 1983), 55.

48. Ervin Sinkó, *Optimisták: Történelmi regény 1918/19-böl,* vol. 2 (Novi Sad: Forum Könyvkiadó, 1965), 337–38. My translation differs slightly from, and incorporates more of the original Hungarian text than, the English excerpt in *György Lukács: His Life in Pictures and Documents,* ed. Éva Fekete and Éva Karádi, trans. Péter Balabán and Kenneth McRobbie (Budapest: Corvina Kiadó, 1981), 108. A similar portrait of Lukács in the spring of 1919 appears in Anna Lesznai's autobiographical novel in the figure of Commissar László. On the eve of his trip to the Czech front to join the Red Army, László attends a meeting of the Budapest Sunday Circle, where he defends a decision having more to do with faith than reason:

> "As I've said, I know and acknowledge the value of skepticism. The intellectual has always been closer to me than the member of any other social group. And nonetheless I maintain that skepticism can function as a dangerous hindrance, likewise the intellectual skeptic who cannot identify with the momentum of the masses. We live in a time when unanimous action is all-important. . . . Today thinking is a more exciting task than ever. Every day we have to make concrete decisions. This is a heavy responsibility, especially if one is handed a certain measure of power. It is electrifying and often a painful task: electrifying agony, that exists, too. Yet I cannot remain in Budapest. The acceptance of danger and of action having to do with sacrifice is more important than the most important decision. Can you understand this? So, my decision was the right one." (Lesznai, *Spätherbst in Eden* [Karlsruhe: Stahlberg, 1965], 620)

49. See Katja Mann, *Unwritten Memories* (New York: Alfred A. Knopf, 1975), 72–73.

50. Thomas Mann, *The Magic Mountain,* trans. H. T. Lowe-Porter (New York: Alfred A. Knopf, 1958), 443–44.

51. This is pure conjecture on my part, as we have no concrete evidence other than Seghers's text. We do know, however, that in later life, incidentally much like Brecht, Seghers did not hide a certain antipathy to both the person and work of Thomas Mann. The GDR writer Stephan Hermlin, a close friend of Seghers and an admirer of Mann, claimed that she "hated" Mann from "deep in her soul," and that her feelings "may have had to do" with Mann's "difficulties with Jews," since Mann "had a Jewish wife, thus had half-Jewish children, and was homosexual." See Eberhard Röhmer, "Nicht gleichwertig, aber verwandt: Gespräch mit Stephan Hermlin," *Argonautenschiff: Jahrbuch der Anna-Seghers-Gesellschaft* 4 (Berlin: Aufbau Verlag, 1995): 158–59. Hermlin told me much the same about Seghers's attitude toward Mann during my (unpublished) interview with him in Berlin-Pankow in June 1994. If Hermlin was correct about the reasons for Seghers's "hate," then we can assume that Mann's depiction of the "ugly" Jew Leo Naphta in *The Magic Mountain* may have aroused similar feelings in her many years ear-

lier. Lukács, as is well known, was a lifelong admirer of Mann's work and assumed tactful restraint whenever he was asked whether Naphta was modeled on him. The topic has received ample attention in the secondary literature. For Lukács's final elaboration on the subject shortly before his death, see Lukács, *Record of a Life,* 93–95.

52. *György Lukács: His Life in Pictures and Documents,* 119.

53. See Löwy, *Georg Lukács: From Romanticism to Bolshevism,* 154–67.

54. See Kadarkay, *Georg Lukács: Life, Thought, and Politics,* 279–95.

55. On Lukács's intellectual debt to Szabó, see Löwy, *Georg Lukács: From Romanticism to Bolshevism,* 80–84.

56. *György Lukács: His Life in Pictures and Documents,* 114.

57. Edit Hajós, born in 1889, studied abroad in France and Switzerland and became a physician. She was a close friend of Lukács, a member of the Sunday Circle, and the first wife of Béla Balázs, with whom she lived in an open marriage until 1918. Balázs based on her the main character in his drama *Dr. Szélpál Margit* (1909), as well as numerous other figures in his early writings. After their separation in 1918 she traveled in the Soviet Union, joined the Bolshevik Party in 1919, and married a Russian. Thereafter she lived in Vienna, Berlin, and, after 1933, London. In 1948 she returned to Hungary, where she was arrested by the Rákosi regime and spent seven years in prison. After her release in 1956 she returned to London, where she worked as a translator and published her prison memoir, *Seven Years Solitary,* under the name Edith Bone in 1957. She died in London in 1975.

58. Victor Serge's account of a conversation with Lukács in Moscow in Serge, *Memoirs of a Revolutionary, 1901–1941,* trans. Peter Sedgwick (London: Oxford University Press, 1967), 187–88.

59. As described by the wife of Lukács's friend and supporter the German writer Paul Ernst, Lukács's living quarters in Vienna consisted of

> a camp bed, a wash basin, a brown chest of drawers, a faded couch, a huge desk, and bookcases and chairs. The whole room was so topsy-turvy and crammed that we had to climb over each other. An iron stove radiated stifling heat. Somewhere Lukács rose, and, struggling his way across the room, greeted us with a helpless smile. . . . Lukács refused to talk about his works of philosophy and aesthetics, which we so admired. To our horror, they were lost in the drift of events. Saddest of all, he expressed no regret over this. (Quoted in Kadarkay, *Georg Lukács: Life, Thought, and Politics,* 288)

Lukács's situation as a political exile is described with greater understanding in the memoirs of Count Mihály Károlyi, a liberal aristocrat who was president of Hungary during the first revolutionary government between November 1918 and March 1919, and who spent the rest of his life in exile:

> George Lukács, the Marxist philosopher of European standing, was living in Döblin, near Vienna. I visited him often, as I had a deep admiration for his intelligence and moral integrity. The son of wealthy Hungarian Jews, he gave

up a comfortable living and chose a faith which rendered him an outcast in his circle. His parents, true to the family solidarity of the race, were trying to supply him with money, which he stubbornly refused. He lived in destitution. I often found that the so-called "materialists" were ready to sacrifice material advantages for an ideal, whilst the main aim of the pious was worldly comfort. (Michael Károlyi, *Faith without Illusion: Memoirs,* trans. Catherine Karolyi, introduction by A. J. P. Taylor [London: Jonathan Cape, 1956], 229)

60. Quoted in Kadarkay, *Georg Lukács: Life, Thought, and Politics,* 286. Trotsky's 1929 memoir includes his wife Natalia's firsthand account of the abduction, a much longer and more detailed report than the description in Lukács's letter, but hardly differing in the essentials. See Leon Trotsky, *My Life: An Attempt at an Autobiography* (New York: Pathfinder Press, 1970), 539–49.

61. Trotsky, *My Life,* 549.

62. Siegfried Kracauer, "Eine Märtyrer-Chronik von heute," *Frankfurter Zeitung,* 13 November 1932.

63. Balázs, entry January–May 1920, "Tagebuch," 23.

64. Balázs, entry 26 October 1920, "Tagebuch," 23. The diary entry also refers to Lesznai's lament that "Gyuri [Georg Lukács], who could tie together the threads coming from so many different directions, says he has no time because he is making the world revolution. But perhaps this, too, has its deeper meaning" (23).

65. See the discussion of Radványi's influence in chapter 4.

66. *The Lukács Reader,* 158.

67. *The Lukács Reader,* 161.

68. Kracauer, "Eine Märtyrer-Chronik von heute."

69. *The Lukács Reader,* 161.

70. Lukács, "L'art pour l'art und proletarische Dichtung," *Die Tat* 18 (June 1926): 222; quoted in Kadarkay, *Georg Lukács: Life, Thought, and Politics,* 283.

71. Lukács, "The Genesis and Value of Imaginative Literature," in *Reviews and Articles from "Die rote Fahne,"* trans. Peter Palmer (London: Merlin Press, 1983), 73.

72. *György Lukács: His Life in Pictures and Documents,* 123.

73. Anna Seghers to Inge Diersen in the early 1960s, quoted in Diersen, *Seghers-Studien: Interpretationen von Werken aus den Jahren 1926–1935,* 316.

Chapter 6

1. Martin Buber, *The Legend of the Baal-Shem,* trans. Maurice Friedman (New York: Schocken Books, 1969), 13.

2. Quoted in Anna Lesznai, "Tagebuch, 1912–1927," in *Georg Lukács, Karl Mannheim und der Sonntagskreis,* ed. Éva Karádi and Erzsébet Vezér (Frankfurt am Main: Sendler Verlag, 1985), 138.

3. Hans Mayer, *Der Widerruf: Über Deutsche und Juden* (Frankfurt am Main: Suhrkamp Verlag, 1994), 282.

4. Walter Jens, "Anna Seghers," *Sinn und Form* 42 (1990): 1169.

5. See Kurt Batt, "Erlebnis des Umbruchs und harmonische Gestalt: Der Dialog zwischen Anna Seghers und Georg Lukács," in *Dialog und Kontroverse mit Georg Lukács,* ed. Werner Mittenzwei (Leipzig: Reclam Verlag, 1975), 204–48.

6. This distinction is not based on genre per se, for the aspect of storytelling is of course a fundamental principle in Seghers's novels as well.

7. Walter Benjamin, "The Storyteller," in *Illuminations,* ed. Hannah Arendt, trans. Harry Zohn (New York: Schocken Books, 1969), 101.

8. Regarding Soviet writers, the case of the master storyteller Isaac Babel, purged in 1939, comes to mind. After being criticized at the Congress of Soviet Writers in 1934 for his lack of productivity, Isaac Babel is reported to have said: "Speaking of silence, I cannot avoid talking about myself, a past master of that art." Quoted in Isaac Babel, *Lyubka the Cossack and Other Stories,* ed. and trans. Andrew R. MacAndrew (New York: New American Library, 1963), 281.

9. Benjamin, "The Storyteller," 102.

10. Letter of 1 September 1938 to Prinz Löwenstein, in Anna Seghers/Wieland Herzfelde, *Gewöhnliches und gefährliches Leben: Ein Briefwechsel aus der Zeit des Exils, 1939–1946,* ed. Ursula Emmerich and Erika Pick (Darmstadt and Neuwied: Luchterhand Verlag, 1986), 197.

11. Letter of early 1945 to Wieland Herzfelde, in Seghers/Herzfelde, *Gewöhnliches und gefährliches Leben,* 63–64.

12. Bertolt Brecht, entry 4 November 1947, in *Journals, 1934–1955,* ed. John Willett, trans. Hugh Rorrison (New York: Routledge, 1993), 373.

13. Letter of 28 June 1948 to Georg Lukács, in Seghers, *Über Kunstwerk und Wirklichkeit,* vol. 4, *Ergänzungsband,* ed. Sigrid Bock (Berlin: Akademie Verlag, 1979), 153–54. The passage quoted refers to Seghers's publishing difficulties at the time in the Soviet Union as well as in the West. *The Dead Stay Young,* published in the United States and England in 1950, was Seghers's last work to appear with a major publisher in English translation.

14. See Jürgen Kuczynski's recollections of his trips to the Soviet Union with Seghers in April–May 1948 and in the summer of 1949, in Kuczynski, *"Ein linientreuer Dissident": Memoiren 1945–1989* (Berlin: Aufbau Verlag, 1994), 47–54.

15. Seghers, *Über Kunstwerk und Wirklichkeit,* 4:154.

16. Letter of 23 September 1938 to the Soviet publisher Ivan Anissimov, in Seghers, *Über Kunstwerk und Wirklichkeit,* vol. 2, *Erlebnis und Gestaltung,* ed. Sigrid Bock (Berlin: Akademie Verlag, 1971), 16.

17. Georg Lukács, *The Theory of the Novel: A Historico-Philosophical Essay on the Forms of Great Epic Literature,* trans. Anna Bostock (Cambridge, Mass.: MIT Press, 1971), 11–12.

18. Lukács, *The Theory of the Novel,* 11–12.

19. See note 16 to this chapter.

20. Pertaining to this topic, see the discussion of Heiner Müller's use of Seghers material in Helen Fehervary, "Landscapes of an *Auftrag,*" *New German Critique* 73, special issue on Heiner Müller, ed. David Bathrick and Helen Fehervary (winter 1998), 115–32.

21. Lukács, *The Theory of the Novel*, 51–52. Whereas Anna Bostock translated Lukács's use of the German term *Novelle* as "short story," I have adjusted the translation by substituting the term *novella*.

22. Lukács, *The Theory of the Novel*, 50. Anna Bostock's translation of the term *der Erzähler* (he who recounts) as "the narrator" unfortunately eclipses the aspect of storytelling, which is as important in the context of this particular passage as it is in Walter Benjamin's essay "Der Erzähler," accurately translated by Harry Zohn as "The Storyteller" (cited in note 7 to this chapter).

23. Christa Wolf first raised the question of why Seghers often relied on material from tales and legends, "even in times of great danger, as in Paris." Seghers was typically evasive, saying she had "invented" some themes and found others "in existing *Märchen* and tales." See Wolf, "Ein Gespräch mit Anna Seghers" (1965), in *Die Dimension des Autors: Essays und Aufsätze; Reden und Gespräche, 1959–1985*, vol. 1 (Berlin: Aufbau Verlag, 1986), 286.

24. Lukács György, "Zsidó miszticizmus," in Lukács, *Ifjúkori müvek, 1902–1918* (Budapest: Magvetö Kiadó, 1977), 556–57.

25. Lesznai, "Tagebuch, 1912–1927," in *Georg Lukács, Karl Mannheim und der Sonntagskreis*, 129–31.

26. Béla Balázs, entry 12 July 1921, "Tagebuch," in *Georg Lukács, Karl Mannheim und der Sonntagskreis*, 127.

27. The personal inscription in the copy of Balázs's *A Fekete Korsó: Uj Játékok* (Budapest: Kner Izidor, 1919) that he evidently gave to Radványi reads: "For László Radványi, the same who was my secretary in the second week of the Commune, with love, Béla Balázs, Bp. [Budapest], 1919, apr. 5." (ASA lib. 6135).

28. See document 31, "Märchenvorträge in den Schulen," in Georg Lukács, *Taktik und Ethik: Politische Aufsätze I, 1918–1920*, ed. Jörg Kammler and Frank Benseler (Darmstadt and Neuwied: Luchterhand Verlag, 1975), 274.

29. See the chapter "Fathers and Sons" in Arpad Kadarkay, *Georg Lukács: Life, Thought, and Politics* (Cambridge, Mass.: Basil Blackwell, 1991), 3–27. On the fairly unique circumstances of Jewish assimilation in Hungary and the more or less successful Jewish-Hungarian symbiosis at the end of the nineteenth century, see John Lukacs, *Budapest 1900: A Historical Portrait of a City and Its Culture* (New York: Grove Press, 1988), 84–107; on the rise of antisemitism after 1900, see 187–208.

30. See Lesznai's autobiographical novel *Spätherbst in Eden* (Karlsruhe: Stahlberg, 1965).

31. Seghers, "Bauern von Hruschowo," in *Der letzte Mann der Höhle: Erzählungen, 1924–1933* (Berlin: Aufbau Verlag, 1994), 154–55. Page references henceforth in the text. Instead of translating the "Bauern" in the title literally as "peasants" or "farmers," I have tried to avoid ambiguity as to meaning by using the more specific term "woodcutters." Clearly, the inhabitants of Hrushovo would have grown crops as far as was possible on the mountain terrain and kept livestock.

32. See the compelling discussion of Seghers's approach to the thematization of the Holocaust in her prose in Jochen Vogt, "Was aus dem Mädchen geworden

ist: Kleine Archäologie eines Gelegenheitstextes von Anna Seghers," *Argonautenschiff: Jahrbuch der Anna-Seghers-Gesellschaft* 6 (Berlin: Aufbau Verlag, 1997): 132.

33. An especially telling example is *Die drei Bäume* (The Three Trees), written in 1940 and first published in Mexico in 1946.

34. Lukács György, "Balázs Béla: Hét Mese," in *Ifjúkori müvek, 1902–1918,* 711, 712, 717, 713–14.

35. Leon Trotsky, *My Life: An Attempt at an Autobiography* (New York: Pathfinder Press, 1970), 6.

36. For a discussion of this thematic in *The Revolt of the Fishermen,* see chapter 5.

37. See David King, *Trotsky: A Photographic Biography* (Oxford: Basil Blackwell, 1986).

38. Seghers, "Sagen von Artemis," in *Reise ins elfte Reich: Erzählungen, 1934–1946* (Berlin: Aufbau Verlag, 1994), 60. Page references henceforth in the text. Seghers's detailed physicalized representation of Artemis in this pose was clearly inspired by the Hellenistic sculpture *Artemis dit Diane de Versailles,* which the author must have seen during her visits to the Louvre while she was in Paris between 1933 and 1940. The sculpture represents Artemis in a tunic that ends above the knee. Her right foot is to the back with its heel off the ground. Her left foot is forward, and the left knee projects slightly below the hem of the tunic. Her right arm is raised, its hand over her shoulder holding the quivers she carries on her back.

39. The copy of Kipling's *The Jungle Book* in Seghers's library contains the personal inscription "for Rod from Tschib," as well as a small pencil drawing, presumably by her (ASA lib. 2459: Rudyard Kipling, *Stories from the Jungle Book* [Bielefeld: Velhagen & Klasing, 1917]). The library contains two other works by Kipling: *Schlichte Geschichten aus den indischen Bergen* (Weimar: Kiepenheuer, 1914), with the ex libris "Netty Reiling" (ASA lib. 2545); and *From Sea to Sea: Letters of Travel* (New York: Doubleday, 1899) (ASA lib. 5549).

40. Seghers, "Die schönsten Sagen vom Räuber Woynok," in *Reise ins elfte Reich: Erzählungen, 1934–1946,* 26. Page references henceforth in the text.

41. See the account in Trotsky, *My Life,* 142ff.

42. Trotsky, *My Life,* 218.

43. See the reference to Batt's essay in note 5 to this chapter.

44. Albeit not without his stepson Ferenc Jánossy's deportation to Siberia. See the account in Kadarkay, *Georg Lukács: Life, Thought, and Politics,* 308–9; on Lukács's situation during these years, see pages 299–341.

45. See notes 10 and 16 to this chapter.

46. As Béla Balázs wrote in his diary in 1921, "Gyuri said it's the very tone of the *Märchen* that 'saves him.'" See note 26 to this chapter.

47. Walter Benjamin, *Understanding Brecht,* trans. Anna Bostock (London: New Left Books, 1973), 119.

48. Benjamin, *Understanding Brecht,* 119. Here and elsewhere I modify the translation of the title of Seghers's story.

49. See Reiner Steinweg, *Das Lehrstück: Brechts Theorie einer politisch-ästhetischen Erziehung* (Stuttgart: Metzler Verlag, 1972); *Brechts Modell der Lehrstücke,* ed. Reiner Steinweg (Frankfurt am Main: Suhrkamp Verlag, 1976); and Wolfgang Schivelbusch, *Sozialistisches Drama nach Brecht* (Darmstadt and Neuwied: Luchterhand Verlag, 1974), 9–25.

50. See the summary of Manfred Wekwerth's last conversations with Brecht, in Bertolt Brecht, *Die Maßnahme: Kritische Ausgabe,* ed. Reiner Steinweg (Frankfurt am Main: Suhrkamp Verlag, 1972), 262–66.

51. See the reference in note 20 to this chapter.

52. Mayer, *Der Widerruf: Über Deutsche und Juden,* 278.

53. See note 14 to this chapter.

54. Seghers, "Das Argonautenschiff," in *Die Hochzeit von Haiti: Erzählungen 1948–1949* (Berlin: Aufbau Verlag, 1994), 138. Page references henceforth in the text.

55. See Robert Graves, *The Greek Myths* (London: Penguin Books, 1992), 603–6.

56. See Frank Wagner, "Deportation nach Piaski: Letzte Stationen der Passion von Hedwig Reiling," *Argonautenschiff: Jahrbuch der Anna-Seghers-Gesellschaft* 3 (Berlin: Aufbau Verlag, 1994): 117–26.

57. Seghers, "Wiedereinführung der Sklaverei in Guadeloupe," in *Die Hochzeit von Haiti: Erzählungen 1948–1949,* 110–11. Page references henceforth in the text.

58. Seghers, "Das Versteck," in *Steinzeit: Erzählungen 1967–1980* (Berlin: Aufbau Verlag, 1994), 338.

Chapter 7

1. "Die Erlösung ist der limes des Fortschritts." Manuscript 490, Walter Benjamin Archive, appears under "Neue Thesen K" in Benjamin, *Gesammelte Schriften,* vol. 1, no. 3, *Anmerkungen der Herausgeber* (Notes by the Editors), ed. Rolf Tiedemann and Hermann Schweppenhäuser (Frankfurt am Main: Suhrkamp Verlag, 1974), 1235.

2. Letter to Irene Witt, 7 August 1947, quoted in *Anna Seghers: Eine Biographie in Bildern,* ed. Frank Wagner, Ursula Emmerich, and Ruth Radvanyi (Berlin: Aufbau Verlag, 1994), 159.

3. Walter Benjamin, *Gesammelte Briefe,* vol. 5, 1935–37, ed. Christoph Gödde and Henri Lonitz (Frankfurt am Main: Suhrkamp Verlag, 1999), 559.

4. Benjamin, *Gesammelte Briefe,* 5:633.

5. Benjamin, *Gesammelte Briefe,* 5:632. Three weeks later, on 13 January 1938, Benjamin once again mentioned to Alfred Cohn "Anna Seghers, whom I now see quite often." Benjamin, *Gesammelte Briefe,* vol. 6, 1938–40, ed. Christoph Gödde and Henri Lonitz (Frankfurt am Main: Suhrkamp Verlag, 2000), 16.

6. Benjamin, *Gesammelte Briefe,* 5:521. The editors provide no explanation of Benjamin's deliberately vague reference to a "suggestion" by Seghers belonging to "the realm of the spoken word." This may have been a reference to the political

purpose behind Seghers's radio play *Der Prozeß der Jeanne d'Arc zu Rouen 1431* (1937, The Trial of Jeanne d'Arc at Rouen, 1431), which she apparently wrote in the wake of the first Moscow trial in August 1936 and had broadcast by Flemish Radio in early 1937. See my discussion of the play and the circumstances surrounding it in chapter 8.

7. See, for example, Frank Leschnitzer's description of a half-hour speech delivered by Seghers without notes in the large, packed hall of the Berlin Philharmonie in 1930: "All the while I listened to these artfully composed sentences that seemed to have been 'constructed' in a most sophisticated way I thought to myself (and was certainly not alone in this): 'Any moment now she'll stumble and fall out of her construction!' But with incredible calm and without any obstructions or hesitations, the magically fairy-tale-like, intricately woven stream of her speech flowed on." Quoted in Friedrich Albrecht, *Die Erzählerin Anna Seghers, 1926–1932* (Berlin: Rütten & Loening, 1975), 272.

8. The essay appeared in the October 1936 issue of *Orient und Okzident,* but to Benjamin's chagrin the actual publication of the 1936 issue was held up until June 1937.

9. *Die neue Weltbühne* 34, no. 19 (12 May 1938): 593–97.

10. Benjamin, "Eine Chronik der deutschen Arbeitslosen: Zu Anna Seghers Roman 'Die Rettung,'" in *Gesammelte Schriften,* vol. 3, *Kritiken und Rezensionen,* ed. Hella Tiedemann-Bartels (Frankfurt am Main: Suhrkamp Verlag, 1972), 531. Page references henceforth in the text, preceded by *CA.*

11. This theme even more obviously pervades Seghers's *Transit.* Beckett of course was in southern France later, in Roussillon, waiting for the war's end. According to one biographer, *Waiting for Godot* is a metaphor for the long walk into Roussillon. Deirdre Bair, *Samuel Beckett* (New York: Harcourt, Brace, Jovanovich, 1978), 386.

12. See Benjamin, "Krisis des Romans: Zu Döblins 'Berlin Alexanderplatz,'" in *Gesammelte Schriften,* 3:230–36. The review first appeared in *Die Gesellschaft* 7, no. 1 (1930): 562–66.

13. According to a letter written late in her life, Seghers had known Benjamin "fleetingly in Berlin in peacetime." The reference occurs in a letter to Ernst-Ullrich Pinkert (ASA letters, file 1384). Since Seghers's response to Pinkert's letter of 5 December 1981 is incorrectly dated 17 December 1980, it is possible that she actually meant she had known Benjamin in Paris "in peacetime" rather than in Berlin. This is more likely since she would have encountered Benjamin "fleetingly" at the Paris writers' congresses and other events involving the German exiles. This would also explain her use of the term "peacetime," that is, Paris before the German invasion, whereas she would have referred to the years in Berlin as "before exile." There is another inconsistency in Seghers's letter, written late in her life when she frequently suffered from memory lapses, in that she refers at one point to being "told" of Benjamin's suicide "as far as I know, while I was still in Paris" and at another point notes that "this is more or less what was written to me," presumably when she was already in Pamiers near Le Vernet, that is, after she had crossed the demarcation line with her two children in September of 1940. On Seghers's escape

to the south of France, see Jeanne Stern's recollections: "Das Floß der Anna Seghers," in *Über Anna Seghers: Ein Almanach zum 75. Geburtstag,* ed. Kurt Batt (Berlin: Aufbau Verlag, 1975), 77–91; and "Die Dame mit dem Turban," *Neue deutsche Literatur,* no. 6 (1981): 5–19.

14. Benjamin, *Gesammelte Schriften,* 3:63.

15. Seghers, "Revolutionärer Alltag," in *Über Kunstwerk und Wirklichkeit,* vol. 2, *Erlebnis und Gestaltung,* ed. Sigrid Bock (Berlin: Akademie Verlag, 1971), 50.

16. See Manès Sperber's account: "Unlike the comrades of the faction and the majority of the political emigrants, Anna lived with her husband and children in a villa at Bellevue near Versailles rather than in a Paris hotel garni. We liked to visit her on Sundays and were very well received. The return to the city, to a room that was usually not made up on Sunday and then appeared even more miserable, was scheduled as late as possible." Sperber, *Until My Eyes Are Closed with Shards,* trans. Harry Zohn (New York: Holmes & Meier Publishers, 1994), 66. Arthur Koestler was in the same communist writers' faction, or caucus, within the Schutzverband deutscher Schriftsteller (Association for the Defense of German Writers) in Paris and wrote in his autobiography: "The Caucus met privately once a week. Only one of its members was a writer of international standing: Anna Seghers, author of *The Fishermen of St. Barbara* [published translation of 1929: *The Revolt of the Fishermen*] and *The Seventh Cross,* whom I admired, and still admire, both as a novelist and as an attractive and charming woman, but with whom I never found any personal contact." Koestler, *The Invisible Writing: An Autobiography* (Boston: Beacon Press, 1955), 231. In his chapter on Alexander (Sándor) Radó ("Homage to a Spy," in *The Invisible Writing,* 301–9), Koestler noted that Radó's and his wife Helene's "closest friends and neighbors were the writer Anna Seghers and her husband, Dr. Radvany [*sic*], who had an apartment in Bellevue or Meudon [Bellevue—H.F.]. They, too, were of course Communists and, by a curious coincidence, Radvany too was a Hungarian married to a German wife" (302). The Hungarian geographer and cartographer Sándor Radó monitored the German army's Russian campaign as head of the Swiss branch of the Soviet Union's European intelligence network and in this capacity contributed greatly to Allied military successes. Due to his efforts to cooperate with British intelligence during this time Radó was recalled to Moscow after the war and imprisoned. In 1955 he was allowed to return to Hungary, where he worked in an academic post as a geographer and cartographer. The exchange of letters after his return between Anna Seghers and Radó and Helene Radó gives evidence of his continuing trauma (ASA letters, file 1403). Radó's memoir, *Codename Dora,* trans. J. A. Underwood (London: Abelard, 1977), challenges other published histories of his case, particularly *Handbook for Spies* (London, 1949) by Alexander Foote, who worked with Radó in Switzerland and subsequently recanted his work as a Soviet spy.

17. See Benjamin's reference to his participation in the Freie Deutsche Hochschule as well as the editorial note in Benjamin, *Gesammelte Briefe,* 5:245–46. Seghers's library contains no first editions of Benjamin's works, only the following:

Einbahnstraße (Frankfurt am Main: Suhrkamp, 1955); *Lesezeichen: Schriften zur deutschsprachigen Literatur* (Leipzig: Reclam Verlag, 1970); and *Walter Benjamin zu Ehren,* ed. Siegfried Unseld (Frankfurt am Main: Suhrkamp, 1972) (ASA lib. 1082, 1501, 834).

18. On the Svendborg conversations, see Benjamin, "Conversations with Brecht: Notes from Svendborg," in *Understanding Brecht,* trans. Anna Bostock (London: New Left Books, 1973), 119. See also Brecht's letter of April–May 1937 asking Benjamin for more information about the Laterne-Cabaret suggested by Seghers for the Paris production of *The Rifles of Señora Carrar,* and asking him to find out whether Helene Weigel might stay with Seghers in Bellevue outside Paris during the play's run. Brecht, *Letters, 1913–1956,* ed. John Willett, trans. Ralph Manheim (London: Methuen, 1990), 254.

19. In Seghers, *Über Kunstwerk und Wirklichkeit,* 2:16.

20. Anna Seghers/Wieland Herzfelde, *Gewöhnliches und gefährliches Leben: Ein Briefwechsel aus der Zeit des Exils, 1939–1946,* ed. Ursula Emmerich and Erika Pick (Darmstadt and Neuwied: Luchterhand Verlag, 1986), 40.

21. Seghers/Herzfelde, *Gewöhnliches und gefährliches Leben,* 42.

22. Seghers/Herzfelde, *Gewöhnliches und gefährliches Leben,* 41–42.

23. Chapter 1, consisting of an introductory frame and eight sections, appeared in issue 6 of *Internationale Literatur* (June 1939): 6–34; the first four sections of chapter 2 appeared in issue 7 (July 1939): 49–65; and the final three sections of chapter 2, 5–7, in issue 8 (August 1939): 8–25.

24. Seghers/Herzfelde, *Gewöhnliches und gefährliches Leben,* 35.

25. See note 1 to this chapter.

26. Anna Seghers, *The Seventh Cross,* trans. James A. Galston (Boston: Little, Brown & Co., 1942), 6. Page references henceforth in the text, preceded by *SC.* Referring to the *limes* years later (and as already noted in chapter 1), Seghers drew a parallel between the architectural display of Roman power and the labors required by subsequent strivings of the Christian church:

> As children we were told that across the blue chain of hills beyond the Rhine the Romans had drawn their *limes,* the boundary between the Roman Empire and the wilderness. That stirred up something in me. . . . On the walls of the cathedral's great crypt we were shown the drawings of apprentices from the Gothic period, and were told how the cathedral's towers were built even earlier—by means of circular wooden stairways for the mules that hauled up the building materials. All that played a part in my relationship to the arts. (Achim Roscher, "Wirklichkeit und Phantasie: Fragen an Anna Seghers," in *Also fragen Sie mich! Gespräche* [Halle: Mitteldeutscher Verlag, 1983], 52–53)

27. Carl Zuckmayer, "Grußwort," in *Anna Seghers aus Mainz,* ed. Walter Heist (Mainz: Verlag Dr. Hanns Krach, 1973), 12.

28. Friedrich Nietzsche, *The Birth of Tragedy and The Case of Wagner,* trans. Walter Kaufmann (New York: Vintage, 1967), 63. Page references henceforth in the text, preceded by *BT.*

29. As discussed in chapter 6, dogs and hounds appear similarly disturbing in *The Most Splendid Tales of Woynok the Brigand* and *Reintroduction of Slavery in Guadeloupe.*

30. See note 1 to this chapter.

31. Manuscript 471, Walter Benjamin Archive, appears under "Das Jetzt der Erkennbarkeit" (The Now of Perception), in Benjamin, *Gesammelte Schriften,* vol. 1, no. 3, *Anmerkungen der Herausgeber,* 1237: "Der Historiker wendet der eignen Zeit den Rücken, und sein Seherblick entzündet sich an den immer tiefer ins Vergangene hinschwindenden Gipfeln der früheren Menschengeschlechter. Dieser Seherblick ist es, dem die eigene Zeit weit deutlicher gegenwärtig ist als den Zeitgenossen, die 'mit ihr Schritt halten.'"

32. Benjamin, "Theses on the Philosophy of History," in *Illuminations,* ed. Hannah Arendt, trans. Harry Zohn (New York: Schocken Books, 1969), 255. My translation of the title as "On the Concept of History" is in keeping with the title "Über den Begriff der Geschichte" used in the standard Suhrkamp Verlag critical edition of Benjamin's *Gesammelte Schriften* edited by Rolf Tiedemann and Hermann Schweppenhäuser. Page references henceforth in the text, preceded by *CH.*

33. Gershom Scholem, *The Messianic Idea in Judaism* (New York: Schocken Books, 1971), 238.

34. Scholem, *The Messianic Idea in Judaism,* 41.

35. The passage occurs in chapter 6 of the novel and would not have been available to Benjamin in published form. The serialization of the novel in *Internationale Literatur* in the summer of 1939 included only the first two chapters. See note 23 to this chapter.

36. Claude Lévi-Strauss, *Tristes Tropiques,* trans. John Russell (New York: Athenaum, 1968), 24–25.

37. Anna Seghers, *Transit,* trans. James A. Galston (Boston: Little, Brown & Co., 1944), 94–96. A similar, shorter passage occurs on page 304. Page references henceforth in the text, preceded by *T.*

38. See *Anna Seghers: Eine Biographie in Bildern,* 90.

39. See Momme Brodersen, *Walter Benjamin: A Biography,* ed. Martina Dervis, trans. Malcolm R. Green and Ingrida Ligers (London: Verso, 1996), 250–62.

40. See the recollections of Jeanne Stern, who helped Seghers and her two children escape across the demarcation line: "Das Floß der Anna Seghers"; and "Die Dame mit dem Turban."

41. Letter to F. C. Weiskopf, 23 November 1940, quoted in *Anna Seghers: Eine Biographie in Bildern,* 104.

42. In fact Benjamin died from an overdose of morphine. It is unclear whether Seghers assumed at the time she wrote her novel that he had shot himself, or whether she simply decided to invent her version. In her response to a letter of 5 December 1981 from Dr. Ernst-Ullrich Pinkert asking whether the reference in *Transit* is to Benjamin's suicide, Seghers confirmed this, saying she learned at the time that Benjamin "left occupied France with a few acquaintances in order to escape across the Spanish border. . . . He was apprehended so as to be handed over

to the Germans. By taking his own life Walter Benjamin avoided this fate." ASA letters, file 1384.

43. Like Seghers's father Isidor Reiling, who with his brother Hermann ran one of the most successful business ventures in art and antiquities in the Rhineland, Benjamin's father Emil Benjamin came from the Rhineland and after arriving in Berlin dealt for a time in art and antiquities, primarily as an auctioneer. On Isidor Reiling, see Friedrich Schütz, "Die Familie Seghers-Reiling und das jüdische Mainz," *Argonautenschiff: Jahrbuch der Anna-Seghers-Gesellschaft* 2 (Berlin: Aufbau Verlag, 1993): 151–73. On Emil Benjamin and other family members, see Brodersen, *Walter Benjamin: A Biography,* 6–19; and Walter Benjamin, *Selected Writings,* vol. 1, ed. Marcus Bullock and Michael W. Jennings (Cambridge, Mass.: The Belknap Press of Harvard University Press, 1996), 490–91.

44. See the pertinent discussion in chapter 6.

45. See Schütz, "Die Familie Seghers-Reiling und das jüdische Mainz," 151–73; and Frank Wagner, "Deportation nach Piaski: Letzte Stationen der Passion von Hedwig Reiling," *Argonautenschiff: Jahrbuch der Anna-Seghers-Gesellschaft* 3 (Berlin: Aufbau Verlag, 1994): 117–26.

46. Seghers/Herzfelde, *Gewöhnliches und gefährliches Leben,* 42.

47. For an intriguing account of the complex political situation in which Jewish communist exiles found themselves in Mexico in the 1940s, and how it was linked to the circumstances of their escape from France, see Marcus G. Patka, *Zu nahe der Sonne: Deutsche Schriftsteller im Exil in Mexico* (Berlin: Aufbau Verlag, 1999).

48. Josephus, *The Jewish War,* ed. E. Mary Smallwood, trans. G. A. Williamson (London: Penguin Books, 1981), 220.

49. Smallwood, introduction to Josephus, *The Jewish War,* 11.

50. See Smallwood, introduction to Josephus, *The Jewish War,* 9–24.

51. Josephus, *The Jewish War,* 27.

52. Josephus, *The Jewish War,* 31.

53. Letter of 12 July 1941 from Mexico to Wieland Herzfelde in New York, in Seghers/Herzfelde, *Gewöhnliches und gefährliches Leben,* 44.

54. Interview with Ruth Radvanyi, Berlin, June 1995.

55. Smallwood, introduction to Josephus, *The Jewish War,* 24.

56. See Alexander Stephan, *Anna Seghers, "Das siebte Kreuz": Welt und Wirkung eines Romans* (Berlin: Aufbau Verlag, 1997), 208–80; also *"Das siebte Kreuz" von Anna Seghers: Texte, Daten, Bilder,* ed. Sonja Hilzinger (Frankfurt am Main: Luchterhand Literaturverlag, 1990), 171–208.

57. Andromache's devotion to her slain husband Hector has been the subject of numerous adaptations since Euripides. When asked in 1960 about the character Marie in *Transit,* Seghers compared her to the title figure of Racine's *Andromache:* "Two men fight over a woman, but the woman in fact loves a third man, who is already dead." Letter to a reader, 7 March 1960, in Seghers, *Über Kunstwerk und Wirklichkeit,* vol. 4, *Ergänzungsband,* ed. Sigrid Bock (Berlin: Akademie Verlag, 1979), 160. In the GDR Seghers often gave partial, even misleading answers to questions about her earlier work. Since she rarely relied on the Greek myths (*Tales*

of Artemis and *The Ship of the Argonauts* are very freely rendered exceptions), I opt in favor of the argument, which I also make in previous chapters, that her mythic characterizations essentially drew on Judeo-Christian legend concerning events in Palestine in the first century. Like so many of her female characters who serially bear the names of early Jewish Christians (Anna, Marie, etc.), the widow of the implicitly Jewish Weidel bears what for Seghers was the originally Jewish (Mirjam) Hellenized name Marie. Regarding the imagery of the ship voyage, it is significant that the ship in the final image of Seghers's *The Revolt of the Fishermen* of 1928 is the *Marie Farère*. See my discussions of the novella and this particular scene in chapters 2 and 5.

58. A more appropriate comparison can be made to the writer Lion Feuchtwanger, who made the life of the first-century chronicler the subject of his Josephus trilogy (*Der Jüdische Krieg,* 1932; *Die Söhne,* 1935; *Der Tag wird kommen,* 1945). Making the most of an already successful writing career, Feuchtwanger continued to be prolific in exile in California, where he remained until his death in 1958.

59. Seghers, "Abschied vom Heine-Club," in *Über Kunstwerk und Wirklichkeit,* vol. 1: *Die Tendenz in der reinen Kunst,* ed. Sigrid Bock (Berlin: Akademie Verlag, 1970), 205–6.

60. Seghers, "Abschied vom Heine-Club," 206.

61. Seghers, "Abschied vom Heine-Club," 207.

62. The letter consists of two handwritten sheets, dated Passy, 27 May 1848, and is addressed to Heine's mother Betty Heine. The letter appears as no. 813 on page 46 in the third volume of Heinrich Heine, *Briefwechsel,* 3 vols., ed. Friedrich Hirth (Berlin: Propyläen Verlag, 1920). The collection is found in Seghers's library and contains the ex libris "Netty Reiling" (ASA lib. 3048).

Chapter 8

1. Related by the writer Erwin Strittmatter, "Anna und ich," in *Über Anna Seghers: Ein Almanach zum 75. Geburtstag,* ed. Kurt Batt (Berlin: Aufbau Verlag, 1975), 257. According to Strittmatter, Brecht made his comment in the fall of 1952, on the day he and Helene Weigel met with Seghers in Berlin-Weißensee to talk about the Berliner Ensemble theatre adaptation of Seghers's radio play *The Trial of Jeanne d'Arc at Rouen, 1431.*

2. Handwritten letter to Helene Weigel from Prague, 19 August 1956, BBA 893/05–07. The letter ends with the words: "Dear Helli, tell me, whatever it is, that can help you, so that I can do it for you. . . . Don't forget that Netty [Anna Seghers] will be there for you."

3. Heiner Müller, *Krieg ohne Schlacht: Leben in zwei Diktaturen* (Cologne: Kiepenheuer & Witsch, 1994), 112.

4. John Willett, *Brecht in Context* (London: Methuen, 1984), 205.

5. Manès Sperber, *Until My Eyes Are Closed with Shards,* trans. Harry Zohn (New York: Holmes & Meier Publishers, 1994), 68–69. Sperber's account continues: "Others who had thought or pretended they were fighting for freedom in exile

did the same thing, but the reason I have said so much about Anna Seghers here is that I lovingly admired her when we and all our companions were still young and that it sometimes seems to me as if she passed away at an early age soon thereafter. 'The dead stay young'? If I think of the princess of poets of the German Democratic Republic, I must doubt this" (69). See the entirety of Sperber's very interesting recollection of his relationship to Seghers in the mid-1930s (66–69; also 104). There is a dignity in Sperber's disappointment that is missing in more petty diatribes, as in John Fuegi, *Brecht and Company: Sex, Politics, and the Making of the Modern Drama* (New York: Grove Press, 1994), which goes to town on debunking Seghers as well as of course Brecht. See the corrective compilation of this work's 621 erroneous assertions in John Willett, James K. Lyon, Siegfried Mews, and Hans Christian Norregaard, "A Brechtbuster Goes Bust: Scholarly Mistakes, Misquotes, and Malpractices in John Fuegi's *Brecht and Company,*" *The Brecht Yearbook* 20: *brecht then and now,* ed. John Willett (1995), 259–367. See also Fredric Jameson, *Brecht and Method* (London: Verso, 1998), who writes that Fuegi's book "will remain a fundamental document for future students of the ideological confusions of Western intellectuals during the immediate post–Cold War years" (31).

6. See my discussion of the MASCH at the end of chapter 4. On Brecht and the MASCH, see Werner Hecht, *Brecht-Chronik* (Frankfurt am Main: Suhrkamp Verlag, 1997), 296.

7. Brecht, *Letters, 1913–1956,* ed. John Willett, trans. Ralph Manheim (London: Methuen, 1990), 133. With his comment about Radványi alias Schmidt, Brecht evidently meant that "Schmidt is no Korsch," which indeed at the time he was not. See also the letters numbered 167 and 169, to Weigel and Margo von Brentano respectively, 132–34.

8. See Brecht, *Letters, 1913–1956,* 254.

9. Anna Seghers, "Helene Weigel spielt in Paris," in *Über Kunstwerk und Wirklichkeit,* vol. 2, *Erlebnis und Gestaltung,* ed. Sigrid Bock (Berlin: Akademie Verlag, 1971), 51–53. Seghers's review made implicit reference to another exiled Viennese-born Jewish actress, Elisabeth Bergner, who reached the height of her career as the lead in Max Reinhardt's 1924 production of *Saint Joan* in Berlin. The support of George Bernard Shaw helped the exiled Bergner make a successful career in England in the 1930s, albeit the shift from her native German to English, and from stage to screen, made her rely all the more on an atmospheric acting style. Meanwhile Helene Weigel, who had last appeared before packed houses five years earlier as the lead in Brecht's *The Mother,* had few prospects in the theatre. With this in mind, Seghers pointed to the precision of Weigel's acting, "a singularly sharp, incorruptible contour, which has nothing of the blurred, indistinct contours of bad photographs touched up with paint, whereby they resemble even more those spiritist photos with which one makes magic" (52).

10. Seghers's second essay, "Die Sprache der Weigel," appeared in *Theaterarbeit: 6 Aufführungen des Berliner Ensembles* (Dresden: VVV Dresdner Verlag, 1952). Strittmatter tells how Brecht once tried unsuccessfully to learn from him the art of telling stories while cracking nuts open with a knife. The scene took place in Berlin-Weißensee in the fall of 1952 while Weigel was preparing the title role in

Brecht's *The Rifles of Señora Carrar.* Seghers, who was also present, turned to Brecht and said: "Now you can see what you're asking of Helli onstage. Not only does she have to mend fishnets; while she's doing that she's even got to babble your lines." Strittmatter, "Anna und ich," 257. On Seghers's and Weigel's relationship in particular, see Helen Fehervary, "Helene Weigel and Anna Seghers: Two Unconventional Conventional Women," *The Brecht Yearbook* 25: *Helene Weigel 100,* ed. Judith Wilke (2000), 75–94.

11. Brecht, *Journals, 1934–1955,* ed. John Willett, trans. Hugh Rorrison (New York: Routledge, 1993), 282. The details of Seghers's accident, after which she suffered from amnesia, have never been fully explained. The official medical report ruled out foul play, suspected by Brecht as well as many in Mexico at the time. See *Anna Seghers: Eine Biographie in Bildern,* ed. Frank Wagner, Ursula Emmerich, and Ruth Radvanyi (Berlin: Aufbau Verlag, 1994), 136–39; and Lenka Reinerová, *Es begann in der Melantrichgasse: Erinnerungen an Weiskopf, Kisch, Uhse und die Seghers* (Berlin and Weimar: Aufbau Verlag, 1985).

12. Hecht, *Brecht-Chronik,* 733–34, 750. Brecht's letter of 30 March 1941 accompanied a bound photocopied typescript copy of his *Gedichte im Exil.* The book contains the dedication "A.S. in Kameradschaft b 1945" (To A.S. in solidarity b 1945) (ASA lib. 695). (The initials provided by Brecht evidently did not daunt the censors.) The Anna Seghers library collection has three copies of Brecht's *Svendborger Gedichte* published by Malik Verlag in London in 1939. Two of them, one probably sent by mail, one personally given to Seghers while she was in Paris, contain the dedication "Anna Seghers in Kameradschaft brecht" (To Anna Seghers in solidarity brecht) (ASA lib. 518, 692, 2867). A comprehensive study of the FBI's surveillance of Seghers, Brecht, and others is found in Alexander Stephan, *"Communazis": FBI Surveillance of German Emigré Writers,* trans. Jan van Heurck (New Haven: Yale University Press, 2000).

13. ASA letters, file 1670.

14. Brecht, *Journals, 1934–1955,* 373. Translation modified.

15. Brecht, *Letters, 1913–1956,* 439–40.

16. The room Seghers occupied in Weißensee in 1950 was even later referred to as her room. Hecht, *Brecht-Chronik,* 943. It was Seghers who, together with Aragon and Konstantin Fedin, nominated Brecht for the Stalin Peace Prize in the spring of 1955. See Werner Mittenzwei, *Das Leben des Bertolt Brecht oder Der Umgang mit den Welträtseln,* vol. 2 (Frankfurt am Main: Suhrkamp Verlag, 1987), 629. Seghers had already received the Peace Prize, as well as the GDR Nationalpreis, in 1951. She was particularly active in the World Peace Council and a member of its executive board. On Seghers's and Weigel's efforts on behalf of Heiner Müller in 1961, see Helen Fehervary, "Landscapes of an *Auftrag,*" *New German Critique* 73, special issue on Heiner Müller, ed. David Bathrick and Helen Fehervary (winter 1998), 121–23; and Fehervary, "Helene Weigel and Anna Seghers; Two Unconventional Conventional Women," 87–89.

17. Related by Jürgen Kuczynski in his *"Ein linientreuer Dissident": Memoiren 1945–1989* (Berlin: Aufbau Verlag, 1994), 52. Ulbricht's question was inspired by Stalin's earlier critique of Fadeyev's novel *The Young Guard* (1947). When Ilya

Ehrenburg, like Kuczynski a close friend of Seghers, heard about the negative review of the novel that subsequently appeared in *Neues Deutschland,* he asked for a meeting with Ulbricht. In Ehrenburg's, Seghers's, and Kuczynski's presence Ulbricht then repeated his "But where's the Party?" whereupon Ehrenburg evidently said: "Yes, Comrade Ulbricht, that's what we also asked ourselves during the war." And with that, according to Kuczynski, the subject was closed (53).

18. See her letter of 14 June 1950, in . . . *und leiser Jubel zöge ein: Autoren und Verlegerbriefe 1950–1959,* ed. Elmar Faber and Carsten Wurm (Berlin: Aufbau Verlag, 1992), 384–86. On Erich Wendt, see page 493.

19. See the correspondence in *Allein mit Lebensmittelkarten ist es nicht auszuhalten: Autoren und Verlegerbriefe 1945–1949,* ed. Elmar Faber and Carsten Wurm (Berlin: Aufbau Verlag, 1991), 297, 300.

20. Entry 11 July 1951, in Brecht, *Journals, 1934–1955,* 438.

21. On page 18 of Anna Seghers, *Die Linie* (Berlin: Aufbau Verlag, 1950) (Brecht's personal library, BBA).

22. In September and October of 1951 Seghers in fact visited China, where, at the invitation of the government, she also met with Mao Tse-tung. See *Anna Seghers: Eine Biographie in Bildern,* 184–85. Upon her return to Berlin she must have found an especially interested listener in Brecht. Having studied sinology and East Asian art at the University of Heidelberg in the early 1920s, Seghers had a rudimentary knowledge of the Chinese language, and she held a lifelong interest in Chinese philosophy, art, and culture and the revolution under Mao. A comparison of these aspects in Seghers's and Brecht's works has yet to be made. On Brecht's *Garbe* project, which Heiner Müller saw himself as continuing in 1956 with his play *Der Lohndrücker,* see Stefan Bock, "Die Tage des Büsching: Brechts *Garbe*—ein deutsches Lehrstück," in *Dramatik der DDR,* ed. Ulrich Profitlich (Frankfurt am Main: Suhrkamp Verlag, 1987), 19–77.

23. See Hecht, *Brecht-Chronik,* 1021.

24. See my discussion of these narratives in chapter 6.

25. David King, *Trotsky: A Photographic Biography* (Oxford: Basil Blackwell, 1986), 248–49.

26. Isaac Deutscher, *The Prophet Outcast: Trotsky, 1929–1940* (London: Oxford University Press, 1963), 333.

27. Deutscher, *The Prophet Outcast,* 334.

28. Deutscher, *The Prophet Outcast,* 332.

29. Deutscher, *The Prophet Outcast,* 393.

30. The Seghers's library includes this work: Joseph Fabre, *Procès de Condamnation de Jeanne d'Arc: D'Après les textes authentiques des procès-verbaux officiels,* traduction avec éclaircissements (Paris: Delagrave, 1848) (ASA lib. 3311). The 1431 protocols were recorded in French and subsequently translated into Latin, from which the Fabre translations were made.

31. Dreyer made his film in the wake of international protests surrounding the trial and sentencing in Boston of the Italian American immigrants Sacco and Vanzetti, who died in the electric chair in August 1927. The case inspired a number of artistic works, among them Seghers's stream-of-consciousness narrative *Auf*

dem Weg zur amerikanischen Botschaft (1929, On the Way to the American Embassy) and the trial and execution scene in Brecht's *Rise and Fall of the City of Mahagonny* (1929). The film is documented in Carl Dreyer, *Four Screenplays* (Bloomington: Indiana University Press, 1964).

32. ASA file 601.

33. Béla Balázs, *Der Geist des Films* (Halle/Saale: Verlag Wilhelm Knapp, 1930), 59–60.

34. For the transcripts of the Dewey Commission trial, see *The Case of Leon Trotsky* (New York: Harper, 1937).

35. Quoted in Deutscher, *The Prophet Outcast,* 369.

36. See Joseph Pischel, "Nachwort," in Lion Feuchtwanger, *Moskau 1937: Ein Reisebericht für meine Freunde* (Berlin: Aufbau Verlag, 1993), 117.

37. Feuchtwanger, *Moskau 1937,* 76–81.

38. Pischel, "Nachwort," in Feuchtwanger, *Moskau 1937,* 117–18. Brecht was more positive in his personal response to Feuchtwanger. Evidently comparing it to André Gide's indictment of Stalinism, he described Feuchtwanger's book as "the best of what European literature has said on this matter." Hecht, *Brecht-Chronik,* 517.

39. Seghers, *Der Prozeß der Jeanne d'Arc zu Rouen 1431* (Leipzig: Reclam Verlag, 1985), 15. Page references henceforth in the text. Where the same phrasing occurs in the stage version adapted for the Berliner Ensemble, I have consulted, but do not always adhere to, the published translation of the theatre adaptation: *The Trial of Joan of Arc at Rouen, 1431* (Anna Seghers), trans. Ralph Manheim and Wolfgang Sauerlander, in Bertolt Brecht, *Collected Plays,* vol. 9, ed. Ralph Manheim and John Willett (New York: Pantheon Books, 1972), 147–87.

40. For László Radványi's analysis of these developments in his dissertation, which must have informed Seghers's understanding of the period, see Ladislaus Radványi, *Der Chiliasmus: Ein Versuch zur Erkenntnis der chiliastischen Idee und des chiliastischen Handelns* (Budapest: MTA Filozófiai Intézet, 1985), 40–59. See my discussion of the dissertation in chapter 4.

41. Some antisemitic posters, beginning with the Polish and White Russian propaganda against Trotsky during the Civil War, are depicted in King, *Trotsky: A Photographic Biography,* 110ff. See also the discussion of antisemitism in relation to Trotsky, and his response to it, in Deutscher, *The Prophet Outcast,* 257–59.

42. Peter Altmann et al., *Der deutsche antifaschistische Widerstand 1933–1945* (Frankfurt am Main: Röderberg, 1975), 87.

43. The indirect communication between the imprisoned Schaeffer in Germany (with whom she studied sinology in Heidelberg in the early 1920s) and the exiled Seghers in Paris is a moving testimony to the extraordinary circumstances of the time and the no less extraordinary spirit of those who became its victims. As Seghers recalled much later: "In exile I received a letter from a chaplain in the Luckau prison. He asked me to send him my Chinese dictionary, saying that the prisoner Philipp Schaeffer would be happy about this and it would make his life easier." Quoted in *Anna Seghers: Eine Biographie in Bildern,* 42. Schaeffer was released after his initial five-year prison term, whereupon he continued his under-

ground work in the resistance. He was apprehended a second time after helping a Jewish couple escape from an apartment raided by the Gestapo. On Schaeffer's courage and continued devotion to the teachings and practice of Buddhism during his second incarceration until his execution in February 1943 in Plötzensee, see Karl Heinz Biernat and Luise Kraushaar, *Die Schulze-Boysen/Harnack-Organisation im antifaschistischen Kampf* (Berlin: Dietz Verlag, 1970), 138–39. Seghers had a photograph of Schaeffer clipped to a bulletin board in her study in her apartment in Berlin-Adlershof. Next to it was a photograph of Argentinian-born Tamara Bunke, a GDR citizen who went to Cuba in 1961, joined Che Guevara on his mission to Bolivia, and two months before Che's death was fatally shot during an attack by the Twelfth Infantry Regiment of Manchego as she and others crossed the Rio Grande. See *Tania, the Unforgettable Guerrilla,* ed. Marta Rojas and Mirta Rodriguez Calderon (New York: Random House, 1971).

44. Letter of 2 November to Julius Hay, in Seghers, *Über Kunstwerk und Wirklichkeit,* vol. 3, *Für den Frieden der Welt,* ed. Sigrid Bock (Berlin: Akademie Verlag, 1971), 310.

45. See Altmann et al., *Der deutsche antifaschistische Widerstand 1933–1945,* 56ff.

46. Seghers, "Hans Beimler" (1937), in *Über Kunstwerk und Wirklichkeit,* 3:154.

47. Seghers, "Helene Weigel spielt in Paris," in *Über Kunstwerk und Wirklichkeit,* 2:52–53.

48. See Mittenzwei, *Das Leben des Bertolt Brecht,* 1:652–54. Brecht wrote in his journal on 23 November 1938: "finished LIFE OF GALILEO. it took three weeks." Brecht, *Journals, 1934–1955,* 19.

49. The quotation from Brecht is taken from Brecht, *Life of Galileo, The Resistable Rise of Arturo Ui, The Caucasian Chalk Circle,* translation of *Life of Galileo* by John Willett (New York: Arcade Publishing, 1994), 93. The quotation from Seghers is my translation of the passage in Seghers, *Der Prozeß der Jeanne d'Arc zu Rouen 1431,* 82. Compare the German in Brecht: "Schließlich ist der Mann der größte Physiker dieser Zeit, das Licht Italiens, und nicht irgendein Wirrkopf. Er hat Freunde. Da ist Versailles. Da ist der Wiener Hof" (*Leben des Galilei* [Frankfurt am Main: Suhrkamp Verlag, 1963], 132) and in Seghers: "Immerhin war dieser Mann Jahrzehnte der berühmteste Kopf Europas, der Dekan der Pariser Fakultät, bei allen Kirchenprozessen gab sein Gutachten den Ausschlag" (82).

50. Walter Benjamin, "Conversations with Brecht," in *Understanding Brecht,* trans. Anna Bostock (London: New Left Books, 1973), 119. Translation of the title modified. I discuss the narrative at length in chapter 6.

51. At the time of Brecht's visits to Paris their conversations must have involved exchanges about their own writing. One of these worked in Brecht's favor when he later wrote "The Job," a story quite similar to a story by Seghers, "Der sogenannte Rendel" (1940, Alias Rendel), based on a newspaper account about a woman in Mainz, Seghers's hometown. In both Seghers's and Brecht's stories, after her husband's death a woman takes over his job as a factory guard, posing as

a man and the father of her two children. After Brecht's version appeared posthumously in 1962, Seghers told the Brecht scholar Ernst Schumacher that in Paris Brecht once asked her for advice on what he might write in order to make money. "I didn't know myself," Seghers told Schumacher. "At the time I was working on several projects, it was always a problem of where to place your work, and as he was sitting there and I looked at him, I suddenly thought to myself, that man Brecht is a kleptomaniac, you've got to be careful; apparently I wasn't. I must have told him that I had written a film story, actually a film novella, for Hans Richter who had landed in Switzerland, because that's what Brecht then wrote up." Ernst Schumacher, "Mit Anna Seghers im Cecilienhof," *Sinn und Form* 35, no. 6 (1983): 1154–55. In an interview in 1978 Seghers was more defensive of Brecht: "I don't see anything wrong in Brecht's having then taken the incident and written his own piece. Brecht didn't want to steal anything from me." Achim Roscher, "Wirkung des Geschriebenen: Gespräche mit Anna Seghers," *Neue deutsche Literatur,* no. 10 (1983): 72. Seghers's story, as well as two drafts and an informative essay by Alexander Stephan, are found in *Argonautenschiff: Jahrbuch der Anna-Seghers-Gesellschaft* 3 (Berlin: Aufbau Verlag, 1994): 87–114. See also the extensive discussion in Stephan, *Anna Seghers im Exil* (Bonn: Bouvier, 1993), 56–124.

52. See Hecht, *Brecht-Chronik,* 617.

53. Entry 19 September 1939, in Brecht, *Journals, 1934–1955,* 36.

54. Entry 7 November 1939, in Brecht, *Journals, 1934–1955,* 37.

55. Brecht, *Werke: Große kommentierte Berliner und Frankfurter Ausgabe,* ed. Werner Hecht, Jan Knopf, Werner Mittenzwei, and Klaus-Detlef Müller, vol. 6, *Stücke 6,* ed. Klaus-Detlef Müller (Berlin and Weimar: Aufbau Verlag; Frankfurt am Main: Suhrkamp Verlag, 1989), 411.

56. Entry 17 December 1941, in Brecht, *Journals, 1934–1955,* 182. Brecht first mentioned the project in a journal entry of 7 July 1940 in Finland. Here, too, in this first formulation of his concept, we find remarkable similarities to the theme of Seghers's radio play, especially as regards the voices Jeanne hears and the political composition of the trial, even if Brecht opted for an explicitly contemporary setting: "a young french girl in orleans who is looking after a petrol station in the absence of her brother dreams day and night that she is joan of arc and suffers her fate. for the germans are advancing on orleans. the voices joan hears are the voices of the people, what the blacksmith says and the peasant. she obeys these voices and saves france from the foreign foe, but is defeated by the enemy within. (the court which finds her guilty is made up solely of clergymen who sympathise with the english.) the victory of the fifth column." Brecht, *Journals, 1934–1955,* 78–79.

57. Entry 19 December 1941, in Brecht, *Journals, 1934–1955,* 183.

58. Entry 19 December 1941, in Brecht, *Journals, 1934–1955,* 183.

59. Seghers, "Rede auf dem II. Deutschen Schriftstellerkongreß 1950," in *Über Kunstwerk und Wirklichkeit,* vol. 1, *Die Tendenz in der reinen Kunst,* ed. Sigrid Bock (Berlin: Akademie Verlag, 1970), 82–83. Seghers erred when she suggested the 1431 trial "was recorded word for word in Latin." In fact it was recorded in French and thereupon translated into Latin. Maximilian Scheer, who published a play as well as a novel about Ethel and Julius Rosenberg in the early 1950s, must

have argued this side of the cold-war issue when he succeeded in persuading Berlin Radio to air Seghers's play. As he later wrote in his memoir, recalling somewhat dismissively Seghers's provocations in 1950, he had thought it "wrong to blow it up into a major international case. I mentioned it with high marks to the Radio management, got no disturbing questions, had it produced, and just to make sure, made an exception and first had it played for the management. It went through, was broadcast, and some time later Brecht put on the stage version of the radio play in his theatre." Maximilian Scheer, *Ein unruhiges Leben* (Berlin: Verlag der Nation, 1975), 252. According to Scheer, Seghers described her attempts to have the play broadcast in the four occupation zones with the words: "People didn't really dare do it, be it the French [occupation forces] or the others. They said it could be misunderstood" (252).

60. ASA file 601. The production was directed by Benno Besson, with costumes and set by Hainer Hill, Käthe Reichel as Jeanne, Erwin Geschonnek as Bishop Cauchon, Georg Peter-Piltz as Jean Beaupère, Paul A. Krumm as Jean de la Fontaine, Regine Lutz as the loose woman, and Ekkehard Schall as Eugene the peasant lad. In the expanded production after April 1954 in the Theater am Schiffbauerdamm the role of Jean de la Fontaine was played by Carl Weber, Jean Beaupère by Fred Düren.

61. See *Der Regisseur Benno Besson,* ed. André Müller (Berlin: Henschel-Verlag, 1967), 26.

62. Brecht, *Werke,* 9:85, 87.

63. Brecht, *Werke,* 9:102. Brechtians may wish to ascribe folksy passages such as this and the aforementioned to the *Stückeschreiber* himself. I am more inclined to believe Benno Besson, who said Seghers wrote the expanded dialogue in the folk scenes (see note 61). Moreover, the cited passages are characteristic of Seghers's writing style. It would be useful to consider that Seghers's early use of folk dialogue, as in her novel *Der Kopflohn* (1934, The Bounty) about the rise of National Socialism in a rural Hessian community, may well have influenced such (later) developments in Brecht's own work. On this aspect, see Fehervary, "'Die gotische Linie': Altdeutsche Landschaften und Physiognomien bei Seghers und Müller," in Jost Hermand and Helen Fehervary, *Mit den Toten reden: Fragen an Heiner Müller* (Cologne: Böhlau Verlag, 1999), 113–35.

64. Brecht, *Werke,* 9:122–23.

65. Brecht, *Werke,* 9:123.

66. For a discussion of these concepts as they pertain to Seghers's short prose narratives, see chapter 6.

67. See note 43 to this chapter; see also *Anna Seghers: Eine Biographie in Bildern,* 41–43.

68. See Friedrich Schütz, "Die Familie Seghers-Reiling und das jüdische Mainz," *Argonautenschiff: Jahrbuch der Anna-Seghers-Gesellschaft* 2 (Berlin: Aufbau Verlag, 1993): 151–73; and Frank Wagner, "Deportation nach Piaski: Letzte Stationen der Passion von Hedwig Reiling," *Argonautenschiff: Jahrbuch der Anna-Seghers-Gesellschaft* 3 (Berlin: Aufbau Verlag, 1994): 117–26. Seghers's most famous response to her personal loss is her autobiographical narrative *Der Ausflug*

der toten Mädchen (The Excursion of the Dead Girls), which she wrote in Mexico in 1943–44. Soon after she finished it she wrote two further narratives pertaining to the Holocaust: *Post ins gelobte Land* (Post to the Promised Land) and *Das Ende* (The End). The three narratives first appeared in the volume *Der Ausflug der toten Mädchen und andere Erzählungen* (New York: Aurora Verlag, 1946). On the circumstances surrounding her work on these narratives, see Anna Seghers/Wieland Herzfelde, *Gewöhnliches und gefährliches Leben: Ein Briefwechsel aus der Zeit des Exils, 1939–1946,* ed. Ursula Emmerich and Erika Pick (Darmstadt and Neuwied: Luchterhand Verlag, 1986). On the assumptions underlying Seghers's approach to the thematization of the Holocaust, as exemplified by her short text *Zwei Denkmäler* (1965, Two Monuments), see Jochen Vogt, "Was aus dem Mädchen geworden ist: Kleine Archäologie eines Gelegenheitstextes von Anna Seghers," *Argonautenschiff: Jahrbuch der Anna-Seghers-Gesellschaft* 6 (Berlin: Aufbau Verlag, 1997): 121–36.

69. László Radványi (Johann-Lorenz Schmidt) held a professorship at the National University in Mexico from 1944 to 1952.

70. Georg Hermann Hodos, *Schauprozesse: Stalinistische Säuberungen in Osteuropa 1948–54* (Frankfurt am Main: Campus Verlag, 1988), 108.

71. On 16 November 1952, one week before the Berliner Ensemble premiere of *The Trial of Jeanne d'Arc,* Seghers sent a cable protesting the death sentences in the Rosenberg trial, in response to a request of 6 November 1952 from Paul Robeson and Howard Fast: "I am dismayed by this monstrous decision . . . and by the rejection of an appeal to the Supreme Court. In the name of the progressive German writers I demand the suspension of this sentence. For it stands in violation of human rights and the best traditions of the American people. Anna Seghers, President of the German Union of Writers." ASA letters, file 469. Seghers also wrote a second letter of protest (ASA letters, file 468) and a short essay on the topic on 7 June 1953 (ASA letters, file 470). Brecht sent a cable to Einstein, Hemingway, and Arthur Miller; its text appeared in *Neues Deutschland* in January 1953: "could you and other scientists still do something for ethel and julius rosenberg. i have read files. they are innocent." Brecht, *Briefe,* ed. Günter Glaeser (Frankfurt am Main: Suhrkamp Verlag, 1981), 688. See also Brecht, *Briefe,* vol. 2, *Anmerkungen,* 1129.

72. In a letter of 15 November 1952 to Carl Orff, Brecht wrote: "we are putting on a play by Anna Seghers, rather sooner than planned, since the Ensemble is going on tour in Poland in December." Brecht, *Letters, 1913–1956,* 513. This may have been the official explanation for having rather hurriedly scheduled the premiere for November 23. If the Berliner Ensemble had not been able to perform the play until after December, the political impact of the production as countertrial would have been lost.

73. Artur London, *The Confession,* trans. Alastair Hamilton (New York: William Morrow, 1970), 266. Page references henceforth in the text.

74. ASA file 601.

75. BBA 370/15.

76. ASA lib. unnumbered.

77. Translation modified to include the phrase "about Anna Seghers, about

Egon Erwin Kisch and his wife," which, curiously, the translator deleted, substituting the word "others." Compare the German version of the same sentence: "Sie fragen mich über Anna Seghers aus, über Egon Erwin Kisch und seine Frau, die sie beschuldigen, in Paris und in Prag Zusammenkünfte trotzkistischer Intellektueller veranstaltet zu haben." Artur London, *Ich gestehe: Der Prozeß um Rudolf Slansky,* trans. Willy Thaler (Berlin: Aufbau Verlag, 1991), 51. Seghers's particularly close relationship to Egon Erwin Kisch and his wife Gisl Kisch deserves further research.

78. BBA 728/62–64. Whereas a secretary typed most of her correspondence on a German typewriter, Seghers herself must have typed this single-spaced three-page letter on the Remington typewriter she brought back with her from exile, suggesting she considered the content of the letter to be both urgent and private. I discovered the letter in a file in the Bertolt-Brecht-Archiv in December 1995 and received permission from Seghers's daughter Dr. Ruth Radvanyi to publish it. See Fehervary, "Brecht, Seghers, and *The Trial of Jeanne d'Arc*—with a Previously Unpublished Letter of 1952 from Seghers to Brecht," *The Brecht Yearbook* 21: *Intersections* (1996), 20–47; the text of the letter appears on pages 35–38. All subsequent text citations refer to this publication. I have been unable to find out why this letter, crucial to both Seghers and Brecht scholarship, was not previously acknowledged by Brecht scholars. Even Carl Wege's excellent twenty-two-page commentary on the 1952 Berliner Ensemble theatre adaptation, published in 1992 in Brecht, *Werke,* vol. 9, *Stücke 9,* 374–96, makes no mention of it.

79. BBA 728/62–64; 370/15.

80. Brecht, *Werke,* vol. 9, *Stücke 9,* 377. See also Brecht's later notes, in Brecht, *Werke,* vol. 24, *Schriften 4: Texte zu Stücken,* 407.

81. Brecht, *Werke,* vol. 9, *Stücke 9,* 375.

82. ASA files 862, 1196, 1291, 1337; ASA letters, addendum 1/40.

83. ASA letters, file 1337.

84. An egregious example of misplaced praise and criticism regarding the theatre adaptation of Seghers's radio play is Hellmuth Karasek's review of the 1960 Peter Palitzsch production in Ulm (*Theater heute,* October 1960, 5–6). See the discussion of this and other misreadings in Fehervary, "Brecht, Seghers, and *The Trial of Jeanne d'Arc*—with a Previously Unpublished Letter of 1952 from Seghers to Brecht," 20–47.

85. ASA letters, addendum 18/7.

86. *La passione di Giovanna d'Arco* (n.d.) is found in Seghers's library with a personal inscription dated Paris, 6 December 1950, and signed "Ihr Peter" (ASA lib. unnumbered). The content, style, and signature using the formal "you" suggest this was not her son Pierre Radvanyi, whom she called Peter, but her nephew Peter Szondi, the later renowned literary scholar, who also studied in Paris at the Sorbonne. Peter Szondi's mother Lilli Radványi Szondi was László Radványi's sister; his father was the psychoanalyst Leopold Szondi. For accounts of the family's five-month incarceration in the concentration camp Bergen-Belsen in 1944, see Lili [Lilli] Szondi-Radványi, "Ein Tag in Bergen-Belsen" (translation of "Egy nap Bergenben"), *Szondiana: Zeitschrift für Tiefenpsychologie: Sonderheft Leopold*

Szondi zum 100. Geburtstag, March 1993, 43–60; and Karl Bürgi-Meyer, "Leopold Szondi als Flüchtling in der Schweiz: Biographische Skizze," *Szondiana: Zeitschrift für Tiefenpsychologie,* no. 1 (1995): 68–87.

Seghers's frequent mention of Dreyer's film continued to have its effect. In 1974 Frankfurt Kammerspiel Frank-Patrick Steckel asked to interview her for a production of *The Trial of Jeanne d'Arc at Rouen, 1431*—"in the radio play version, *not* in Brecht's version," he wrote. ASA letters, file 1565. The timing of Steckel's 1976 production suggested the Federal Republic's campaigns against urban guerrillas such as the Baader-Meinhof group; Jeanne d'Arc appeared onstage in a pantsuit, and the theatre program quoted Seghers: "Focusing on Johanna in 1976 means discovering aspects of this figure different from those of 1936." *AZ,* 14 Oct. 1976. In 1979 an authorized GDR stage production of the radio play by the Kreistheater Annaberg used stills from the Dreyer film and excerpts from the 1450–56 rehabilitation hearings. ASA file 601.

87. See note 40 to this chapter.

88. ASA letters, file 933.

89. ASA letters, file 933.

90. Christa Wolf, "Gesichter der Anna Seghers" (1992), in *Anna Seghers: Eine Biographie in Bildern,* 8.

91. Hans Mayer, *Der Turm von Babel: Erinnerung an eine Deutsche Demokratische Republik* (Frankfurt am Main: Suhrkamp Verlag, 1991), 202–3.

92. See Georg Lukács, *Record of a Life: An Autobiographical Sketch,* ed. István Eörsi, trans. Rodney Livingstone (London: Verso, 1983). Lukács's negative comments at this point in his life about both Seghers and her husband stemmed in regard to her from what I conjecture to have been his unfavorable opinion of her GDR-affirmative novel *Das Vertrauen* (1968, Trust). See Lukács, *Record of a Life,* 93: "I was on friendly terms with Anna Seghers until fairly recently. Our correspondence, too, was always very friendly. It was only when she succumbed to Ulbricht's latest literary fashion, in what was to my way of thinking a completely mindless and superfluous manner, that our friendship just died a natural death. . . . Yes, her husband was a Hungarian, but one of the unpleasant kind. I didn't think he was completely kosher—I mean, he always slavishly followed the Party line. In that respect I think he had an unfortunate influence on her." Jürgen Kuczynski made similar comments regarding Radványi in "*Ein linientreuer Dissident": Memoiren 1945–1989,* 70. Radványi's greater distance to Lukács in his later years is evident in the terseness of his own statements about the elder philosopher as recorded in Éva Gábor, "Egy 'elfelejtett' vasárnapos emlékeiböl," *Világosság,* no. 7 (1980): 449–52. Radványi's (i.e., Johann-Lorenz Schmidt's) testimony in the GDR case against Paul Merker is presented in Jeffrey Herf, "Dokumentation: Antisemitismus in der SED: Geheime Dokumente zum Fall Paul Merker aus SED- und MfS-Archiven," *Vierteljahreshefte für Zeitgeschichte,* no. 4 (1994): 635–67. See also Wolfgang Kießling, *Partner im "Narrenparadies": Der Freundschaftskreis um Noel Field und Paul Merker* (Berlin: Dietz Verlag, 1994). The larger complexity of Radványi's connection to the Merker case and, as Kuczynski relates, another case in 1958 is still unknown and deserves further research. Regarding Heiner

Müller's interview autobiography, see Müller, *Krieg ohne Schlacht: Leben in zwei Diktaturen* (Cologne: Kiepenheuer & Witsch, 1992; expanded 1994). References and passages pertaining to Seghers are indicated in the index. See my discussion of some of these passages in "Landscapes of an *Auftrag*," 115–32; see also Fehervary, "Helene Weigel and Anna Seghers: Two Unconventional Conventional Women," 75–94.

93. *Tausend und ein Tag: Orientalische Erzählungen,* ed. Paul Ernst (Leipzig: Insel Verlag, 1925), 460–61 (ASA lib. 4112).

Index

Social History, Popular Culture, and Politics in Germany
Geoff Eley, Series Editor

(continued from pg. ii)